To Ed

[handwritten inscription, illegible]

DON STOLZ

THE
OLD LOG
THEATER & ME

ISBN 10: 1-59298-309-X
ISBN 13: 978-1-59298-309-4

Library of Congress Catalog Number: 2009937538

Printed in the United States of America

First Printing: 2009

13 12 11 10 09   5 4 3 2 1

Cover and interior design by James Monroe Design, LLC.

A special thanks to Anita Anderson O'Sullivan, Cindy Rogers, and Robin Schoenwetter.

Beaver's Pond Press, Inc.
7104 Ohms Lane, Suite 101
Edina, MN 55439–2129
(952) 829-8818
www.BeaversPondPress.com

BEAVER'S
POND
PRESS

To order, visit www.BeaversPondBooks.com
or call (800) 901-3480. Reseller discounts available.

Dedication

"Why don't you get a real job" is a question that was never asked by my wife, Joan, or by any of my sons: Peter, Dony, Tommy, Timmy, or Jon. This book is dedicated to them.

Contents

Foreword

Don asked me if I'd "care to write a Foreword to his autobiography." Care to write?! I'm thrilled and honored beyond words. No man in the history of American Theater has achieved more than Don Stolz. I'm not exaggerating. And, because of the changes in our industry over the last 60 years, his achievements will never be matched in the future.

The man has devoted his life and career to just one theater for over sixty years! He built it up from a shoestring summer stock company, which entailed presenting 13 plays for a run of one week each to the most Professional, attractive and entertaining Dinner Theater where some of his productions have run for over a year.

I tell you, if this man had had the same career in England he would have been knighted by now for "services to the theater." That means he'd be Sir Don Stolz. No, "Sir" is not good enough for Don's services to the Theater. In England he would have been elevated to a Lordship. Lord Stolz of Excelsior! Or Baron Stolz of Minnesota!

And it's not as though this genius is content with running the place and producing the plays. No, he directs most of the productions, acts in the plays whenever he's allowed and, on top of this, steps forward every night to address the audience! Lord Stolz of Energy, maybe.

So he's got all this amazing talent and you'd think that was enough. But no! He's also thoughtful of others, generous and has a twinkle in his eye whether things are good or bad. And more! He sustained the happiest of marriages for over sixty years to his beloved Joan who was as determined a trouper as Don himself. If marriages are "made in heaven" that was certainly the case with Joan and Don and I'm sure she's up there still keeping an eye on Don and the Old Log—and the running expenses!

Could there be more? You betcha! Five sons! And each one followed Don into the Entertainment Business. Somehow Peter escaped to Hollywood but Tom, Tim, Dony and Jon have all been part of the Old Log since they were in diapers with Tom playing the lead (he's been great in all of my plays!) in most of the productions. Prince Tom of Excelsior!

Don has produced many of my plays over the last 25 years, and it's been a real privilege for my wife and me to dine at the Old Log and then sit in the Theater and hear the audience laugh fit to bust. Yes, that is Don's talent—for over sixty years he has given the audiences what they want and at prices they can afford.

Don's life story will be an inspiration to any young person aspiring to a career in the Theater and a reminder to the rest of the readers as to what can be achieved by determination, dedication, and a generosity of spirit that has touched all of us who have had the delight of working with him. Here's to the next 70 years at the Old Log—OK, I'll settle for 50!

Ray Cooney, playwright, producer, director, and actor
Ray has earned a reputation as the finest writer
of comedy in the last 75 years. He has been responsible
for over thirty West End productions plus over
forty productions for The Theater of Comedy.

HOW IT STARTED

When it comes right down to it, my father is to blame for this whole thing. I mean the thing of my being in theater. Not that that was ever what he had in mind.

My father was a Methodist Minister. Which means, of course, that my mother was a minister's wife, which is an occupation to be avoided if you possibly can. Their three children, Frederick, Dorothy Jeanne and me, as members of the pastor's family, were expected to participate in every Easter, Thanksgiving, Christmas and Pentecost play, program and pageant—and my father made it quite clear that, regardless of how talented and skilled we might feel we were, we should never expect, nor would we ever receive, leading roles.

The Reverend Fred Stolz spent his childhood in Grand Rapids, Michigan. He attended Baldwin-Wallace College, studied speech under Dr. Comstock of Northwestern, and completed his studies of theology at Garrett Biblical Institute, the Seminary of Northwestern.

His parents, immigrants from Switzerland, were determined that he and his brother, Karl, would receive a good education. Karl had an illustrious career as an author of religious books and as Dean of the School of Religious Education at Hartford, Connecticut.

I've known few men as well educated as my father. He spoke German, read Hebrew and Greek and was a fine student of Latin. After ordination, he decided he could best fulfill his life's mission by going to the uncivilized, backcountry of the Southwest. A missionary to the Indians and the pioneers—the frontier.

Dexter, Kansas, was his first assignment; he still had dreams of the frontier. When he finally arrived in the small town of Capron, Oklahoma, I'm sure he found it a little different frontier from the one he had anticipated.

I remember little of Capron; I was little more than a baby. I do remember that the entire town was devastated by a tornado, and as far as I know, no one thought enough of Capron to rebuild it. Pawnee was my father's next "charge" (as the minister's assignments were known), and it was here that he fulfilled his desire to work with the Indians. There wasn't a single Indian in Pawnee's Methodist Church, but the people on the reservation soon learned that they had a friend in the Methodist parsonage. (As did the African Americans, who were not allowed to spend the night inside Pawnee's city limits).

Dad made it a point to get acquainted with the minister of their squalid little village outside of town, and the black minister became a regular visitor to our home to borrow books from my father's library. I remember Pawnee as my family's favorite assignment. In the 1920s and '30s the Oklahoma Conference of the Methodist Church had established a pattern of moving their ministers every two years. In spite of this, we stayed in Pawnee for four years. In the four years that we were there, my father led the effort to build a beautiful and modern new church. Despite this, not all of the congregation favored the Rev. Fred Stolz, for when they asked him to join the Ku Klux Klan, he refused saying he did not understand how anyone who called himself a Christian could possibly be a member of the KKK. This was in 1924.

After the four years in Pawnee, we moved to Miami (Oklahoma, of course), then to Waynoka, in the western part of the state. There were three points of special interest: the desert-like sand hills to the west, the well-maintained Santa Fe Railroad station in downtown, and a new airport immediately to the north of town. The airport had been built to accommodate the travelers from the West Coast. They would board a plane in Los Angeles, fly to Waynoka be bused from the airport to the Santa Fe Railroad where the evening "Chief" would be waiting to take them overnight to Chicago. We used to go to the airport just to watch as the wonderful Ford Trimotors landed.

I'm not sure that I remember the exact order of small towns in which we next lived—Cleveland, Guthrie, Britton. It was in Guthrie that I entered high school and played trumpet in the high school band. Mr. Kleinstauber, teacher of speech and elocution, asked me to join the debating club. I was the only male member. Looking back, I think he wanted me to be a member so that when the team went out of town for a tournament, no one could suspect any dalliance, for after all, the minister's son was a part of the team. The youngest member of the senior class, I graduated valedictorian. I thank heaven that there remains no copy of the speech I gave at the graduation ceremony.

As I approached my junior year, my family and I realized that if I hoped to enter college, I must have a better job than the occasional odd jobs. I had taken both typing and shorthand already efficient in both. At the suggestion of a friend, Dick Adams, I applied for a job at the local branch of the Fairmont Creamery, where Dick's father was president. I was hired. I was to work two hours every day after school, five hours on Saturday. The pay was $2.00 a week.

Some time after the first week I was there, Mr. Adams came to me and said that everyone in the office knew I had been hired at only fifteen because I was a friend of his family. The only way to offset this was for me to become the fastest typist in the office. To accomplish this, I was to stay an hour after work each day, an hour for which I would not be paid, until I had, in fact, become the fastest typist. It seemed fair. I did it. The ability to take shorthand, transcribe and type saw me through college.

When I enrolled at Oklahoma City University, it was in the pre-med course. My father didn't disapprove—not at all—but, still with the hope that I might see the light, hear the calling and follow him into the Methodist ministry, he suggested that I take a few speech courses from his friend, Professor Wayne Campbell.

During our childhood, my father had insisted that we take "reading lessons," as oral interpretation was called in those days. He was pleased that when I was entered by the school in the county's humorous reading contest, I won first prize the two years I was entered.

Wayne Campbell was head of the speech department—in fact, he was the whole department. Unfortunately, he was also the head (and the whole) of the theater department. The cards were further stacked against my medical career when I went to the University's employment service for secretarial work and they assigned me to Wayne Campbell as his personal secretary.

Campbell was an unbelievably talented man. He had been a successful actor, graduated from the Trueblood School of Oratory and found his way into academia. He was much sought after as a speaker. He would dictate the speech to me, I would transcribe it, then drive him to the engagement, where he never once took my typed script out of his pocket. When finally I asked him about it, he told me that it was only in this method that he felt prepared.

It was in the second week of my freshman year, when Campbell announced that the first play for The College Players, which included everyone he could find who would act (and several who couldn't), was to be the timeless, immortal *Everyman*. The next day when he dictated his first two pages, he announced: "And by the way, you will play 'Goods and Riches.'"

Campbell also reminded me that being his secretary included my creating some sort of stage setting for the production out of the old gray drapes. Junior, Rolland Swain, would handle the lighting. I remember it as my first experience of working more than two days without sleep. On the afternoon of the performance, as soon as I crawled into the big gray box which represented the chest in which Everyman would find his goods and riches, I was immediately asleep. Orville Sherman, who played *Everyman*, remembers to this day that he had to knock on the box to get me to answer my cue.

During the next four years, I was—I believe—in every play that the department presented. And I created every set.

There are three plays that I remember vividly. *The Fool*, in which playwright Channing Pollock reveals what happens when a young minister, just assigned to a wealthy church in New York, tries to live his life in those years of the national Depression, in the way in which he thought Christ would if he had faced the same challenges. In the thirties, *The Fool* was the most performed play in America; there were over a hundred professional companies touring the country. Then, in my junior year, we did Shaw's *Candida* in which I played Marchbanks. I had designed, built and painted what I thought was a lovely set (looking back it was probably just short of horrible), so I went to a downtown furniture store and talked them into letting us use furniture which I thought the production and the set deserved. Campbell, delighted with my Marchbanks, then looked for another play in which I would play a prominent role. He decided it should be *Night Must Fall* by Emlyn Williams. Campbell had an enormous hit. Tom Heggen, the critic for the campus newspaper, wrote the most glowing review that an actor could ask for. Someone from the theater department at the State University in Norman saw the production and immediately started making arrangements for us to bring *Night Must Fall* to their theater. We did. Breathtaking response. The Norman student body suggested to their theater department that they arrange for me to be a guest star in their next two productions. That, of course, did not happen.

It was about then that my father realized what a mistake he had made, for he recognized that I was beginning to find theater almost as interesting as comparative anatomy.

I think it was in organic chemistry during my third year, that I, too, was beginning to realize that theater might just be a little more fun. I completed my pre-med course, was accepted by the University of Oklahoma School of Medicine, even though they were not too happy to have another prospective student without money. Four years of undergraduate education had been—well—difficult. I was poor. I don't think I realized it. I know I didn't care.

Before entering O.C.U., I had been awarded a one-year scholarship by the president, a scholarship covering tuition—a scholarship that he had intended to renew each year. But he died in six months into my first year. Like so many students in those years, I had absolutely no income other than what I earned. The four years were

The Wedding of Dora Cooper, daughter of Dr. and Mrs. Cooper, and the Reverend Fred Stolz. Taken in Dexter, Kansas in 1913.

Don's mother, older brother Frederick, and Donald.

The new Methodist Church, Pawnee, Oklahoma.

Devil's Roost.

strenuous but not unhappy. Not only did I work as Campbell's secretary, but I also worked as a dishwasher in the house where I roomed and boarded, and took occasional jobs wherever I could find them. Each day my lunch was a Coca-Cola and a sack of Planter's Salted Peanuts. I wasn't thrifty, I just didn't have any money. During those years I honestly cannot remember buying anything except food. Not anything. Except a bicycle. Needing transportation for my summertime downtown jobs, I purchased a bicycle from Sears Robuck. I paid $3.00 down and a dollar a week until it was paid off. The bicycle was a life saver but it was almost a life ender. Besides attending class, taking care of the University's stage, doing odd jobs and being in "those ridiculous plays," I was tired. Not exhausted, tired. And sleepy. Late one afternoon, I was riding down 23rd Street to my favorite restaurant where you could get a breaded veal cutlet meal for 35 cents. Finally, I reached that gentle but long hill just before the café. I could coast. I did and promptly went to sleep, which resulted in my running into the back end of a parked car. I was thrown over the handlebars onto the car, slid down the back of the trunk catching my neck on the protruding license plate. Though I was bleeding, I could make my way into a nearby barbershop, where the barber, still not believing what had happened, applied a pressure bandage and called an ambulance. I didn't board the ambulance until the barber promised to take care of my bike.

The federally funded N.Y.A. campus jobs limited the hours a student could work, so I always had to find additional jobs. In the summer I found full-time jobs, trying to save enough to pay the upcoming fall tuition.

In my junior year, despite working and not spending much—I didn't have much to spend—I found myself unable to pay my room rent at the fraternity house, so I arranged a loan of $40 from the Liberty National Bank, where I was employed as a messenger.

That afternoon, I was to give the stage a thorough cleaning, so I changed my clothes, leaving my just acquired $40 in my trousers, which I had hung in the stage right organ loft, a space I always used as a dressing room. A few hours later, when I climbed the steps to the loft to again change clothes, I found that someone had taken the money. The solution was obvious; what had been my private dressing room was now my bedroom, my closet and my study. I continued living there until graduation.

When I graduated, it was with a BFA in theater and Professor Campbell's blessing as one of his very favorite students. I don't remember his ever mentioning the difficulties and disappointments that might be ahead.

My decision not to attend medical school was made easier by the fact that I had been employed by WKY, Oklahoma's finest, largest and best radio station, as a staff actor. In the late '30s, big, commercially successful stations often produced dramatic shows. This resulted in a secure income.

When, in 1938, the station had announced that they were to hold auditions for a new staff of actors, I applied and was hired as the station's juvenile actor. It was then that I first met Terry O'Sullivan, already established as the station's leading and most popular announcer. He immediately became their leading male actor.

After a few months, WKY was asked to produce a series of network shows called "Southwestern Stars." The next spring when the very popular network production, *Lights Out* took a summer break, WKY decided to produce its own replacement—an adventure/mystery titled *Devil's Roost* with Terry O'Sullivan playing Eric Stewart and Don Stolz playing Bill Walters, two adventuresome young amateur detectives. It was an instant hit, and local production became regional network with shows three times a week. What was to be a summer replacement became a fall and winter regional hit. Thirteen weeks, twenty-six weeks—it was going to carry me through to graduation.

The writer, Nafe Abedear, was a marvelous and gifted man— the fastest writer I have ever met. I swear he could write a 30-minute script in 37 minutes. Each week he would ask the few of us who were still in school if we would like to have him cash our checks for us. Of course we were happy and grateful. Then, suddenly, our dear friend disappeared. The station soon discovered that each week he was cashing checks written for actors who weren't on the show. The writer discovered that the station had discovered this minor embezzlement and decided the best solution was to disappear. Management decided the solution for the show was to hand the task of writing to a young continuity writer who until that time had never written a line of dialogue. He protested that there was no way he could write three 30 minute shows a week—he had never done it and couldn't do it. He protested, he pleaded, he cried. Each show the script—such as it was—was delivered closer and closer to broadcast time. Never was any of them reviewed by the station management. There were nights when the only scripts available were the stencil and the second sheet. Finally when his pleas for help brought no help—he took the only action he felt was possible. He got all of the characters that comprised ***Devil's Roost*** into the big cave, the headquarters of the villains being pursued.

(Into scene)

(There is a microphone standing in center. On one side stand Terry and Don. Terry has just finished reading off the mimeographed stencil; Don is holding the second sheet. On the other side of the microphone stands the announcer. He quickly takes the mimeographed stencil from Terry and reads the following lines. There are several other actors who have been looking over Terry's and Don's shoulders.)

Sound: A giant explosion

Announcer: *(as sound of explosion fades into background)* It was truly a horrendous explosion of such force that it completely destroyed the giant cave in which John Walters and Eric Stewart had taken refuge An explosion killing all who were inside—the Cincinnati mobsters pursuing Eric and John and the peace officers who were hoping to intervene. It was an explosion that also killed Eric Stewart and John Walters. There is no more Devil's Roost.

Music: Theme is played.

(During the above the actors look mournfully to each other.)
Announcer: *(As theme fades)* Stay tuned for the late-night news.
(Mic is now off)
Announcer: *(To actors)* Sorry. It's too bad. The audience is
  going to raise hell.
Terry: Yes, they will.
Don: I wonder what's happened to Nafe Abedear. *(This is
  almost to himself)* *(Now to actors)* Well, it's been fun. *(They
  ad lib answers)*
Announcer: *(To Terry)* You have the news, don't you?
Terry: That's right.
Announcer: We'd better get in there before there's another
  giant explosion. *(To Don)* I'll call you.
(Everyone leaves)

It was the end of the show. The young continuity writer was
fired, and I was out of a job. But only for a short time. As soon as the
weather turned warm that year, Terry hired me to play the juvenile
lead in a tent show production of a melodrama titled, as I remember,
They Done Her Wrong. I'm not sure about that title; it may be a
reflection of how we did. On the center pole of the tent was a padlock.
With the purchase of a ticket to see ***They Done Her Wrong***, each
audience member was given a key. If the key unlocked the padlock
on the center pole, that fantastically lucky person would receive
$100.00. Which was an amount greater than we had taken in for
two weeks. But there was no danger; the padlock might just as well
have been welded to the pole—no key in the world would have
unlocked it.

And there was the experience early in the run when the young,
a-little-more-than pleasingly plump ingenue fainted so heavily in my
arms that we both fell off the stage onto the ground in front of the
platform. The audience was so delighted that Terry insisted the fall
be repeated in every performance.

Then there were the periods between shows when we rested on
the part of backstage that extended behind the tent. It was there that
we listened to the stories told by the wonderful and handsome lead-

ing man, Guy Runyon—(and he really was wonderful)—stories about how only a few years earlier an actor could build a successful career just by working the tent shows that traveled out of Kansas City. Terry had hired Guy to direct our show. He had had years of experience playing these shows and knew all the devices to make them work. As a director, he insisted that the beginning of your line should top in energy and volume the line that had preceded it.

When fall came, I was off to Northwestern University graduate school in Evanston.

The Adventures and Misadventures in Securing a Master's Degree

Actually, it was a campaign for which I had spent months preparing. I knew Theodore Fuchs, an established Broadway lighting designer, had been added to Northwestern's staff as the head of the lighting department. I purchased the book which he and McCandless had recently published, read it and studied it until I could come close to delivering it word for word. I had also learned that the Dean of the school was Doctor Dennis. I found article after article that he had written concerning Oral Interpretation, and within those articles he referred so often to the poetry of Lew Sarrett, who for some reason I do not yet know was not in the school of literature, but in the School of Speech and Theater. I found his poems easy to read and easy to recall.

I was ready, come what may. Most fortunately my interview was with the man already an academic legend, Dean Dennis.

(Sitting behind a desk is a nice looking, studious looking man of 65. There is a knock at the door)

Dean: Come in.

Don: *(Enters)* Thank you.

Dean: Stolz—Don Stolz? Right?

Don: Yes, sir.

Dean: *(Examining application—not for the first time)* I have found your application for admission to the Graduate School of Speech and Theater to be interesting. Last June you graduated from Oklahoma City University with a BFA in Theater and also a completion of a pre-med discipline. Unusual.

Don: Not really, sir, not for one who changed his mind about his chosen profession.

Dean: I see. Changed your mind.

Don: Yes, sir.

Dean: The thing I find most interesting is that you have already done a lot of work as a professional radio actor, and you've also done a season of professional work on stage.

Don: Yes, sir, that's correct.

Dean: Then my question is, if you're already working professionally, why do you want to come and do graduate studies at Northwestern?

Don: Would you repeat the question?

Dean: If you've already started working as a professional actor, why do you want to come here?

Don: *(Hesitating a little)* Well, to get my Master's Degree.

Dean: Why?

Don: Well . . . I can answer that. It's because my father's graduate degrees are from Garrett and Northwestern.

Dean: So if this doesn't work out, you're prepared to blame your father.

Don: I've already blamed my father.

Dean: What?

Don: It was nothing … just an attempt at humor.

Dean: Your attempt was a little feeble.

Don: I thought so too, sir.

Dean: Well. If we accept your application and approve entrance, how do you intend to proceed?

Don: My goal is to complete the necessary work and courses to receive my Master's Degree in one year.

Dean: In one year? Do you mean one year, twelve months—or one year, nine months?

Don: One year—nine months.

Dean: It's never been done. It can't be done.

Don: I've prepared myself for this. With respect, Dean Dennis, I think—I really think I can do it.

Dean: We'll see. We'll see quickly. Before we can accept your application for admission, you must take and pass the same exams we give our graduating students when they enter graduate studies. First there's a platform exam.

Don: A what?

Dean: A platform exam. Thirty minutes of performance before a faculty committee. If you're a professional actor, you should be able to come up with something. Then there's an exam in lighting; another in scenic design and construction; another in costuming and makeup; also in theater literature. I will schedule the exams. You can pick up the schedule tomorrow morning. You'll take the tests and I'll see you back here a week from today.

Don: Thank you.

Dean: You may leave now.

Don: Thank you. *(He walks to the door)*

Dean: Stolz …

Don: Yes, sir?

Dean: I question your judgment, but I do admire your spirit.

Don: Thank you.

One week later, I was back.

(Knock)

Dean: Come in. Sit down.

Don: Thank you.

Dean: I have the results of the tests.

Don: All of them?

Dean: All of them. First, the exam on stage lighting.

Don: Yes?

Dean: Professor Fuchs has reported that you achieved the highest score of any student who has ever taken it.

Don: Good. I read his book.

Dean: Scenic Design and Construction? Doctor Mitchell reports "Good." He didn't write a book.

Don: But McCandless did. And at OCU I designed and built every set they had for four years.

Dean: I see. *(Continues)* Costume design and makeup.

Don: *(With some apprehension)* Yes . . .

Dean: Miss Prisk reported "this young man seems to have an idea about what he's doing."
Theater Literature. You seemed to have knowledge of every play on the exam. How did that happen?

Don: Well, a little over a year ago, I wrote requesting a list of the required plays.

Dean: You have prepared. Now we come to the platform exam. Now as you know, this is my field—Oral Interpretation. I understand from Dr. Cunningham ...

Don: The Chairman of that committee?

Dean: Yes. He reported that you presented a thirty-minute memorized rendition of Robert Browning's "Andrea Del Sarto," correct?

Don: Yes, sir. Did he like it?

Dean: Stolz, that is not a question that we ask in Academia.

Don: Sorry. Did I pass?

Dean: *(Takes a long time in answering)* Dr. Cunningham reported that in all his years here at Northwestern, it was the best platform exam he had ever witnessed.

Don: *(No comment, just a release of suspense)*

Dean: He had one criticism.

Don: Oh?

Dean: He thought dramatic monologues were too easy for you and recommended in your future studies here that you be allowed to study and deliver only what Dr. Cunningham calls "pure poetry."

Don: Pure poetry?

Dean: Keats and Tennyson. The result of all the tests? You can take whatever graduate courses we offer. It would be unfair and unjust not to allow it.

Don: Thank you.

Dean: It's not improper for me to ask—do you have funds for
   this?

Don: I've saved enough for my first semester's tuition.

Dean: What about room and board?

Don: Oh—I'll find work.

Dean: Doing what?

Don: Taking dictation and typing.

Dean: You intend to work your way through graduate school.

Don: Yes, sir.

Dean: A full course toward a degree in nine months and
   working at the same time.

Don: I think I can do it.

Dean: God help you. And I mean that.

Don: Thank you.

Dean: I have one word of advice for you as an actor. Don't
   even audition for any of the plays here at Northwestern.
   Good luck. And remember, I'm watching. And I think,
   hoping.

When I applied for a job at the employment office at Northwestern they sent me to be a secretary taking dictation and typing for
Edwin S. Mills, a retired vice president of the Carnegie Illinois Steel
Company. The office had warned me that he was a terror and like all
others who had been sacrificed to work for him, I would probably last
only a week or ten days. I was still working for him nine months
later.

I had been reporting to his home for only two weeks when he
recommended me as a secretary for Mrs. Mills as well as himself. He
liked me. I'm not sure what it was—the fact that I could take dictation
as fast as he could talk or that I refused to let a letter be mailed that
wasn't perfectly typed. For me they were pleasant days even when he
was threatening to sue both Postal Telegram and Western Union
because he felt they had been casual in the delivering of his messages.
There was only one thing wrong with the job: even between them, the

Mills did not have enough work to enable me to meet my expenses. As a result, I was constantly looking for work.

One morning, walking down Foster Street to class, I noticed a man painting the outside trim of his frame house. As a professor of literature, he knew nothing about what he was doing, so I immediately went to him and said that I needed work and I knew how to paint. I've never seen a man so relieved. As the next few weeks progressed, not only did I paint the outside trim, but I was also turned loose on three rooms on the interior. Two days after finishing the work I was just ready to present my bill when I heard that the young professor had suddenly and unexpectedly died. From what, I do not know. Several days later, I gathered my courage and went to call on the young widow. I, clumsily, I'm sure, attempted to express my condolences and told her that under the circumstances there would be no bill. When she thanked me, she smiled gently and said, "My husband and I had planned this work, had budgeted for it. I want you to take my check—I'm sure, that you as a student, are much more in need of the money than I am at this time. Thank you, anyway."

At Annie May Swift Hall, the general office of the School of Speech and Theater, and the only performance area they had, I was told what courses I should take if I were serious about getting a master's in nine months—something that had never been done and probably wouldn't, they kept reminding me. Their suggested courses became the assigned courses. And I liked every one of them. At least looking back on it now, I think I liked every one of them.

Advanced Oral Interpretation—Dr. C. D. Cunningham. I have no recollection of what the other members of the class were assigned, but I do remember his turning to me and saying, "You will work on Keat's 'Ode to a Grecian Urn.'" I was not thrilled. Not at first. It became a work in progress—studying form, rhyme, rhythm, meter, consonance, alliteration, all the ingredients of prosody. It became a magnificent challenge and I became an ardent admirer of Keats. And of C. C. Cunningham. He loved poetry. One morning during class, this master of interpretation, a legend in the academic world, stated that he would gladly give everything he had accomplished if he could but write two good lines of poetry. I still wonder if he ever really tried.

Lighting—Dr. Theodore Fuchs. It was exactly what I had anticipated. He was again and again surprised that I already knew the material.

Children's Theater—Miss Winifred Ward. She and Charlotte B. Charpenning of the Goodman Theatre faculty were accepted as the pioneers and leaders in this branch of theater.

Costuming—Miss Prisk. No one was ever better organized.

Theater Design—Lee Mitchell. Graduate students whose major was design were each scheduled to design a set for an Annie May Swift auditorium production. One or two of the sets that year were unbelievably bad. Each time this happened, Mitchell had the perfect critique for the student: "A very interesting set." Learning to use that phrase was probably the most important thing I picked up from Mitchell.

Then there was Advanced Acting. Alvina Krause. Even today, years after her death, she remains an icon in academic theater. Hardly three weeks into the class I met disaster. Miss Krause was starting her lecture concerning the deeply meaningful entrance speech of Orestes, and telling how it should be delivered. Mentally I disagreed, but I certainly did not intend to give any indication of my thoughts. But apparently I did something, for she immediately stopped her presentation.

Alvina: Obviously, Mr. Stolz, you don't agree with my interpretation.

Stolz: I'm sorry, Miss Krause.

Alvina: You do disagree, don't you?

Stolz: I'm sorry, yes, I do.

Alvina: I'm not going to ask you how you think it should be done.

Stolz: Thank you.

Alvina: But I'm going to give you a chance to show us. You will memorize Orestes' speech and deliver it before the class tomorrow morning.

Stolz: Memorize it and give it tomorrow morning.

Alvina: That is correct. Right here in this class.

As you might possibly recall, this speech of Orestes is not short. I memorized it that night and delivered it the next morning. I think I would have been all right with Miss Krause, if at the end of the speech I hadn't received a standing ovation. From that moment on, I was Miss Krause's forgotten student.

Then there was Doctor Clement Ramsland—Tim—the new head of the theater department and the professor of Theater Directing. It was his first year at Northwestern—they had hired him from the Humanities Department at the University of Minnesota. He knew more about stage blocking, the positioning and movement of actors on stage, than any man in academia or the professional theater. He could change the entire meaning of a scene by repositioning the actors.

When auditions for the first play of the year were announced (***The Warrior's Husband***), I, acting against the suggestion that Dean Dennis had made when he approved my acceptance into graduate studies, read for Dr. Ramsland, who was to direct the play, and the rest of the audition committee, and was given the role of Sapiens, who was the Warrior's Husband. Miss Krause, who was a member of the committee, was not pleased, but it mattered not. For the first time in the department's history the play was not presented in Annie Mae Swift Hall, but in the new auditorium across campus, Cahn Auditorium. It was a colorful and fun production that won the approval (and attendance) of the general student body, most of whom had never before attended the department's productions. Miss Krause was no more pleased when I was given the lead role in Ramsland's next directorial presentation.

When the Christmas holidays came, I decided to hitchhike back home to Britton, Oklahoma. I was tired, hungry, with absolutely no money and no hope of immediate work. So for the first and only time in my life, I telephoned home and asked my parents if they could possibly send me any money. My father wired all that they had—it was not quite four dollars.

With the "not quite four dollars" in my pocket, I picked up my already packed suitcase and headed for home. After thumbing a number of short, but quick, rides, I was stranded, until a very pleasant lady driver stopped and asked me where I was going. When I told her I wanted to reach Highway 66, she then told me that was exactly where she was going. I picked up my suitcase and got in. After driving for 15 or 20 minutes she stopped and told me that it had been very pleasant and was so glad that she could help me on my way. Where she had taken me was 66th Street, which had nothing to do with Highway 66. After she drove off, I went into a nearby filling station to ask for the shortest and quickest way to join Highway 66. They told me that I could either go back four miles, or if I was really wanting the shortest and quickest way, I could walk across the city dump, about a two-mile journey, and there would be Highway 66.

Since by now it was becoming twilight, I decided on the dump. I entered on the only road that crossed the dump to the other side. Actually it was little more than a dirt path used only by dump trucks bringing garbage. I walked something more than five minutes; the twilight was darkening into dusk. As it grew darker, there began to appear on either side of the narrow road, thousands of rats. I was only mildly relieved when I saw that they had little interest in me; they were too busy looking for more available food. As I continued to walk, I was determined not to attract further attention by revealing my fright or starting to run. I walked. Was there any way that my suitcase could be of help in case the situation worsened? The walk of "only two miles" was an eternity. Finally I was through the dump and standing on the edge of Highway 66 ready for some serious hitchhiking to Britton, Oklahoma.

In 1939, hitchhiking was a safe and usually quick way for young people to travel, but on this December cold and rainy day, it was different. No driver was eager to pick up a wet passenger and his wet suitcase. By 8:30 I was fortunate to have reached the main street of Rolla, Missouri. By now it was really raining and it seemed colder than at any time during the day. Nothing was open. The streets were dark except for the light post on every corner. Wisely, I thought, I decided to take refuge in the doorway of one of the stores. I had been there maybe ten minutes when a police car stopped directly in front of me. The officer got out and walked to where I was standing. Very politely, he said:

Police: Good evening.

Don: Good evening, sir.

Police: May I ask, what are you doing?

Don: Waiting until it stops raining.

Police: And then?

Don: Then I hope to get on my way to Oklahoma.

Police: Hitchhiking?

Don: Yes, sir.

Police: Do you know that in Missouri it's against the law to hitchhike?

Don: I'd heard that, yes.

Police: But everyone does it, right?

Don: Yes, sir.

Police: Now I have to ask: how much money do you have?

Don: What do you mean?

Police: I mean, how much money do you have?

Don: I have some.

Police: As much as $5.00?

Don: Not quite.

Police: Under $5.00. If you don't have at least $5.00 on you, then legally you're a vagrant.

Don: Oh.

Police: And I'm sorry to say, that means I have to put you in jail.

Don: Jail?

Police: Just remember, son, there it's warm and dry. So just get in the back seat of the car and we'll be on our way.

The jail was a brick building, perfectly square with no attached addition and no out buildings. A square brick building. The policeman opened the door and I went in. Inside the square was one large cell, surrounded by a wide hall that surrounded it on all four sides. In the cell were two prisoners who had obviously made that cell their home: their own radio, their own books, magazines and newspapers several packages of food and their laundry hanging on a line stretched from one corner to another.

The policeman pointed to a cot in the hallway and said, "That's yours. It would be a good idea for you to get dry as soon as you can." As soon as the outer door was closed, the two guys in the cell decided they could now talk:

First guy: Welcome.

Second guy: Yes. Glad you're here.

First: How long are you in for?

Don: I don't know.

First: Oh, that's too bad.

Second: Yes.

First: What are you in for?

Don: Vagrancy.

First: Oh, that's too bad.

Second: Yes.

Don: How long are you two in for?

First: We don't really know.

Second: No, we don't. We've been here for two months now.

Don: Oh.

First: Yes, two months.

Don: What are you in for?

First: Vagrancy.

They didn't laugh and neither did I. The next morning, the same policeman opened the outside door, bringing food to the two guys in the inner cell. After a minute or two he came back in with a breakfast for me: two fried eggs, bacon, two slices of toast and a coffee in a tin cup. In all the years since, I have never tasted coffee as good as it was that December morning in jail.

After I had finished eating, the officer said, "Okay, pick up your things. You're out of here." My two jail mates said goodbye, wished me well, and I was back in the police car headed for Route 66, leading south out of town. When we were well outside the city limits, the policeman said: "Remember now, it's against the law to hitchhike in Missouri, so don't you start doing it until I've turned around and am out of sight."

What a blessing that policeman was.

Once I reached Britton, my father and mother put me to bed and called the doctor. I had pneumonia. I don't remember being even uncomfortable, but it was several weeks before the doctor would hear of my hitchhiking back to Evanston. Classes had started again, but I had telephoned the theater office to tell them I would be returning a week late.

The first day I was back, I discovered that I had been assigned to direct a one-act play. It was a chore that all theater graduate students were given; the student is to select his choice of plays— either a one-act or one act of a full-length play. During my absence, someone on the faculty decided I should direct one act of **Peer Gynt**. I was not pleased, but felt it was better to go ahead. Looking back, I suppose pique played a part in my decision, but I set Peer Gynt in Dogpatch, the comic strip home of the Yokum family, and Peer Gynt would be L'il Abner, and his mother would be Ma Yokum. Everyone seemed to think it was creative and fun, except a few of the faculty. They objected most to L'il Abner and his mother carrying a jug around containing Dogpatch Kickapoo Joy Juice. Ramsland and Cunningham found it "amusing and clever." I did not win the directing award and Bob Ratcliffe, as L'il Abner, did not receive the award for acting. Truly I did not mean to be a smart-ass, but I guess I really was.

Much more important to my education and future work was a class I was assigned when the second semester arrived. It was called "Prosody" and was taught by Lew Sarrett. Sarrett was an established and much published poet; there are few anthologies that do not include several of his poems. Why he was in the School of Speech rather than one of the schools studying other forms of literature, I never knew. The class was an evening lecture class of three hours. It met only once a week with little homework. It was a lecture class; we sat there taking notes as we listened to one of the most inspiring teachers I had ever known. Prosody, aesthetics, ethics, writing—he covered them all. It was no wonder that fellow faculty member C. C. Cunningham thought of Lew Sarrett as the most brilliant of a star-studded faculty.

The final exam—a surprise: each of us in the class was to write a short story, not a poem—a short story. Sarrett read and wrote a critique of every story. He liked my story. I was as happy as a pig in Dogpatch mud.

The last of the nine months was rapidly approaching. Two weeks before the end of the second semester I had a call from Dr. Cunningham asking me to meet him in his office.

Cunningham: Come in.

(*Stolz enters*)

Cunningham: Sit down.

Stolz: Thank you.

Cunningham: In my mailbox I found this letter. From the business office of the University. In it they tell me that I, as your academic advisor, should know that you have not paid your second semester tuition. Is that true?

Stolz: Yes, sir, I'm afraid it is.

Cunningham: They go on to tell me that if you have not paid your tuition due, that I, as your counselor, should not allow you to take your remaining comprehensive exams—the final step in your achieving your Master's.

Stolz: *(Dejected)* I see.

Cunningham: Do you have the money to pay this bill?

Stolz: No, sir.

Cunningham: Is there any place you can borrow it?

Stolz: No, I'm afraid not.

(Pause)

Cunningham: I'm sorry.

(Pause)

Cunningham: If I had it, I'd lend it to you. But there have been … well family … *(lets it fade out)* I've kept my eye on you. You've done well. Unbelievably well. I guess I even understand why you took time to be in all those plays. My friend, Lew Sarrett, liked your short story.

Stolz: Thank you. That's almost as good as passing the comprehensives.

Cunningham: Yes, it is. *(Pause)* Well—*(Pause)* I think I've found a way around this. It might work. Your last exams are tomorrow, aren't they?

Stolz: Yes, sir.

Cunningham: All right. I'll put this letter back in the envelope—put it back in my mailbox and forget to pick up my mail until late tomorrow afternoon.

Stolz: You won't get in any trouble?

Cunningham: How can an old Oral Interpretation professor get in trouble for not remembering to pick up his mail?

(Pause)

Stolz: I don't know how to thank you.

Cunningham: Just pass those tests. That's all the thanks I need.

And I did. It would be several years before I could even attempt to pay the tuition payment that was long overdue. Achieving a Master's Degree from the Northwestern School of Speech in nine months suddenly brought to mind the question that comes to so many students today. What now? Where to from here?

ALL RIGHT,
BUT FOR ONLY ONE SHOW

Two months before the end of the second semester, Theodore Fuchs had recommended me as a lighting designer and technical director for a theater in Southern Illinois. I thanked him and graciously, I hope, told him I had other plans—not completely formed—but other plans. As I recall, it was the same week that Dr. Ramsland asked me to go to the Old Log Theater in Minnesota as an actor. For months he had told all of us in the Foster Street Apartment about this new theater that had opened in 1940. It was a professional company; they did thirteen plays in thirteen weeks; he had directed ten of them and in the coming summer of 1941, he would direct them all. I don't know why I turned him down; acting was what I wanted to do. I can't think of any time since when I have been so undecided on what I should do.

It was late afternoon the day I heard that I had passed the last of my comprehensive. Since the graduate students' final exams were not complete until two or three days after the close of the rest of the University, I went home to the empty apartment on Foster Street. I was tired, hungry and uncertain. I solved all three by going to bed. Just before two the next morning, the bedside phone rang.

Stolz: Hello.

Ramsland: Hello, this is Tim.

Stolz: *(Sleepily)* Who?

Ramsland: Clement Ramsland.

Stolz: Oh.

Ramsland: What are you doing?

Stolz: Sleeping.

Ramsland: Have you finished your comprehensive?

Stolz: The last of them.

Ramsland: Good. Well, I'm in Minneapolis, actually, out at the Lake. Remember I told you about the new season at the Old Log?

Stolz: Your second year.

Ramsland: That's right. And I asked you to come as one of the resident actors.

Stolz: Tim …

Ramsland: And you turned me down. Well, I'm calling with a different offer. I've just discovered that when I came to Northwestern I signed a contract that required me to teach the summer session which means, of course, that I can't be here at the Old Log. So Bob Aden, company manager, and Deborah Tighe, the primary financial backer, authorized me to call you and offer a position of actor/director.

Stolz: *(Silence)*

Ramsland: Don,

Stolz: Yes?

Ramsland: It would be great.

(Silence)

Ramsland: What do you say?

Stolz: I thank you, I really thank you, Tim, but no.

Ramsland: Why not?

Stolz: I don't know why not.

Ramsland: Don, they're desperate for a director and I promised to help them. I'll tell you what to do. Come here and direct the next play. That gives them a couple of weeks to look around. How about that?

Stolz: Tim … *(Pleadingly)*

Ramsland: After the encouragement I've given you the past year …

Stolz: Nine months.

Ramsland: All right, nine months. Anyway, I think you owe me this. Just do the next show.

Stolz: All right.

Ramsland: Good. There's a ticket waiting for you at the Evanston Station.

"A ticket waiting for me at the Evanston Station." It didn't take me too long to realize how sure of himself he really was.

Later that morning I went to the Evanston train station, picked up my ticket and caught the Hiawatha for Minneapolis. I was really pleased to find on the same train an old friend from Oklahoma City University, Tommy Heggen, who in a few years would become famous as the author of the war's greatest play and motion picture, *Mr. Roberts*. His family had moved to Minnesota and he finished his education at the University of Minnesota. Together we found our way to the club car, where Tommy demonstrated that his old school reputation as a "good drinker" was not to be taken lightly.

After what seemed, under the circumstances, to be too short a journey, at 5:30 p.m. the Hiawatha pulled into the Milwaukee station in Minneapolis, where there was a young man waiting to take me to Excelsior, the home of the Old Log. I said a reluctant goodbye to Heggen and followed the young man to an International Station Wagon. As soon as I got in he informed me that we were to go to the Viking Room at the downtown Radisson, where we would meet another passenger for the Old Log—a passenger who, by the way, never showed up.

The Viking Room was glorious—the town's most popular meeting place. My escort suggested that I order a rum collins, it was one of the drinks for which the room was famous. In Oklahoma, which was still a dry state, my occasional drink was home-distilled corn liquor with a 3.2 beer chaser. During the nine months in Evanston, I had graduated to the very cheap bourbon, Wilkins Family, ordered from a Howard Street off-sale. To this day I remember the delight of my first rum collins.

It had started raining. When we finally arrived at the Old Log, the rain had become a downpour. Rain at the old Old Log was something that once you experienced, you would never forget. It formed a river the flowed down from the parking area, through the back door of the theater and down the aisle to form a pond that, as the evening progressed, covered the footing of the first three rows.

I waded down the path to the box office where I met one of the most intelligent and personable women I have ever known, Deborah Tighe.

(The box office in the old theater. Back of the counter is Deborah Tighe)

(Don enters, briefly looks around and approaches counter)

Don: Hello.

Deborah: Hello.

Don: I'm Don Stolz.

(At this moment a couple of customers arrive and approach counter)

Deborah: *(To Don)* Excuse me. *(To customers)* May I help you?

Customer: Yes, thank you. I'd like to pick up my tickets. The name is Harry Bullis.

Deborah: *(Who knows Harry very well)* Certainly, Harry. And Mrs. Bullis. Now—*(finding envelope)* here they are. Two tickets, that's $1.70.

Harry: *(Handing her two one-dollar bills)* And thank you.

Deborah: *(As she gives him 30 cents in change)* Thank you. Have a good evening.

Harry: *Taming of the Shrew*—I'm looking forward to it.

Deborah: *(Now she turns to Don)* What did you say your name was?

Don: Don … Don Stolz.

Deborah: Oh, yes, you're the boy that Bob hired for the pop stand.

Don: Oh?

Ramsland: *(Enters)* He's not the boy for the pop stand, he's your new director.

Deborah: Director? He's just a child.

Ramsland: *(Not displeased with this)* Well, he's a very talented child. Come on, Don, let's go into the theater. *(Picks up programs, hands one to Don)*

Deborah: Tim?

Ramsland: Yes?

Deborah: I don't understand it, I looked in the theater a few minutes ago, there must be thirty people in there and I've sold only eight tickets.

Ramsland: Well, I've been standing at the back door and letting them in.

Deborah: You what?

Ramsland: Well, I told you we weren't ready to open, so I've been letting people in to see our last rehearsal.

Deborah: Not ready to open? *(During this, Ramsland and Don enter the theater)*

Ramsland: *(As they move in)* Have a good trip?

Don: Fine.

Ramsland: I like that train. A hell of a lot better than driving from here to Chicago.

Don: An old friend of mine was on the train. I knew him at Oklahoma City University. His name is Tom Heggen.

Ramsland: An actor?

Don: No, a writer. At least that's his goal. Had a good time.

Ramsland: In the club car?

Don: In the club car. Man, can he drink.

Ramsland: Here we are. We'll sit here in the eleventh row. Leaves plenty of room for the audience in front of us. *(They sit. Don looks at his program)*

Don: Big cast.

Ramsland: *Taming of the Shrew* is a big show. I cut it down as much as I could, but ...

Don: *(Still looking at program)* Bob Aden plays Petruchio.

Ramsland: He's good. You met Bob when he was casting in Chicago.

Don: I remember. *(Reading)* Louis Lytton.

Ramsland: Good character man. He was with us last summer.

He was selling newspapers on Hennepin. A newspaperman brought him out to us.

Don: *(Reading)* Betsy Nash—Kate.

Ramsland: A Wayzata socialite. She's all right.

Don: *(Still reading)* Chuck Nolte.

Ramsland: High school boy—fine actor. You'll like him. His father is a dean at the University of Minnesota.

Don: The University of Minnesota. I remember Lew Sarrett—you know at Northwestern—telling us that there was one of the great teachers of oral interpretation at the University of Minnesota I think his name was Rarig.

Ramsland: Sarrett was correct. Rarig is great.

Don: Tim?

Ramsland: Yes?

Don: *(Finding name on program)* Don Stolz …

Ramsland: It's just a small part.

Don: I know, but what do you do about it tonight?

Ramsland: We just skip it. You'll learn the part and go on tomorrow night.

Don: What time's the rehearsal?

Ramsland: You don't need a rehearsal. Just learn the part and go on. You don't need a rehearsal.

Don: I see.

That was my introduction to the Old Log Theater. I probably should tell you that the production was just as bad as the weather.

When the critic came out two nights later, it was still rough. He reviewed the play under the headline: "Shrew Tames Actors." As Bob Aden wrote sixty years later, "and Don's life would never be the same again." He was so right.

In Bob's book, *The Way It Was*, he included an article written by Deborah Tighe for *Countryside Magazine*; it chronicled the beginning of the Old Log Theater:

"On May 31, 1940, if you attend our show, you will witness the birth of a theater—a theater which we hope will grow to a ripe old age. Upon you, our audience, depends largely whether this theater will succeed or fail. Audience reactions are the thermometer of opinion for a theater, its measure of popularity and effort. We take pride in being able to say we are the first theater to be created on the shores of Lake Minnetonka, and the first summer repertory theater in the State of Minnesota. Our hope is that you, our audience will likewise take pride in being able to take part in this creation. This theater and its members are dedicated to producing good plays. It is in this spirit and for this purpose that we present to you this theater."

"We present to you this theater." As I have said so many times, the Old Log does belong to the audience. To you.

The actors, in 1940, all lived in a "loose-joined" old house that was once a speakeasy and meeting place for ladies of the evening. To many of the conservative elders of Excelsior, this location confirmed what they already had imagined actors to be. Other citizens were more understanding.

At the end of that first season, 1940, Bob Aden wrote Mr. and Mrs. Harry Kuechle, from whom they leased the property:

"Whether we earn much or not at the end of this season is really not of prime importance. What matters is that we will have laid the groundwork for a really successful season. And this, in itself, will have been an achievement."

So, returning to my arrival at the Old Log in 1941 . . .

In *The Way It Was*, Bob writes:

"Don Stolz, quickly adapting to the Old Log, began to put some of his expertise in stage lighting to use, and redesignd our whole system. There was so much to do everywhere and not enough hours for the task. One midnight, when Don seemed to be missing and had us worried, we searched till we found him ... fast asleep, cradled safely in among the struts and rafters, with one hand still clutching a spotlight."

Now that's the way Aden remembers it; I'm just not sure. I suppose anyone who can go to sleep while riding a bicycle can go to sleep in the rafters.

The first play I directed at the Old Log was Sidney Howard's ***Ned McCobb's Daughter***. What a fortunate choice Bob had made;

the resident company was perfectly suited to their roles. It would have been difficult to find better choices even in New York; it was a play we all loved. In the *Minneapolis Star*, John Sherman, theater critic for the paper, wrote:

"There comes a time in the life of most repertory theaters when months of work and preparation, sweat and tears suddenly 'jell' as if by magic, to produce a play that comes close to perfection—one of those occasions when casting and staging and script and performance all merge into a brilliant, close-knit unit. The Old Log reaches one of those milestones this week . . . young Donald Stolz has done an uncommonly deft job of direction, and his 10 players have made one of the strongest acting ensembles I have yet seen."

The "one" play I had promised Tim Ramsland to direct was done. Now I was free to do whatever I hadn't planned. After the opening night performance, two days before the review appeared, the actors knew that **Ned McCobb's Daughter** was a winner. They all started pleading with me—and pleading is the apt word—to remain at the Old Log. When I did not give an immediate answer they said, "well, at least stay for the next show." And it seems, after that, the only thing that got me away was World War II.

In this summer of 1941, the entire company lived in a rented house known as The Old Backbay Grocery, which it had once been. Not far from the theater, it is today the site of the Georgetown Manor Apartments. Bob and Deborah had hired a cook and housekeeper, Reeney Bunn. Bob wrote, "In her forties, black, small and bespectacled, she ruled us with adamantine will, moral probity and delightful humor."

When a young high school age apprentice with the desire to learn the "actor's craft" was to move in, the house was already filled beyond capacity. As an example, there were four of us sleeping in the screened side porch. There was no room in the manor. Reeney had an easy answer; he could move into her attic room with her. She would hang a sheet between the two beds "and everything would be fine." It was fine with young David Moore, as well. It was fine with everyone until the weekend when Dave's father and mother appeared and saw the living condition. That was the end of David's career at the Old Log. Temporary end. It would be thirteen years before Dave Moore, soon to become the Twin Cities favorite television newscaster, would next appear on the Old Log stage in the hit play, *The Moon is Blue.*

Bob and Deborah were so encouraged by the 1941 season that by the end of the summer, they had decided that the Old Log should go on tour through Minnesota, North Dakota and perhaps Wisconsin and Iowa. Anywhere that it could be booked. Bob had gone to the Actors Equity office in New York and through them had hired four splendid, mature and experienced actors. They were to be paid $15.00 a week plus room. I was to direct, then travel with the show as stage manager and lighting technician. We non-Minnesotans in the company all purchased several sets of heavy long underwear, but as the tour progressed, they were never used—though when we reached Bismarck, we were snowbound for two days by an early blizzard.

I remember the tour quite well; some things I remember vividly. Like the night when enroute to Bismarck we stopped for coffee at a small café. A big poster on the wall announced that next week the town would be honored by a visit of the world's finest polka band, Whoopee John Wilfahrt. I could not believe that anyone with that name would continue without having it changed. When I laughed, the waitress said, "Don't dare make fun. Whoopee John is the best known person in the Upper Midwest."

Also the night we drove into Bismarck and saw a big—an enormous—big red lighted "P" atop the tallest building in town. One of the locals informed us the Big P stood for pimps, prostitutes and the Patterson Hotel.

Later on our tour, back in Minnesota, New Ulm, and the marvelous theater, Turner Hall. Beginning with the balcony loge, the seats were permanent. The "orchestra" (the main level seating) was a flat floor covered with sections of seats that could be folded down upon one another and pushed under the loge, leaving a hardwood, level floor for athletic events. The stage was like that of a nineteenth century opera house with even a prompter's box in the downstage footlights. The house scenery was 18 feet tall, precisely tapered toward the top so the weight would be on the lower part of the flats. The stage crew was wonderfully trained and closely knit. Most of them were teachers or professional men who proudly donated their time to the Turner projects. What a delight was our engagement in New Ulm. One of our last bookings was to be Rochester, Minnesota, the Mayo Auditorium, an unbelievable facility with a good union crew.

Early Sunday morning, Bob Aden and I left the Kahler Hotel and walked the short distance to the Mayo. The date was December 7, 1941. While we were working with the crew, getting the set up and the furniture in place, the sound man came from his booth, where he had been listening to the radio, and said in a tone and manner I shall never forget: "All of you must come in here and listen to this broadcast." It was the attack on Pearl Harbor.

Over 600 tickets had been sold for the evening performance, fewer than a hundred attended. How the play was acted, how the play was received, not one of us remembers. Most of us can't even recall which of the two plays we presented. As one of the actors later said, "It was a macabre and awful experience."

On Monday the troupe returned to Minneapolis and after a very elegant farewell at the Nicollet Hotel, I left for Oklahoma where I immediately enlisted in the Navy.

There Was No Doubt What To Do:
Enlistment

In reviewing my enlistment papers, and seeing that I had a BFA from Oklahoma City University and an MA from Northwestern, the Navy recruiter decided that I should go to one of their Midshipmen Schools. But while they were waiting for a place at one of the schools, they wanted me to go someplace and take a course in trigonometry. Just make certain that I kept the Navy informed about where I was and how they could reach me. Where I went was Oklahoma City University and took up quarters in the men's on-campus dormitory. The next day I went to downtown Oklahoma City because I had heard that KVOK was looking for an announcer. An announcer I had never been, but I got the job. Several months later a new station manager fired me because I "sounded too much like a real person." In those days, announcers were to sound like announcers.

As for the course in trigonometry, it was a breeze. Mathematics has never been difficult for me—except the mathematics required to balance my checkbook. Trigonometry was no more difficult than looking up a number in the city telephone directory.

In the spring I had not heard from the Navy, but I had heard from Bob Aden who wanted to know if there was any way I could return to Minnesota and direct the 1942 season. And could I convince Cleda Villines (the actress I recommended and they had hired in 1941) that she should return as well.

I wrote the Navy and told them where I was going and caught

the train for Minneapolis.

Molly George was back as Administrator. A new designer had been hired, Tom Russell, who had been designing, building and painting sets for professional theaters for 30 years.

The opening play for the 1942 season was *Peg O' My Heart*, starring Cleda. Out of the seven-member cast, four were new members of the company.

Earlier in the spring, Aden had gone to New York to hire actors for the 1942 season. And he had done well. As Bob reported: "Larry Hugo and his wife came to us after recent engagements in New York with Helen Hayes and Gladys George. Bert Jeeter, fey, gentle and rail-thin, came from a stock company in England and most recently from the production of *The Daughters of Atreus* in New York. Brook Fleming had worked with Orson Welles and had a short time before been a trapeze performer with the Ringling Brothers."

Bob had found a handsome and talented young juvenile in the amateur theater world of Minneapolis. Cleda Villines, the Oklahoma City University student whom I had recommended for the 1941 season, was returning for 1942, as was the unbelievably talented Evelyn Snapp. All that was needed was a character man to replace our beloved Louis Lytton, who had decided to "skip" the summer because he had gotten a job with the Anti-Defamation League, and he felt strongly that they needed him perhaps as much as did we.

I can't recall the exact time I arrived in Excelsior, but I do know it was some time Tuesday evening, because I remember very well Bob handing me the manuscript and telling me that he had already given the "sides" to the actors. In those days, professional stock and repertory actors did not work with "books" but from sides. The sides were 8 1/2" by 5 1/2," half of the regular size typewriter paper. On those sides would be typed the actor's line, preceded by his "cue," which in most cases gave the actor absolutely no idea as to why he was saying what he was saying—that he would learn the first day of rehearsal.

I remember that it was Tuesday night when I got the manuscript, for it gave me a whole day to read the script and "block" the action. In other words, tell each actor where he was to be and when, and where he was to move. I tried never to go into the first day of rehearsal without having blocked the entire play. That full day before Thursday rehearsal seemed a luxury. All during the last season we opened on Wednesday, and started rehearsal for the next play the next morning at 10:00. As a result, there was no Wednesday night during the entire season when I slept more than three hours.

The company was housed and fed in the Sampson House in downtown Excelsior. Bob Aden wrote, "The hotel was a decaying relic of the 1890s resort days, but it was to provide a comfortable and homey atmosphere for the company." By the time I arrived from Oklahoma City, all available rooms at the Sampson House had been assigned, so I, along with a number of others, was sent to the Swee-ney Boarding House in the next block. The only room left at the Sweeney's could be entered only by climbing out a window in the upstairs hall to the almost flat roof of the porch, and then crawling back in a window at the other end. The room had, however, one enormous advantage: my night time study and preparation of the script would have absolutely no interrupting visitors.

Three days before rehearsals were to start (two days before I arrived from Oklahoma), a gray-haired man in his fifties arrived at the theater with a young woman whom he introduced as his daughter. Though that relationship was certainly questionable, it was apparent that the man had had considerable experience in small stock companies and tent shows. Bob needed a character man, and here he was. When Bob told me of this new addition to the company, he also informed me that the girl, Donna, almost never spoke. This was the company with whom I started rehearsals the last Wednesday in May for *Peg O' My Heart*. It was a capable cast—a good cast and a charming play, which even in 1942 did not seem unbearably dated.

Aden almost never asked me what plays should be scheduled; that he had determined during the winter months. Nor do I remember his ever telling me what actor should be cast in what role. That was my job. But I do recall that early in June 1941, he came to me with an idea on which he wanted my opinion. Let me quote directly from Bob's book:

"Something else was in the wind, something big. John Salisbury, on his radio show had interviewed one of the top strippers in the country, June March, thought she was indescribably great, and wanted us to do **White Cargo** with June as Tondeleyo. Don and I were all for it, and when we met June we were totally won over by her charm and simplicity.

"June and her sister, Evelyn, were the children of a leading man and leading lady in the waning days of tent shows and weekly downtown stock. As the movies grabbed hold and live theater dwindled, burlesque began to flourish, and Ivy de Marco decided, when her husband died, that her daughters had to help out. There was no better possibility of salvation than with the new rage. Blessed with rhythm, long legs and great "meal tickets" (June's word for breasts), both girls were natural strippers, so Ivy became an obnoxiously strict stage mother and the girls highly paid stars under the names of June March and Gay Knight. How these girls remained unspoiled and virginal is a mystery and a tribute to Ivy. When June, Don and I worked together, we became fast friends and stayed fast friends for many years. She could bring out the fun and insouciance in both of us, and there was little we liked better, for example, than the buying of a jar of pickled pig's feet, going to the Alvin Theater, sitting in the front row, and eating the pig's feet during the performance of one of June's friends, that week's star stripper.

"Now more than sixty years later, I still meet men who say to me, 'You know, the first play I ever saw at the Old Log was **White Cargo** with June March. I told my parents I was just going to the Excelsior Amusement Park. They never did find out where I had actually gone.'"

Bob Aden as Witzel, bitter and vile-tempered, was nothing short of marvelous; he made enough of an impression that he was offered a Warner Brothers screen test. The difficulty was that they demanded he be on the spot in Hollywood, but would not assign a date. It was easy for Bob to decide he was needed at the Old Log.

White Cargo with June March and Bob Aden was a tremendous success. As Bob Aden wrote 47 years later: "And what a hit! We ran it for two weeks to standing room only and even had to turn people away night after night. Then we took it to downtown Minneapolis and ran it for a week at the Alvin, that wonderful old North Seventh Street home of the Bainbridge Players, striptease burlesque, and latterly movies."

Deborah and Bob had decided that the run at the Alvin should coincide with the Aquatennial, the Minneapolis Summer Festival. One of the leading actors in *White Cargo*, thinking he had the week off, had taken a job as stage manager of Al Sheehan's great show, The Aqua Follies, which played summer after summer at Theodore Wirth Park. Aden and Al Sheehan reached, without difficulty, a compromise: the member of the cast would appear at the Alvin and I would take his place as stage manager at the Aqua Follies.

I can't leave the summer of 1942 without mentioning two more things. When *The Moon is Down*, the play about the Nazi invasion of Norway, opened in New York, Aden immediately started a campaign of phone calls, letters and telegrams to John Steinbeck, the author of the book from which the play was written. Bob by-passed the producer of the play, the director, and went directly to the author of the novel. After weeks of continued bombardment, Steinbeck finally arranged for the Old Log to be the first theater outside of New York to present *The Moon is Down*.

It was a sensation and in Minnesota, the American home of the Norwegians, how could it not be a great box office success? Just as with *White Cargo*, it was necessary to hold the play over for a second week.

Finally, during the summer of 1942, Sinclair Lewis, at that time Minnesota's most famous novelist and playwright, was almost a daily visitor to the Old Log. Originally he wanted to direct one of his own writings, with his mistress at that time in the leading role. As the summer progressed, he decided he would rather direct Shaw's *Candida* with Don Stolz playing Marchbanks. There was enough talk about it that Minneapolis columnist, Virginia Stafford, wrote, "Sinclair Lewis is now considering *Candida* as his choice to direct

White Cargo; Don Stolz, Joe Tomes, Bob Aden, Ken Senn, Louis Lytton, Carl Shelton, and Dan Stapleton.

for the final play of the summer season."

Why it never happened, I do not know.

At the end of the season, the Navy still had not called me to duty, so I wrote telling them I was going to New York and as soon as I had an address, I would send it to them. Bob wanted to visit his mother living in New York, so the two of us took the train together. I stayed as a roomer in a household that included the silent screen star, Lila Lee, and her young son, playwright-to-be Jimmie Kirkwood, and a delightful character woman, Edna West.

As I remember, it was the day after I arrived that I called my cousin, Robert Stolz, who was a senior executive with Macy's (as was his wife). Knowing the vagaries of the theater profession, Bob suggested that I apply for a job at the store. I did, and after a week of training, was named night manager of the men's store. Regardless of how important the title may sound, it really meant that I was in charge of the stock boys who worked nights. It also allowed me to make rounds during the day to all the theater agents and radio networks.

The second week I was in New York, I obtained an audition with Marge Morrow, talent director for CBS Radio network. One week later, I was on the air playing a role in *Let's Pretend*, the network production for children.

Most actors dislike or even hate "making the rounds," but thinking back across 60 years, I recall that I enjoyed it. I even called regularly on the Brown Brothers agency, an office most actors wouldn't enter alone.

In September and November (now remember that this is 1942, with a great many young men already in the service), I was lucky. I was scheduled to be one of the leading actors in *Henry Aldrich*, was on call-back for the boy in *The Great Big Doorstep*, and had been called into Marge Morrow's office so she could tell me she had left CBS for Warner Brothers and wanted to know if I was available for motion pictures.

The day after visiting Ms. Morrow, I discovered that at last, I had not been forgotten by the Navy. They wanted me to report to the Midshipman's School at the University of Notre Dame. Despite the promising activities in New York, I was glad. In World War II. we thought we knew what we were fighting for. And we did.

Since transportation had been arranged from point of enlistment, I left New York and went home to Oklahoma. After a two-day visit with my father and mother, I boarded the Santa Fe to Chicago, where I transferred to the South Shore Line to South Bend, where I was to find a whole new world.

THE BATTLE OF SOUTH BEND

The South Shore train from Chicago arrived at the South Bend station—then located in downtown South Bend—where about sixty of us got off, and were told that soon transportation to Notre Dame would be arriving. The transportation turned out to be two stake body trucks. In the orders we had received from the Navy some 15 days earlier, we had been informed to bring as little as possible with us, so there was little luggage to be thrown aboard the trucks, and there was plenty of standing room for those of us who in less than 50 minutes, would be magically transformed into apprentice seamen.

Once aboard the truck, I began to seriously listen to the various conversations and learned that all were graduates of colleges and universities across the country. I also soon discovered that most of their studies had been in mathematics, engineering, physics or other science—many already with graduate degrees. I didn't take a survey, but I am willing to wager that there wasn't another Fine Arts graduate in either truck. I began to seriously question if the Navy knew what they were doing when they sent me to Midshipmen's School. I was apprehensive. Personal failure seemed just ahead. The one thing that all aboard both trucks had in common was a dislike for the University of Notre Dame. A dislike, without reason, which I shared.

Aboard the same truck was a solemn looking young man who was as silent and removed as I. I later learned though a college graduate, he had enlisted in the Navy and had served as a sailor aboard a destroyer. He had been sent to Midshipmen's School because the officers aboard the destroyer felt he would be an excellent officer. They were correct. Robert Sweitzer became the best Navy officer I ever knew—and during the months and years ahead, one of my dearest friends.

Once on campus, we found that where we were to be quartered, and with whom, had already been determined. It had been done alphabetically. I was to be in Section 36, assigned to a room on the second floor of Howard Hall, and my roommate would be Albert Stokes. The following day when we were given our textbooks, Stokes told me that it was the first time since grade school that he had a textbook. Never, he declared, regardless of which level of schooling, had he ever owned a textbook. He had been raised in an orphanage, soon developed into an unbelievably talented football player, was taken by a Texas high school, and then recruited by Texas State, where he became a Little All-American football star.

My immediate thought was that here was a guy who might be in for more trouble becoming an officer than someone with a BFA. It was not a fear unknown to him. Soon after classes began, he grew more and more discouraged. And despite the help that three of us were giving him, he felt certain he would never make it. The Navy had also reached the same conclusion, and with wisdom and consideration, which we were delighted to see, they removed Stokes from Midshipmen School and because of his football skill and record, turned him into a physical training Chief Petty Officer at another location.

To most new sailors, one of the surprising things was the efficiency and cooperation between the Navy and Notre Dame. Though we were at the other end of the campus, we marched on the same sidewalks as the University students; we walked to their separate classrooms; we dined in the same dining hall (where I eventually learned to like the German hot potato salad); we used the Rockne building. I remember one day during swimming instruction, here was a Protestant swimming in the Rockne pool and across from me was a midshipman wearing the Star of David on a chain around his neck. Though the Midshipman School, the University and the University NROTC all used the same facilities, there never seemed to be a conflict or any confusion of schedule.

The classes? What I had expected, I'm not sure, but they weren't as difficult for me as I had anticipated. I began to realize that quite possibly I was going to make it.

After thirty days as apprentice seaman, the 75% of us still remaining were named Midshipmen and, on the next Saturday night, were allowed for the first time to go into downtown South Bend. I need say no more about Saturday night in downtown South Bend.

Sundays were different. Never anywhere have the men and women in the service been better treated than they were by the people in South Bend. If you were in the service, it was impossible to go to any church in the city without being asked to Sunday dinner. I attended the West Side Methodist Church where I soon learned that the minister was a friend of my Uncle Karl. He immediately asked me to act as a liaison between the church and the Midshipmen School. I soon began, at his request, to act also as an assistant pastor occasionally preaching the morning sermon. I thank God that there is absolutely no written record of what I may have said. When our class graduated from Midshipmen School as young Ensigns, Larry Ackman, from Minneapolis, also the son of a Methodist minister, and I were placed in charge of the ceremony at the church.

One Saturday morning, as our ninety days were coming close to an end, an inspection of the whole Midshipmen School was scheduled before we were dismissed for the rest of the day. Each section was standing at attention in front of their respective halls. Our company officer was a young ensign, Charlie Reed, loved by all of us except for two men in the section; both of them standing on either side of me. It was the day on which the officers had just changed their cap covers from blue to white. Ensign Reed was proud of this group; except for the two, all had done well. As he strutted back and forth in front of us, he was a combination of a cute bantam rooster and a Virginia gentleman lawyer. Just as he passed the end of the line where his two non-believers and I stood, a bird dive-bombed and hit Mr. Reed's new white hat cover. The man to the right of me said in voice loud enough to be heard by everyone in the section, "Even the birds know."

As graduation day approached, those of us who were to be commissioned were interviewed and asked to what part of the Navy we would like to be assigned. It was a good public relations move, but it didn't mean a thing. We were sent where they wanted to send us where they thought we would best contribute. I was surprised when orders finally came, that I was to be retained as an instructor in the Navigation Department. Some time during the next day the Seamanship Department arranged a trade. So a man who had never been out of the sight of land was to teach seamanship.

Next to the fact that I had "made it," the most pleasing part of becoming an officer meant that I could get rid of those ridiculous pants with thirteen buttons and the heavy wool "watch" shirt, the uniform of the apprentice seamen and midshipmen.

And it was spring. I remember well my first Saturday night as a new Navy officer. I was wearing my new dress whites, the most comfortable uniform that any service ever had. I had a date with quite a pretty young lady. We had visited the officer's club on the second floor of the hotel. I was now in the lobby of the hotel waiting for her to return from the ladies' room. As I stood there, I couldn't but reflect on how lucky a young man I was—I had received my commission, I had been retained as an instructor, I had a date with a pretty girl and, for the first time in months, I had a few dollars in my pocket, and I felt very good about my new dress whites. It must have been obvious how I felt because two middle-aged, Helen Hokanson-type women, passed me, took one look, realized how self-satisfied I was and then one of them said in a voice just loud enough for me to hear, "Isn't it remarkable how much like uniforms they're making these play suits nowadays?" Never had there been a more appropriate squelch.

Bob Sweitzer, whom I mentioned earlier, was also now an Ensign, and had also been assigned to the Midshipman's School as a Company Officer, a position for which I couldn't even imagine anyone as well qualified. He was firm and stern and knew well the value of discipline, but administered it with compassion and

Ensign Donald Stolz

Joan Marie Fuller

understanding.

During our Midshipman weeks, Bob and I had developed a fast friendship; so, when it was necessary for us to find quarters off campus, we rented a large room at a home on West Jefferson.

One spring night, when Bob was on "guard" duty, another recently commissioned officer suggested it would be fun to go on a double date. His beloved-at-that-moment had a car and would drive. It was fun. At the end of the evening, the young chauffeur suggested we finish the evening with a coke at the Marmain Drug Store. Shortly after she parked, another car parked next to us. In it were five young girls. Our chauffeur of the night noticed them and then said of one of the passengers of the other car, who were by now entering the drug store, "There goes that Joan Fuller. Everybody likes her but me. I can't stand her." Then she turned to me and said, "I suppose you'd like to meet her."

That, of course, was a challenge that no one could possibly resist, so we, too, entered the drug store and I was introduced to the "Horrible Joan Fuller," whom I found to be one of the cutest, prettiest, and most pleasant girls I had ever met. I managed to get her telephone number from a friend of Joan's brother, who was also enjoying the Marmain that evening.

I, apparently, was not as subtle as I had hoped, for when I telephoned Joan Fuller the next evening to ask if she could have dinner with me in the dining room of the Hoffman, she said she would ask her mother and I should call back the next day. The next day, I received a not particularly eager "yes."

As spring turned into summer, Sweitzer and I were two of the young officers invited daily to meet at the Studebaker family (still in the automobile manufacturing business) swimming pool. I was tremendously pleased to see that Joan, who was a dear friend of Mary and Lillian Studebaker, was also a daily visitor to the pool. It was an idyllic summer. At no time since then have I had as much leisure. On occasion, not too often, I felt a little guilty. Here the country was at war, I was in the Navy, and I was having the best time of my life. Please note "on occasion."

Ever since arriving at the Midshipman School, I, along with most of the other men, had found my dislike for Notre Dame beginning to diminish. You couldn't but admire their efficiency, their commitment to ethical and moral values. When fall came, my conversion (not to Catholicism but to the spirit of Notre Dame) became almost complete. At the first home game of the Fighting Irish, the Midshipmen, all feeling as I had when I first arrived, every single one as a united body, loudly cheered the football team opposing Notre Dame. Loudly and enthusiastically. The next day a sports columnist for the *South Bend Tribune* wrote a scathing column about the rude and unappreciative Midshipmen who were given tickets by Notre Dame and still roared with approval at every good play made by the opposing team. The column received an immediate reply from the President of Notre Dame, in which he revealed that the Navy had paid for and delivered the tickets and as long as he was President of Notre Dame, the Midshipmen could root for any team they wanted to support.

It is little wonder that the Navy and Notre Dame are still and will continue to play one another in a game that always beautifully illustrates what college football should be.

Joan returned to Stephens College, the Studebaker girls returned to their schools, but dinner invitations to Bob and me continued. How we got through Thanksgiving, I don't know. Bob accepted an invitation to dinner for both of us; I, not yet knowing this, accepted a different invitation for both of us; and then Joan's mother and father invited the both of us. In all three cases the dinner time was different, so Bob and I made all three. It was two days before either of us ate again.

Theater, certainly, was not foremost in my mind … not until a midshipman from Minneapolis remembered my connection with the Old Log and suggested it might be a great idea for me to direct a production with Midshipmen and officers as the cast. The female characters would be solicited from St. Mary's. I remember a charming little play, **Spring Dance**, and I remember a number of the rehearsals. Little more. One thing more, it was presented in Washington Hall, and I loved the place.

When Joan returned to South Bend for Christmas vacation, I presented, and she accepted an engagement ring. The following spring, Joan and her mother insisted that Joan's father, Gus, had no idea that there was any significance to the ring she was wearing, and I must—MUST—"ask him for her hand in marriage." Imagining how a father might feel about his daughter just barely 18 years old, I approached Gus with great apprehension. He was reading the Sunday edition of the *Chicago Tribune*.

Gus: Well, Don, how's the Navy?

Don: Uhh … fine.

Gus: You heard from Bob since he was transferred? Sea duty, wasn't it?

Don: Yes, sir. He's aboard the *New York*.

Gus: That's a battleship, isn't it?

Don: One of the older ones. One of the best ones.

Gus: Did he say what his duty is?

Don: He was in communication, but he's being assigned to navigation.

Gus: I'm sure Bob is a very capable officer.

Don: I agree.

Gus: Well.

Don: Yes, sir.

Gus: Pleasant day.

Don: Yes, sir.

Gus: What are you and Joan going to do today?

Don: Probably go see the Donahues and the Studebakers.

Gus: I'll tell Joan to take one of the cars.

Don: Thank you, but we can ride our bikes.

Gus: No, take one of the cars.

Don: Thank you. *(pause)* Er …

Gus: Yes?

Don: Well …

Gus: Yes?

Don: Well—

Gus: Yes—

Don: Lillian and Joan thought I should ask you ...

Gus: Ask me what?

Don: *(After a pause)* For permission to marry Joan.

Gus: *(Pause)* You've got to be kidding.

Honestly, that's all he said. He just sat there, stunned. So I decided it was a conversation best continued by Lillian and Joan who were waiting in the next room.

How Gus arrived at his eventual answer, I have never cared to find out. It was "yes." The Fuller family within three weeks was to move to California where Gus was to supervise the construction of a new munitions facility for the government. For the Fullers, it became a frantic and stressful time of wedding preparation.

My responsibility was to take a crash Catholic instruction course from Father Carey, whom I had met through the Donahues. He was a wonderful man, a cheerful outgoing priest, a gentle leader. I think Bing Crosby must have patterned every character of a priest he ever played after Father Carey.

Instruction went very well, or at least somewhat well, until one afternoon, Father Carey said:

Carey: You're doing fine, Don.

Don: Okay.

Carey: One very important thing.

Don: Yes?

Carey: You do realize that whatever children you and Joan have, you're required to raise them Catholic.

Don: Oh?

Carey: How do you feel about that?

Don: Not too good.

Carey: Why?

Don: Well, I'd just hate for them to grow up thinking they're right and everyone else is wrong.

They did grow up thinking they were right and everyone else is wrong—not about religion, but about theater—an attitude they may have inherited from me.

Note: When I told my parents that Joan and I were getting married and she was Catholic, neither showed any sign of displeasure. Instead, my father said, "It is not good for family members to be going to different churches, so I suggest you strongly consider becoming Catholic. It is usually too difficult for them to change."

As the date for the soon to be performed wedding came closer—after all, there was so much to do in three weeks—everyone became more frantic and more upset, to the point where I think Joan was hoping I wouldn't pass my Wasserman or Father Carey would refuse to marry us. The date was to be June 14; the location was be in the sacristy at the Notre Dame Cathedral.

I asked the Methodist minister, with whom I had worked so many Sundays to be my best man, but he wisely declined. He would certainly attend but because of the circumstances such a role might be viewed as adversarial.

The ceremony was short. The reception at the LaSalle Hotel was beautiful. I'm sure that I did not properly fulfill my responsibilities. Though my father had performed hundreds of marriages, it was the first wedding I had ever seen and the first wedding reception I had ever attended.

During the next few months, my joy of being married grew; my appreciation of South Bend increased; and I was beginning to feel the mystical, spiritual thing that is Notre Dame. But I also felt everything was too perfect; I knew that I was not doing my share of World War II, so I went to Captain Burnett and told him I was going to request a transfer to the Chaplain Corps if I didn't get sent to sea.

A year and a half later, while I was at sea, Father Carey baptized our first child, Peter Robert Stolz.

When earlier I wrote about my entrance into the Navy at the Midshipmen School at the University of Notre Dame, I indicated that many of us arrived with suspicion, dislike or even hate for Notre Dame. I know of no one who, having earned his commission, left there without having had his view changed. So, you can understand how meaningful it was when years after the war, it was decided to have a reunion of all who, after being commissioned, were retained as either teachers or company officers.

The reunion committee found the Alumni Association of Notre Dame eager to help plan the event. Our requirements were simple. All we wanted to do was drink, eat and talk, and have a place to sleep. Reservations were made at the Morris Inn for the returnees and their wives.

The event was a rewarding, marvelous gathering of dear associates, most of whom we hadn't seen for years. After three days, when it was time for us to leave, we were determined to have another reunion soon again. Almost every year since then, several of us have arranged to return to Notre Dame for reminiscing, for renewal and for worship. Attending mass at the beautiful Basilica of St. Mary's was always a part of our being there.

I wanted to include Notre Dame in this accounting because to me and my family, Notre Dame has become a spiritual near-mystical sanctuary to which we want to make a yearly retreat. So much of our emotional and spiritual life is tied there.

The Sollitt Company, of which Joan's father was a vice president, built many of the buildings, including the football stadium and Rockne Gym.

Joan attended the St. Mary's academy and Prep School just across the highway.

I received my commission, afterward teaching at the Midshipman School.

Joan and I were married in the sacristy of the Basilica; two of our children were baptized at Notre Dame.

Our visits to South Bend and the University have continued. Going with Joan and me the last several times have been Dony and Jon. In a miraculous way, it has become as special to them as to Joan and me.

Certainly on these trips we visited other South Bend attractions: the magnificently restored Morris Theater, the rebuilt adjacent Palais Royale dance hall, the Studebaker Museum and the cemetery where Joan's family are all buried. But the center spine of the trip has been the campus.

Since we always stayed at the Morris Inn, it is, to me, little wonder that Dony and Jon spent long nighttime hours at two places: the Grotto and the old on-campus cemetery. Jon, always interested in architecture and landscaping, has become so familiar with every building, that during his last visit he was acting as an unofficial guide to those wanting to tour the campus.

Notre Dame is part of our lives.

Proceed Independently—
San Francisco Port Director
Proceed Independently—Task Force
Commander, Okinawa

I received orders to report to Astoria, Oregon, where I would become a part of the crew of a soon-to-be-commissioned Troop Transport Attack Ship. The A.P.A.'s were all built on the same hull as the light aircraft carrier. They were 455 feet long, with a single screw propeller. They were equipped with four twin 20 mm, four twin 40 mm, and one 5-inch cannon. They carried 14 landing craft and were designed for a crew of 530 and a troop transport of 1,525. Notwithstanding that they were hastily built, they were good ships that, though they were single screw, maneuvered nicely.

Joan and I made train reservations to the West Coast and started on our way. It was a long trip. One afternoon, Joan and I, sitting opposite in coach seats, were playing double solitaire. She was going through the cards "both way."

(Don, of course, is in uniform. Both he and Joan look very young. Especially Joan, who was very young. A Chief Petty Officer comes by, then stops to watch the game.)

Chief: Afternoon, sir.

Don: Afternoon.

(Play continues as Chief watches)

Chief: *(Finally)* Pardon me, sir, but could I see you for a moment at the end of the car?

Don: Certainly. *(To Joan)* I'll be right back. *(He and the Chief* *walk to end of car)*

Chief: Pardon me, sir. I don't know where you picked that girl
up, but she's cheating the hell out of you in that card
game.

I thanked the Chief and told him that I knew what she was
doing, but it was just easier that way.

When I first reported to the soon-to-be-commissioned, *USS
Fond du Lac*, APA 166, I was assigned to the First Lieutenant's
department, the group in charge of damage control. Before the shakedown cruises up and down the west coast were completed, the
Captain, for reasons not necessary to cover here, had thrown the
Navigator, a full commander, a transfer from the Merchant Marine,
off the ship. Two weeks later, not for the same reason, the Captain
dismissed the new Navigator, a full lieutenant. The Captain and a
new Executive Officer gathered all deck officers in the wardroom and
explained that they were giving a test in piloting, maneuver board and
navigation. It all was material I'd been teaching at Notre Dame, so of
course Ensign Stolz was the winner. Had I known what the prize was
to be, I would have done my best to do less. I was now the Navigator
of the APA 166, a position that on the personnel list showed a full
Commander with a full lieutenant as an assistant. I would have
jumped ship except I had become acquainted with the bridge Quartermaster and Chief Quartermaster and I knew that they knew everything that I didn't know.

Our Chaplain, the Reverend Peter Carr—knowing that the
mission of the *Fond du Lac* was to carry troops to where they were
needed, and provide the landing craft to get them ashore—and realizing that we would never have much opportunity for on-shore
recreation, took all the funds allotted and all the grants donated for
physical games equipment, and purchased books for the ship's library.
The *Fond du Lac* had the biggest and best floating library in the
Pacific. And the men aboard became readers, serious readers. The
Navigation Quartermaster read a book a day. I shall always remember the joy of reading *The Origin of the English Language*.

The shakedown cruises just off shore were over; the ship was

APA 166

Ensign Stolz on bridge.

informed that our orders were at the San Francisco Port Director's Office and they were to be picked up immediately. In the Navy it is tradition that the navigator pick up the orders. On the way to the Port Director's Office, I was worried, but felt secure in the belief that the *Fond du Lac* would be one ship in a large convoy. As the Navigator, three times a day I would send into the senior ship present what I thought was our position, and the senior ship present would then tell me, three times a day, how wrong I was. Being told I was wrong, I could endure; that was easy.

The Port Director had me sign for our orders; I was reminded that they were not to be opened until I had them in the chart room aboard ship. The anticipation you can well imagine. I could hardly wait until I was up the gangway, had saluted the quarterdeck and climbed to the chart room. The first two words of the orders "proceed independently."" Finally recovering from that, I read the next three words "to Espirito Santos." Someone who had never been out of the sight of land was responsible for guiding this ship, with 2,000 men aboard, across the Pacific to an unknown land. Thank God for the Quartermaster and the Chief Quartermaster.

In the months ahead, I found that regardless of our destination, what port, our Captain, being a four-stripe Annapolis man, liked to follow the old Navy tradition of arriving at that destination right at dawn. Thank God for radar. Almost always, when we arrived at a destination, we were met by a pilot who guided the ship through the channel to anchorage. As soon as the pilot was aboard, I was officially relieved of duty, but I always stayed on the bridge until I heard the pilot actually say something to the Captain that would reveal, definitely, that we were where we were supposed to be.

On March 27, 1945, we left Layte Gulf in company with Task Force 51.132 of the Fifth Fleet bound for Okinawa, which was anticipated to be the most important and most deadly of all Pacific invasions to date.

At 0236, Easter Sunday morning, the *Fond du Lac*, along with the other ships of the convoy, entered Okinawa harbor. At General Quarters, I, as navigator, was to take the con of the ship on the

bridge until the Captain appeared. There being no assistant navigator and with the quartermasters having other General Quarters
assignments, there was no one of authority in the chart room. For
the first several hours I managed. When the Kamikaze attack began
at dawn, the SOP signaled "Proceed Independently." It was the most
frightening moment of my Navy life. I knew not how to "proceed
independently," I had no idea where we were, except for help from
the radar room.

Though the Captain had been called several times, he had not
appeared from his emergency cabin; the Kamikaze planes were
attacking the convoy. The anti-aircraft from the ships was, with its
tracer bullets, reassuring but still most awesome. At almost 0600,
one of the suicide planes had selected the *Fond du Lac* as its target. It
was sighted early by the 20 mm gun crew mounted directly over the
Captain's emergency cabin. No one could have slept through that.
Captain Creehan came roaring out of his emergency cabin wearing
only his BVDs. Not the Navy issue of shorts and t-shirts, but his
BVDs.

Captain: Stolz!
Stolz: Yes, sir.
Captain: What was that?
Stolz: Twenty millimeter gun fire.
Captain: Whose twenty millimeter?
Stolz: Ours.
Captain: What were they firing at?
Stolz: An enemy plane. Thank God they got it.
Captain: Why wasn't I called? Captains don't sleep through
battles.
Stolz: No, sir.
Captain: I'll relieve you from the con as soon as I can put on
my pants.

"Captains don't sleep through battles" became the mantra of the
officers and the crew of the *Fond du Lac*.

"I'll relieve you as soon as I can put on my pants," was mine.

When the boats were lowered away and the army and marine

units climbed down the rope ladders into the landing craft and started for the shore, I was again filled with apprehension, admiration and a prayerful heart for their safety.

Later, after twenty-one more voyages, on October 22, we embarked, with 1,500 troops aboard, for a top-secret mission. The destination we were not to know until several days later. When the orders were made known, we learned that we were headed for an invasion of the Japanese island Sasebo. We were to prepare for the most difficult and deadliest assignment yet.

The ship's doctors, Sperow and Heiny, were to make certain that the hospital space aboard our ship was prepared to handle casualties that might be returned to the *Fond du Lac*.

It wasn't until the day before we were to attack and land that we received word that an armistice had been agreed. We proceeded to approach the island exactly as had been planned. As we entered the narrow channel that led to the inner harbor, the ship was at General Quarters and the troops armed. Every Naval officer was wearing his 45 side arms, prepared for the unexpected. The Japanese pilots were taken aboard and we entered Sasebo without incident.

After a few days in Japan, the *Fond du Lac* left for a series of destinations: Lingayen, back to Sasebo, Guam, San Pedro, Leyte Gulf then back to San Francisco. The war was over; my time in the Navy had earned enough "points" that I was released from active duty. I signed over the confidential charts to the new Navigator and packed for home.

I was out of the Navy, and I was home for Christmas. What a wonderful Christmas it was with Joan and two little boys, Peter and Dony.

A Hasty Decision

With the war over and me out of the Navy, my sickness (a madness for theater) immediately returned. I started looking for work—primarily radio and motion pictures. But as it quite often turns out, while pursuing these careers, what I found was a role in a play being produced in one of the smaller Los Angeles theaters. It was a terrible script, but it was work. The playwright was a very successful author of radio scripts for, as I remember, Folger's Coffee. I played the part of a taxi driver, who, for two and a half acts was the most engaging and likeable person in the cast. Suddenly, in the third act, I, without any forewarning, was revealed as the guy who had been killing everyone. But it still was work.

I also was lucky enough—though I didn't consider myself lucky—to get bit parts in three different motion pictures for Republic. I don't know anyone, including me, who ever saw them. In one, I remember opening and closing a prop elevator door. At the suggestion of my old friend, Terry O'Sullivan, who was doing very well, I started auditioning for radio commercials as well as roles in shows. My fondest audition memory: not following the usual method, the agency had informed all who were to audition that they were to have three minutes. Here, I thought, is a great chance. What they were selling was laundry soap. I wrote three commercials—one for a young businessman, another for a cowboy and the last for a minister. When I had finished delivering them at the audition, the advertising group in the booth told me that they were looking for an older voice, but if I wanted a job writing commercials, they would give it to me. In the years since, there have been more than a few times when I have thought, "that is the way I should have gone."

Then came another audition. This time for a role in a daily radio drama. When I stood in front of that microphone and read, I was wonderful; it was a part for which I was absolutely perfect. But you know how actors are—there isn't a part ever written for which they aren't perfect. With a musician, you can show him a piece of music and he can tell you whether or not he can play it. Either he can or he can't. That does not happen with actors. As I just said, "there isn't a part ever written for which they aren't perfect."

When I didn't get the role, I was so upset I went home to Van Noord Street and told Joan we were going to go to Minneapolis and reopen the Old Log. There was no way the poor girl could possibly have known what that meant. As a matter of truth, I didn't know either. I first called Bob Aden and asked him if he was going to reopen the Old Log, and he replied that he was never, ever, returning to Minnesota. (I thank God that, in the next years, that did not prove to be true.) When I asked Bob if he, then, would sell me the theater, he replied, "Send me a dollar and it's yours." Had I known then what I know now, I would have negotiated for a better price. My next call was to Harry Kuechle to see if he had rented the building for the 1946 season. He replied that of course not, he was saving it for me, as he had promised he would. Of that promise I have absolutely no memory; it must have been some time during the farewell party after the 1941 tour was cancelled because of Pearl Harbor.

By now, not only did we have Peter, a little boy of not yet two, but also our second, Dony, just a baby. We made what preparations we could for Joan to join me in Minnesota, then I got on my way.

I was in Excelsior only three days when I had a telephone call, forwarded by Joan, from the Chaplin Studios in California, offering me a thirteen-week contract. I had absolutely no hesitancy in telling them that too many arrangements had been made at the Old Log. I never considered the offer as an omen that I had made the wrong choice. Why I was so eager to reopen the Old Log, I really don't know; my only explanation, "I thought it was important."

Since his work for the government was completed in California,

Mr. and Mrs. Fuller had moved back to South Bend, the home office of Sollitt Construction. Had Gus been in California, he may very well have asked, "Why—why is theater important?" To which I would probably have answered something vague such as "Theater is a celebration." (Note: I realize that today the word "celebration" is rarely used, except in memorial services for those who have just died.) A celebration of what we have been, a celebration of what we are, a celebration of what we hope to be. "Theater is a summary of what we are." Gus would have accepted it even if he would have preferred something better organized and a little more meaningful.

If he were to have asked me exactly what kind of a theater I hoped to operate, that answer might have gotten a little vague, too. I knew I hoped to operate a professional theater that was commercially successful. Commercially successful: in 1946 we didn't even know— or even had heard—of a professional company that was subsidized, living on grants, or any other of the "not for profit" plans. Professional theater was commercial theater. Usually, the more commercial, the better. In graduate school, I had noted that of all the plays that were considered to be classical theater, every one of them had been a box office success during the lifetime of the author. Even in reviewing the plays of William Shakespeare, I noticed that the ones that today we consider his great works were the ones that were big successes when presented in his day; his plays that we consider his lesser works, were less successful when presented at the Globe. So it's easy to say, "the more commercial, the better."

Theory aside, it was time for some realistic decisions. What kind of a "celebration" did I want to perform? Where, in the past Bob and Deborah had decided the season of plays, now this challenge was mine. Thirteen plays, thirteen productions. I soon decided there was little time to act other than "soon," preferably "immediately."

Selecting and scheduling thirteen plays for the summer of 1946 was entirely different from selecting thirteen plays today. The Burns Mantle summary of the 1945–46 season in New York shows 38 new plays, 48 musicals and revues and 20 plays that had opened the previous season but were still running. Nor were we as tightly limited by the number of characters in a play. Equity required only that we have at least six union actors in the cast. If our resident company were well suited to the leading roles in a play, we would produce it regardless of how many other actors were required. It was this that led us in those early years to schedule such plays as Maxwell Anderson's *High Tor* and *Winterset* and Julian Thompson's *The Warrior's Husband*.

While today most professional theater rights to produce an established play are gotten primarily through either Samuel French, Inc. or Brandt & Brandt (now Bob Friedman), in 1946 there were at least three other agencies to be approached: Century, Vanguard and Dunwood.

In selecting the thirteen plays for the summer of 1946, I decided to follow the pattern of two comedies, one serious play, two comedies, one serious play, etc., until we were at 13. Even in 1946, I was aware that though a playwright labels his work as "serious," it does not mean that it is necessarily a good play. For me, if a "serious play" did not contain some nobility or beauty of character, it was discarded. The Old Log, I felt, had no time for the tragic writing of hopelessness; if the play revealed a tragic situation, but expressed the hope that if we searched, we might possibly find a solution—then that play was carefully considered. A serious play without beauty, nobility of character or hope had little chance at the Old Log.

Before I reached Minneapolis, I had the first two plays of the '46 season selected, *Claudia* (a comedy) and *The Silver Cord* (not a comedy).

During my initial telephone conversation with Mr. Kuechle, he had told me that when I reached Minneapolis, I should come directly to his office at Double Wear Shoe Company on Lake Street, and he would take me out to the Old Log in Excelsior. I had ridden with Mr. Kuechle before and was not looking forward to the drive. We had not left Lake Calhoun before I noticed a change.

*(In car, Mr. Kuechle driving. The car has stopped and
Mr. Kuechle is gesturing for another car to proceed, giving them
the right of way.)*

Don: Mr. Kuechle,

Kuechle: Yes?

Don: That was very nice.

Kuechle: What was nice?

Don: Signaling that other car to go on, when actually you had the right of way.

Kuechle: Oh.

Don: I noticed we've just started on our way to the Lake and you've done that, oh, at least three times.

Kuechle: Well, I've done it deliberately. I used to get in the car and think the road was mine.

Don: I remember.

Kuechle: What?

Don: *(Recovering)* I mean, once we're behind the wheel, we all are inclined to feel that way.

Kuechle: True. Last summer I started measuring the time it took to reach Excelsior. If I drove as fast as I could and insisted at every corner that I had the right of way, the drive took 20 to 25 minutes. And I'd get home mad at every other driver that was on the road—and the rest of the world as well. Sometimes I didn't recover until after dinner. Then I found that if I took my time, was pleasant to other drivers—which, by the way, I've come to enjoy—when I got home, it was seldom more than 30 minutes from the store. And I'd be happy. When did you say Joan was getting here from California?

Don: Probably another seven or eight days.

Kuechle: I'm looking forward to seeing her and the two little boys. Well, I suppose in the next two or three days we should sign some kind of a lease for the theater.

Don: Whenever you say.

Kuechle: You're to pay me 10% of the gross each week, due each Monday. Mike and I—you remember Mike, of course.

Don: Mike Smith, your maintenance man.

Kuechle: Right. Well, Mike will take care of the grounds except the immediate area surrounding the theater. He and I have gone over the theater property—the two outhouses are all right; they got through the winter. Mike connected the well; you can get water at that outside faucet. The pop stand is all set.

Don: And the theater?

Kuechle: It's ready—except my gondola is still on the stage.

Don: Your what?

Kuechle: Gondola. Right from Venice. Except we added a little motor. We've had a lot of fun with it the last several summers. Hired a singing gondolier. Took our guests around the little island—all over the pond.

Don: It sounds fun.

Kuechle: Mike promised he'd get some help and they'd have the gondola off the stage by tomorrow morning.

Don: Speaking of the pond, how are the swans?

Kuechle: They're there all right. And the Muscovy ducks, too. By the way, Grace wanted me to tell you that if you wanted the recipe for the peanut sauce that she served on hamburgers at the pop stand …

Don: The logburgers. Would be great.

Kuechle: She'll like that. Do you know yet what play you're going to open with?

Don: *Claudia*.

Kuechle: Is it any good?

Don: I certainly hope so.

Kuechle: Don, everyone is glad you're back. I think you're going to have a wonderful season.

Mr. Kuechle was a wise and shrewd businessman, but there was no way he could have foreseen what would happen the summer of 1946.

When Joan and the two boys joined me, we moved into an abandoned cottage in back of the theater. It was located just where the stage of the new theater is today. There was a bathroom, but no

Don, Joan, Peter, and Dony (on grounds at
The Old Log Theater).

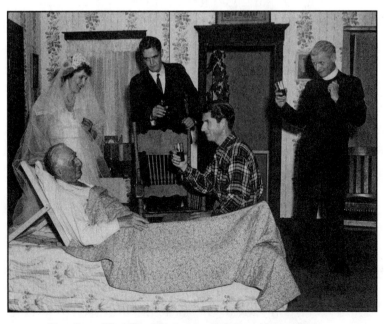

They Knew What They Wanted; Louis Lytton, Maxine Stetson,
Dan Stapleton, Joe Tomes, and Ken Jones.

stool. A shower, but no water. We found some pipe in the not-used-for-years greenhouse beside the theater, strung the pipe the sixty feet or so across the lawn from the theater's outside faucet to the cottage. In the meantime, Dan Stapleton had walked into Excelsior, purchased a used toilet stool from West and Hedla Plumbers, gotten in a cab and brought it home. The pipe running on top of the lawn may have seemed strange, but it had one wonderful feature. After a warm sunny day, one was able to take a hot shower. The surrounding grounds were beautiful and we enjoyed them.

I thought we had neat, but small living quarters, until I overheard Deborah ask Bob Aden, "Does Joan's mother know how she's living?"

Contrary to Mr. Kuechle's forecast in May, the summer of 1946 was a complete disaster. As I had planned, the season opened with the play, *Claudia*. Joan and I, without help, designed, made and painted the set. It featured a large stone fireplace, with the stone having been made of stuffed and then painted, gunny sacking. The audience, doubtlessly not as sophisticated as today's, thought it was wonderful. All things considered, I guess it was.

I had managed to assemble a good company: Maxine Stetson, Cleda Villines, Evelyn Snapp, Joe Tomes, Louis Lytton and Ken Jones, were happily available and happily returned. And I had asked my friend, Dan Stapleton, from OCU and Northwestern to join us. And another Northwestern Alumni, Richard Lang, was the new box office manager. Early in the season, Dick Lang had asked Joan to assist him in the box office, and my sister, Jeanne, had come up from Oklahoma to help in any way that she could and play whatever ingenue parts might be available.

It was in July that we met and immediately hired, two Minneapolis actors who were known and highly respected in local theaters— Duke (Warner) Lahtinen and the unbelievable Ken Senn. Both immediately became important to the Old Log family.

We did 13 plays in 13 weeks as scheduled. I don't know how we did it. We even thought we were having fun. The seventh play of that 1946 season was *They Knew What They Wanted*, a charming play by Sidney Howard. On the third day of rehearsal, I realized that we were doing an absolutely abysmal job with the whole thing. It was then that I decided we should, in the five days of rehearsal remaining, find a real Chinese young man to play the Chinese houseboy. The audience would be so attracted by him, they would be distracted from what a lousy job we were doing and we'd get by. With this in mind, I went to the Nankin Café, a Chinese restaurant in downtown Minneapolis and found an attractive young man, who agreed to be in the cast for $25. In those years, $25 was a lot of money. The truth is, in theater, $25 is still a lot of money. Anyway, the young man agreed to the terms and said he would be at rehearsal the next morning at 9:30. He didn't show. The next afternoon I went to the other Chinese restaurant in downtown Minneapolis. Again I found a nice looking Chinese man; again the terms were accepted with the promise he would be there the next morning. He did not show.

It was at this point that Dick Langehinrichs, our box office manager, came to me and said, "Don, you're wasting very precious time and very precious money. I can do a great Chinese makeup and you have your problem solved, and we will have saved twenty-five dollars." There was nothing to do but agree.

On opening night, Joan and I were standing in the wings when Dick made his first entrance. His makeup combined with his receding hairline was miraculous. I whispered to Joan, "He almost looks Chinese, doesn't he?" Her reply: "Well, I can tell you one thing, he comes within $25 of it." In the next almost seventy years, whenever we have wanted something at the theater that we could not afford and have settled for something cheaper, that line became our answer: "Well, it comes within $25 of it."

In the middle of the summer, the polio epidemic hit. Unless you were here to experience it, there is no way you can even imagine what it was like. Schools closed, movie theaters closed, churches closed, the only thing not closed was the Old Log. And we probably would have been if we'd had enough money to buy a lock.

By September, we had lost every dollar we had saved during my years in the Navy. We were broke and owing money. I sold the car—

giving me enough money to pay a few of the bills that absolutely could not be postponed, promised the others I'd be back the next summer, and had enough money left for Joan, Peter and Dony to fly back to California. I think they must have taken Northwest Airlines, because I hitchhiked back to the West Coast and almost beat them there.

It was that winter in California that one of the disappointments, about which Professor Campbell had never warned me, came into my life. Some way or other, I had landed a small role in a new play written by Keith Winters, who a few short years earlier had received the Pulitzer Prize for his play, **The Shining Hour**, and was currently working as a writer for Twentieth Century Fox. He had just finished a new play, which he himself was going to produce and direct. He had assembled a good Hollywood cast that included Patricia Morrison's father and Olivia DeHaviland's mother. At the first rehearsal, Keith explained that the title of the play, **Worse Things Happen at Sea**, was an expression in his homeland England, that was used when everything seems hopeless. You are supposed to just shrug your shoulders, gather your courage and say, "Oh, well, worse things happen at sea."

As rehearsals continued in Los Angeles, we all became convinced that we were part of a great venture that after would travel to Broadway where we all would have worthwhile and pleasant work for at least two seasons. When we opened the show, the reaction of the audience confirmed the view we already had. In the audience was the drama critic of *Daily Variety*, the only publication in Los Angeles at that time that really affected the destiny of a play.

The morning after the opening night, we members of the cast all gathered—on the corner of Hollywood and Vine—the first drop off point of *Daily Variety* to read what we knew was going to be a glorious review that would take us all to stardom in New York.

No matter how many years I may spend in theater, I will never forget the review. I shall quote it in its entirety. The headline read: **Worse Things Happen at Sea**—then followed—"written, produced and directed by Keith Winters." Below that it listed the cast, then the entire body of the review, of which I leave out not one word.

"After seeing last night's opening performance at the Vine Street Theater, the title, *Worse Things Happen at Sea*, seems hardly likely."

Disappointment or not, suddenly it was spring. Spring, 1947. After the disastrous 1946 season and after the closing of *Worse Things* ... I don't know why we ever returned to the Old Log. I've never been quite sure. I think it was the fact that I'd promised Mr. Kuechle and the several merchants to whom I owed money, that we would.

In the next couple of years we had made enough money that we could rent a small house in downtown Excelsior. It was an easy walk to the theater, only a mile and a half. In the meantime, Mr. Kuechle, probably not wanting Joan's mother to see where she had been living, had traded the cottage to Mr. Jerow for a case of bourbon. All Mr. Jerow had to do was move it from Lot 109 to Lot 105, just up the road. Years later, we purchased the very neat cottage that Mr. Jerow had made of the shack.

During those years, the Excelsior Catholic Church, St. John's, was an old but well-maintained building on the corner of Courtland and First Street. Father Cushing, an elderly priest and accomplished orator, was the pastor. When you attended mass on a summer Sunday, you knew these things: it would be hot, Father would condemn the University of Minnesota as the center of the state's Communists, and if neighborhood dogs barked as they always did, he would scathingly tell the congregation that in future they must leave their dogs at home.

Father Cushing was a good priest. He was strong in faith, firm in his convictions and a good homilist except for the many times he addressed the problems of the University and neighborhood dogs. Regardless of how warm the weather, Father Cushing meticulously dressed as the liturgical season required. One year on Corpus Christi Sunday, Joan, Peter, Dony, Tommy and I were sitting on the aisle. At the end of the service, Father Cushing, dressed in elegant observation of the day, led the procession down the aisle. When he passed our family group, three-year-old Dony said in full voice, "Boy, look at the costume that guy has on." In the memory of every member of the congregation, it was the only time when Father Cushing was known to smile when inside the sanctuary.

Dony always felt close to and friendly with the church and the members of the church's vocations. It was only a few weeks later that he was sitting in our car parked in downtown, Minneapolis, when two sisters (in those days still in their habits and veils) passed by. Wanting to express his love and respect for them, he leaned out of the window and said, "Hello, Cousins." Despite Dony's devotion, it was his younger brother, Tommy, who became an altar boy.

EXCELSIOR:
A WHOLE DIFFERENT COUNTRY

Though in no way was the Old Log a project of the City of Excelsior, the theater company always had a warm affection for the village and its town folks.

In the forties, whenever an Excelsior citizen died, it was still customary that every business in town be closed during the hours of the funeral or memorial service. In the late forties, the fifties and even half way through the sixties, Excelsior was a farm community, not yet a bedroom for Minneapolis.

It was a city rich with legends: the Excelsior High football team won every game in those years, never had a point scored against them and, according to those who played on the team, no running back ever got past the Excelsior defensive line.

The innumerable stories about the early days on Lake Minnetonka, told by Ray Mason, Vic Bacon and Russ Gray, were repeated by everyone in the community.

Vic liked to tell of his buying his home just across the street from the property that was to become the Old Log Theater parking lot. The transaction—rather, the negotiation—took place long before anyone even dreamed of a theater. Included in the property under negotiation was the small pie-shaped piece across Meadville Street from the lot on which stood the house under consideration. When Vic told the seller that his price was too high, the man replied, "Well, remember, you're getting that piece of property across the street." To which Vic replied, "That piece of property is nothing but a swamp not worth a thing." The seller replied, "Swamp or not, I promise you that you can sell it for $5,000." "You're crazy. Nobody would pay anything for it." The buyer played his ace: "Oh, yes, they would. Harry Kuechle would; you just put up a sign 'free dumping' and Harry Kuechle will buy it."

Ray Mason always asked Russ Gray to tell about the way he handled the carload of Minneapolitans who parked at Gray's lake-shore home, spread their picnic lunch on his lawn, and even used his rowboat. According to Ray, Russ never said a word, but did get their license number. On Monday, Russ traced the owner's name and address and picked up Ray Mason and a couple of other friends and drove into Minneapolis, where they had a picnic on the lawn of the couple that had taken over the Gray property the Sunday before.

In downtown Excelsior, there were three year-round restaurants (Melba's, Bill's and Hasty Tasty), three drug stores, three hardware stores, a butcher shop, a combination electrical and plumbing shop, a dime store, three clothing stores and even a department store. Though the paddle wheel had vanished from the Lake, the fabled Blue Line Café was still serving the best chicken meals in Minnesota. The Excelsior Amusement Park, with its romantic dance hall across the street, still opened every summer, though the blue-haired ladies wearing tennis shoes, who had just moved to Excelsior, showed up at the Excelsior Council meetings to protest its existence.

In addition to the three year-round restaurants and the Blue Line Café, there was our favorite summertime café, the Anchor Inn. Though it was roofed, it was in fact an outdoor café. Its booth seats had been salvaged from the streetcars that years before had carried passengers from Minneapolis to Excelsior. The menu went from the customary hamburger to a full walleyed pike meal for 35 cents. No wonder we ate there. As did most of the local residents. Whenever Joan's father and mother came from South Bend to visit, they looked forward to having dinner every night at the Anchor Inn.

Excelsior was a parochial city; in many ways it still is. That is one of the reasons that I loved Excelsior and always shall. Though there is today no hardware store within the city limits, in those long ago days, Aldritt's Hardware was the Stolz family favorite.

One lovely early summer morning, some years ago, Joan and I traveled from our lake house in the incorporated city of Greenwood—a city of 600, with no business district, no police department, no fire department, not one single place of business except a theater (and what kind of business is a theater?). Anyway, we drove from Greenwood into the center of downtown Excelsior, a distance of just less than a mile and a quarter, to purchase a dime's worth of nails at Aldritt's Hardware Store. If it had been a nickel's worth, I would have made the trip alone, but if the purchase was ten cents or more, it took the approval of both of us.

It was not a Saturday morning, so, of course, the only clerk in the store was Mr. Aldritt himself. Everyone in town—well, almost everyone, called Mr. Aldritt "Link," but since we had lived here only fifteen years, for me it was still "Mr. Aldritt." There was only one other customer—a lady—ahead of us, but Joan and I knew there would be a little wait. Mr. Aldritt not only greeted each customer, waited on each customer, but also liked to discuss affairs of the city with each customer. Finally her purchases were completed and the talk was over. It was our turn.

Mr. A: Good morning, Don, Mrs. Stolz:

Don: Morning, Mr. Aldritt.

Joan: *(with above)* Good morning.

Mr. A: That lady that was just here ...

Don: Yes?

Mr. A: That was Mrs. Winter, wasn't it?

Don: That's right.

Mr. A: And she lives over there on Meadville Street by you, doesn't she?

Joan: Just two doors away. Practically next door.

Mr. A: Now the Winters are that family who live in California in the winter and come here for the summer. Is that right?

Don: California in the winter, Excelsior in the summer.

Mr. A: That's what I thought. Well, she's a very nice lady for just summer folk.

For years, most of the businessmen with stores or offices on Water Street met at ten every morning at Bacon's Drug Store for coffee and to catch up on the news of the city. Whenever he wasn't scheduled to fly, Phil Hallen, a pilot for Northwest Airlines, living at Excelsior at the Gables, would join them. The others never thought of him as "just summer folk" or even as "someone who sleeps here"; he was accepted as one of them.

Not thought by this group as "one of them," but quite often in the drug store at the same time as they, was Donnie, an elf-like older urchin that everyone in town knew. One fall day, Donnie overheard the businessmen discussing a birthday party they had attended; they, in turn, overheard Donnie's remarks that in all his fifty-seven years he had never had a birthday party.

I don't know where but Excelsior that the following would happen. After Donnie had left the drug store, Phil Hallen, the pilot, told Vic Bacon that all of the "guys" had thought it would be nice to give Donnie his first birthday party. He, Phil, would buy a cake at the bakery across the street, they would meet at Bacon's where they would buy their usual morning coffee. Vic thought it a great idea and said he'd furnish the candles; Phil purchased a card, which all the men signed.

The next morning, Phil casually asked Donnie the date of his birthday. The group set a time for the gathering and all was ready.

Things went even better than they had dreamed. They had Donnie blow out the candles, cut the cake and distribute pieces to all present. Then Phil handed the birthday card to Donnie, who immediately opened it, looked surprised, turned to Phil and asked, "Where's the money?"

One of the businessmen present at Donnie's birthday party was a regular at the ten o'clocks; Jerome Studer, an earth-moving contractor. Even in the fifties, what is now the theater parking lot was still a swamp. Mr. Kuechle, realizing its value, was steadily working to have it filled in. Anyone who had clean fill and was looking for somewhere to deposit it was welcomed by Mr. Kuechle. As soon as the stacks of clean fill were high enough, Mr. Kuechle would call

Jerome and have him come over and push the fill into the swamp.

Late afternoon in late May, Jerome arrived with his caterpillar tractor to push what had been accumulated into the swamp. He had no more than started the job when his tractor was the property of the swamp; swamp water and mud were clear up to the base of the saddle. In some way, Jerome was able to walk to solid ground. After trying for more than an hour to pull the tractor out with the aid of the truck on which it had been hauled, Jerome decided he needed a mechanical advantage (a block and tackle). To accomplish this, he selected what he unthinkingly considered the point with the most strength—the N & SL railroad track that ran immediately adjacent to the theater property. He took from his trunk a heavy chain and laid it across the tracks, then brought it back under the track between the ties.

Stolz: What happens if a train comes by?

Jerome: That's a good question. You stand here, and if you see a train coming, you stop it.

Stolz: All right, but how …

>*(Before I could ask how I was going to stop the train, he was on his way down to the tractor. The block and tackle worked. But instead of pulling the tractor out of the swamp, it was pulling the tracks still attached to the ties into an "S" curve. I shouted at Jerome—told him what was happening. He looked at the curved track.)*

Jerome: If I had my tractor out, I could probably bring it up here and push the track back in position.

Stolz: What are you going to do?

Jerome: I'm going down to the depot and tell them I was over at the theater and when I left there, I looked right and left to make certain there was no train coming, and I noticed that some way or other the tracks had been bent into almost a perfect "S" and they had better call the dispatcher in Minneapolis and tell them not to send any train out until it's fixed.

Stolz: What do you want me to do?

Jerome: Stand here by the track and if you see a train coming, you stop it.

Stolz: All right, but how ...

This time before I could even ask the question, Jerome was in his truck and on his way to the Excelsior depot. I stayed at my post. What I could have done should a train come down those tracks, I don't know. I kept thinking of all the Keystone Cops comedies I had seen in which someone is tied to the railroad tracks.

No train came. A repair crew was sent to the scene. I've always felt certain that Jerome hadn't fooled the superintendent at the Excelsior depot. The superintendent was smart enough to realize that the easiest way to handle the situation was to accept the story he'd just been told.

Jerome, I must tell you, was a member of the legendary football team that I mentioned earlier. He played in the backfield, both on offense and defense. One day I asked him whether he preferred running on offense or tackling on defense, he confirmed the statement I made earlier by saying, "I don't know—I never had to make a tackle—no running back from the other teams ever got past our line." His future brother-in-law, Anson Mason, was one of the stars of the line that played both ways.

Try Again the Next Season
1947– 49

Despite vivid memories of the disaster of 1946, we did reopen the Old Log the summer of 1947. The first play was **Here Comes Mr. Jordan**, which is all we have to say about the opening. Someway, despite his statement that he was never returning to Minnesota, we were able to get Bob Aden back for a repeat of **White Cargo**, again starring him and June March. It was the only play of the summer for Bob, though June did remain for most of the season, giving a wonderful performance of Sadie Thompson in **Rain**, with Joe Tomes and the Lahtinens. One of the memorable productions of the summer was **Ah Wilderness** by Eugene O'Neill. Memorable not necessarily because of the quality of the production, but from an occurrence the Friday night of the week's run. I was playing the young boy, sitting on an overturned boat on the beach, waiting for his girlfriend to appear. While waiting, the character was to recite poetry. I had just finished a lovely bit of verse when someone in the audience broke wind. It was a blast that could have been heard to Kuechle's dock. Things were all right; the audience could not have been better behaved. For the moment. I waited then most foolishly delivered the next line from Mr. O'Neill's script—"Gee, that was a peach." At that point the audience lost it and became something less than well behaved.

In addition to building a company of good actors, we had been able to hire an excellent and experienced designer/painter, Herb Gahagan. For a stage the proscenium of which was only 22 feet, he

Here comes Mr. Jordan; Louis Lytton, Carl Shelton,
and Joe Tomes.

Rain; Betty Odell, Sue Lahtinen, Louis Lytton, Joe Tomes, June March,
Marion Cooper, Carl Shelton, Stephen Wray, and Dan Stapleton.

Philadelphia Story; Angel Casey, Dan Stapleton, Louis Lytton, and Lois Schall.

Night Must Fall; Don Stolz and Maxine Stetson.

produced appropriate and beautiful sets. A picture of his setting for **Philadelphia Story**, elegant, but simple and tastefully furnished, today hangs in our lobby. In the picture are actors Angel Casey, Dan Stapleton, Louis Lytton and Lois Shaw. Herb's designs set a standard of quality that we have striven ever since to maintain.

During the summer, my friend, Tom Heggen, from Oklahoma City University, now living in Minneapolis and having attended the University of Minnesota, became a regular visitor to the Old Log. Though Tom had seen my performance at O.C.U. in **Night Must Fall** and strongly recommended that we produce it at the Old Log, he came not so much to see the shows but to visit with Joan and me. He had become quite fond of Joan and the boys. He told us that his short stories written about his experiences aboard a Navy cargo ship during World War II were being made into a play called **Mr. Roberts**, and it was to be directed by Josh Logan. In the play was a part for me. All I had to do was come to New York.

Needless to say, when we closed **Two's a Crowd**, the last play of our 1947 season, I was off to New York. But I soon learned that, after the war, New York had changed.

All of the young men who had not been there during my first trip were now back. Things were tough, but far from despair because I knew Tom wanted me to play the character named "Stolz" in **Mr. Roberts**. Though the producer, the director and the author all knew that the script was long, at the first reading with actors, we all were surprised to find that it ran 4-1/2 hours. Josh Logan and Heggen were reluctant to cut a word; they liked what they had. They found the solution by arranging for the English playwright, director, producer and actor, Emlyn Williams, to cut an hour and a half. He did. The first scenes to go, and he was correct in his judgment, were the ones in which Seaman Stolz appeared. Originally Heggen had written them as separate short stories for the *New Yorker*.

I was offered one of the many sailor parts, but declined—not in pique but—in hopes that my former radio work would soon reappear.

As I said, things were tough. I continued "making the rounds" to offices of agents and producers. One morning I had just finished watching the ice skaters at the Radio City rink and had turned to walk down 48th Street, when I was approached by a man who appeared to be in his early forties. He was neatly dressed and well groomed. He stopped me and very quietly said:

Man: Pardon me, I'm embarrassed to have to do this, but I'm terribly hungry. Could you help me?

Don: *(Never having seen anyone who looked so hungry)* I have eighty cents in my pocket and if you won't be insulted, I'll give you half of it.

Man: You have eighty cents and you're going to give me half of it?

Don: If you want it, yes.

Man: Hell, I can do better than that. *(He reaches into his side pocket, pulls out an enormous roll of bills, takes a dollar bill off the roll and hands it to Don.)* Here. Take it.

Don: Thank you. *(Takes the one dollar bill.)*

For some reason it reminded me of a time shortly after I had made my first journey into New York. I was getting tokens for the subway and handed the booth clerk a dollar; when she handed me the change I automatically said, "Thank you." To which she asked, "How long have you been in New York?"

And for a reason that is apparent, it also reminded me of an occasion when Dan Stapleton and I, after missing breakfast, had gone into a Bickfords for lunch. After spending some time trying to figure out what we could best buy with the small amount of money we had, Dan turned to me and said, "Don, do you think we'll ever have enough money to come into Bickfords and order whatever we want?" You know, some day I still intend to do that.

Besides looking for a job, I was also looking for a place to live—a place for me and Joan and two little boys. I don't remember who suggested that the best apartments for the money could be found in Long Beach, Long Island, especially in the fall and winter off-season.

I soon found and rented an inexpensive basement apartment.

When I describe it as a basement apartment, that is exactly what it was. Very basement. The next week when Joan arrived, she was—I don't think "appalled" is too harsh a word. The landlord was no less appalled at the prospect of having two small children in her basement, so she returned my deposit and referred me to a friend of hers who was renting a "lovely garden apartment." It was truly lovely, the rent was less than reasonable, the landlady loved children, and we could move in immediately. Another crisis in my life when I had the good fortune of running into the right people. We were even more fortunate than we knew. We found Long Beach to be a warm and welcoming community. It was 90% Jewish, 10% Irish Catholic, with Duke Ellington and his family being the one family neither Jewish nor Catholic.

As weeks went by, Joan and I grew more and more fond of Long Beach. In a thrift store, we found a wicker stroller designed to seat two children side by side. Whenever we could, which was quite often, we would seat Peter and Dony side by side and go for a ride along the walkway off the beach. It was almost impossible to go for even a block without someone stopping us to admire our little twins. This continued to puzzle us because Peter, though only a year older, was decidedly larger than Dony. This continued to puzzle us until Joan figured out that they thought Dony, who was still wearing his long curls, was a little girl twin.

I enjoyed the one-hour train trip into Manhattan and back; again I had time for reading. During the months we lived in Long Beach, I re-read most of Shakespeare's plays. I say "re-read"—some of them I had never read before.

Christmas time in Long Beach, because of the large Jewish population, was different. On the main business street of the town, the only Christmas decorations—really "holiday" decorations—were cardboard wreaths on the lampposts, with each wreath reading "Shop Locally."

We, along with a few other families in town, had a traditional Christmas tree. Joan and I knew that Peter was too young for a tricycle, but we bought him one anyway. He loved it. He immediately turned it over on its side and spun the back wheels. I don't remember what we gave Dony, but I do remember what pleased him the most were the glass ornament decorations on the tree. Finally we convinced him he was not allowed to touch them. He obeyed. He didn't touch them; he would pull up his undershirt and then rub his stomach across the glass ball. We should have known then that he was a manipulator.

During the winter, we had visitors almost every weekend. Dan Stapleton and Carl Shelton, (another OCU actor) would get on the train, each holding his own bed linen (we had no extra) and a bottle of Wilkins Family Whiskey.

When the Great New York Blizzard of 1948 hit, I, by luck not by judgment, caught the last train from Manhattan to Long Island. Not even in Minnesota have I since seen so much snow. It covered the streets so completely you would never know they were there. On the second day of the storm there was a knock on the door. We knew it couldn't be either Dan or Shel, but had absolutely no idea that it would be Joan's mother, who, in some way, had struggled through the five blocks from the station to our apartment. As she stood on the stoop, she looked like the Abominable Snowman. After two days, she and Joan took the train into Manhattan to visit Gus, Joan's father, who had wisely decided to spend the days of the storm in the Commodore Hotel.

Joan and I seldom went out at night—we had little money and two young children, but we had one of the happiest winters of our lives. We would listen to the radio, then I would read aloud from *The Brothers Karamazov*, then play double solitaire until time to go to bed. We, of course, had no television; few families did. But our landlady had friends who invited us to a New Year's Eve party at which we watched, on their small TV, the celebration of the New Year at Times Square.

During the weeks of spring, I really started planning the upcoming summer of 1948. I called the Seymour Hotel in New York and reserved a small suite: sitting room and bedroom. I had selected the Seymour because Aden had always stayed there and held his auditions there. The Seymour was a good middle-class hotel, but it certainly was not a venue that impressed auditioning actors, so they were not particularly careful about what they wore for the interview. This seemed particularly true of the young ladies who often arrived at the Seymour wearing pants or slacks. On more than one occasion I would ask that they go home, put on a dress and then come back for the audition. Not one of them ever seemed offended by this request, but I wasn't comfortable with the situation.

After several years at the Seymour, Joan and I decided that one of the reasons for their dress and grooming was the hotel. The spring after that, I called the Plaza and told them, if they approved, I would like to hold auditions there. The Plaza said that was perfectly all right as long as I told prospective actors to stop at the desk before coming up to my suite. The change of hotels brought a remarkable change. Every prospective candidate, male and female, came to the Plaza well groomed and properly dressed.

One spring during audition time, I had a telephone call from the lobby. It was the director of the Mountain Playhouse. Though we had never met, we had many mutual actor friends. He said he knew we were busy auditioning, but if we could give him a few minutes, he would like to come up and meet us. He knocked a few minutes later. As I opened the door he started to introduce himself and then saw Joan sitting on the couch knitting. Without another word he swept by me, rushed over to sit beside her, and asked where she had gotten the argyle pattern she was knitting. He loved to knit, would knit for hours.

The discussion of his knitting led to his telling us that he had been first a costumer then had become a director of the Mountain Playhouse where he had been for years. When I asked what plays they intended to do their next season and asked which one of those he was particularly looking forward to directing, he replied none of them. He didn't really care for directing and the reason he did it was because it was the only job he could find where he could knit while he was working.

Despite our visitor, who really in no way interfered, our Plaza

Hotel auditions were successful.

To our company, I added three New York-based actors: Guy Aubury, who had come from Minneapolis and as a boy had acted in the Bainbridge Stock Company; Bea Roth, a splendid young actress well established in Network radio, had several years of stock experience and the year before had appeared on Broadway in *The Survivors* with Louis Calhoun, Hume Cronyn and Guy Aubury—the same Guy Aubrey we had just hired; and Kelly Flint, a beautiful true leading lady who also had Broadway experience.

When I scheduled *The Glass Menagerie* to be the opening play of the season, Francis Hidden of the Phillips Agency told me that I absolutely must get Mary Perry to play Amanda. She insisted that though Mary was always working, she felt certain that we could get her for a week of rehearsal and a week run for a modest price. I had great hope and great anticipation, for Mary was a veteran of a number of Broadway successes, had understudied Laurette Taylor in the Broadway production of *The Glass Menagerie* and had starred in productions of the play in cities from Boston to Los Angeles.

Later that spring when I arrived back in Minneapolis, the first thing I did was call on John Sherman, the critic of the *Minneapolis Star*.

Sherman: I'm glad you're back.

Don: Thank you. Glad to be here at the Old Log.

Sherman: Do you have your season set?

Don: I know the opening play.

Sherman: Oh?

Don: *The Glass Menagerie*.

Sherman: *The Glass Menagerie*?

Don: I have Mary Perry coming in to play the mother.

Sherman: She understudied Laurette Taylor, didn't she?

Don: That's right. And then went on tour. The legend is that she was scheduled to play the role in the motion picture but at the last minute someone decided they needed a bigger name.

Sherman: Mary Perry—Good. You'll play the son, of course.

Glass Menagerie; Don Stolz.

Petticoat Fever; Kelly Flint, John Galavarro, John Salisbury, Orville Sherman, Jeanne Stolz (Don's Sister), and Vicki Benson.

Time of Your Life; Bea Roth, Ken Senn, Louis Lytton, Guy Arbury, Don Stolz, and Orville Sherman.

The Warrior Husband; the cast including: John Salisbury, Maxine Stetson, Mary Droning, John Galavarro, Jeanne Stolz, Henry Allen, Ebba Nelson, Don Stolz, Tom Millot, Ken Senn, Kelly Flint, Bea Roth, Marian Couper, and Guy Arbury.

The Front Page; Joe Seger, Fresty Jenstad, Walt Johnson, Brad Morison, and Dick Kleeman.

The Front Page; John Sherman and George Geise.

The Front Page; Virginia Safford.

Don: Tom. That's right. Guy Arbury—years ago he played several boys roles at the Bainbridge Stock—he'll do the Gentleman Caller. And Bea Roth, a nice young actress, is playing the daughter. Arbury and Bea will be here for the entire season.

Sherman: *The Glass Menagerie*—that's your opener?

Don: You sound a little … doubtful?

Sherman: I don't remember ever knowing of a stock company that opened its season with a dramatic or serious play. Especially by Tennessee Williams. And with a small cast.

Don: That's the reason I selected it. The union won't require me to have the minimum of six actors for the opening.

Sherman: Four—and you're one of them. I follow your reasoning. I just hope it works.

And with great luck it did work. *The Glass Menagerie* was such a hit that we had to hold it over for a second week and the 1948 season was off to a great start.

The next three shows: *January Thaw*, *State of the Union* (we had a fine production starring our new leading lady Kelly Flint, Ken Senn, Guy Arbury and John Salisbury, a radio personality from the Twin Cities), and *Petticoat Fever*, all did well. Then came the second blockbuster of the season, William Saroyan's *The Time of Your Life*. Though we were again told that summer stock doesn't do Saroyan, it turned out to be one of the productions on which our reputation as a theater presenting serious plays was built. I played Joe, Ken Senn played Tom and Guy Arbury played Nick, the owner of the bar in which the play is set. Louis Lytton was perfect as Kit Carson; Kelly Flint was beautiful and heart breaking as Mary L. As I have said so many times, nothing makes a director a good director quicker than a good script, a good cast, and the right audience.

Two weeks later our production was *Warrior's Husband*, a delightful comedy about Amazon warriors over-protecting their men. Nothing demonstrates better how things have changed than to simply say there were twenty-six actors in the cast. Regardless of how good the play might be—regardless of how funny—twenty-six

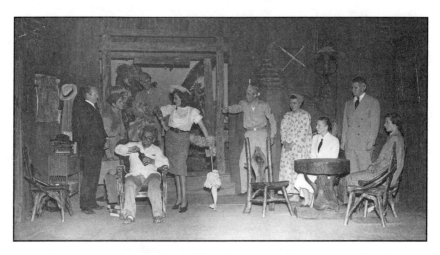

Rain; June March and Joe Tomes.

The Heiress; Guy Arbury, Maxine Stetson, Diana Kemble, and Warner Lahtinen.

Anna Christie; Wayne Campbell, Kelly Flint, and Guy Arbury.

people in the cast is just something that today we couldn't do.

The second week in August we opened the play that established box office records that wouldn't be broken for years. As the program cover read, "Don Stolz Presents the Old Log Company in *The Front Page*, featuring members of *The Minneapolis Star* and *The Minneapolis Tribune*. "The featured staff members" were George Rice, Bradley Morrison, Bob Murphy, George Guise, Bower Hawthorne, Dick Kleeman, John K. Sherman, Sarah Lee Luther, Joe Seeger, Virginia Safford, Barbara Flanagan, Margaret Foley, Gideon Seymour, plus Ed Ryan, the Sheriff of Hennepin County. Ed played the dumb sheriff with magnificent authority. The whole cast was good. Guy Arbury played Hidy and I played Earl Williams, the condemned man.

We rehearsed several hours a day for several weeks; never has there been a more dedicated cast. As soon as *George Washington Slept Here* opened, I gave *The Front Page* my full attention, handing the chore of directing *Skylark* over to Orville Sherman, an actor I had brought to the Old Log from Oklahoma City University.

Some time during the last week of rehearsal of *The Front Page*, someone in the cast suggested that with John Sherman in the cast, I, though also in the cast, should write the review for the *Star*. In my mind I wrote it during the opening night performance. There was opportunity, for Earl Williams, the character I played, spent most of the night hidden in a roll top desk. In the review, I, of course, gave Don Stolz a tremendous review though I did report that many of the audience thought that my best performing was done while hidden from view. I then thought of every phrase that actors dislike having been used by critics, and applied every one of those phrases to one of the newspaper cast members. I saved the best for John Sherman, who was absolutely wonderful as Bensinger, the hypochondriac reporter for the *Chicago Tribune*. I put him at the very bottom of the review with the words that actors most hate to have written about them: "Also in the cast was John K. Sherman."

I turned in my copy; it was published the next afternoon with the headline "Stolz Thinks Stolz is Wonderful." At the bottom of the review were five identical portraits of me, each the size of a post-age stamp. The next week when Sherman wrote his review of *Double Door*, he arranged for the last line: "Also in the cast was Don Stolz," to be printed in type so small one needed a magnifying glass to read it. Payback can be extremely satisfying.

I can't leave the 1948 season without telling that the star of *Double Door* was Maude Sheerer "acclaimed as one of the nation's best in the unusual field of 'playreading.'" Maude possessed strong focus and great poise.

The season of 1948 was a glorious one for the Old Log Theater. A season that added great strength to whatever foundation we had built in previous years.

With the success of the 1948 season giving me courage—perhaps false courage—I started early planning the season for 1949. I made two decisions: I would start a school of apprentices and would bring my old friend and mentor, Professor Wayne Campbell, here from Oklahoma City to be organizer, director and teacher. He happily agreed; he and his wife drove up and were soon settled in a rather cute cottage I had managed to rent for them. The second big decision was to open the season with a show that would immediately bring an audience. And I found it—June March as Sadie Thompson in *Rain*. It did everything I hoped it would. As Minnesota's favorite strip artist, there was little question of June March's ability to draw an audience. Warner Lahtinen played the Rev. Alfred Davidson with spiritual and sexual fervor, Susanne Moran (Mrs. Lahtinen's stage name) played Mrs. Davidson. Though Wayne Campbell had already started his apprentice classes, he offered himself to be cast; he was a great Joe Horn.

The fourth show the summer of 1949 was *The Heiress*. Needing to add to our company, but not having time for a casting trip to New York, I telephoned a beautiful young actress whom we had auditioned in New York the year before. When I told her that her first show would be *The Heiress*, she eagerly agreed and would leave immediately for Minneapolis. When she arrived, we could hardly believe it was the actress we had sent for; she had had a rough year, there was no doubt. She was a delight in rehearsals; on stage she was as beautiful as we had remembered her to be. The audience loved her.

After the performance on opening night, when I was passing out "sides" for the next show, I met what was really a shocking surprise.

Don: A wonderful performance tonight. Wonderful.

Actress: Thank you.

Don: And here are your sides for the next show. Rehearsals tomorrow morning at 9:30, remember.

Actress: Don, we have to talk.

Don: Yes …

Actress: I can't be in the next play—I have to go back to New York.

Don: Is anything wrong?

Actress: Yes, there is. I have been here for two weeks now and I haven't been able to get any man in this company to go to bed with me. Sex is very important to me, so I'm going back to New York. I'm sorry.

Before I could explain to her that we were all too married, too moral, or too tired, she was gone. We did the next play without her.

In the middle of July, Professor Wayne Campbell made evident his long years of professional acting when we cast him as the father in *Anna Christie*. It was an example to the entire cast and company to see a man of his age still capable of playing a show in summer stock. It was an inspiration. He continued his acting classes for the apprentices, and at the end of August we starred him in the popular *The Man Who Came to Dinner*.

Royal Eckert, who was a combination of set designer, utility actor and dear friend, kept a very complete scrapbook of the 1949 season. In it is found a review by John K. Sherman with this closing paragraph:

"Director Don Stolz, probably one of the hardest working men on Minnetonka's shores, merits an extra round of applause at this season's end, for giving so generously of delight and satisfaction in the Old Log's 1949 presentations. This year, more than ever before, a path has been worn to the barn theater's doors, and few have regretted contracting the Old Log habit."

It was so encouraging that we began to think most seriously about a winter season in the old Palace Theater on Hennepin Avenue. When this plan proved impossible, we began looking for other opportunities.

"How and Why"
I Still Don't Know

There is no question I can think of that is more often asked of me by young actors, than "What was it like doing thirteen plays in thirteen weeks? What was summer stock like in those years?" As I look back in an answer to that question, I can't believe what it was like and you probably won't believe it either, but my answer is as accurate as I can make it.

The first week of the season, by comparison, was easy—despite having a new cast and perhaps even a new designer. We started rehearsal on a Monday and had until a week from Wednesday to put it together. And of course in that first week, there were no plays in the evening. Beginning with the second week, things were different. Much different.

Each week, in preparing for rehearsals, we had to go to the American Express office, immediately adjacent to the Milwaukee Railway station to pick up the script and the "sides." The package came from the playbroker COD, the COD including the royalty for the opening week.

On Thursday morning, after the opening Wednesday night, rehearsals on the next play would begin at 9:30. We would rehearse until 12:30, take a lunch break until 1:30, and rehearse until 3:30. Most actors would go home for a short nap before dinner and a return to the theater for the night performance.

Remember, before the first rehearsal on Thursday, the director had prepared by reviewing the playwright's purpose in writing the play, the setting requirements, and conversations with the designer about entrances, their locations, furniture and its placement.

Before the first rehearsal, the director must determine which in his stable of actors would play which role. It was our practice at the Old Log to attempt to stagger the heavy lead roles, which had an influence on when a play was scheduled in the season. If you had two plays both of which had difficult and long roles, for, let us say, the leading lady, it would be best to not schedule the two plays back to back.

Fridays and Saturdays the rehearsal schedules were the same as Thursdays 9:30 to 12:30 and 1:30 to 3:30. On Sundays, if things had gone even reasonably well on Thursday, Friday and Saturday, there was no rehearsal until 12:00 noon, but it ran straight through to 5:30.

As soon as the Sunday night performance was over and while the actors were gathering their wardrobe and clearing the dressing room, the designer and his helpers (the director, the box office assistant and an actor or two who might not be in the next show) started immediately to strike (take down) the current stage set, to bring in the setting for the next show and to start putting it up, hoping that it would be completed by next Wednesday night. Sunday night's "strike" almost always lasted until rehearsal Monday morning.

Though the days were strenuous, endless and exhausting, I, thinking it all worthwhile, really enjoyed them. In his notebook, referred to earlier, Royal Eckert incudes as his dedication, the following quote:

"There is no place I would rather be than right here, right now."
Don Stolz
(old) Old Log Theater,
2:00 a.m. any strike night
Summer 1949, 50, 51, etc."
And it was true. I don't explain it, I just say "it was true."

Monday morning—rehearsal on what part of the next setting might be up, with chairs representing the furniture placed in the proper locations.

Monday night—the stage belonged to the crew, who attacked with new energy, having slept most of Monday daytime. The crew usually worked straight through until rehearsal at 1:30 Tuesday afternoon.

As the actors started Tuesday rehearsal, the crew again tried for a quick few minutes of sleep before dress rehearsal began at 7:30 that evening. If we were lucky and things went well, dress rehearsals were usually over by 1:00 a.m. Wednesday. Wednesday afternoon—a quick run through before opening the show that night. After the performance, I once again handed out the "sides" for the next play. Rehearsal started at 9:30 the next morning, and we started the process all over.

Remember that some time during that busy schedule the actors had to learn lines and, with the help of the director, determine wardrobe and find a few moments to pray for deliverance.

This we did for thirteen weeks. How? I can only answer by saying we thought what we were doing was important and we were young. When those two ingredients are present, you can do anything, especially when you know that after thirteen weeks, you can rest.

In *The Way it Was*, Aden writes, "One thing about weekly stock is that the rapidity of production heightens the perception of change of pace and versatility. A number of different skills are developed and honed. The ability to remember a long and complicated role, the ability to give the character life and depth, the sense of unity and comfort that leads to ensemble work, and if the company jells at all, the wonderful *espirit de corps* that forms from all of the above. But of all the rewards that come from constant hard work in comedies, in front of many different live audiences, nothing beats that of timing. The sense of timing in the theater comes mostly from practice before an audience."

There are people who say that playing stock results in paraphrasing, trite characterizations and sloppy technique, but these statements come from actors who have never had the experience of working stock or had worked for companies completely undisciplined. This was not the Old Log.

How did I, as the director, use the 6 1/2 days of rehearsal?

Thursday morning rehearsal would start with a brief, and quickly delivered, review of the purpose of the play, each character's relationship to that purpose, the style we hoped to obtain, the unusual difficulties that the script might bring, an explanation of the floor plan and the placement of the rehearsal "chairs." Then immediately began blocking. "Blocking"—telling the actor where and when to move. Beware of the rehearsal where the director allows the actors to "roam" at will. This is especially true if you have only 6 1/2 days.

We seldom—SELDOM—allowed ourselves the luxury of sitting down and "reading" the play.

After blocking the first act, we attempted, on that first day, to repeat the first act three times. We had found that in repeating the lines with the action three times, the actor is prepared to go home, study his lines and come to the next morning's rehearsal having memorized, not perfectly, the first act.

Friday morning rehearsal began with a repeat of Act One with someone "on book," thus allowing the actors to be prompted as they discovered how much they had succeeded in their previous night's study. After this run through, we would start Act Two. In those years, almost all plays were written in three acts, with the combined second and third acts only slightly longer than the first act alone. With the second act shorter, we could usually block it and repeat it three times before Friday's rehearsal was over.

Saturday rehearsal began with a run through of Act Two, hoping that the lines had been mastered some time between Friday's rehearsal and Friday night's performance of the play then running. A run through of Act One. Then with any remaining time, block Act Three.

While there was no Sunday morning rehearsal, with the thought of church attendance, most of the actors used Sunday morning as a time to "nail down" their lines.

Monday morning usually began with several repeats of Act Three, then went on to a running of Act One and Act Two.

Tuesday—Morning and early afternoon were spent in continuing to study the role and lines, completing selection of wardrobe and a quick prayer to St. Genesius.

Tuesday night—dress rehearsal. No more need be said.

Wednesday afternoon—quick run through.

Wednesday night—Opening Night.

Later Wednesday night—a short visit to the nearest bar.

Thursday morning—start the process all over again with the next play. Prayers of thanks that you were still alive.

What of the theater building in which we were working and in which the audience viewed our work?

The grounds were beautiful.

The theater, a converted stable, had great rustic charm. The box office was a converted tack room with a magnificent stone fireplace.

The only "facilities" were two shabby but clean outhouses. As clean as an outhouse can be. No running water save for a shallow well outside the building. That's not quite true—when it rained we had water that ran in the back door right down to the three rows in front of the stage.

There was no air-conditioning; we attempted to cool the building on especially hot days by hosing water (from the well) over the roof, hoping the evaporation would have some cooling effect. The one large fan in the rear of the auditorium was so noisy it had to be turned off during performance.

Certainly there were cool nights. We had no heat; the fireplace had no effect on the auditorium. Whoever was working in the box office could have a small electric heater beneath the counter, but it and the box office lights had to be turned off before we could turn on the stage lights. Pat Cunningham, Excelsior's friendly electrician, had even tried to give us extra power by wiring around the parking lot lights directly to the fuse box.

Despite everything, it was a place we grew to love. The porch leading into the box office became a favorite place to meet after rehearsals, after the play and any other moment when we weren't working. We would sit on the log railing and discuss and settle the problems of the world.

I can't remember an actor, particularly in the early '40s, who wasn't truly patriotic. Though there were certainly opposing political views, seldom was there any political discussion; there were more important subjects such as plays, playwrights and fellow actors.

I remember a number of us were sitting on the porch when an imposing but gracious 55-year-old lady, who had just married our ancient character man, Uncle Louis Lytton, joined us and reported: "Louis and I have been talking and we want you to know that we are well aware that you young people are wondering and sometimes even joking about what our relationship might be. Well, I want you to know that I married Louis thinking he was a damn good man and I have not been disappointed."

Despite what Mr. and Mrs. Lytton thought, their relationship was a subject that was never brought up.

Don't Take The Other Actor's Line

The 1950 summer season. John K. Sherman: "Under Don Stolz's direction, the Meadville troupe opened its 1950 schedule Wednesday with a strong and well-knit performance of Robert Sherwood's tense play, *The Petrified Forest*, about the gunman and the intellectual. There's good ensemble work in the production and really outstanding work from Mary Seibel as a profane and frustrated waitress. The Old Log is off to a flying start."

Mary Seibel was a student at St. Catherine's who had been an apprentice at the Old Log. To illustrate how close the entire Old Log company was, when our oldest son, Peter, was hospitalized for a tracheotomy, Mary and her sister came out to the lake, picked up our two youngest children, Dony and Tommy, and took them home to their mother to be taken care of, assuring her that they would take care of changing the boys diapers.

By the time we opened the second Wednesday in June, it was already an uncommonly hot summer. In 1950, most homes did not have air-conditioning any more than did the Old Log Theater. We realized, however, that by midnight there were people who were exhausted from trying to sleep in a hot bedroom and would get up to enjoy the night air, so we scheduled what we called "the Midnight Matinees." Hot weather or not, it achieved at least a modest success. I must add, however, that some of the strangest groups that ever entered a theater showed up.

On July 12 we again wanted to vary our presentation, so I

scheduled three one-act plays: *Hello Out There* by William Saroyan, *Ile* by Eugene O'Neill, and *The Long Goodbye* by Tennessee Williams. Though the productions were praised by both critics and audience, our experience has never shown that audiences are much excited by an evening of one-act plays.

The Torchbearers, a legendary comedy about amateur theater as practiced by high society of Philadelphia, was funny for everyone but the audience. One of the newspaper critics told me "Just keep on giving it until they start coming out and laughing."

Our ninth offering of the 1950 season was *Winterset*, set atop a mountain peak. How we performed it on our small stage, I am not quite sure.

In our employ we had a teenager who would dedicate his life to theater. His name: Tommy Millott.

Tommy was put in charge of gathering props and even making arrangements with a local trucker to pick up the furniture that had been selected to be in the next show. To do all this, Tommy traveled by bus and streetcar. He was also to be on book backstage and, on occasion, was given a small role to play. One summer night, Millott became aware that on stage something was wrong; somebody had forgotten what to do or more importantly an actor had failed to make an entrance. Tommy was frantic. The problem had to be immediately corrected. He picked up the master script (which he should never have put down) to find out whose entrance it was. He found the place and uttered in a voice that could be heard in the front row—"Oh, God—it's me!" and rushed on stage.

The last play of the 1950 summer season was *Born Yesterday* and I mention it not just because Ken Senn was absolutely terrific in the lead, but also because it was the only play we have ever presented in which my wife, Joan, played a role. Joan was the manicurist; the manicurist had but one line. Every night—every night—just as she was about to give her line, Senn would say "Oh, I know what you're about to say—" and then give the line. We have never been able to get Joan back on stage again.

CABARETIN' AND PLOWING NEW FIELDS

Sometime during the winter months, Dardy Orlando, one of burlesque's biggest stars, was booked into the Red Feather, downtown 4th Street. Monty Perkis, the nightclub's owner/manager, had years before imported a collection of reproductions of famous nudes. To everyone he said, "my collection's worth over a million dollars if I had the originals." He built a small 12-foot proscenium stage at the end away from the street. Monty thought the stage perfect for both the band and the performance of Miss Orlando. In no way, she told Monty, was she going to appear on that stage with a five-piece band on the small stage behind her. It became an argument of enormous proportions. Finally, the day before they were to open, Monty and Dardy agreed they would turn the decision of band on the stage/band off the stage to an outside authority. As soon as they had agreed, Dardy, who knew of me from her friend, June March, named me. Monty, who had met me some weeks earlier, agreed. I had little trouble making my decision; there was no way that Dardy's beautiful act (and it was beautiful) should be ruined by a bunch of musicians playing behind her. Monty accepted the decision without question. Dardy was so delighted that the next week she presented Joan with her charm bracelet with her ten-year extensive collection of "charms." Dardy remained a friend for the years that followed, as did Marty.

Sometime during the discussion of Dardy's show, Monty got the idea of presenting, on that same small stage, what he called "Comedy Capsules," which meant 90 minutes from a famous comedy. On that 12-foot proscenium stage, the Old Log presented, if you can believe it, *Three Men on a Horse*, with a cast of nine and three sets,

The Voice of the Turtle and *The Drunkard*, a cast of twelve with multiple sets.

One night, when Joan and I came into the Red Feather for a drink, and I'll never forget Monty asked us, "Well, where have you two been—out cabareting?" We liked Monty no matter what his background.

In the first week of June 1951, the *Minneapolis Star*, on its entertainment page, carried a story with this headline: "Old Log Theater Season to Open with 14 Week Schedule June 13." The story under the headline told that the first play would be "the famous comedy, *Harvey*, starring Minneapolis' favorite comedian, Ken Senn."

The 1951 season included a sharp production of *Private Lives*, and a truly dramatic *Detective Story*, by Sidney Kingsley. *Detective Story* starred Warner Lahtinen who gave a fine performance. The review read "Ably supporting Lahtinen is the largest cast in many seasons on the Old Log stage. Some 34 people make appearances including old standbys Ken Senn, Mary Ellen Fedora, Al Gregory, Rupert LaBelle, Anita Torcum and Herschel Welsh. Royal Eckert has outdone himself on this production in the way of set designing. Both he and Director Don Stolz deserve special applause for this show."

Toward the end of the summer, Bob Aden and Deborah Tighe Aden returned to Minnesota, and we persuaded him to perform in the last week of the season. We would produce whatever play in which he wanted to appear. Little did we expect that he would come up with *What Price Glory*, a World War One drama. It opened September 12; also opening September 12 was the 1951 season of rain. The water flowed in the back door and made its way to the first few rows where it formed a small Lake Minnetonka. During one of the scenes of *What Price Glory*, one of the military hats was knocked off the head of one of the armed forces and fell into our front row lake. I remember being on stage later in the performance and watching the hat as it floated from the front of the first row around the first row into the second and then back to in front of the first. It added a certain Naval effect to the army on stage. It would not be unfair to refer to *What Price Glory* as "interesting but a disaster." But the rest of the season had been good.

So good that we were sold out almost every Saturday night, althouth the Midnight Matinees, which we continued to hold, were not attracting that many customers. What we needed were more seats in the theater. The theater benches held 278 people—if they were friendly. During the winter we developed the idea that if we built a stage box on the one end of the building, we could then remodel the audience section, adding the space that had formerly been the stage. I made an appointment with Mr. Kuechle and showed him not only the plans on how the building would be remodeled, but also how it could be paid for. We would continue paying our ten percent of the gross, and every time the sales went over our old capacity, he would get 50%. It was remarkable how quickly the whole thing was paid for. Somewhere I should probably note that from 1946 on, we never missed a rental payment to Mr. Kuechle; and never did Mr. Kuechle enter the theater without first buying a ticket.

The changes to the building were not the only preparation I made. During the winter I had received several hundred 8" x 10" photographs with attached resumes from New York actors. In early spring I sorted through these, selected the ones I thought would fit our company, then went to New York for interviews and auditions. I was looking primarily for three actors: a young ingenue/leading lady, a young leading man, and a mature leading man.

I knew the ingenue/leading lady I wanted—Lois Nettleton, whom I had met when she had played the Lyceum Theater in *Darkness at Noon* with Edward G. Robinson, the same role she had played in New York opposite Claude Raines. After several seasons of stock she had gone to New York and three weeks later landed the role of the daughter in *The Biggest Thief in Town*.

When I told an agent in New York that I was hoping to hire Lois for the 1952 summer season, the agent told me I was dreaming, that Lois was one of the most popular, most respected and most sought after actresses in New York. When I telephoned Lois and told her the plays scheduled for the season, she accepted immediately. When asked by an agent why in the world she would do that, Lois replied that she wanted to learn to play comedy and her friends had told her that the place to do that was at the Old Log.

So now I was looking for the young leading man and the mature leading man. In two days, conducting interviews at my hotel room, I had seen over 110 actors, and had hired John Compton, a very handsome young man with considerable experience including a Broadway juvenile lead in *Ryan's Girl*. When discussing the details of his coming to Minnesota, John asked me if it would be all right if he brought his wife of only a few months with him. He showed me her photograph and said that though she was not yet an actress, she would like to do small roles. She was beautiful. The year before she had been named the national Miss Oleo-Margarine. This is not a joke.

Still no mature leading man.

The morning of my third and last day in New York, I had packed my suitcase, gathered all of the leftover resumes and was ready to check out when the room telephone rang. It was a call from an actor, Bill Hughes, who just arrived back in town after a tour in Margaret Webster's *Hamlet*. I told him I had to catch my plane; he replied that he was in the hotel lobby and could come up immediately. It was a short and hurried interview during which he told me that on graduating from Harvard, he was lucky to have been hired for the touring company of *The Male Animal*, had any number of Broadway shows and loved to act. As time ran out, I said, "Bill, I do have to leave now for the airport. After interviewing over a hundred actors, you seem a perfect choice. Is there any reason why I shouldn't hire you?" He looked at me, smiled, "There are at least a dozen reasons why you shouldn't hire me, but I'm not going to tell you a one." Since he didn't tell me, I hired him. And in the years that followed, I never learned a one of the "dozen reasons" he claimed.

The 1952 season opened with John Patrick's new comedy, *Lo and Behold*. John Sherman reviewed our play with this opening paragraph:

"It is a healthy thing for an old institution to have a rebirth now and then, and this week the Old Log Theater becomes the new Old

Log with the addition of a large stage house, a lengthened auditorium, new audience benches, a hard surfaced floor and elegant sanitary facilities."

When he wrote this, John knew well exactly what the "elegant facilities" were. We had moved a small yard workshop from the Kuchele's extended yard to a spot back of the theater; and run a water pipe from the well faucet beside the theater. The small building already had a door at each end, so all we had to do to provide both women's and men's "elegant facilities" was to build a separating wall in the middle and then install a toilet bowl and a wash bowl in each side. Looking back, I can't believe that Rupert LaBelle and I did it. One memorable afternoon with the job drawing to a close, I was nailing a board on the separating wall. Rupert was holding my hammer while I got down on my hands and knees.

> **Don:** "All right, Rupert, I'm all settled. Please hand me my hammer."
>
> **Rupert:** Your hammer? I don't remember where it is.
>
> **Don:** You're holding it—it's in your right hand.
>
> **Rupert:** Oh, yes—here it is.
>
> **Don:** Thank you. Now if you would please hold your hammer on the other side of this board while I'm trying to secure it.
>
> **Rupert:** Oh, hell—now I can't find my hammer.
>
> **Don:** Rupert … it's in your other hand.
>
> **Rupert:** It is—isn't it?

Despite everything, Rupert and I worked well together.

As the summer progressed, we tried to make the really quite crude "elegant facilities" at least entertaining by posting a sign in each and changing the sign each week. Such terribly clever phrasings included "Purchased at the Estate of the Late William Randolph Hearst" And "Please Do Not Flush During Performance."

Another paragraph in Sherman's review read: "Don Stolz's perseverance in keeping the Old Log rolling through fat years and lean is beginning to pay off. Energy, talent and money expended over a long period has firmly established a reputation for service and quality in theatrical goods." I always hoped that there was more truth in this paragraph than there was in Sherman's "elegant sanitary facilities."

John Compton and Bill Hughes made their first appearance at the Old Log in *Lo and Behold*—appearances heartily approved by both critics and audiences. Lois Nettleton's first appearance at the Old Log was in the fourth play of the season, **Shadow and Substance**. And watching it, you knew why Edward G. Robinson had said, "Miss Nettleton is well on her way to being Broadway's brightest young star."

The first play in which June Tolley, John Compton's wife, appeared was the second show of the season, **The Curious Savage**. June played Fairy May, one of the "guests" in the Cloisters home. There wasn't a person in the audience who didn't recognize that she was beautiful. And a little off. On opening night, when the phone didn't ring when it was supposed to, Fairy May without hesitation said, "Ding a Ling" and answered it. Most in the audience did not perceive this as a grievous error but thought anyone called Fairy May must have extra senses and thus anticipated the phone call. Oh, well.

We soon learned that Bill Hughes, as he established himself as the Old Log's leading man, was not only a superb actor, but also one with exceptional powers of memorization. After Wednesday, opening night, I would hand to each actor his sides for the next show. Remember, the actor's line was preceded by only a few words, which were his cue. When rehearsals started Thursday morning at 9:30, Hughes would show up knowing the entire play. He knew what he was to say, but on occasion had no idea why he was saying it or when. It certainly did not lead to easy rehearsals for the director or the other actors. When opening night of the new play would arrive, Hughes was always so confident of his control of the role that he would sit backstage reading the newspaper. As his years at the Old Log progressed, I started calling him "America's oldest leading man," to which he would always reply "Directed by America's oldest juvenile." We still hear from Bill, but not often enough.

I mention the eighth play of the summer, because it was and remains one of my favorites, **The Biggest Thief in Town**, a brilliant

Guest in the House; Lois Nettleton and Bill Hughes.

The Biggest Thief in Town; John Varnum, Ken Senn, Bob Edwards, Joe Young.

comedy written by Dalton Trumbo. This is the play that when it played in New York with Ed Mitchell and Walter Abel, Lois Nettleton played the ingenue lead. When it opened in Boston, both critics and audiences were carried away and predicted one of the longest runs in Broadway history. Hardly three weeks into its Boston tryout, several newspaper reporters recalled that its author, Dalton Trumbo, was one of the accused communists on the Hollywood Black List. This was all Walter Winchell needed; it became his personal vendetta to destroy what he kept calling communist propaganda. By the time the play came into New York, Winchell had been successful; *The Biggest Thief in Town* closed after a heartbreakingly short run. Unless honesty, ethics and morality are in the sole possession of the Communist Party, not one of us at the Old Log could ever detect one word of "communist propaganda."

The synopsis of scenes reads: "All three acts occur in Bert Hutchins undertaking establishment in the small Colorado town of Shale City. Above the town and very close to it, towers a dark mountain. Atop the mountain stands John Troybal's enormous palace, which he calls Mount Miracle. The spotlight outside John Troybal's wide-windowed bedroom may be seen at night from the front windows of Bert's establishment."

Bert Hutchins, played by Ken Senn (who by then was Minnesota's favorite actor), knowing that Troybal's health and old age are making him a primary prospect, had arranged with one of Troybal's staff to turn out the visible spotlight at the very moment of Troybal's death. The plan is to be the first to appear at Mount Miracle, claim the body, and take it to the local mortuary for what will become the most expensive funeral in the history of the state.

On one of the nights when the town's editor, its druggist and its doctor have all gathered at Bert's establishment for their "weekly drinking," the light suddenly goes out and they are on their way to Mount Miracle.

Our production was a huge success. In the years since, we have done the play five more times, the latest in 1973.

The thirteenth play of 1952 was a beautiful production of *A*

Streetcar Named Desire. Our production was one of which even today I am most proud. May Ellen Fedora played Stella Kowalski, and Barbara Davies, having returned from New York where she had been offered the leading role in the touring company, played Blanche DuBois. Otto Stohr, a fine actor whom we had frequently used, was Mitch, and Robert Aden was at his very best as Stanley. It was so long ago that I was young enough to play the paperboy who knocks at the door. Barbara Davies was truly remarkable. She opened the door, and with haunting loneliness and passionate longing said, "Oh, young, young man." In just these words was the soul of every feminine role that Williams had ever written. If ever you have been a producer, director, actor or stage manager, you have heard line readings that were so special you shall never forget them. This is one of them: "Oh, young, young man."

Design for Living was the fourteenth show of the season and scheduled as the last. And we were having fun and making money. Well, not losing money. Not giving up the attraction of presenting three one acts in an evening, we selected *The Last of My Solid Gold Watches* by Tennessee Williams. It is difficult to believe that this is not what inspired Arthur Miller's *The Death of a Salesman*. The second of the one acts was *The Respectable Prostitute* and the third was *If Men Played Cards as Women Do*. It was a fun combination of material, and I still insist we did not lose money. At least not much.

The Script Isn't As Bad As You Think It Is

After the season of 1952, still hoping that some arrangement might be worked out with Paramount Pictures concerning the rental of the Palace Theater, and with the realization that it was becoming increasingly difficult with our growing family to move back and forth to either New York or California, we rented a small but attractive bungalow in the 5200 block of Fremont Avenue in South Minneapolis. It was only two blocks to the streetcar route and only a few more to Annunciation Catholic Church where we attended 8:00 mass every Sunday.

The only remaining problem was making a living. I have often said that "In those days it was vulgar what I would do to make a dollar," and I guess that may still be true today.

Only ten days after the close of the season, I had a telephone call from Minneapolis Honeywell saying that in their search for an actor for an "industrial show" they were planning, they had called John Sherman at the *Star* and he had suggested they call me. When they replied it probably wasn't anything I would be interested in doing, Sherman had answered that our season was over and he felt certain I would be interested in anything. Honeywell called our home and asked if I could come to their office the next Tuesday morning.

Tuesday Morning! In the conference room was an oblong table around which were seated seven Honeywell executives. In charge was Herb Bissell, having come to Honeywell from his job in advertising and marketing at Ford Motor Company, just one week earlier. Herb introduced all present and passed out copies of the proposed "Wrong Way, Right Way" skit. Sitting on my right was the young man who had written the script. After we finished the read-through, there was silence. Finally Herb Bissell said, "This script is terrible. What do you think, Mr. Stolz?"

Remembering that the author of the "terrible script" was sitting immediately on my right, I replied, "Well, I certainly don't think it's as bad as you do."

Mr. Bissell threw his copy on the table in front of me and said, "Well, take it home and re-write it. We'll meet again Thursday morning at 10:00."

End of meeting.

It was to be the first script I had written for a company. The script was approved, rehearsals began and, a week later, we started the tour. I had great experience playing the lead in the six states in which Honeywell wanted to present it.

Before we had played the last city, I received a telephone call from, Al Whitman, a Vice President of Campbell-Mithun advertising agency. He asked if I would be interested in producing and directing a show that the Hamm Brewing Company planned for the next meeting of their distributors.

When I started work at Hamm's, I learned that just as my job at Honeywell had included the coaching of the company speakers, at Hamm it also included re-writing speeches prepared by their executives. I remember well my first meeting with Odd Moe, Hamm Vice President in charge of the meetings. Odd told me to have a seat and immediately started reading what he had written. On finishing, he, with dislike for what he had just read, said, "It's not very good, is it? In fact, it's awful."

"Well, it doesn't sound much like you. What do you really want to tell your distributors?" I asked.

Mr. Moe put the script down and started talking. What he said was exactly what he should say. "That's what I want to say, so see what you can do."

I went home and wrote what I had just heard Odd say, and took it back to him the next morning. After reading it, he looked up and said, "It's wonderful. How did you do it?"

"All I did, Mr. Moe—I remembered what you said yesterday, and just wrote it down."

The next year, when the distributors meeting came around, Mr. Moe handed me a script and said, "Take it home and re-write it like you did last year."

The third year, after the meeting was scheduled, Mr. Moe telephoned me. "You know what I want to say—just write it."

The Hamm meetings I enjoyed enormously. Especially the one for an anniversary celebration, when I dramatized their long and romantic history. In their history were the legends of immigrants arriving from Germany with tags that read, "Send me to Hamm Brewing, St. Paul, Minnesota"; draft horses that drank beer instead of water; dormitories and lunch rooms for the workers; Mrs. Hamm who may have escaped injury from a group of Indians by offering them a dinner when they came to the back door of her home. And a modern legend: if you were an employee and your child graduated from high school in the top third of their class, the brewery would assist financially in their college education. What a wonderful musical their history could be. The Hamm bear, the heart of their advertising, was not the only lovable ingredient of the Hamm Brewing Company.

The business meetings were held at the St. Paul Auditorium. It was a venue that had developed one of the most talented and cooperative union stage crews in the nation. They were proud, hard working and fun. The crew always included the Den Bleyker brothers, who were third-generation members of the International Association of Stage and Theater Employees (IASTE). The last night of the Hamm distributor meeting was an evening of dancing and entertainment, always held at the Prom Ballroom in the Midway. For the distributor organization it was the social event of the year. For this event, we always tried to hire stagehands with whom we had worked that day at the auditorium. Over the years, the Den Bleyker brothers became fellow workers and close friends.

One year we had prepared, in our shop at the Old Log, a small moveable wagon set piece for the Prom stage. We had carefully designed and built it so that when it was necessary to move, it would barely roll past a permanent mike pipe that hung from the stage ceiling. The night of the show, as Harold Den Bleyker and I were standing off stage watching as the "Old Log Wagon" rolled past, but barely missing the pipe, I proudly turned to Harold:

Don: See, Harold, that's how well we do things at the Old Log.

Harold: Just remember, Stolz, no amount of skill will ever replace outhouse luck.

It should be pointed out here that these social evenings were always formal and the entertainment always clean. Let me say that there is nothing as conservative and morally correct as a beer distributor when his wife is present. One year the entertainment for the Prom Ballroom was Nancy Wilson, a wonderful vocalist, and Larry Storch, the comedian. Both Larry and his agent were told by Hamm's that there absolutely must not be one single bit of "off-color" material. Though Larry had agreed, when he made his entrance that evening, the first five minutes were the raunchiest I had ever heard. At that point, one of the Hamm's executives, a man no larger than I, went out on stage, picked up Larry, carried him off stage, returned to apologize to the audience, and introduced Miss Wilson who most obligingly lengthened her act to fill the evening.

And there was Red Owl. I can't remember how many years I worked on every meeting they had—meetings for store operators, department heads, truck drivers—all of them. In preparation for the Red Owl meeting for store operators, Ford Bell told me he wanted me to work with their new president on his speeches. Ford led me into the office of Jim Watson. After introducing me and telling Jim why I was there, he left to return to his own office.

After a short pause, Jim said, "I'm sure that you're wondering how a young man like me can be the president of a company like Red Owl. Well, the fact that Ford is married to my sister didn't hurt a bit." It was a moment of admiration that immediately established a friendship that I have cherished ever since. Less than two years ago, at a large social gathering at Lafayette, Jim announced to all who would listen—"Don is a close friend; for years he wrote every speech I ever delivered." It may not have been quite true, but it was typical of Jim to state it.

During these years, Ford Bell and I had become good friends. Often during the summer months, he and his wife, Eleanor, would invite Joan and me to come to their pool for a swim, always followed by a delicious lunch.

One afternoon, present were a number of the Fords' close friends. One of them was a member of the Dupont family. Sitting beside the pool, Ford remarked that he was saddened by the fact that in all the activities he loved, his skills were decreasing:

Ford: It is truly sad—my golf game, as you saw yesterday, is bad and getting worse; my tennis is one double fault after another; and my swimming hasn't the slightest semblance of grace.

Dupont: Ford, you've got to change the way you live.

Ford: Oh? How do you mean?

Dupont: At our age, knowing that our athletic skills are going to decrease, we should get interested in activities that we've never done before. That's what I've done. You remember, I've never played tennis before—not until this spring. And then the most important example—I'm taking piano lessons.

Ford: Piano lessons? Are you any good?

Dupont: No—that's the point. I'm terrible. Improvement is the only thing possible.

Whether Dupont's advice had a great deal to do with Ford's decision to make another motion picture, I'm not sure. But I do know the project began immediately.

It had been years since Ford, as a young man, had written, directed and filmed a motion picture with young friends that even today is still a Wayzata legend. Ford's mother endorsed his efforts even though she knew Ford's father would disapprove. As soon as Bell, Senior, departed for his Minneapolis office, the cast would gather at the Bell swimming pool and filming would begin. Mrs. Bell and Ford had arranged for Mr. Bell's secretary to call when Ford Senior left his office to return to the Lake. When the call came all cameras, lighting equipment and cast immediately disappeared.

On his new film venture, Ford generously asked me to work with him. Our first step was a trip to Chicago to seek the advice of one of his old and dear friends, Colleen Moore. Yes, the retired motion picture star who, during her years as a Hollywood star in dozens of films, had built an unbelievable doll's house that today can be visited in the Chicago Museum of Science and Industry, where it has been viewed by decades of admiring visitors.

Ford never flew. Well, seldom flew. For him it was even better to walk; so he had designed a bus that included his sleeping quarters. On our trip to Chicago, we took The Milwaukee Road. Ford had booked a bedroom for Joan and me, and two bedrooms with the connecting wall removed for himself, for he had the habit of spending much of the night walking around the combined rooms.

We boarded the train at 11:45 p.m. At midnight we were west of Minneapolis. All train routes had been altered by high water between St. Paul and Chicago. We arrived at the Union Station in Chicago two hours late, but patiently waiting was the driver that had been engaged by Ford to meet us. Also waiting were Joan's mother and father who had come to Chicago from South Bend to spend the day with Joan.

Ford and I were driven to Colleen Moore's home, an apartment with a beautiful view of Lake Michigan. It was almost midday when we arrived at the building. There was only one person in the lobby, the elevator operator. He stood about four feet eleven. Ford immediately and somewhat majestically entered the elevator and said to the operator, "Miss Moore's floor, please." The elevator operator looked up at Ford and asked in a manner barely short of rude, "Is Miss Moore expecting you?"

Now if you have ever met Ford you must remember that he was

a tall, good looking, impressive, even imposing man, not accustomed to having his orders or even his suggestions questioned. With a look that would wither an ordinary man, Ford rose to full height and in his best Cathedral voice replied, "Of course, Miss Moore expects me—I am Ford Bell." With this announcement he made no greater impression than if he had said, "I am Don Stolz."

The elevator man, I thought, reluctantly, took us to the sixth floor. Each apartment occupied an entire floor. Separating the apartment from the elevator was a small hallway. Ford walked to the entrance to ring the bell, looking back at the elevator operator who stood there still challenging and refusing to leave the sixth floor before he knew if it was true that Ford Bell was expected.

No one answered the door. Ford looked back at the elevator operator who still stood there, now with a look that only one who knows he is right can manage. Ford again pushed the doorbell. Still no answer. I knew that Ford was beginning to wonder if our late arrival could have changed Miss Moore's plans. Again the challenging looks between the two men. Two more rings. The action remained the same. Had the operator been correct, I don't know what he hoped to do in case all was a lie. I could have taken the operator. Ford would have smashed him with one blow.

Again the doorbell. Again the exchange of challenging stares, stares, each time becoming more glaring. This time the door opened and there stood Miss Moore who threw her arms around Ford as she said with great delight, "Ford, Honey—it's wonderful to see you." Even before answering her, but while embracing her, Ford turned to give the elevator operator a last look—now a look of triumph and victory and said only one word: "See." Victory after being challenged is sweet and dear.

The next week, Ford, his son Fordy, and I went to Hollywood, where we hired actresses and a motion picture director to come to Minneapolis to work on the film Ford had written. The rest of the cast, including his nephew, Sam Bell, who played the lead, was from this area. They completed the film, had an invitation-only showing at the Wayzata motion picture theater, where it had excellent reception. But to my knowledge, the film has never been released. Ford was a remarkable man whom I enjoyed and greatly admired.

Honeywell executives had been so pleased with my coaching of their speakers, that when I suggested a course of "Public Speaking as Related to Selling" for their school for sales engineers, they asked me to present a projected outline. The outline was approved. I taught this course for years at their "school" building at 28th and Nicollet. Many of these sessions were conducted during our Old Log summer season, which resulted in even less sleep. I sometimes conducted the class after being up all night, still dressed in scene-paint-stained clothes.

Sometime during my Hamm Brewing and Minneapolis Honeywell work, Graybar, the local representative of Hot Point Appliances called me for help with their annual meeting for Dakota Montana Utilities, presented at the Fox Theater in Billings, Montana. Each year I would catch the late afternoon train and find, already aboard, the Hotpoint executives who had caught the train in Chicago, the city of their home office. We would have dinner together and then start our first rehearsal. Those were fun trips.

These were the early days of what became my extensive work in "industrial theater," all of which I found most gratifying. There is no better audience, no more eager audience for new ideas, nor audiences more open minded than a group of businessmen.

But there were still the days when "I would do anything to make a living." I painted scenery for the Masonic Temple; I designed a complicated front curtain for the World Theater; I stage managed amateur shows; I taught drama and speech classes—including a speech course at the Technical High School in downtown Minneapolis. One of my students enrolled for five consecutive semesters. She gave the same speech every time for five semesters.

And there was still theater.

When You're Grown, Do You Want To Be an Actor?

A family's working hours, regardless of what might be the business or profession, has, I know, a great influence on family routines and activity. And I am equally sure that every family, again regardless of business or profession, feels that their family life is especially influenced by father's occupation. So please, I beg of you, forgive me when I say that our being in the theater seems to have placed special demands and stresses on the time we had to spend together. In our case, we attempted to make the family a part of the activity at the Old Log as soon as possible. I always considered it a blessing—perhaps it was not. Perhaps a mistake, I don't know. I do know my mistake was that I've always tried to govern by affection and example even when the situation really required discipline.

Some of the few times I futilely attempted discipline, I remember quite well. Our oldest, Peter, was in his second year of school at St. Thomas Church School on 44th and Upton. I was awakened very early one morning by some slight noise coming from the first floor library/office. When I went down to investigate, I found Peter sitting at my desk writing something—a something he quickly hid in the desk center drawer. Sitting in an armchair half asleep was his brother, Dony.

Peter: *(As he quickly hides what he's writing in the center drawer of the desk)* Hello.
Don: What's going on?
Peter: Nothing.

Don: You were writing something.

Peter: Oh?

Don: Weren't you?

Peter: *(With hesitation)* Yes.

Don: What was it?

Peter: Oh, just an assignment from the teacher.

Don: I want to see it.

Peter: *(Getting it out of the drawer)* I have to write it 500 times, "I won't say shit on the playground again."

Don: I see. My next question—what is Dony doing down here?

Peter: Well, you don't think I want to write it all alone.

Don: To make clear what you are writing and why, you will be on probation for two weeks.

All probation meant was that he come home immediately after school and remain in the house for the rest of the afternoon. It was during the second week that Peter said to his mother, "Mom, I don't understand why you ever married that man."

The combination of the nun's assignment to write that sentence 500 times and my endorsing it with an attempt at discipline, resulted in making the offending word a permanent part of Peter's vocabulary.

It was later, in his homeroom at St. Thomas, when that same nun was very understanding and helpful. Joan and I and Blake and Dorothy Cox were scheduled to spend the weekend in Duluth. Blake was the Campbell Mithun executive on the Zinsmaster Bread account. Since I was producing their commercials, he had scheduled a Saturday afternoon meeting to discuss the new approach to their advertising. We would spend Saturday and Sunday nights in Duluth, and come back to Minneapolis Monday afternoon.

It was the first time we had ever left the boys with a sitter over-night. As we were getting ready to be picked up by the Coxes for the trip, Peter asked what we were going to do in Duluth. We told him that we were having a business meeting on Saturday, and probably another meeting on Sunday afternoon. When he asked what we were going to do Sunday morning, I replied that we were going to go to church of course.

Monday morning, it was obvious to the good nun that something was wrong with Peter. When she asked him what was troubling him, he told her that his mother and father had gone to Duluth for the weekend. She replied that she thought that was very nice, to which Peter said, "But you don't understand, Sister, Sunday morning they attended the Dulutheran Church."

Our baby sitter was always Mrs. Erickson, who lived with her daughter and son-in-law just two doors north of our house. When Mrs. Erickson was no longer available, we called Peter Pan, an efficient and trustworthy agency, which provided women to sit and care for children. Can you imagine such a company existing today?

When both Joan and I were to be away, we, of course, left a phone number at which we could be reached. One afternoon I received a call from the Peter Pan lady.

Peter Pan Lady: Mr. Stolz …

Don: Yes?

Lady: You know your little dog—what is it—Nina?

Don: Yes.

Lady: Well, she has just bitten Dony. I don't think it's serious, but I thought you should know.

Don: Thank you. Let me talk with Dony.

Lady: He's right here.

Dony: *(Taking phone)* Hello?

Don: Nina bit you?

Dony: It's all right. I don't need any stitches. *(At five, he was already well acquainted with stitches.)*

Don: Well, why did Nina bite you?

Dony: I think it was because I bit her first.

Later that afternoon when I drove the Peter Pan lady home, Dony asked if he could go along. When we arrived at the lady's home …

Peter Pan Lady: Good afternoon. Thank you, Mr. Stolz.

Don: Thank you.

Lady: *(Turning to Dony in the back seat)* Goodbye, Peter. It's been nice being with you.

Dony: Thank you.

Don: *(Being gracious as usual)* Oh, this isn't Peter, this is Dony.

Lady: Why that little devil—he told me he was Peter, but that's all right. I didn't call him Peter. I called him by his nickname.

Don: And what is his nickname?

Lady: He told me his nickname was "Aucky."

And you know what Aucky means.

Whatever, as soon as the children could walk and talk, they went to the Old Log Theater.

Dony was only two years old when I decided that a little boy would be a great addition (as well as a distraction from a scene that I didn't feel was going well) to the crowd scene in Maxwell Anderson's **Winterset**. It was, or seemed to be, a good addition even on the night when two-year-old Dony was tired of standing. Turning to the one member of the cast that he knew the best, he said, "Orono, pick me up." I don't think many in the audience ever believed that was a line written by Maxwell Anderson.

Our fourth boy, Timmy, was not yet three years old when I started taking him to daily rehearsals. One of the reasons was because we had lost our baby daughter shortly before Tim's birth. At three, he would sit next to me and watch the morning three-hour rehearsal without making a sound or making a move. Lunch together, and then back for the afternoon rehearsal. Each day, when we drove home to Edina, I was always surprised to hear what he thought of the day's viewing. In those days we were still doing weekly stock, so it is easy to imagine the many hours we spent together. During lunch break, little Timmy would step through the closed curtain, face the empty theater, and deliver a speech of welcome to the Old Log.

Quite often, Harry Kuechle, who, it must be said, loved theater, would bring lunch for the entire cast. We would eat together in the theater dining room. On occasion it was ground beef, which we were to use to prepare beef tartare. Almost always he would bring a small sack of special treats for young Tim, and as he handed them to Timmy, he would tell the rest of the company, "These doughnuts are for Timmy, not to be shared with the rest of you." After eating lunch, Timmy, taking his doughnuts with him, would go backstage, step through the curtain and say to the dark auditorium: "Welcome to the Old Log Theater."

One day, Angus Duncan, the company's juvenile, who always coveted the doughnuts, sneaked backstage, made sure that Timmy hadn't seen him and when Timmy stepped through the curtain to voice his welcome to the imagined audience, Angus crept up directly behind the curtain and in his deepest, most frightening voice said, "Huh, huh, hum, I'm going to get you."

Three-year-old Timmy replied to the unseen figure: "You may get me—but you're not going to get my doughnuts."

Those were great days.

In the fall of one of those years of the early '60s, we had taken Tim with us to the place where we were to vote, the Wooddale School in Edina. Without warning, Tim stepped through the curtain that masked the stage and announced, "Welcome to the Old Log Theater."

Later that year when the whole family were guests at the opening of the Guthrie Theater and we were all backstage to visit their production stage manager, Rex Partington (the husband of our leading lady, Cleo Holladay), Timmy, with the permission of Rex, went up on the stairway leading to the on-stage balcony of the set for Hamlet, stepped out on the balcony and announced to that part of the audience still in the building, "Welcome to the new Old Log Theater." This remark he had not sought permission to give, but Rex was delighted.

Again, perhaps because he was born shortly after the death of our daughter, both Joan and I were always a little apprehensive and probably a little over protective of Timmy, guarding against his ever feeling that we had been disappointed when he was not another little girl. Whatever the circumstances, he came to our bed every night; he did not start there, but once three o'clock came around, he was there and welcomed. It happened every night until we moved into our new lake house at 5120 Meadville, when his bedroom and Jon's were immediately adjacent to ours. Despite Tim's example, in all those years little Jon never once crawled into bed with us, or even suggested it. His was a free spirit, even then.

As I said, Timmy always started the night in his own bed. It was a routine: after dinner, I would put him in bed, read him a short story, kiss him goodnight and leave for the theater. From Thanksgiving until the middle of February, what Tim wanted to hear was *The Night Before Christmas*. One January night—late January—Timmy and I had been late coming home from rehearsal, dinner then was late, and putting Tim in bed was late. I was ready to leave immediately for the theater, when he asked, "Aren't you going to read to me?" "Well, what would you like to hear?" *The Night Before Christmas.* I should have known. Frustrated by the need to get underway immediately, I grabbed the book—opened it without much care and there on the page where I had opened it was a picture of the father of the house who had heard Santa and his reindeers and was leaning out of the window to look below. Timmy, with the quick understanding of children, realized I was somewhat irritated at the delay, so seeking to calm the situation, he looked at the picture and said, "There's that poor, sick man." I had to ask, "What makes you think he's sick?" "Well," he replied, "it says right there in the book that he threw up the sash."

Sometimes we just don't realize what we are reading to our children.

As I mentioned, Tim's habit of coming to our bed every night continued until we moved into our new home—on Lake Minnetonka, 5120 Meadville. Peter had his room upstairs; Dony and Tommy had their room, complete with fireplace, upstairs, young Tim and Jon's bedroom was immediately adjacent to the master bedroom downstairs. Joan and I decided it was time to talk to Tim about his nocturnal visits, so we said, "Timmy, you are now right next to our room, you are not a young boy now and I think you will agree that it's time for you to start spending the entire night in your own bed." Timmy, without hesitation, agreed. It was the first night—3:00 in the morning:

Tim: Daddy?

Don: Yes?

Tim: Will you come in and sleep with me?

Some weeks later, again in the middle of the night, another call. This time, for the very first time ever, it was little Jon.

Jon: Daddy?

Don: Yes?

Jon: I don't feel well. Will you come in and sleep with Timmy?

As is true in most families, the older boys are always impressing their younger brothers with slightly exaggerated stories of their knowledge, their athletic accomplishments, their physical strength. Almost from the time they could walk, both Timmy and Jon were subjected to these fulsome tales by Peter, Dony and Tommy. One night, when Timmy was just five, Vern Gagne dropped by our house at 5120 Meadville to talk about a project on which we both were working, the purpose of which I do not recall.

I knew that Timmy, who was already in bed, would want to meet this wrestler who was the champion of the world, so I got Timmy up and took him into the family room to meet Mr. Gagne.

Vern: How do you do—Timmy—?

Don: That's right, Timmy.

Timmy: How do you do. Are you the strongest man in the
world?

I wondered, how in the world Vern would answer this. If he modestly says, "Oh, no," then this little boy is going to be terribly disappointed. If he answers, "Yes, I am," then this same little boy is going to think how conceited Vern is. After only a second or two, Vern came up with absolutely the perfect answer.

Vern: Some people would say that I am.

Timmy: Well, they're wrong. My brother Tommy is.

During these years, Rupert LaBelle was our family confidante, our sons' mentor, grandfather, best friend and guide. Dony and Rupert were especially close. Rupert, when Dony was only five years old, had already named him as his replacement. Dony was to be the Old Log Theater's box office manager. And that's exactly what happened.

Rupert's opinion that Dony should be the next manager of the box office was never questioned. From an early age, Dony already knew how to get money and what to do with it. When he was five, Joan and I had decided that for some minor infraction of family rules, Dony should be punished. Neither of us was about to spank him; the solution seemed to be taking away his "allowance" for three weeks. It was really quite a harsh punishment because he was receiving the royal sum of five cents a week. One day during this three-week period of torture, I came home from my daily performance of a dog and cat on television to find Dony all smiles. It was obvious that I had been at least semi-forgiven.

Joan: Dony, show your father what you have.

Don: What is it?

Dony: My new prayer book.

Don: It's very nice. Where did you get it?

Dony: I bought it at school.

Don: How much was it?

Dony: Twenty-five cents.

Don: Without an allowance the past two weeks, where did you get the twenty-five cents?

Dony: *(Pausing a few seconds, to make certain he had his figures straight.)* Well, you remember that ten cents I had saved?

Don: *(Of course I remembered it. When anyone in the family saved any money at all, we all remembered it.)* Yes.

Dony: Well, do you remember Peter Spellissi?

Don: Yes. *(Of course I did. How could you ever forget a boy who had a name like Peter Spellissi.)*

Dony: Well, Peter had written a post card to Axel and I promised if he would give me a dime, I would guarantee Axel would read it on the air.

Don: All right, you had the dime you saved, you got a dime from Peter Spellissi, where did you get the rest of the twenty-five cents?

Dony: Well, I told Peter if he'd give me another nickel, I would deliver it for him and he wouldn't have to buy a stamp.

That same year, as Christmas approached, all Dony could talk about was the electric train that he hoped to get from Santa Claus. With the family being on a limited budget, Joan and I explained to Dony that Santa just might not be able to bring him the train that he wanted. The second week in December, we were still hearing about the train and were still giving him the same explanation.

On Friday, when several of us were appearing at WCCO Radio in the weekly drama, Ed Viehman suggested that it would be great fun if we were to take Marge, his wife, and Joan, and go to the Radisson's Flame Room to hear George Goebel. The next night when he picked us up, I asked if he could stop at the Dairy Store. When he asked why, I said I wanted to cash a check. No. Ed said, the Flame Room always "comped" him because he mentioned them on the air. To which I replied, "Well, they know I can't mention them on the air, so you had better stop at the Dairy Store."

George Goebel was at his best, and his best was great. Ed Viehman laughed uproariously at every joke—and immediately wrote it down in a small notebook. He was always looking for new material. At one point, Ed's response was so prolonged that he was late in opening his notebook. Goebel looked at him and said, "That's all right; take your time. I'll wait for you."

It was a glorious evening. After the second show—we stayed for both—Ed asked the waiter for the check. To Ed's request, the waiter said, "The bill is already taken care of."

"Oh, no, I certainly didn't expect that. Are you sure?"

"Well, I thought so—I'll go back and check for sure." Well of course when he returned—"I guess I was mistaken," as he placed the bill on the corner of the table. Viehman finally turned to me and said, "It was a pretty good thing that you stopped to cash a check, because I haven't a penny with me." When I paid the bill, I noticed that it was still marked "comp."

The next evening at our family dinner at home, Dony asked if we had a good time seeing George Goebel. We replied that it had been a wonderful evening.

Dony: How much does it cost to spend an evening like that?

Don: Well, *(reducing the amount somewhat)* about $26.00.

Dony: You know, I just don't understand things. If you can spend $26.00 for a night like that, I can't see why Santa Claus can't bring me an electric train.

He got the train.

Early Christmas morning, it was not yet dawn, older brother Peter came into our bedroom and announced, "Dony is downstairs playing with the train, but I haven't been down yet." Peter remembered well that the rule was "no one is to go downstairs to the Christmas tree until Joan and I are awake and ready. It was the rule, but I can't remember even once when it was actually observed. Just as with other families, we tried everything. One year I had secretly brought home from the station a life-sized cardboard Santa Claus, which we placed at the bottom of the stairway. In the light of early dawn it proved effective; when enough light came that they could see that it was only a cardboard figure, they delayed no longer their attack on the tree and everything around it.

The Christmas after the train, Joan and I, after being up most of the night getting everything erected and under the tree—at the last minute we remembered a child's play grocery store, which was still in its box. The first line of the instructions read: "If one is normally adept, this play store can be assembled in one hour and fifteen minutes." This was a challenge to one's adeptiveness. One hour and fifteen minutes. I worked diligently in an attempt to prove "normally adept." I completed the project in one hour and ten minutes. A victory.

Anyway, Joan and I decided that this year there would be no early tree visiting. We would sleep on the floor right outside their bedroom door. We were so tired that sleeping on the floor seemed a treat, even though we were joined by our dachshund, Nina, who insisted on sleeping between us. We had been asleep on the floor less than two hours when I awakened to hear whispering at the door:

Dony: Mom and Dad are asleep on the floor right outside our door.

Peter: Well, step over them.

Dony: I can't. They're too wide.

It was time to give up and all of us go downstairs together.

Another Christmas I remember well. It was Christmas Eve morning and I had been working trying to clean the basement before Christmas. I kept thinking of Joan's and my failure to find the only present Dony had asked for. What was that year's most advertised and therefore most popular toy for boys was a genuine service issue leather 45 automatic holster with an excellent toy copy of a service 45 automatic. It was so popular that by the time Joan and I had started looking for this "wonderful gift," there wasn't one to be found anywhere. Thinking about it that Christmas Eve morning, I went upstairs and told Joan that I just remembered one place we hadn't shopped, a little hardware store on Lake Street. Joan expressed great doubt that that little store would even have carried such a ridiculous toy, but I decided to rush to Lake Street before the store closed at noon. They were still open. I rushed in still dressed in my basement cleaning clothes.

Clerk: Merry Christmas. Can I help you?

Don: I sure hope so. I'm looking for one of those imitation 45 automatics in a genuine service issue holster—you know what I mean. I've looked everywhere and it's all one of my sons wants for Christmas.

Clerk: Sure, I know what you're looking for. We have one left. One.

Don: Thank heavens. I thought I'd never find one this late. How much is it?

Clerk: (*Looking at how I was dressed and taking note that I was desperately shopping at the very last minute*) Well, we have only one left, so I'll sell it to you for half price.

Don: Oh, wonderful.

Clerk: Why don't you look around and see if there isn't

something else you'd like to buy?

Don: Thank you. I noticed those little shoe shining kits. How much are they?

Clerk: We have dozens of those left—so how would a dollar each be?

Don: I'll take three of them.

Clerk: Good. Anything else?

Don: There's a nice clothes basket. I could carry everything in it.

Clerk: You can have that for 75 cents.

Don: Thank you.

It was only then that I realized that here was a man filled with the Christmas spirit and wanted to help this poverty stricken man furnish a good Christmas for his family. Then I remembered that the only money I had was a fifty dollar bill. I could not ruin his day by letting him know I had that much money.

Don: *(To clerk)* Oh—just hold all this stuff for me. I guess I left my billfold in the car. I'm parked just around the corner. I'll be right back, I promise.

I had noticed that there was a bank across from where I had parked. I went there, got change for the fifty and went back to the store. The clerk had everything all packed in the laundry basket. A basket we still have.

I hope that clerk still remembers with joy helping a poor family have a better Christmas.

Dony knew how to—well, the only word I can think of is "manipulate." A year later, during Christmas vacation, I was working at home—writing a script for someone. Joan was at a meeting of the Junior League. Dony's brothers, Peter and Tommy, were not home, and Dony decided he wanted to go ice skating at the public rink two blocks away. He kept asking me to go with him. Finally I said, "Dony, it's only two blocks away; you walk there and you'll find a lot of your friends already skating."

Finally he agreed. He was gone less than fifteen minutes when the phone rang.

Don: Hello?

Dony: *(It was Dony at the other end. He was crying.)* You'd better come get me.

Don: Did you fall down? Are you hurt?

Dony: No, but you better come get me.

Don: *(I thought perhaps he'd gotten in a fight.)* Did you get in a fight with anyone?

Dony: No, but you'd better come get me. *(Still crying)*

Don: All right, stop crying and I'll get in the car and drive down and pick you up.

Dony: Good. And bring your skates with you.

Rupert knew what he was doing when he selected Dony to be his apprentice in the box office.

Our 1954 season closed with our third production of **White Cargo**. The play immediately preceding **White Cargo** was **The Frogs of Spring**, a not so simple comedy by playwright Nathaniel Benchley. It starred Bob Aden, Dolly Wheaton, Walter Boughton and Bebe Shopp, the former Miss America. Included in the cast were nine-year-old Peter Stolz, eight-year-old Dony Stolz and seven-year-old Tommy. Young Barbara Flanagan, who was, in 1954, already one of the city's two favorite columnists, asked for an interview with the young Stolzs. For Barbara it must have been an interesting afternoon. We collected the boys at the big swing in the middle of the spacious green lawn. Peter was riding his new bike and was wearing a crepe hair goatee.

Barbara: Do you enjoy acting?

Peter: I guess it's all right.

Barbara: Well, when you're grown up do you want to be an actor?

Peter: Oh, no.

Barbara: Well what do you want to be?

Peter: I want to be the Pope.

Barbara: I see. Well, Dony, do you enjoy acting?

Dony: Oh, yes.

Barbara: Do you want to be an actor when you grow up?

Dony: Maybe.

Barbara: Well, what do you like to do when you're not on
stage?

Dony: I like to kill frogs.

He had never killed a frog in his life and hasn't to this day. We did think for a while that Peter really did intend to become at least a priest. About once a week he would serve mass in his bedroom. The host was represented by cut out circles of paper which, with proper ceremony, he served to the kneeling Tommy. Peter was always followed by Dony who carried a tray on which to recover the paper hosts.

Interview of the Stolz children by Barbara Flanagan.

Never Doubt the
Power of the Sheriff

I was born into this world a Democrat and remained one through Franklin Roosevelt and Harry Truman—clear up to Dwight Eisenhower, when I became a Republican. A conservative Republican. But I am also a union member—a proud union member. Three unions. It may seem a strange combination, but for me, never an uncomfortable one. In the early 1960s, I was elected president of the American Federation of Radio and Television Artists Twin City Local. After my administration, Old Log actor and activist in the Republican Party, Ken Senn took office—to my knowledge, the only two Republicans ever to be president of any AFTRA local. I said, to me, it was never an uncomfortable position.

When I came into the business, what so many producers did to so many actors was a crime. The union, Actor's Equity, was absolutely necessary. As was the Stage Hands Union. When I first came to Minneapolis, the head of IASTE would call me because they needed extra hands and they knew I needed extra money. I remember working with a crew unloading trucks at the old Lyceum Theater, pushing scenery through the only accessible entrance—a second-story window. The temperature was below zero, we were paid $2.00 an hour. Those were union wages.

When I, long before that, had started producing plays for the stage, I was told again and again, "Don, there are two things you must avoid whenever possible: the Stage Hands Union and the Musicians Union." Avoid them? They were my friends.

Whenever we do anything in Minneapolis, I call the unions first. I couldn't always do what they wanted, but we always found a compromise. Their members I respect, admire and enjoy. Every minute I've ever worked with them has been a good one. Among the many "special occasions," there remains one that I shall always remember.

Late in 1949, our season at the Old Log over, we decided to attempt to book a four-state tour of one of my favorite productions, **The Glass Menagerie**. Mary Perry, who had understudied the role in New York and who had played Amanda beautifully at the Old Log, agreed to join the cast. Barbara Davies was to play the daughter, her husband, Bill Nelson, was to play the gentleman caller, and I repeated my role as Tom. It was a good cast, a good production.

The day our tentative schedule was printed in the *Minneapolis Tribune*, I received a phone call from the gruff voiced Bill Donnelly, head of the local Stage Hands Union.

(Telephone rings)

Don: Hello.

Bill: Don?

Don: Yes.

Bill: This is Donnelly—Bill Donnelly.

(pause)

Bill: Head of the Stage Hands Union.

Don: Oh, sure.

Bill: I see in this morning's paper that you're taking that show of yours, the Tennessee Williams thing, on tour.

Don: Yes.

Bill: I don't think that's going to work. Where are you going to get your scenery?

Don: *(Not too certain of where this is leading)* We'll just build it here at the Old Log, the same way we always do.

Bill: I don't think that's going to work.

Don: Oh?

Bill: The Trib story listed a bunch of places you're going where there's a union stage.

Don: That's right.

Bill: Well, you just can't do it. If you go into those theaters, you're going to have to have scenery with the IASTE label stamped on the back.

Don: Bill, you know we can't afford that.

Bill: Well, you'll have to find a way. Every piece of that scenery has to have the seal.

(Pause)

Bill: I don't want to stop the tour, so I have this suggestion. You and your guys come down to our shop—you know, there on Nicollet Avenue. You build the scenery, we'll put the stamp on. All you have to pay is work dues covering the hours that you're there.

Don: You serious?

Bill: It's a solution, isn't it?

Don: It's an unbelievable offer.

Bill: So …

Don: Bill, you know I can't even afford the lumber and the canvas.

Bill: Aw, hell, we'll furnish everything. And then I'll bill you some time after the tour.

When we went on tour, it was with our IASTE labeled set. About seven months after the tour, I received a memo from Bill: "scrap lumber, scrap canvas—no charge."

After the end of our season in 1950, the Stolz family, then with three children, stayed in Minneapolis with the hope of opening a winter season in the old Palace Theater on lower Hennepin Avenue. A beautiful building. There were many reasons why that did not materialize, so we settled for a ten-week winter season at the Woman's Club on Loring Park. As soon as our schedule was announced, the Musicians Union called. Since we were doing only straight plays and no musicals, I had seen no reason to call them. They told me that regardless of our schedule, there must be three men in the pit for every performance. The union had an established minimum for every theater and nightclub in the city. I replied that it was impossi-

ble for me to hire any musicians, that I would be lucky if I were able
to pay the actors. They held firm, saying that if we didn't agree, they
would picket outside the auditorium at the Woman's Club and they
doubted very much that the ladies of that organization would care
much for that arrangement. The next day, I was still wondering what
to do when the phone rang.

(Phone rings)

Don: Hello.

Ed: Don, this is Ed Ryan. Can you have lunch with me
tomorrow?

Don: Why yes, thank you.

Ed: The Anglaise Café, 12:15.

Don: I'll be there.

(Both hang up)

Don: *(to audience)* Ed Ryan was the Sheriff of Hennepin County.
I had gotten to know him because when we had done ***The
Front Page*** at the Old Log with all the newspapermen,
six-foot-six Ed had been talked into playing the dumb
sheriff. Though a very bright and intelligent man, it was a
role he played with considerable authority. Anyway, when I
arrived at the Anglaise, already there were Ed Ryan, the
host, Stan Ballard, head of the Twin Cities Musicians
Union, and Jack Jorgeson, the top man in the local
Teamsters.

Ed: So, all right. Even before we order, I'd like to get this
settled. Now, we all know that the Old Log is coming
into town for a short season at the Woman's Club, right?

All: *(agree with a sound of some kind)*

Ed: Now as I understand it, there has been a previous
discussion about musicians playing for those shows. Right?

All: *(some sound meaning yes)*

Ed: All right. You first, Don, you say that there is no way in
the world that you'll be able to pay the musicians, right?

Don: That is correct.

Ed: And, Stan, you maintain that you have to have musicians there regardless of what the production is, right?

Musicians Union: I know it may sound unreasonable, but you see in our contracts we state that there will be musicians wherever there is any production in any theater or any night club. We break it here; we have no control anywhere.

Ed: All right. *(Turning to head of the Teamsters union)* What do you think, Jack?

Jack: I think the way to solve this thing is for the Teamsters union to buy enough tickets each week to pay for the musicians. *(Turning to Don)* When do you open and how much are the tickets?

The Teamsters saved our season. For several years after, the Teamsters would take a night at the Old Log—the regular one on Lake Minnetonka. They were the best dressed, best behaved audiences we ever had. And the Musicians Union—we've never since had a disagreement and we have used them whenever we possibly could.

The season they saved was a memorable one. We did ten different productions in ten weeks at the Woman's Club.

"Meet Me at Scheik's Café"
—Count Dracula

As some of you well know, the Woman's Club has its important weekly meeting every Tuesday during the winter in their beautiful theater auditorium. They were kind, generous and certainly supportive of our season. They had basically only one requirement: no scenery or props were to remain onstage or offstage after Sunday night's performance, and no scenery, furniture or props were to be brought in until after their meeting Tuesday afternoon. When you know that we opened on Wednesday night, you can immediately understand when I say it was a memorable season. There is more. According to the National Weather Service, those ten Tuesday nights, when the scenery was to be moved in, were the ten coldest Tuesdays in the history of the State. I used to pray to God "If you're going to take me soon, please do so before another Tuesday night/Wednesday morning."

How we survived, I can't quite recall. I only faintly remember loading the scenery from the second floor of a downtown warehouse, where it had been built and painted by our designer, Tom Russell—then taking the scenery to the Woman's Club and getting as much of it set up as we possibly could for the late Tuesday night rehearsal. a rehearsal that was repeated early Wednesday morning and afternoon. Still we managed to present some good shows. And one or two that were not so good, I'm sure.

One of the two I remember with at least a little pride was the drama, *Edward, My Son*, written by Robert Morley and Noel Langley. The leading role was portrayed by Ken Senn, already known as the area's finest comedian. He proved in this production of *Edward,*

My Son, that he was a brilliant dramatic actor, as well portraying beautifully the love of a father for his son.

The second of the two, *Night Must Fall*, was the hit of the season. On Saturday night we were sold out—all 660 seats, while Catherine Cornell on tour and playing at the Minneapolis Lyceum had only 600 in her audience that same night. Jack Cornelius, advertising genius and the head of the local BBD&O office wanted to get investors and take our production of *Night Must Fall* into New York.

Just remember, Sheriff Ed Ryan and the Teamsters Union had saved the season.

The ten-week season at the Woman's Club had been so impressive, so "moderately" successful, and so much fun for not only the Old Log cast and crew, but also for members of the theater board as well. One of them, Wayne Fish, an extremely successful seed broker who officed in the Rand Tower, decided he wanted to be a part of this fun and gratification that was show business. He decided to take the Old Log on tour with two plays, *Dracula* and *John Loves Mary*.

In reviewing a pre-tour invited audience performance of *John Loves Mary*, John Sherman wrote:

"Stolz is an old expert at casting, and in *John Loves Mary*, he has assembled a cast that fits the play like a glove fits the hand, a cast moreover that works as well together as its individuals work separately. Marian Kate as the starry-eyed sweetheart, baffled by her soldier hero's reluctance to marry her, has charm and magnetism, and you never saw a prettier girl in a sorrier situation. The stalwart and winning performance of Dan Stapleton is certainly one of his most engaging roles."

I remember *Dracula* vividly. As we started casting, preparing for rehearsals, we discovered that we had no one available to play Abraham Van Helsing. When Bob and I reported this to Wayne Fish, he sent us to Chicago to see what we might find there. We interviewed three men—that's all that responded to the casting notice at the Equity office and the ad in the newspaper. The first could hardly talk, the second looked as if he had just played one of the seven dwarfs. For years after, Bob kept insisting that he "knew" that the man was attempting to color his hair with black shoe polish.

Bob and I were wondering what to do next when in came Rupert LaBelle. He was perfect. I was convinced that there was no way in the world we would ever be able to hire him. He was at the height of his career as Chicago's favorite radio actor, appearing regularly on every major radio show that originated in that city. In New York, his success had been no less, extending into the early days of television. Rupert, I couldn't imagine why, agreed to the three-week contract. We had our Dr. Heising. Two days later, when Mr. LaBelle arrived in Minneapolis, I picked him up at the depot. On the way to Excelsior he asked if we would be going anywhere near the theater. When I told him I was going there to pick up a few props, he asked if he could come along.

Luckily for us, when Rupert first saw the Old Log, it was a beautiful early spring day. You know how winning, how seductive Lake Minnetonka can be under these conditions. When he got out of the car and stood in front of the original Old Log, Mr. Labelle's first words were "I know my contract is for three weeks only, but I'm staying here for the rest of my life."

And he did.

The first time I introduced Rupert to Mr. Kuechle, Mr. Kuechle asked, "Oh, are you an actor?"

With pride, Rupert answered, "Yes, I am. I'm a member of one of the world's two oldest professions, both of them ruined by amateurs."

Back to **Dracula**. Our cast starred Bob Aden as Count Dracula, our new character man, Rupert LaBelle as Abraham Van Helsing and Mary Ellen Fedora was beautiful as Lucy Seward. Also on the cast were Old Log favorites Marilyn Dean Hagerman, Al Gregory and Royal Eckert.

James Grunke, one of the designers from previous summers had designed, built and painted the set incorporating a scrim portrait, which hung quite high in the upstage left back wall. At one point, Count Dracula was to be revealed behind that scrim. So high was the scrimmed portrait that it was necessary for Aden, as the Count, to climb a stepladder to properly get behind the portrait. It was extremely effective, until every night when Bob, ordinarily most coordinated, would miss a step and then clatter down the other steps of the ladder. There wasn't a person over ten in the theater who didn't know exactly what had happened.

The show, **Dracula**, had been booked into Turner Hall, the New Ulm lovely old theater. The setting in such a romantic place of heritage could not have been better. At exactly the proper moment, when a rigged bat is supposed to fly through the set, a live bat flew out of the set, through the audience and back on the set, and then out of view. It was absolutely unbelievable. The audience was thrilled, frightened and wondering. When asked after the play how we had trained the bat to perform so perfectly, Bob Aden answered, "It was with great difficulty and persistence."

It was a strenuous but delightful tour. The day we returned to Minneapolis, Aden telephoned Joan and asked us to meet him and Deborah for dinner at Schiek's Café. Schiek's had become a legend with its talented sextet performing short versions of popular musicals. The music combined with the authentic German atmosphere and food made it the area's most popular restaurant. Joan eagerly accepted Bob's invitation.

When we arrived, the elderly but very dignified maitre'd welcomed us. When we told him we were to join Mr. Aden, he replied, "Oh, you're guests of the Count." He led us to the table where Aden and Deborah were sitting. I couldn't believe what I was seeing; Bob had worn his Dracula costume, complete with sash and medals. As we sat down, he quickly whispered, "Just call me 'Count.'" If ever there was royal service, it was at our table that night, and when the entertainment started, one section was dedicated to "The Count who was present." I have not since dined with royalty.

When our next season began, we knew that our new friend and fellow actor, Rupert LaBelle would, besides acting, be in charge of the box office.

BLESS UNION CREWS

In the years since Bill Donnelly's unbelievable action of providing the set for our *Glass Menagerie*, I have never said one word against the Stage Hands Union. When producing in Las Vegas and Hawaii, I may have felt that their charges were a little excessive, but they were always good and skilled co-workers. It was sometimes a little irritating when the stage hands made more than the actors. Oh, well! When you don't have union stage hands on the job, the chance of things going wrong has been enormously increased.

We were on tour with the gang from Harley Davidson Golf Cars (for years we did their motorcycle shows as well, but more about that later). One stop on our tour for the golf cars was the resort on Lake Lanier outside of Atlanta. It was a low budget tour so no advance man from the company had been sent to the resort to check out the space and equipment. When we arrived late on a Sunday evening, Ray Komischke, our musical conductor, and I asked to see the room in which the show was to take place early the next morning. We were taken to the room by a houseboy, who very proudly told us that he had everything set up exactly like the outline he had received from Milwaukee. And he was partly right. At one end of the room was the relatively small but adequate platform stage. The necessary 200 chairs were properly arranged with a center aisle. In that aisle facing the back wall—the back wall—was a slide projector and on the back wall, the screen.

> **Don:** *(To the houseboy)* Oh, I see, you haven't arranged the slide and screen. Are these left over from your last show?
>
> **Houseboy:** *(Showing sheet)* No, this is for your show—it says

right here on my work sheet "rear screen projection."

Ray: Don, you come back and straighten it out later. I think the important thing right now is to see the piano.

Don: *(Hardly able to contain himself)* We'll get this projection business worked out some way. *(To houseboy)* We've noticed you haven't moved the piano in yet. Isn't that on your worksheet?

Boy: Yes, it is, but I couldn't find it.

Ray: Couldn't find the piano?

Boy: I know it's around somewhere; I saw it last week, but I can't remember just where.

Ray: Since the show's 8:00 tomorrow morning, don't you think it might be a good idea if we started looking for it?

Boy: *(Checking his worksheet)* That's right. That's what it says—show Monday morning 8:00 a.m. Since I know the building, I'll lead the way.

(The two pantomime looking while Don talks directly to the audience.)

Don: After searching every public room at the resort, we still hadn't found it.

Boy: Well, I guess that's it. We've looked everywhere. I know I saw it somewhere last week.

Ray: How far is it to Atlanta?

Boy: Why?

Ray: We have to have a keyboard at 8:00 tomorrow morning regardless of what we have to do to get it.

Boy: It's almost midnight. There's nothing open, believe me.

Ray: Then we'll open it.

Boy: Even if you do, you'll need a truck to get it out here.

Ray: Then we'll find a truck.

Boy: I'm afraid, sir, that you'll just have to accept the fact— *(suddenly seeing something)* There it is! There's the piano You see it? Right out there in the middle of the yard.

Don: Where?

Boy: Under that tarpaulin. I knew I'd seen it somewhere.

That's where we left it last week.

Ray: You mean you left a piano outside in this Georgia heat and humidity for a week?

Boy: Well, we had it covered. You can see that. It's a good piano, I promise you. We painted it white just a month ago.

(As they go supposedly to look at the piano, Don turns directly to audience)

Don: Unless you yourself have spent a week under a tarp in Georgia heat and humidity, there is no way you can even imagine what that piano sounded like after the tarp had been removed and Ray played the first chord.

(Don rejoins the other two)

Ray: *(Stunned. Looks at boy)*

Boy: Sounds a little strange, doesn't it?

Ray: Never in the long history of civilization has any piano sounded so bad. It is terrible.

Boy: It's all we have. Looks nice white though, doesn't it?

Ray: Is there any way to get a piano tuner out here?

Boy: Between now and 8 o'clock tomorrow morning—no way.

Don: All right. Get whatever help you can find here at the hotel and get this thing up to the meeting room.

Ray: Don, it can't be used.

Don: Ray—

Ray: And don't give me any of that crap about "the show must go on."

Don: Even if it is crap, I'm afraid in this case it's true. *(To boy)* After you get the piano up there, you and I will do something with that projector and screen.

(They disperse.)

Ray and I agreed to meet at 6:30 the next morning to see if there was any hope at all for the piano. In the meantime, I had gone to the engineer on duty and borrowed a set of allen wrenches with the hope that one of them might fit the string pins and maybe Ray could do something. The next morning—well, there is no way you will believe it, because I didn't believe it and I was there. After six hours in that air-conditioned meeting room, the loose strings had pulled up with the result that it was almost in perfect tune. I tried to convince Ray that our prayers had been answered. He maintained it was the air-conditioning. We compromised by agreeing that it was both.

Beware of a resort with no union crew.

And sometimes even then things can go a little wrong.

We were doing an industrial show for Country Kitchen, which at that time had been recently purchased by the Hospitality Group of the Carlson Companies. The location was a lovely golf resort in Florida, which—and don't think it was a coincidence—at that time was managed by the same Radisson Hospitality Group. Curt Carlson was present to get better acquainted with the men and women of Country Kitchen, as well as to see how the resort was progressing.

The setup—a simple one, really—had gone well and the union crew of three had easily and good-heartedly worked through the brief rehearsal. One man on the backstage switchboard, the other two to operate the two follow spots. The catering manager, a non-union man, had told the crew, without our knowledge, that the show was nine o'clock the next evening, after dinner. There was no way they showed up for a nine o'clock show in the morning. Well it was easy. The show was simple. I was familiar with the type of dimmer system we had backstage. The only problem was the two follow spots. So I told Joan (my wife almost always went with the industrial shows), "You can run the follow spot. It's incandescent, not arc. You won't have any problem at all." I was just finishing my instructions when I discovered Mr. Carlson standing right beside us.

Mr. Carlson: You say Joan is going to operate one of these follow spots?

Don: That's right.

Carlson: Well, what about the other? Who's going to operate it?

Don: I don't know.

Carlson: Well, if Joan can operate one of those things, I
certainly am capable of handling the other. Just show me
how to turn it on and how to adjust it.

And he did operate it. And well. I am certain that Curt Carlson, the legendary Radisson Hotel impresario had more fun at that meeting than he ever did at any convention he ever attended.

And he wasn't even union.

As was said that day, this stage business, acting or crew, is fun.

RECOMMEND THE BEST

Sometime between the 1952 and 1953 seasons, we, Joan and I, were able to buy, on contract for deed, an 85-year-old lakeshore cottage on Meadville Street, two blocks from the Old Log Theater. During the summers that followed, it became the scene of our happiest, most joyful times. And the saddest.

It wasn't long before we were able to buy a small motorboat. Dony had already had an old double-end wooden rowboat and the boys also had an "X" boat for sailing. The motorboat Joan and I purchased was old and it was small. It was the smallest in-board motorboat on Lake Minnetonka. It would go for days on one tank of gas. We discovered, however, that it would not go as far as we thought. One afternoon, Joan and I decided we deserved a couple of hours on the lake. It being a weekday, there were no other boats around—a perfect day for a ride. I never even thought of checking the gas tank. We were on our way. We were having a wonderful time when we paid for my assumption that, as always, we had plenty of fuel.

We were marooned in the widest part of the lake; we had no paddles, no oars, there was not a boat in sight. We were wondering—seriously wondering—what to do when we saw at a considerable distance an enormous cruiser just leaving its dock. The cruiser was headed directly for us. When it came long within hailing distance, it looked as big as the Titanic. A genial face looked down at us and asked, "Do you need any help?" It was Clint Morrison. When I replied that in a way I didn't quite understand, we had run out of gas, Clint replied, "I'll throw down a line and tow you over to Wayzata."

For years after, whenever I ran into Clint on the street, without even pausing in stride, he would say, "Have you been out on the lake lately?"

Each year we "moved" from our home on Washburn on Mother's Day and "moved" back to Minneapolis when school started. The boys swam, fished and sailed. Joan had many delightful hours sunning on the long dock, which extended 30 to 40 feet into the lake. It was idyllic.

Early in May, I telephoned the Chicago Equity office and made arrangements to audition actors for the upcoming Old Log season. We had already hired Louise Buckley from New York as our mature leading lady, but we still hadn't found an ingenue.

In the '50s, the Chicago Equity office was in the apartment of the organization director, a beautiful and delightful widow, Marge Dare. Her husband, Frank, had been the director of the office, and at his death, it seemed proper to the board of directors to place Marge in control. It was an arrangement that worked well for both producers and actors.

On the day set for my interviewing and reading actors, Marge arranged for her niece, Ro Sussman, to help with the auditions. Ro was lovely, efficient and helpful.

At the end of the afternoon, I left for the airport with an armful of 8" x 10" photographs and resumes, but with absolutely no answer to my need for a young ingenue. The only young lady who looked like an ingenue should look, was Ro Sussman, who was her aunt's secretary.

The next morning I telephoned the Equity office:

Ro: Good morning, Actors Equity.

Don: Is Miss Sussman there?

Ro: This is she.

Don: This is Don Stolz—the Old Log Theater.

Ro: Oh, yes. You were here yesterday.

Don: Well, I'm still looking for an ingenue.

Ro: Oh.

Don: And I've been wondering, do you act?

Ro: Yes, I do.

Don: Are you already signed for the summer?

Ro: No, I'm not.

Don: Well, why didn't you audition yesterday?

Ro: I didn't think it would be proper since I'm Marge's niece.

Don: Proper or not, would you be interested in coming to the Old Log?

Ro: Yes I would—very much so.

Don: I'll send a contract. We need you beginning with the second show.

Ro: What is the second show?

Don: *The Joyous Season.*

With her first show at the Old Log, Ro became an audience favorite. During the years she was at the Old Log, every 14-year-old boy in Excelsior fell madly in love with her, including Clellan Card's son, Michael.

The Joyous Season was the second play of the 1953 season; the first play was *Mr. Roberts*. It was, in many ways, a remarkable production, which included Dave Moore as Ensign Pulver. Dave was a charming, gifted, well-trained actor, which you already know if ever you watched him on Channel Four.

I had first become acquainted with Dave during his short apprenticeship at the Old Log in 1941, but really came to know him because of the television work I was doing, primarily at Channel Four. I so admired his work that when Charlie Johnson, head of what was hopefully called "The News Department," came to me, I reached out.

Don: Hi, Mr. Johnson

Charlie: Hi. *(hardly more than a grunt)*

Don: You seem … down.

Charlie: Well, hell—we've just been turned down again.

Don: Turned down?

Charlie: To anchor our news department. First it was that other guy, and now it's Walter Cronkite. He was all ready to accept the job—anchor for the 12:00 noon, the 6:00

and then the ten. He called just now—said he'd changed his mind. Something about he thinks he has a future with CBS. Screwed again.

Don: That's too bad.

Charlie: You know, I feel like just forgetting this big name stuff and getting some local guy to take the job. Trouble is, I can't think of anyone local.

Don: Just forget the big name?

Charlie: Right.

Don: Why don't you try Dave Moore?

Charlie: Dave Moore ... you're the second person who has recommended him.

Don: Try him.

Charlie: I think I will.

And you know—he did. And Dave became the star of the station.

At the time, I had been working in television for several years. One of my earliest jobs at Channel Four was producing, with Bradley Morrison, Jr., a "Sunday Night Review of the Week's News." We wrote it, put it together, produced it, directed whatever announcer would be reading our copy. I was also the on-the-air weatherman.

Every Sunday late afternoon, the National Weather Service would deliver a formal forecast to the station; I would study it, decide what I was to forecast, and go on the air. Things went well. One memorable Sunday—it had been relentlessly raining for three days—everyone was wondering when the rain would end. When the forecast from the bureau was delivered, it showed that rain had already stopped in the Dakotas and everything was moving east. I noted the speed at which the storm was moving, found how many miles were involved, and arrived at the conclusion that the rain would leave Minneapolis at 1:14 a.m. on Monday. Thinking "what the hell," I went on the air that Sunday evening and confidently forecasted "The rain which has been with us for three days now will stop at 1:14 tomorrow morning."

There were people who stayed up all night to see how wrong I would be. In the morning *Tribune*, one of their columnists reported that Stolz had missed it by only four minutes.

As Harold DenBleker had said several years before, "No amount of skill will ever replace outhouse luck."

When it was decided that Cedric Adams should start making his way into television, he hired me to be his television advisor and also write several "special shows," which he would be doing on Channel Four. I was working with Cedric in his office when I received a telephone call from the hospital that Joan and I were now the parents of a baby girl. We couldn't believe it—a girl. Cedric was almost as excited as I—there has never been a man with a greater curiosity and sense of awareness. As soon as congratulations had been given, he said, "Don, a girl in the Stolz family. I know the perfect name for her, 'Stella.'"

Can you imagine? Stella Stolz. I didn't have time to ask him if he was serious, I was already on my way to the hospital.

During this time, my primary work in television was as producer of commercials for Campbell-Mithun.

Newspaper columnist Bob Murphy had an idea for a television show, one that would show interesting film footage taken by amateurs. Channel Four scheduled it with me as the narrator and conductor of the interviews with the filmmakers.

Early in the spring each year that comprised the 1950s, we, at the Old Log, knew we'd have a visit from Paul Gilmore and his daughter on their drive from Dubuque, Iowa, to their theater on Highway 61, 14 miles north of Duluth. Mr. Gilmore had been a dashing, distinguished and nationally popular actor for years—a former star.

According to the legend that was relayed to me, when Gilmore was a young actor playing leading roles, the troupe played a series in Dubuque. Present at every performance was the young teenage daughter of one of the city's most influential and affluent families, the Coopers, whose Cooper Wagons were rated with the Studebaker Wagons of South Bend.

After her very first attendance of the play starring young Gilmore, the daughter fell madly in love. The couple, even though the daughter was not yet of age, eloped. Of course the Cooper family gave chase, brought her home and had the wedding annulled. When they learned their daughter was pregnant, they put her in a convent where the baby was born and named Virginia. Both the young mother and baby Virginia remained in the convent for years.

As soon as Virginia was of independent age, she told the Coopers she was going to find her father. It wasn't a difficult task because her father, though certainly older, was still a nationally popular actor. Since then, father and daughter were never separated. In the early fifties, they purchased a Quonset hut located just off the highway and called it Theater 61. Presenting romantic comedies, father and daughter played the two romantic leads. It seems weird. It was weird. But they had such charm and self-assurance that they made it work. Or made it almost work.

When their season closed each year, they would again stop at the Old Log and would compare audiences and box office results. Then they would drive on to Dubuque, where they lived happily in the Cooper mansion.

Each of these several years, the Gilmores, Virginia and Paul, would talk to us about our taking over their Duluth theater. Finally, we agreed to lease the theater. I selected and directed a number of shows, and sent the cast, under the leadership of Walter Boughton, north. The combination of running the Old Log and appearing daily on *Axel and His Dog* television show prevented my spending much time away from Excelsior.

Deep Blue Sea

As the 1954 season at the Old Log got underway, I had no idea of the television show that would be developed before the summer was over, a show that changed many lives.

One of our first plays in 1954 was **The Moon is Blue**, not particularly approved by the Catholic Church. We starred Dave Moore, Ro Sussman and Walter Boughton, who after several summers here and winters at Ripon College, became head of the Dartmouth Drama Department. Dave Moore again proved to attract and delight audiences.

The dramatic hit of the year was Eugene O'Neill's **Desire Under the Elms**, starring Dolly Wheaton and Ro Sussman. I played the son, Eden. The Old Log has done more Eugene O'Neill than any other theater in America, with the exception of the Long Wharf, a theater dedicated to his plays.

In early August, I had a telephone call from WCCO-TV, asking if I would be interested in playing the dog, Towser, on a new show for children, starring Clellan Card as Axel, the same zany, colorful character that he had done for so many years on radio. Axel, now, however, is no longer the janitor but a delightful man who lives in a tree house with his dog. I don't know who suggested me; whether it was Harry Jones who was to produce and direct the show, or Clellan, whom I had first met at WCCO Radio. I admired Clellan, loved his outrageous humor, and knew it would be fun.

August 5, 1954, **Axel and his Dog** opened. As the dog, I wore a long "dog" sleeve that resembled, in theory, a dog's leg and paw. That was all that was ever seen of Towser.

I reported early at the studio for a rehearsal to find there was none. Clellan had played Axel for years on the radio, and I didn't need one—all I had to do was bark. But the real reason there was no rehearsal was that at the last minute, there were just so very many details not yet settled.

For weeks the station had been announcing that this new show would be telecast on August 5 and urged the kids to send in riddles and "knock-knocks" that Axel might read on the air.

The show went well. As the end of the 30 minutes approached, it was time for Axel to read one or two of the riddles that had been submitted. In the hectic minutes preceding the opening show, the post cards had been gathered but not pre-read by Harry Jones, not by Axel, not by anyone.

Filled with the joy of knowing that the first episode of a new show had gone even better than expected, Axel asked for the first riddle. It was handed to him. Its first reading was on the air.

Axel: The first riddle was sent in by little Johnny Dixon. Here it is. "Why did the young chicken cross the road?" (Having told the riddle hundreds of times on radio, Axel, without even pausing, turned the card around and read the answer.) "The young chicken crossed the road because she was laying the farmer on the other side."

This is true. I can prove it. It's a wonder that this first show wasn't also the last. Happily *Axel and his Dog* would continue and become the most popular TV show, local or network, in the Twin Cities for 12 years.

The relationship between Axel and his young viewers was like no other; he was "the best friend" to tens of thousands of boys and girls, and to many, "the only friend I had when I was growing up."

In the weeks and months that followed, the cast and crew of *Axel* grew closer. To everyone who worked the show, it was special. As an example, an old Army buddy of Harry Jones (the director) came to the Twin Cities where he almost immediately became seriously ill and hospitalized in St. Paul's Miller Hospital. The hospital reported that the patient was going to need a long list of multiple

Axel and His Dog; Clellan Card and Don Stolz.

Axel and His Dog; crew: Don Stolz, Clellan Card,
T. Hurd, Bill Dietrickson, and Harry Jones.

transfusions. They needed blood. They would accept any type (being able to trade for whatever they needed at the blood bank).

When we heard this news, the cast and crew immediately volunteered. We agreed to meet at Miller Hospital immediately after the telecast. At the transfusion center of Miller, we all sat on a series of pews waiting our turn. Present were Axel, Harry Jones, Stan Wolfson, Tassles (a floor man) and me. Everyone but Mary Davies who had that afternoon played Carmen the Nurse. When Harry said, "We're all here except Mary. I wonder what's happened to her?" Clellan said, "I know she'll be here. She promised." Fifteen minutes went by, still no Mary. Finally wandering into the area came Mary's first husband—a sweet and gentle man from whom Mary had been divorced for seven years. When I asked him what he was doing here, he very quietly replied, "Well, Mary called and said she couldn't be here, so she asked me if I would sub for her."

The *Axel* show was the "closest" unit I've ever been a part of. If you couldn't make it, you certainly would find a "sub."

In the fall of 1954, shortly after closing the summer season at the Old Log, we were asked to produce two shows at the Lyceum Theater in downtown Minneapolis. The two we selected were *Time of the Cuckoo* and *Rain*, again with June March. The two plays were well mounted, well performed and well received. We looked forward to the upcoming 1955 season without anticipating in any way the sorrow that was ahead.

On August 3, our 2-and-a-half-year-old little Joannie drowned in front of our home on Lake Minnetonka. How we survived, I know not. I remember only how supportive Clellan and Marion and Michael were. They had experienced two losses of children in their family. The closeness of the two families continues today, though only Michael, the youngest of their sons, remains. The support of friends and faith. I witnessed the pain of Joan, Peter, Dony and Tom, and shall remember it always. And I witnessed their faith, and that I shall also remember always.

In 1995, when I was asked to write a play about Axel. Still remembering August 3, 1954, I wrote the first draft attempting to describe that day and those that followed in some detail. I truly felt that Ron Peluso, the director, would ask for a re-write in which would be eliminated this story of our family tragedy. Ron decided that it should not be eliminated—not even reduced.

I don't think I'm up to writing it again. Read the play if you can find a copy.

The play, *Axel and his Dog*, was first presented at the Great American History Theatre in November 1998. It starred Steve Shaffer as Axel and Tom Stolz as me. When I was at the show's opening night, it was difficult for me to realize that, in truth, Steve had become Axel and Tom, in truth, had become me. The past was alive.

In the program, Ron Peluso, as director wrote:

"Most of us in the 'business of theater and the arts' wonder … often aloud … 'What are we doing with our lives?' Of what importance is our work? Does it have any effect on the world around us? After a good deal of soul searching and many years, we may come to understand how a precious moment on stage or screen DOES touch someone in a profound way. It may or may not be understood at first, or we may never have intended it to be so, but our work is out there and it does have an effect.

"Days before opening, the History Theatre received a letter addressed to Axel, WCCO-4, with a request to Please Forward. Well, Mr. Card has not been with us for over thirty years, but the letter was a touching memento. 'Thank you and your friends for being there for two kids who really needed a friend, a companion, an after school buddy.' Axel had indeed touched their lives and 'brought sunshine' to many more in a way that Mr. Card may not have ever imagined. These fans, now in their 40's and 50's signed off 'Wherever you are, God bless you, Axel.'

"Indeed your life has touched many, Mr. Card … and you, too, Mr. Stolz. Thank you both."

Ron, realizing that the audience would wonder about the memory of that day by the children, asked Tom to write a paragraph that he could use in the program.

Tom wrote: A SUMMER'S DAY IN AUGUST 1955

Axel and His Dog at the History Theater, St. Paul. Steve Shaffer as Axel,
Tom Stolz as Don Stolz.

"Another perfect morning on the lake with the sun shining and whole day of fun ahead! First I'll hurry down to the theater and see what the actors are doing, then maybe Peter and Dony will let me ride into Excelsior with them on our bikes. We could stop at the Amusement Park for a ride on the merry-go-round, then head into the Ben Franklin. I wanna buy a new peashooter. Then I'll come home for lunch before sailing with the Kimball boys. I hope they don't tip it … the lake looks scary today. Then hurry downtown with Daddy to the studio. Axel said he'd read Donny's joke on TV today. A perfect day! Mom even has sweet rolls for breakfast. And look, little Joannie is up already. 'Joannie, can you say perfect day? I can't believe how much you can talk. All right, Joannie, I'll give you some of my sweet roll, but first you have to give me a kiss. That was a good one. Bye-bye.' Oh, little Joannie, why didn't I give you your bite of a sweet roll? Your kiss is stolen property … and now I can't give it back.'"

Ron also suggested notes from the author.

"Some time last winter, Ron Peluso telephoned me at the Old Log and asked if he and Tom Berger could come out and talk to me. Apparently he had, the night before, been watching Channel Two, and had seen an episode of *Twin Cities Lost*. It was one of the shows hosted by Dave Moore and included a long segment of my being interviewed by a Channel Two reporter about the years I spent as Towser the Dog and Tallulah the Cat in the Tree House.

"Ron went on to tell that he found Axel funny, and though he had not lived in the area during those early days of Twin Cities television, could sense the enormous love that the children had for Axel. It was a love that lives on still.

"Ron said he had a wonderful idea that he would like to discuss. His wonderful idea was that I should write a play based on the Axel show. He asked if I would be interested.

"As the person who had played Towser and Tallulah, I knew and loved the show. As a close friend of Clellan's, I knew and loved the man who was Axel. I was interested even though I knew that in writing a play there was no way I could at all explain those wonderful days of early television, could tell of the great affection of every man and woman on the crew, could fully thank Channel Four and the staff for their adventuresome spirit and creativity, could even touch on the great loving and lovable, funny and tender, spiritual man that was Axel.

"But thank you, Ron, for asking. Don Stolz"

I did not include the ironic fact that the day Joannie drowned was also the opening night of the play **The Deep Blue Sea**.

Somehow we got back to work and through the winter. It helped that about every night, winter and spring, two old friends, Roger Quinlan and Bob Phelps would show up at our house, uninvited, set up the card table and announce, "We are ready to play bridge."

You Never Have Received
a Valentine?

The 1956 season was another successful summer that opened with an impressive production of *Mice and Men*.

For the middle of the 1957 season, we scheduled Graham Greene's *The Potting Shed*. It featured Edgar Meyer, whom we all knew as one of the company's most reliable actors and newcomer, Ralph Nilson, whom we all knew to be somewhat self-involved. For the only time in the years I worked with Edgar, in the scene with his psychologist, he was lost—hopelessly lost. He needed the help of a fellow actor.

> **Edgar:** *(To Doctor Ralph Nilson)* Eh … eh … eh … Doctor, can't you help me?
>
> **Ralph:** *(Without even a second pause)* No. A doctor can help only those who will help themselves.

Whatever figment of friendship might have existed before, was immediately destroyed. Edgar never spoke to Ralph the rest of the summer.

The most beautiful performance of the 1958 season was Jeanne LeBouvier in the dual roles in *Separate Tables*.

During the winters of '57 and '58 I was appearing not only as Towser the Dog and Tallulah the Cat on the Axel show, but also as Vivian Vulture on "Commodore Cappy," the John Gallos show. One afternoon, Commodore Cappy announced:

> **Gallos:** Boys and girls, remember Valentine's Day is just around the corner—next Tuesday.

Vivian: Valentine's Day—what is Valentine's Day?

Gallos: Well, it's a day when you send and receive special greetings and best wishes. These are called "Valentines."

Vivian: Oh.

Gallos: Haven't you ever received a Valentine?

Vivian: No.

Gallos: Not ever?

Vivian: Not ever.

Gallos: Well—well—maybe someone will send you one some day.

The next three days the station received over 15,000 Valentines for the ugly, hateful, frightening vulture. It is no wonder that now with those kids in their '40s, '50s and '60s, we can refer to them as "Minnesota Nice."

The Valentine venture reminded me of the time that Axel, during one of the film clips when we were off-camera, said to me:

Axel: Wouldn't some fudge taste wonderful right now?

Don: Yes. Yes, some fudge would be wonderful.

(Immediately we were back on camera)

Axel: Tallulah and I have been talking and we've decided to have a fudge contest. To the boy or girl who sends in the best box of fudge, we're going to give a ten-dollar prize.

By the end of the week, thousands of pounds of fudge had been received and were filling to overflowing the WCCO lobby until someone had the idea of sending it to every veteran establishment and nursing home in Minneapolis, something that today could not be done.

The 1958 season at the Old Log was, overall, the most successful season yet.

"The Best Is Yet To Come"
—Robert Browning

By the time the season ended, I was doing so much work in downtown Minneapolis, that I rented a small office in the old but architecturally romantic Violin Makers Building on Tenth Street. Rupert Labelle and I, working out of this office, by spring of the next year, had sold over 10,000 tickets before we announced a schedule or hired an actor.

Rupert: I can't believe it. How many tickets have we sold?

Don: We have reservations for just over 10,000.

Rupert: And they don't even know what plays they're going to see.

Don: And we don't, either.

Rupert: Anyway, that's loyalty to the Old Log.

Don: Yes, it is. So much so that I think we should do more.

Rupert: Well, we can do more—we have several weeks before we open.

Don: That's not what I mean. I think we should do more by having a winter season.

Rupert: A winter season! Where?

Don: We'll build a new building.

Rupert: A new building? I think you're out of your mind. But I'm with you. Do it.

No sooner had we felt committed to this plan than it was announced that Doctor Tyrone Guthrie was coming to Minneapolis, where a glorious new theater building would be built for the presentation of classic plays. I was graciously invited to the first planning sessions and certainly never expressed even a hint of any disapproval. If you believe in the importance of theater, how can you object to a new one coming to town?

If we weren't discouraged by the news of the new Guthrie, we should have been by the presentation of our second 1959 production, a three-set show, *Who Was That Lady I Saw You With*. Our designer for the season was not yet available, so on the recommendation of Maxine Stetson, we had hired a young man from a theater in Chicago. Dress rehearsal day, with only one of the three sets prepared, he came into the afternoon rehearsal to tell me:

Designer: I'm sorry. I have to get back to Chicago. I'm on my way to the airport right now.

Don: *(Stunned)*

Designer: Good luck.

It was good luck that never materialized. On opening night, the next night, the sets were still not finished though we had worked all night in an effort to complete them. It is absolute fact that during the first act opening night, I was in back of the theater painting the set for Act II. Act III was somewhat completed during the playing of Act II. It was midnight before the final curtain. Not a soul had left the theater. This demonstration of loyalty surpassed the demonstration of 10,000 pre-season sales. In my despair, I could recognize nothing but complete failure.

I had explained to Mr. Kuechle our idea of building a new theater on his property, so it was small wonder that during the summer he took me to Chanhassen to see the style of structure that he felt was exactly right for the new Old Log. It was the lumberyard/hardware store, batten and board design by Herb Bloomberg. We started architectural plans for the New Old Log Theater.

Then came the subject of financing the project. Someone suggested that I go to Northwestern National Life, because several years earlier they had been impressed by speeches I had made on behalf of United Way. (At that time it was the "Red Feather Community Chest.")

John Pillsbury and Harry Atwood told the company to prepare the proper mortgage loan. Since we owned the business but not the property, they requested a copy of the lease. The only lease we had with the Kuechles was the one we had prepared in 1946. We were told that a new lease must be written, signed and presented to them. There were three attorneys involved in the "new lease." After working on it for five weeks, they came up with a document that was exactly what we had signed in 1946 without three attorneys. Construction began.

During the last summer season in the old building, there was an occurrence that has become a legend. So much a legend that those of us, who were there and still here, place the occurrence in three different plays with three different sets of actors. I am going to name a play and two actors who probably weren't even there.

Let us for now accept the possibility that the play was *The Golden Fleecing* and that the two actors were Jean LeBouvier and Bob Aden. Even those who disagree and name other actors, all agree that it is something that could well have happened to Jean and Bob.

The Golden Fleecing; Angus Duncan, Rupert LaBelle, Judy Perlt.

The two, Bob and Jean, are playing a scene in which they are seated on a sofa, leaning over the coffee table on which is an open briefcase filled with money. They are just finishing the rapid counting of the money. Bob is still leaning over the briefcase to make certain all monies have been properly re-packed. Jean closes the briefcase, not noticing that in closing it she has caught Bob's tie. When she hurriedly picks up the briefcase to make a quick exit, Bob's tie is still securely caught with the result that she drags him clear across the coffee table.

Whatever the play, whoever were the two actors, both thought it was a wonderful comedic discovery with which I agreed and which they repeated every night for the run of "whatever the play."

In the 1960 summer season, there were bright spots that made me forget—or at least rise above—*Who Was That Lady I Saw You With*. Edgar Meyer and Jean LeBouvier were absolutely the best Franklin and Eleanor Roosevelt who ever played *Sunrise at Campobello*, and a good production of *Look Homeward Angel*. Both plays were meticulously produced. We even purchased new shoes for Edgar as Roosevelt, so if anyone in the audience saw the soles, they would see they had never been walked on. For *Look Homeward Angel*, we hired the head of Dayton's display group to come out and put together a beautiful angel statue. The last summer in the old building also included a simple but charming comedy, *The Golden Fleecing*.

Besides, our first play in the new building was only a few weeks away.

THE NEW OLD LOG THEATER

Months before architectural plans had been completed, finances arranged, permits issued, we began to realize that a new Old Log Theater was not only an enormous change for us, but also for the community. Only four years earlier, our immediate neighborhood had seceded from the governing body known as Excelsior Township to become the incorporated Village (now City) of Greenwood. With that realization, all building permits would necessarily come through the new official Village Council of Greenwood.

Belle Aire Yacht Club, Cochrane Boat Works and the Old Log were the only businesses in the newly formed village; other than these three, Greenwood was residential.

The homeowners that would be the most affected were those who lived on Meadville Street, directly across from the theater property. They were the ones who would realize the most change. Instead of thirteen weeks of traffic coming to and leaving the theater, there would now be 52 weeks. The sound (I don't want to say "noise") coming from the theater from early evening until almost midnight, would also be year round. I could well imagine that there might be some neighbors who would not find this a desirable change. I decided that whatever opposition there might be, would be better faced before the application for a building permit, rather than after construction had started.

I started with the families living directly across the street and called personally on every family on Meadville. After Meadville Street, I systematically called on every household in the newly formed city. I explained what we were trying to do, discussed the problems of increased traffic and noise, answered whatever questions they had and then asked for their support. There was not one person who stated an objection; all encouraged us and wished us well. They were all, and are today, good neighbors. In an attempt to show our thanks, as soon as the new theater opened, we started the tradition of inviting everyone in Greenwood to be our guests at a show, usually between Christmas and New Years.

Construction began. It was the winter of 1959–1960.

Change was not only for the residents of the little village, but much greater change was also to be faced by the Old Log. There was no city water; there was no city sewer. The faucet outside the old building, the colorful outhouse back of the theater now had no place. They were to be replaced by a deep, six-inch well and two modern restrooms. Where before there had been no heat, except for a small electric heater in the old box office, there would now be a furnace. We had no idea there would be six furnaces. A big fan in the back window would be replaced by Trane air-conditioning—air-conditioning that is still operating today. The cozy wooden benches would be replaced by comfortable opera seats.

In going over the building plans with Herb Bloomberg, the architect/builder, Joan pointed out that there was no view of the front entrance of the theater from the parking lot. Herb came back with a new plan that showed the lobby turned so that the main entrance is now visible as one approaches the building. I, as any producer would, asked Herb if there was any way we could increase the depth of the stage box. It could not be done without going to iron beam construction, and for that we did not have the money. The next day I came up with the idea of leaving the stage box the size it was, but building a shed-like addition on the back that would house the dressing rooms and give us a cross over from stage right to stage left. When we asked for an increased gridiron height, we were again told that increased height would eliminate the necessary support. I suggested bringing one side of the gridiron down at a 45-degree angle, that would give increased strength. Herb checked it architecturally; it would work.

As construction neared completion, John Beauford, culture editor of the *Christian Science Monitor* visited Minneapolis. Though his visit to the city had in no way been promoted by what was going on in Greenwood, when he heard of a new theater being built, he asked to be taken to the Lake area so he could see it for himself. In his column a week later, Beauford told of what he had seen and reported that it was the first time in 150 years that a new theater had been built without any drive for funds. Basically, he was correct; he just was not aware of the many "drives" that we had made down to Northwestern National Life to arrange the mortgage loan.

We were proud of the fact that we had made no drive for funds. We have always been proud that we have never taken a dollar for anything other than the purchase of a ticket or a meal. This does not mean that we aren't beholden to a great many people for what they have done. As an example: Several weeks after the old Old Log closed, we loaded the old stake-body truck with scenery and materials that should have been thrown away years before and took them to the Excelsior village dump. The dump was operated by Mrs. Studer. If you brought in one garbage can it was 50 cents. Two garbage cans—$1.00. If you arrived with a truckload, she charged whatever she thought the traffic would bear. Mrs. Studer took one look at the overflowing truck load and said: "Don, I drove past your new building this morning and it's perfectly obvious that you've spent every penny you have. So today I'm going to let you dump free."

Over the years there have been a lot of people who in one way or another have let us dump free, but the Old Log is proud that, as I just reported, we've never accepted a dollar for anything other than the purchase of a ticket.

The new Old Log was to open November 29, 1960.

My anticipation was so great that I had little difficulty in pushing aside thoughts about how I was going to meet expenses that we had never known before. Not the mortgage payments, that was like paying rent. But for the first time we would be paying a janitor; paying the gas bill; paying for maintenance of a beautiful new building with its new seats, new well, new furnaces, new restrooms and

Exterior view of the new Old Log Theater

Interior view (the lobby) of the New Old Log Theater

year-round employees. I didn't know how we were going to do it, but the men at Northwestern National Life were much smarter than I, and if they believed we could make it, why should I be the one to question it.

For the opening play I had selected a recent Broadway hit, *The Marriage Go Round*, authored by Leslie Stevens. Dr. Paul Delville, the Professor of Cultural Anthropology was played by Edgar Meyer; Dr. Content Lowell (the wife of Paul Delville) Dean of Women, played by Jean LeBouvier; Katrin Sveg, the Swedish femme fatale, by Joan Peters; Dr. Ross Barnett, by our Old Log favorite, Ken Senn.

The printed souvenir program for the grand opening of this glorious adventure had, as its cover, a beautiful line drawing of the new building. It is fun to examine a copy of that first program and read the ads of congratulations.

The most significant full page ad was that of Northwestern National Life. It read: "Congratulations and best wishes for continued success. Because of the vision and untiring efforts of Don Stolz and the Old Log Theater company, theatergoers in the Upper Midwest may now enjoy the Old Log's outstanding productions year round. Funds for the new theater were provided by a National mortgage loan. Northwestern National Life is pleased to have played a part in bringing to reality the dream of a new Old Log. Northwestern National Life." For some reason never understood by either John Pillsbury or Don Stolz, Northwestern National Life Insurance company is now known as Reliastar. Not all change is good.

From the full page ad taken by the Wayzata State Bank, "In our tiny more limited world our stage for years has been the Old Log. We have supported it from its inception, partly because it is the frosting on the cake of Minnetonka suburbia, and partly because we like to take our entertainment sans commercials. So, along with Don Stolz, we're busting our buttons over the New Old Log."

Then the theater used a full page to thank Harry and Grace Kuchele. It ended with this paragraph: "We have heard much of love of the theater, but never have we seen it more clearly demonstrated than by these two. It was this and their faith in the future of commercial theater that made possible the new Old Log. Again, I speak for all of us when I say, 'Thank you, Grace and Harry Kuechle. Don Stolz.'"

I also wrote words of appreciation to two very special people, Joan Stolz and Rupert Labelle.

Just as interesting are the small ads taken by firms no longer in existence. Firms such as Mac's Minnetonka Pizza located on Brown's Bay. They made the best pizza I have ever eaten. Edith's Country Show, Mergen's Electric, Laramie Motors, Hart's Café, the Copper Stein Supper Club in Tonka Terrace. These places were special with special people. And the two best known, most frequented firms in Excelsior, the Water Street Super Value and V. G. Bacon Drugs.

The Marriage Go Round played for two weeks, then we opened *Breath of Spring*. This was followed by our first play for children, *The Three Bears*, which brought to an end our first partial season in the New Old Log Theater.

PLAN CAREFULLY THE LENTEN SEASON

Though we had often thought and talked about a plan for operating in the new year-round theater, after we opened *The Three Bears*, we decided to delay for a week the opening of the first play in 1961, *The Pleasure of His Company*. During those few days of rest, we, knowing that it would be difficult to find each year 52 plays that we felt appropriate, confirmed what had been a tentative plan: we would schedule each play for two weeks.

It was during the run of *The Pleasure of His Company* that we learned how truly different operating year-round was going to be. On the second Wednesday of January, the Minneapolis Woman's Club had booked the entire house as a fund-raising event. The Chairwoman of the event (I don't know why I can't say "Chairman") was Mrs. Eugene Larson, an elegant and most proper lady. That Wednesday was the coldest night of the year; the facilities in the ladies room had frozen resulting in a flood of water that soon reached into the lobby. Mrs. Larson came to me in a panic, "What are we going to do?" I replied, "You and I are going to take care of it—I'll get two mops and we'll go to work. Will you help me?" To this, the still proper and elegant woman agreed. We worked—and I mean "worked." We succeeded in our task. Ever after that, she considered me one of her dearest friends and the Old Log had a special place in her heart. Years later, knowing that she had only a few days to live, Mrs. Larson asked her husband to bring her to the Old Log for her last visit.

The second play of this schedule was *Send Me No Flowers*.

In the winter of 1960–61, we were trying to feel our way through the Minnesota cold, so as the Lenten season approached (and in the '60s, Minnesota Lutherans and Catholics were much more observant of the season than they are today), we decided that we should schedule three plays with at least some religious overtones for a run of two weeks each.

Wanting to demonstrate, in an admittedly minor way, our respect and observances of the seasons of both Lent and Passover, we set a six-week "religious drama" schedule. There would be one Catholic play, one play acceptable by the Jewish religion, another Catholic play acceptable by Protestants as well as Catholics.

The first was a gentle play, *The Velvet Glove*, starring Rupert LaBelle as the Monsignor, Marge Snell as the Mother Superior, in whose office at the Convent of St. Paul, the action took place. We brought in the lovely, talented and theatrically well-educated Mary Ingalls as one of the several nuns. The cast included members of what we considered our permanent company: Edgar Meyer, Maury Cooper, Jeanne LaBouvier and Ken Senn. The cast greatly enjoyed the script and played it well. They were fully prepared and well rehearsed. So much so, during the second Thursday night performance, in a pivotal scene between Rupert and Marge, I noticed something odd; it sounded different. She was taking his lines and he hers. It worked well. No one in the audience, no one in the cast, neither Rupert nor Marge, realized that they had done this. The only one who knew was I. I was on book backstage. It was only after I showed Rupert and Marge the script that they would believe what they had done.

The talented Mary Ingalls was the daughter of Mr. and Mrs. Tom Moore, the area's holder of the Coca-Cola franchise, and owner of the downtown Radisson. Mary was married to Dr. Ed Ingalls, a handsome and personable young man, highly respected and regarded as the area's leading obstetrician. Several years after the production of *The Velvet Glove*, Ed and Mary were attending the theater. With them were Beth and Russell Bennett, their long-time and dear friends. When I joined them, the conversation went immediately to the next play.

The Velvet Glove; Rupert LaBelle.

The Flowering Peach

Mary: Are you all set for the next play?

Don: Well, yes—all except for the important male role.

Mary: What's he supposed to look like?

Don: Well, mature—handsome—someone like Ed.

Russ: Why don't you cast Ed?

Don: A great idea. I've never met a doctor who wouldn't like to be on stage.

Mary: Ed can't act. He's never even thought of it.

Beth: Mary, you've always said that Don can teach anyone to act. What about it, Ed?

Ed: Well—

Mary: In no way. Medicine is your field; theater is mine. Not yours.

Ed: Well, it might be fun.

Don: Yes, it would be.

Ed: Would I have to sign a contract?

Don: Sure—and join Equity, but that would be easy.

Russ: Do you have any contracts in your office?

Don: Sure I do.

Russ: Well, I, as Ed's attorney, will witness his signing.

Mary: *(To Ed)* If you agree to this, you'll not only need a new attorney, you'll need a new wife.

Ed: Don't be ridiculous. It would be fun.

Mary: Not for me.

Don: *(Now returning with a copy of an Equity contract)* Here you are, Ed. As you can see the salary isn't very much, but as I heard you say, "it will be fun."

Mary: You sign that, Ed …

Beth: Mary, it will only be for three weeks—

Mary: He signs that and our separation will be forever.

Ed: *(Of Don)* This is where I sign, right?

Don: Right.

Ed: *(Signs it and hands it to Russ)* And now you can witness my signature.

Russ: All right.

Seldom have I seen a woman as hurt and as angry. Medicine was Ed's field; theater was hers. Was hers!

When Beth explained that it all was a joke, Mary still wanted nothing to do with any one of us. The next day, when I telephoned Mary to apologize, she wouldn't even talk. Within a week, Mary had forgiven Russ and Beth. It would be months before her forgiveness included Ed and Don.

The second of our "religious plays" was one we recommended for those celebrating Lent and those celebrating the Passover Season. It was **The Flowering Peach**, Clifford Odets telling the story of Noah, his family and the flood. I do not exaggerate when I say Rupert as Noah was nothing less than marvelous. Maxine Stetson was great as Noah's wife, Esther. Maxine Stetson, if you remember Bob Aden's book, was one of the first actresses hired by the Old Log. Leon Pike answered well the problems of the setting. Though Odets gave **The Flowering Peach** a gentle, philosophical view, included, as well, was a lot of gentle humor. No one in the audience shall ever forget that when the flood was over and the Ark reached a landing on top of Mount Ararat, the daughters and daughters-in-law all were noticeably pregnant.

The religious third play was Eugene O'Neill's **Days Without End**. O'Neill scholars will tell you that as it prepared to open in New York, O'Neill thought it to be his masterpiece. While a few of the critics agreed with him, the majority violently disagreed. When both the critics and the audiences rejected it, so great was O'Neill's bitterness that he never wrote another play for twelve years. O'Neill had written **Days Without End** as a passionate confirmation of his Catholic faith. I don't know when I have worked on a play that interested me more. Edgar Meyer played the principal character; Maury Cooper also played the principal character. Both on stage at the same time, one speaking the word that all the world heard, the other speaking his thoughts that only the audience heard. **Days Without End** is unlike O'Neill's later plays. In a serious vein, the story ends with hope and expression of Christian love and most certainly carried a message of Catholic faith.

Our 1961 production remains the only presentation of **Days Without End** since the New York production. And that's unfortunate.

During the week of Easter, we presented our spring play for children, *Little Red Riding Hood*.

Our first big commercial box office success in the new building opened the third week in July, **Under the Yum Yum Tree**, by Larry Roman. On my first reading of the script, I disliked it, even though there were some humorous bits. I had scheduled it because almost every morning, beginning in early spring, Arthur Godfrey, on his CBS radio show reported that one of the members of his cast (I remember it as Julius LaRosa) was to appear in this wonderful comedy in one of the New England summer stock companies.

No play the Old Log ever did had better national publicity. As I started rehearsal with a very good cast, Jean LeBouvier, Andy Johnson, Maury Cooper and Marilyn Schlampp Joliffe—now using her television name of Mary Ann Woods, I felt strongly that despite all the publicity and a good cast, I just didn't want to do the play. Joan, who listened to Arthur Godfrey every morning, insisted I must. In fact, there was nothing else to do. After three days of rehearsal, I found myself beginning to not only accept **Under the Yum Yum Tree**, but even liking it. Not much. Just a little. In years since, I have grown to feel that plays are very much like people: if you get to know them and work with them, it's surprising what you will find in them.

Under the Yum Yum Tree was an immediate, huge success. It has remained a box office success during the six times we have since scheduled it. All of which proves how little I know.

More serious fare during the 1961 season were Tennessee Williams's **Period of Adjustment**, William Inge's **The Dark at the Top of the Stairs**, and Hugh Wheeler's **Big Fish, Little Fish**. I particularly remember with great affection and even pride, our production of **Dark at the Top of the Stairs** with Edgar Meyer, Maury Cooper, Marge Snell, 12-year-old Tommy Stolz, Mary Lu Wadas and Victor Linoff. It was one of Tommy's first starring roles. A beautiful show,

Under the Yum Yum Tree; Marilyn Schlampp, Andy Johnson.

Dark at the Top of the Stairs; Tom Stolz, Marge Snell,
and Edgar Meyer.

beautifully done.

While in college, I had dreamed of—it would be much less pompous to say "had occasionally thought of"—giving concerts in my own theater. My desire to get more people, more often, into our new theater probably had more to do with my booking our first concert than did the fulfillment of a vague college dream. The concert was an afternoon program on April 1, 1961, by the St. Paul Chamber Orchestra, Leopold Sipe, conductor, with Suzanne Bloch, soloist. One of the trumpet players was Ron Hasselman, who in the following years became a good friend to the theater and me.

The year 1961 ended with the second production of *Under the Yum Yum Tree*, and *Pinocchio*, our holiday play for children. The end of the first year of the new Old Log, and we were still alive and not very much in debt.

THINGS AREN'T ALWAYS
WHAT THEY SEEM

The children's show. The children's show. Rupert LaBelle had a cynical title for them; he called them the "Pop and Piss Matinees." Actor's Equity, the union, likes to call them "Theater for Young Audiences." Let's admit it—their title is more accurate than ours because we present adult actors (all members of the union) with as few children as possible—for obvious reasons—including the fact that they have to attend school. Anyway, the Theater for Young Audiences.

Beginning with our first play for children in the new building, I felt it necessary to have music. Not only to accompany the singers, but also to color and support the action on stage. I did not want to use recorded music as most theaters at that time were doing, so we hired Willie Peterson, from WCCO Radio to play a Hammond organ, which he owned. Willie was marvelous. Before the first rehearsal was over, he had established a "theme" for each character that he would play at appropriate times. Not only was Willie extremely talented, he was also a joy to have at the theater. On the days when we had two shows scheduled, all of us, cast and crew, would gather after lunch in front of the large fireplace in the lobby. It is no exaggeration to say our children loved Willie. One day, when little six-year-old Jon was mildly complaining about something, Willie said to him, "Jon, don't be a little Bluebird Girl—forget it." Jon went to Betty Kuechle, borrowed her daughter's Bluebird uniform, and was wearing it. He stood next to Willie's chair. It was

15 minutes before Willie realized what had happened; the little Bluebird standing beside him was Jon.

As the years went by, we used Willie Peterson for every one of our Christmas shows for children. When he was no longer able to play the show because of terminal illness, Willie suggested we use his wife, Jeanne Arland Peterson, who not only was a fine pianist, but also an organist. She became not only our pianist for all of our industrial shows, but also played every Christmas show and New Year's Eve at the Old Log, until 2006. There is no doubt: she is the greatest.

The world's greatest drama is easier to produce than a play for children. Especially at the Old Log—because whatever settings we have for the young audiences, they must fit inside our somewhat permanent set for the evening adult shows. It isn't always easy. In the early days—the early 1960s before we were more efficiently organized—it quite often meant working all night, the night before opening early the next morning. It was in 1993, as I recall, that Peter, Dony and I (Tom was playing the lead in the show) had worked all Sunday night after the show for adults and it was now 15 minutes before early morning curtain for the children's show. We were exhausted. The three of us stood there hardly able to move. Someone said—"I don't know why we do it—it just isn't worth it." No one answered. Finally I said, "You're right. I promise you this, I won't put you through anything like this again. This is the last kid's show we'll ever do." I had no more than finished the promise when we heard a distant sound. It was children singing a Christmas carol. The three of us staggered to the window to see what it was. It was a long column of children marching from St. John's School. Their bus had failed to pick them up, so they were marching the two miles to the theater in zero weather. Leading the column were two nuns in habit, followed by a young boy carrying the American flag. As I watched and listened, it was with a feeling I shall always remember. As the three of us stood there barely able to hold back the tears, Dony said, "Well, there goes your promise, doesn't it?" He was right. There went the promise. We've been doing children's plays every year since.

The first show for children, as I have already stated, was in 1960 at Christmastime. It was ***The Three Bears***. You remember the story—Pappa Bear, Mamma Bear and Baby Bear—actors all standing erect, dressed in bear cloth costumes made from a hooded pajama pattern that zipped up the front, with booties, mittens and small masks added. They walked and talked just like people. But it did create the illusion. Well, almost created the illusion. In 1960, Vic Bacon—the legendary druggist of Excelsior—lived directly across the street from the theater parking lot. His niece usually spent part of the Christmas holiday with the Bacons. In 1960, this niece was five years old, so of course Vic sent her across the street to see ***The Three Bears***. When she returned after the show, the question was:

Vic: Did you have a good time?

Niece: It was wonderful. There was Pappa Bear, Mamma
   Bear and Baby Bear.

Vic: Now just a minute—you don't mean that they had real
   live bears on the stage?

Niece: Oh, yes.

Vic: Are you sure they were real?

Niece: Yes.

Vic: Real bears?

Niece: Well—I know Pappa Bear was real—and Mamma
   Bear was real, but I'm not sure about Baby Bear.

Vic: What makes you think Baby Bear wasn't real?

Niece: Because I could see his zipper.

I don't care how long you've been in this business; you never really know what maintains the illusion and what destroys it. All I've learned is try to find the zipper in the costume before the audience does.

It was in the same show, ***The Three Bears***, that there was a memorable rehearsal. In the play, Goldilocks' father is out in the woods with his deer-hunting rifle—or bear hunting, if you prefer. The elegantly handsome, just short-of-pompous actor, Joseph Della Malva, played the father. In the middle of dress rehearsal, he stopped, turned front and asked, "I still seem to have this rifle in my hand,

See How They Run; Richard Paul, John Varnum, and Ken Senn.

what do you suggest that I do with it?" Before I could answer, Ken Senn, who was waiting for his entrance off stage right, gave Joe exactly the answer you'd expect Ken to give him.

As I have told you, Ken was the heart and soul of the Children's shows. One Christmastime, he was playing the emperor in **The Emperor's New Clothes**. At that time the Senn family had a bulldog that looked exactly like Ken and followed him everywhere, so it was not a big surprise when Ken suggested that it would be fun to have his dog be a part of the emperor's entourage and a part of the parade in which the emperor reveals his new clothes. The opening morning, the dog made his entrance exactly on cue, came to center stage and vomited exactly in the path that the royal family was to follow.

It was this same dog—and he did look exactly like Ken—that appeared every night in **See How They Run**. Ken played the visiting Bishop and entered from stage left, followed by the bulldog. He called for the family—there was no answer—so he sits on the divan and soon falls asleep. The dog sat on the floor next to the divan, faced directly front toward the audience. A few seconds later, the dog fell asleep and toppled over. We received acclaim as great dog trainers.

But I was talking about the play for children. In changing from one set to another, it's necessary—especially so for plays for children—to make the change as quickly as possible. In ***Rumpelstiltskin***, we took only a few seconds to cover the two upstage center stained glass windows of the castle into the throne room, by the simple device of hanging a bright red velour drape. The change would be made, as I said, in a few seconds. And so it did. Every performance but one.

Willie Quinn, one of our young, loyal and eager workers had the assignment to hang the red drapes. He didn't do it in time—the lights came up and there he was, center stage, his back to the audience, holding the drapes. He slowly turned front to see if what he thought had happened actually had happened. He gasped—the loudest gasp I have ever heard, dropped the drape to the floor, ran offstage and locked himself in the toilet of the women's dressing room. In the meantime the lights came back down, the stage manager rushed on stage and the drapes were hung—but not by Willie Quinn. He remained locked in the women's toilet until late that afternoon.

I wish I knew the name of those two nuns who in 1960 marched their students from St. John's to the Old Log—I'd like to thank them for the 45 years of presenting children's plays that have followed. What these plays have meant through the years—well, late December when walking through a cluster of shops in Wayzata, an older woman stopped me and said, "I have to tell you something. We have always enjoyed the Old Log Theater, but on last Wednesday morning, it was more marvelous than ever.

"I had taken my daughter and her little girl to see your production of ***Robin Hood***; it was wonderful. My granddaughter loved every minute of it, as well as talking with the actors afterward in the lobby. Her mother and I had never seen her so delighted, so pleased, so happy. On the way home, she was sitting in the back seat of the car, still just glowing. We had driven several miles when she asked,

"'Mommy, am I dreaming?'

"'Why no—what makes you ask a question like that?'

"'Because I've had such a wonderful day, and I'm so happy, and I don't want to wake up and find out that it was all a dream.'"

I hope I don't wake up and find it was all a dream.

"Be Careful What You Ask For"— Industrial Theater

Friday afternoon in 1962, Campbell Mithun telephoned to ask if I could meet with them and one of their clients, Trane Air-conditioning, to discuss an upcoming convention. The agency suggested that they thought it might add to the "ambience" of the meeting if we could serve the group lunch on the veranda of the Old Log. Even though we did not yet have a kitchen at the Old Log, I agreed. Friday I thought would be easy because the local country club had a reputation for serving the best shrimp salad in Minnesota.

I called the club and arranged for shrimp salad for the eight people that would be in attendance. When the group from Campbell Mithun and Trane arrived, I proudly took them to the veranda where we had set an attractive table. When our specially arranged lunch was served, the lead man from Trane started turning red and announced that he was terribly allergic to shrimp to the point if he were to eat it, it would probably result in his death. "Did we have anything else?" Well, we did have back in the furnace room a refrigerator, where I found all that was necessary to construct an adequate ham sandwich. I was just recovering from this blow, when the young lady who was serving iced tea dumped a whole container of ice cubes on the bald head of Trane's "next to head man." Any hope in my mind of landing this account vanished. But I was wrong. Trane Air-conditioning became one of our strongest, most loyal and happiest accounts; we worked with them for years. As a matter of fact, we're still working with them. Trane, Toro, Honeywell and Better Homes and Gardens are the three companies for which we have written and produced the most "industrial theater."

After what I thought was a disastrous lunch, the "lead man" and the "second lead man" told us about the meeting they had in mind. Two years before their visit to the Old Log, Trane had established a new residential air-conditioning division they titled "Trane Comfort Corps." It was a structured, controlled and disciplined organization of dealer/distributors who, if agreeing to the requirements, were guaranteed that they would become millionaires within eight years.

The Trane "lead man," Milt Bevington, had spent his time since the concept of the corps, recruiting young, personable engineers, training them in the company's management and sales styles, and helping them establish their own new businesses. With almost military preciseness, these young men were given a dress code of gray flannel trousers and good quality blue blazers on the breast pocket of which would be a truly beautiful emblem of the corps. Their salesmen were to dress in similar style. The mechanics and servicemen were to wear the company-furnished blue uniform, all carrying the Trane Comfort Corps emblem. The corps business and sales plans and customer relationships were just as carefully documented. Some of the young men, though the corps was not yet two years old, were already doing very well, reaching out for that million dollar goal. It had already been discovered that for these young businessmen to follow the organizational plan required long hours, often extending over the weekend. Being a wise and observant man, Bevington realized that some of the young wives were beginning to wonder if this "Trane Comfort thing" they had gotten into was really what their young family should be doing. He decided that the most expedient and best way to answer all of the wives questions, was by showing and telling what would be done by presenting a small musical built around the problems, solutions, requirements and goals of the Corps.

The location for this "showing and telling" would be as first class as the Corps itself: at the Doral Country Club, just outside of Miami, Florida. The final night was to be a black-tie banquet; if you didn't have your own tuxedo, Milt would have rental agents at the hotel to properly outfit you for the dinner/dance.

The job of the Old Log was to become acquainted with the Corps plan, its problems, its difficulties, its goals, and how to attain them. I was to have long and detailed interviews with several of the young managers, combined with several trips to the home office in La Crosse, Wisconsin. For these trips, I would fly to the La Crosse airport, where I would be picked up by a uniformed chauffeur and taken to Milt's office. There I would meet with Milt, Bill Roth, Don Spirduso and usually several other Corps officers. At noon, we would move the meeting to the officer's private dining room. To me, it seemed the way in which business should be conducted.

I wrote what amounted to a two-hour musical with the principal character a new member/dealer of the Corps, his doubtful wife, and his more than doubtful brother-in-law who worked as a service man. The script covered problems and revealed answers with a great deal of comedy combined with statements of policy and commitment. Whatever young wives had come questioning were now convinced disciples.

The show cast included Ray Komischke and his five-piece orchestra (all dressed in Trane Corps uniforms), Bruce Neilson and five other singers, and four additional actors, including the marvelously funny Ken Senn. For years we all had heard that Ken was funny in Excelsior because the audiences had all learned to love him and laugh at anything he did. In the Trane show, titled, "Our Future's Now," Ken got an enormous laugh by answering a question before he even came on stage. He and Bruce Neilson performed a song and dance, which immediately became a part of the Trane Corps legend. Milt Bevington knew what he was doing. And he did it well!

That meeting was the beginning of long friendships with Milt, Spirduso, Bill Roth and others; from most of them I still hear every year.

After a few years, I was approached by the Trane Commercial Division, who were at first a little doubtful because they knew of my affection and attachment to Milt and his residential group.

The president of Trane Commercial was Dick Campbell; my

interview was to be with him.

Dick: Stolz? Stolz? You're the fellow that's been working with that ridiculous Trane Comfort Corps.

Stolz: Yes, that's correct.

Dick: And I understand that you're a friend of Milt Bevington.

Stolz: Yes, I am.

Dick: Well, you might as well understand that I personally don't care for him or his ridiculous Trane Comfort Corps. Trane has spent a fortune promoting that thing with money that would have been better spent in Commercial. You still working with Residential?

Stolz: So far—every year.

Dick: Do you think you could forget them long enough to work with us on our next convention?

Stolz: Yes, sir. I can do it—if you can do it.

Never again did Dick Campbell mention Milt Bevington or the Trane Comfort Corps. What started with doubt became an ideal working relationship combining affection and admiration.

In the next years, the parent Trane Company placed less emphasis on Residential, transferring it from La Crosse to Texas, and concentrated more on their primary field—the one in which they absolutely excelled—Commercial. My work with Commercial brought some of my most joyful business experiences, experiences that still continue. Many of the businessmen I most admire were officers with Trane.

One of these was Tom Mikulina. Over the years, Tom and his wife, Lynne, became dear friends, coming often to Excelsior to visit, have dinner and see the play. I knew that Tom was a connoisseur of fine wines. (A talent I have always held suspect.) After the show I asked if they would like to go over to see Joan and have a drink. At the house I asked with confidence what they would like to drink. I had everything: bourbon, Scotch, vodka, beer—everything. Mikulina said he'd like to have a glass of white wine; exactly what I didn't have. I was about to tell Tom that he'd have to have something else—

For the Trane Comfort Corp; Bruce Neilson and Ken Senn.

Toro's crew, the Gillespie Dancers, Don Stolz, and Ray Carpenter.

and then I remembered the small bottle of wine that I had received aboard a plane on my last trip. With confidence, I opened it, poured it into a wine glass. They, I thought very wisely, added a couple of drops of Coke to give it a little body and color. I served it to Tom, he thanked me, raised the glass, tested the aroma and then said "Delta." I wish I had been quick enough to say, "All right, smart aleck, what flight?" The next time Tom came to Excelsior, he brought me a bottle of Thunderbird.

The format for the Commercial conventions was somewhat different from those for Residential. The Commercial meetings were for the Trane Distributor organization, managers and some top sales people. It seemed well, in this case, to have some of the Trane officers take part in the skit, sometimes playing themselves and at other times assuming other characters. When in the cast, they studied and rehearsed. We often used "monitor" teleprompters to help. I instructed the Old Log actors to forget the teleprompters entirely.

Jim Schultz had come through the company to become the president of Commercial. He was a "fireplug" of a man— short, stocky, strong and direct. Jim, even as president, loved being a part of the opening skit that established the theme of the meeting. This was built on the strong personal relationship he had with the organization. He would play any character, do anything that the script demanded.

One year the opening skit had as its locale an abbey of monks; Jim played the Abbott. Another year the skit opened with two horses and riders entering from the rear of the meeting room. We had made "horses" that fit around the "rider." Rene Schultz and Tom Joseph entered while the instrumental trio played a "gallop." Later, Jim entered in splendid, formal riding habit. The fireplug's legs were as thick as the waist of many people. We split the boots so they would go around the leg, covering the split with material from another pair of boots. Jim coming down that center aisle, tapping his riding crop against his leg delighted every person in the audience. Another year the setting for the opening script was a western saloon. When it was time for Jim's entrance from the rear of the room, he, as the ranch foreman, fired a blank pistol and marched in. Anyone who might have been sleeping was now awake.

At every meeting, shortly after Jim arrived on stage, the skit would end, and Jim would deliver a heartfelt keynote speech in which he would review the past year, outline the goals for the coming year, and then tell how those in the audience would be required to help attain those goals—goals which would take hard work, long hours and personal commitment. Two days later at the end of the meeting, Jim Schultz would return and tell that he expected them all to reach their assigned quota, but then would end with: "I want you to know, and remember, that regardless of what Trane expects of you, your family comes first." Schultz meant it; Schultz lived it.

And then there was Toro; no, I should say, "Before Trane there was Toro." My first work with Toro goes back to the early 1950s. Here my assignment was somewhat different from Trane. Rather than a strong, long continuous two-hour show, Toro required short skits or songs between the scheduled speeches of the officers. Often the meeting began with an opening number with singers and dancers introducing the president, who would start the meeting with a review and keynote address.

My primary job was to write or re-write and coordinate all the speeches, which was not always an easy task, because on some occasion there had been no solid agreement on the points to be made. My coordinating of "views" became so accepted that one of the executives said, "You had as much to do with developing the corporate culture of Toro as anyone."

A lot of my work was done with the head of Toro's A/V department, Ray Carpenter. He was a creative, hard-working man who loved Toro's products and most, though not all, of Toro's officers. When Ken Melrose became President and Chairman of the Board, Ray was so devoted, that if anyone even questioned Ken's approach it was an act of treason. Toro never had an advertising agency that Ray thought was adequate.

Ray had gathered a remarkable audio-visual crew that included Mark Carpenter, Scott Ortho and Buck Pearson. They were hard working and committed to produce the best presentation for the convention. We often rehearsed all day and late into the night before the opening session, with a final run through very early the next morning after two or three hours of sleep.

My son Jon was always a part of the crew. Buck Pearson likes to tell the story that one year (we were always at the Radisson South) we had worked far into the morning hours, gone to our rooms for a short nap and reported back to the ballroom for another run through.

"When it was time to start the run through," according to Buck, "Jon was still in his room. I went to the telephone, called Jon's room and said, 'Get your butt down here to the ballroom immediately. Now!'

"Ten minutes later a man, whom no one knew or had ever seen before, showed up wearing his trousers over his pajamas.

"'I don't know what this is about but I'm here. What am I supposed to do?'

"I had called the wrong room."

At that time, it was Toro's custom to engage an inspirational speaker to appear sometime during the two or two-and-a-half day convention.

To Ray Carpenter, a "hired inspirational speaker" was as suspect as an advertising agency account executive. If the attendees needed inspiration, all they had to do was "listen to their president, Ken Melrose."

Invariably, the inspirational speaker had a list of required equipment or props, all of which was Ray's responsibility to locate and provide. One year, the inspirational speaker, in talking with Ray, was more arrogant and demanding than most. His presentation was built around the idea "to succeed you have to keep chipping away." He needed the trunk of a real tree, fastened, in some way, securely to the stage floor, and an axe to "chip" away at it. It must be a new and unused axe, which he would take home as a souvenir of his successful inspirational appearance.

Ray had had it! He sent his crew out to bring in a green oak trunk, and instructed them to "dull" the new axe. When the inspiration speaker took his first swing at the oak tree, the axe flew backward without the blade even denting the bark of the oak.

When booking yourself as an inspirational speaker, be extremely careful about what you ask for.

Another year, the guest inspirational speaker, in Ray's mind, was just as unnecessary. When we, the crew, first saw him he was already dressed for his "performance." A dark, short man, his white suit and black shoes made him look even shorter and less effective. Ray took one look at him and in sotto voce said to me, "Where did they find him and who hired him?"

The first five minutes were as stumbling and bumbling as his appearance led you to know they would be. Suddenly he changed— he was truly inspirational ... magnificently inspirational. He closed by telling all present to repeat, "I can, I can, I can." It grew to a roar with every salesman in the audience filled with inspiration. "I can, I can."

It was then that the speaker, fired with success, made his only mistake. Sitting in the front row was a man who had not responded at all. The speaker looked at him and said, "Get your hands off your crotch and say 'I can, I can, I can.'" The man with his hands on his crotch, unfortunately, was Wendell Wilke, Toro's biggest distributor.

The up-to-now truly inspirational speaker was, an hour later, at the convention lunch where he had to stand and before everyone, apologize to the offended distributor.

This was one inspirational speaker for Toro for whom Ray Carpenter felt genuine sympathy. And I think admiration.

For every meeting, I took what information Ken would give me and around it write his speech. When he wrote his book *Making the Grass Greener on Your Side*. Ken asked me to write the framework and transition paragraphs. Ken Melrose was great to work with; he brought to everything a youthful enthusiasm.

The Toro two-or three-day meetings always ended with a very formal Award Night. During dinner, state songs would be sung by attendees, a fourteen-piece band would play fanfares for the various awards, as well as play the recipients to the stage. It was always a long evening; the awards were many, but all well earned. It was a strong and emotional way to end the annual convention.

A relationship between the Old Log and Toro still exists. They were one of the sponsors for our summer concerts.

ANYTHING FOR THE THEATER

Peter: Mom, when's dinner?

Joan: Why?

Peter: I have to be at the theater early to set up the pop stand.

Joan: You mean in that old gazebo?

Peter: Don (they never called their father anything other than that—for no reason except perhaps because no one else called me anything other than Don) said we ought to try it. He thought maybe it would add a little atmosphere— give a feeling of an old time stock company.

Joan: He's out of his mind.

Peter: I know, but maybe it will do something. You know, anything for the theater.

"Anything for the theater."

It would be difficult for any one of the five Stolz boys to remember any part of his life that wasn't in the theater. When your father owns and operates a theater presenting live plays 52 weeks a year, and your mother agrees that the family should spend as much time together as possible, where is that time going to be spent? At the theater. Most of the time the entire family was agreeable to that—in fact even pleasant about it—occasionally even saying, "Every family should have a theater of its own." There were other times, however, when being a member of the theater family was limiting, inhibiting and frustrating. This we try to forget.

Sometime shortly after our opening the New Old Log, the New York edition of *Variety* carried a story about our new building and our new "year-round" schedule. The article was read by Terry

O'Sullivan, whom I hadn't seen since 1947 in California. He wrote, asking if the Don Stolz producer of the New Old Log Theater could possibly be his old fellow "star" in the WKY radio show, "Devil's Roost." Terry was now a big star in national television; he had appeared on the *Steve Allen Show* and the *Perry Como Show*, and was now playing Arthur Tate on *Search for Tomorrow*. For three consecutive years he had been voted by viewers as the "best and favorite actor" on daytime television. Terry was a star.

I, of course, answered his letter, and in the letters we exchanged, I promised that the next time Joan and I were in New York, we certainly wanted to meet him for lunch. When we met in the fall of 1961, there was no way that either of us could possibly keep from talking about his coming to the Old Log for a special guest appearance. We even discussed possible plays; the winner was **Critics Choice**. Terry opined that the producer and writer of *Search for Tomorrow* would probably see that Arthur Tate (the role in which he was starring) was in an accident that would hospitalize him for the three weeks necessary for him to do the special appearance with us. It was an exciting prospect for our 1962 season.

The 1962 season opened with a small cast comedy, **Champagne Complex**. As I wrote for the printed program, "We are delighted to have with us the lovely and talented actress, Soni Torgeson, who stars in this week's play, along with Old Log favorites, Maury Cooper and Andy Johnson. And on hand for future productions are Edgar Meyer, Rupert LaBelle, Ken Senn, Marge Snell and more of your favorites from past seasons and productions."

The second play of 1962 was **Sailor Beware**. It was such a success that we immediately scheduled it for a third week. It worked.

The third show after **Sailor Beware** was our first production of **Everybody Loves Opal**. And they did. I say "first production" because in the following years we repeated the play five times. A catalogue description reads, "Opal is a middle aged recluse, living in a tumble down mansion on the edge of the municipal dump. Regardless of her circumstances, Opal remains an optimist and, regardless of how she may be treated, Opal responds with unfailing kindness and an abid-

Everybody Loves Opal;
Marge Snell.

Critic's Choice; Terry O'Sullivan
and Tom Stolz.

ing faith in the goodness of human nature." Opal was played by one of the country's finest actresses, Minneapolitan Marge Snell. To this date I believe—no, let's change that—I "know" that it was not only Marge's great talent that made her so effective as Opal, but her "abiding faith in the goodness of human nature."

Terry O'Sullivan arrived from New York the second week in July when rehearsals began for the upcoming *Critics Choice*. Jean LeBouvier was to play the wife and young Tom Stolz, their son.

Terry was a hard worker and had come to the first rehearsal with his lines learned, which in his case worked out all right. Almost every night during rehearsal period we would take Terry to one of the good downtown Minneapolis restaurants. Wherever we went, he was instantly recognized with the result that the waitresses were competing to see who would be his server. The night Terry was recognized by every waitress and bartender at Charlie's, Joan said, "I don't understand it—they immediately recognize Terry from seeing him on television. I don't think I would recognize my own mother if I saw her that far from home."

As with the other plays in 1962, *Critics Choice* ran for two weeks. It was such a box office success and so popular with all who saw it, that Terry and I started plans for his return in 1963.

In the middle of August we presented *Sunrise at Campobello* again, with Edgar Meyer as Franklin and Jean LeBouvier as Elea-nor. Rolland Beck played Louis Howe, Ann Blager was Sarah Delano Roosevelt. The Roosevelt children were played by Peter Stolz, Dony Stolz, Tommy Stolz and Timmy Stolz. As John Roos-evelt, Timmy had to learn more than a few lines of the French language, because John Roosevelt was studying French in his classes. Timmy received a great review from John Sherman, and the audi-ence—it is fair to say—adored the five-year-old linguist.

Timmy had worked hard—very hard—to learn the lines in French, and as a result, was happy and gratified by the experience. When, six months later, he was hospitalized, the nurses told us that whenever he was worried or lonely, he would recite again his lines from *Sunrise at Campobello*. Memory of a happy time is great solace

Celebration of the Old Log Theater's 25th anniversary; Don Stolz, Jon Stolz, Joan Stolz, and Mrs. Harry Bullis. The woman in the background is Marge Dare (head of the Chicago Equity office).

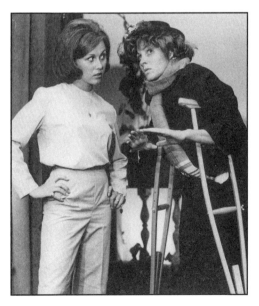

Goodnight Mrs. Puffin; Nancy Nelson and
Jean LeBouvier.

in a time not so happy.

It was in 1964 that the Old Log celebrated its 25th anniversary. It was a happy occasion with representatives from government and the union. With the theater now running winter and summer, 52 weeks a year, Joan and I began to realize that the many trips back and forth during the winter months should in some way be eliminated. The solution, of course, was to sell our home on Moorland and our summer home on Meadville Street and find something close to the theater. When the Kuechles heard of our decision, they suggested we purchase the house and lot next to them. We did. The property had a beautiful view of the lake with 155 feet of shoreline.

For some time we considered having the old farm house on the property remodeled, but instead we decided to have Herb Bloomberg build. I have heard people say that the most trying time of their marriage was when they built a home. Well, they couldn't have had Herb as the builder. He was a delight. I told him exactly what we had to spend, but added that any ideas he had as he was constructing the house, we'd like to hear about even if we couldn't afford them.

Herb designed a house that bent around the same curve the lot had facing the lake. As he was nearing completion, he suggested that since one end of the large upstairs bedroom for two of the boys was immediately adjacent to a chimney, that we should include a fireplace. When I told him I thought it was a great idea, but felt I shouldn't spend another dollar, he replied that he would do it as a Christmas gift for Dony and Tommy. The house was completed exactly at the amount I had told him we had. Not one dollar more. Building a new home with Herb was, for us, a happy experience. And living in the new home was a happy experience.

From Meadville Street the house appeared to be a spacious, though one-story cottage; from the lake side you could see that it was, in fact, a large structure of three floors. The first floor consisted of a game room that contained both a pool table and ping pong table, a sauna, a workshop, a family room with a large, cut-stone fireplace at one end, a dark room—and the most special feature of all, a small theater at one end, complete with stage, front curtain and a lighting control room.

As the boys were growing up, there was production after production on their stage; as the years passed, the grandchildren took over the plays to which the neighbors were always invited. Theresa, Tom and Pat's daughter, and the oldest of our grandchildren, was usually in charge, having written the play, built the scenery and sternly directed her siblings and her cousins. Years later, when we felt we should sell 5120, it was Theresa who was the most upset even though by then she was a practicing doctor in Milwaukee with children of her own.

Living in the new home was a happy experience for quite a number of people outside our immediate family. Looking back to the first few years after moving in, I can remember very few nights that there weren't overnight guests. Truly it went on for years. Somebody was always bringing some unfortunate home with them. Most of the time it was Dony who found the unfortunates. Early in the spring of 1964, he came out of Bacon's Drug Store to find Eddie, a schoolmate of his, standing on the corner with a packed suitcase and tears in his eyes. When Dony asked and Eddie told him that when he had gone home to the apartment shared by him and his mother, he found the only thing remaining in the apartment was this suitcase filled with his clothes. When Dony asked Eddie where he was going to go, Eddie's tears came more rapidly. He "had no idea." Dony told Eddie he did— he was going to go home with him; he knew his parents would welcome him. Eddie lived with us for almost two years, working small jobs at the theater. When he graduated from high school, he enlisted in the Navy. After his Navy time, Eddie got married, started his own little business and his own little family. All of this time he had heard little from his mother. Years passed; Eddie, some way or other, heard that his mother was back in Minneapolis and critically ill. He drove back to Minnesota, picked up his mother and took her back to California, so he and his wife could take care of her.

We always dreaded a little bit, Dony's going to Bacon Drug— for quite often, when he came out, there was someone who needed help. Again it was a classmate standing on the corner with his suitcase. This time it was the son of an affluent family. He reported that he had been told to leave their home. In his words, "I was kicked out." Dony brought him home. I called the boy's parents and got their unfriendly permission to let him stay with us. We didn't hear from the family again until months later when the school year was to begin. His mother telephoned and asked Joan if her son had gotten off to school. That was it—nothing more. Today this boy is happy with a nice family of his own.

Dony was far from responsible for all of our guests. When in 1966, Jeanne LeBouvier broke her leg during the run of **Goodnight Mrs. Puffin**, it couldn't have been more natural than for her to recover and rehabilitate at our place. There was an empty bedroom.

Dony's next rescue did not result in another houseguest, but resulted in one of the oldest and dearest friendships of our entire family. A sophomore at Minnetonka High School, Bob Wang, bright and eager, put together a small rocket. As he was placing it for flight, the rocket took off, entering his head through the soft underside of his jaw, then passing through his head at a point close to his left temple. After long hospitalization, he was left with a limp, little use of his left arm and difficulty in speaking. As months passed, he had re-entered school, but found no recovery from his injuries. Some of his fellow students were no more considerate than some of us adults. They joked about his omission of unnecessary words such as "Going home now" for, "I think I'll go home now."

Some of the faculty wrongly assumed that his mind had been affected. Bob Wang felt he had no friend until Dony adopted him as his friend. They rode around, they hunted. For deer hunting with bow and arrow, Bob would hold the bow with his good hand and pull the bow spring back by holding it in his teeth. Dony and Bob could talk together for hours. It was Dony who suggested we hire Bob as a night janitor. It was a job he did beautifully. By now the community had discovered that Bob's mind and emotions were not only normal but admirable as well.

When Bob told the police that he was working all night at the theater, they issued him a permit to carry a pistol during working hours.

Perhaps it was a year later, at 2:00 a.m. when my bedside phone rang.

Bob: Don?

Don: Yes ...

Bob: Bob. Know the mirror in ladies room? One that covers the whole wall?

Don: Yes ...

Bob: Shot it out.

And he had. Alone in the building, he had gone into the ladies room to clean, had seen his reflection, and thinking it was an interloper, drew fast and shot it out.

In all the years since, Bob has been a dear friend of all the Stolz family and all of Excelsior. He now lives in Mankato but never once has he missed New Year's Eve with Dony at the Old Log. The night, he spends at Dony and Sue's home.

Back to the houseguests at 5120. Dony was not alone in his efforts to offer succor and solace to those in need. When one of Joan's dearest friends was told by her husband that he was seeking divorce, Joan's friend was devastated, suicidal. Joan brought her to 5120 where she stayed for weeks, hardly able to talk or even get out of bed.

We, the Stolz family, almost believe that there was something therapeutically special about our home. But there were limits. Early one spring our young assistant scenic designer was having difficulty with his wife. He asked if he could stay with us until he could solve his problem at home. One of Dony's friends was still there. Two days later, the daughter of one of our old acting couples arrived for a short rest before continuing her bus trip to the West Coast. The boys adjusted their sleeping quarters to accommodate her. As the summer came, our dock was daily filled with sunbathers and our kitchen sink filled with breakfast and luncheon dishes.

Before we realized it, the summer had passed and it was time for young Timmy and Jon to re-enter school. Joan decided it was time to act. She told me that she and the two younger sons were moving down to the little house on Covington, which we had purchased, re-built and just furnished. They would live there until I could tell her we had no guests at 5120. I saw her wisdom and solved it by moving with her into the cottage on Covington.

Some way, I don't remember how, the housing problem was solved and we moved back to 5120.

Our 5120 home was just across the street from the large log cabin where our son, Dony, and his family lived. We liked the proximity and so did our dogs. Our West Highland Terrier spent a lot of time sunning in their yard, most of the time happy just to watch the passing traffic. One morning, however, she took a dislike to a jogger going down Meadville Street. She took after him, caught him, and gave him a little nip on his leg. Without even stopping, the runner jogged right down to the police station to report the incident. He told them where the attack had originated—from where the dog had charged.

When the police knocked, Francie, our daughter-in-law answered the door. With her was their five-year-old daughter, Joannie.

Francie: Good morning.

Police: Good morning. A jogger just reported to us that he was bitten by a little white dog.

Francie: He did?

Police: Do you have a little white dog?

Francie: No, we don't.

Police: Do you know anyone who has a little white dog?

Francie: Almost everyone in the neighborhood has a little white dog.

Police: Well, the jogger told us that this little white dog had a bow of yarn in its collar.

Five-year-old Joannie: Oh—then that's my grandmother's little white dog and he's bitten about a hundred people.

The policeman laughed, told Joannie to tell her grandmother not to let her little white dog do it again, and left.

BACK TO THE BUSINESS OF THEATER

Beginning with 1963, we stopped using the word "season"; we could never make it accurately apply. Our season in the old Old Log had been summer; now we were open 52 weeks a year. Instead of saying "during our 1963 season," it became "the year 1963."

The year hadn't started before Terry and I decided his return should be in the very popular *Seven Year Itch*. We set his schedule and ours to open *Itch* in the second week of July. The Old Log had several adventures in 1963 before that would occur.

For the only time in the long history of the Old Log, early in 1962 we took an audience survey asking what plays they would like to have the Old Log perform. The unlikely winner—the most requested—*Rhinoceros*. We decided "what the hell," so presented *Rhinoceros* as the second play of 1963. I kept a very accurate count: not a one—not a one—of those who had requested it ever attended during its two-week run. Despite that, it was well received and we were happy and even proud to have done it. But it was the end of audience surveys at the Log.

When spring came, Joan and I made hotel and flight reservations for New York. The purpose of the trip was threefold: to see and visit with Terry O'Sullivan, to call on the play brokers to see if any new scripts were available, and to hold a few auditions in an effort to add some good people to our company.

The broker house that we were particularly eager to visit was Brandt and Brandt, from which company we had leased many plays. We had always dealt with a dignified, elegant though warm man, Bill Koppelman. Bill welcomed me and then reported that he was close to retirement and we would, in future, be dealing with the son of the Chairman, a young man just out of college, Bob Freedman. He assured me that we would like this young addition to the company and I should meet him immediately.

Bob Freedman and I talked for hours about everything involved with theater and a lot of things that weren't. After two hours, I remembered that I had scheduled auditions—not at the hotel, but in a rented studio.

Bob: Auditions—you mean for actors?

Don: That's right.

Bob: That must be fun.

Don: You've never attended an audition?

Bob: Not really.

Don: You want to come with me?

Bob: If you don't mind.

I didn't mind. After spending the afternoon—most of the afternoon—in an unattractive studio, I suggested that Bob and his wife, Beth, have dinner with Joan and me. Sometime during the evening, Bob reminded me that he would have a list of new plays ready for me by ten the next morning. The next morning Bob had the list, and said, "You know, this has been a most enjoyable time."

Without even asking Joan, who was with me, I said, "Bob, why don't you and Beth come out to Minnesota, visit us, see the theater and our new home. Bob immediately reached for his weekly planner, and said "All right. Beth and I will be there next Wednesday."

Both Beth and Bob were delightful houseguests. Both loved the Old Log.

In the years since, Bob has sent us copies of every play that he thought would be right for the Old Log. Perhaps almost as importantly, if he hears a new joke, he telephones me immediately to give me his rendition. Bob is a true raconteur. And a dear, dear friend.

Life with Father preceded *The Seven Year Itch*. Ken Senn was father, Ann Blager, mother, Cleo Holladay was Vinnie's cousin and lovely young Bibi Boles was Mary Skinner. The Day children were played by, and this can't be a surprise, Peter Stolz, Dony Stolz, Tom

Stolz and Timmy.

A week before rehearsals for *Life With Father* were to begin, I still did not have an actress to play Vinnie's cousin. I mentioned this to my friend, Brad Morrison, who by then was working for the Guthrie. Brad told me that the Guthrie's production stage manager had a wife who was an actress but not in the Guthrie company. He gave me her number and I telephoned.

Cleo: Good morning. (all of this dialogue is in a Southern voice; that's the only voice Cleo ever had)

Don: This is Don Stolz, director at the Old Log Theater.

Cleo: Oh, yes, the theater that's sorta out in the country.

Don: That's the one. I understand that you're an actress.

Cleo: That's right—yes, I am.

Don: I wonder if you'd be interested in coming out and auditioning.

Cleo: Oh, I sure would. (This is very Southern)

Don: Miss Holladay, where are you from?

Cleo: I'm proud to say I'm from Virginia.

Don: I see. Well, come on out anyway.

She did. And with her performance in *Life With Father*, she became known as "The Queen of the Old Log." Every man in the audience loved her and not one woman objected because they liked her, too.

The four boys and Ken all had to have their hair dyed red for the performance. There was just no way it would work with wigs. That fall, the Stolz boys all started school with noticeable remnants of the dye job.

During the run of *Life With Father*, the Stolz family was having dinner at the Anchor Inn. Also at the Anchor that night were Mr. and Mrs. Sweeney, whom we knew well. As a matter of fact, in one of the early years I had a room at their house as did most of the actors. The Sweeneys also knew all of our children, so when I told them that the next play was *Life With Father* and that all of them would be in it, it was apparent that they thought it fun and exciting. When I asked them what night they would like to attend the play as

Life With Father; (standing) Tom Stolz, Peter Stolz, and Dony Stolz;
(sitting) Ann Blager, Timmy Stolz, and Ken Senn.

our guests, they decided Friday night.

Friday night, the Sweeney family attended the play, but we didn't have the opportunity of talking with them until the next week when we again saw them at the Anchor Inn. The play was mentioned. They did not respond at all as I had expected. In fact, they were obviously disappointed and perhaps even offended. Finally, Mrs. Sweeney said:

Mrs: The play was perfectly all right—if it hadn't been for that terrible Ken Senn.

Don: Ken Senn?

Mrs: Yes. Ken Senn. No matter where he is, he is always swearing.

Don: In the play?

Mrs: Of course in the play.

Don: I don't remember any swearing.

Mrs: It's all through the play—all those—"Oh Gawd." That's Ken Senn.

Don: Oh, well, Ken isn't responsible for that. Those are all in the script.

Mrs: Don't make excuses for him. I know Ken and he's always swearing.

Don: Well, really, those "Oh Gawd's" are not swearing, they're—they're really supplications."

Mrs: Just stop trying to make excuses for your friend.

Don: Well, I'm sorry you didn't care for the play.

Mrs: The rest of it was fine. I just couldn't stand all that swearing.

Don: I'm sorry.

Mr: What's your next play?

Don: *Seven Year Itch.*

Mrs: That's the one with Terry O'Sullivan. I really want to see that one.

Don: Well, I'd be happy to have tickets for you, but I don't think you'd like it.

Mrs: Is there any swearing in it?

Don: (Thinking) No—no, there isn't.

Mrs: Any taking the Lord's name in vain?

Don: No, there isn't. But I just don't think you'd like it.

Mrs: Why?

Don: Well—you know—

Mrs: Oh—you mean "the other?" That's just nature. We'd like to be there Friday.

In *The Way it Was*, Bob Aden wrote that the people of Excelsior strongly held their opinion that the actors of the Old Log—in fact probably all actors—were "disreputable." I wrote that by 1960 this view had been somewhat mitigated. Not eliminated, just mitigated. The people of Excelsior still didn't always understand us; nor did we always understand them.

The Sweeneys accepted the tickets, which I somewhat reluctantly offered, and they thought *The Seven Year Itch* was the best they had ever seen. They waited to see Terry after the final curtain. Mrs. Sweeney asked for his autograph and enthusiastically thanked me that night, not waiting for our next meeting at the Anchor Inn.

"Nor do we always understand them."

The Seven Year Itch was followed by one of those almost forgettable comedies. The Sweeneys, without doubt, could have accepted it, but since Terry O'Sullivan wasn't in it, they didn't show. When I was preparing for rehearsal of *The Trap*, it developed that I had no leading man. Not having time for a casting trip to either New York or Chicago, I telephoned Amelia Lorence, an agent who had formerly worked for the Equity office. I told her what I needed; she sent me John Varnum. John had toured with Vivian Leigh in *Duel of Angels*, had just closed in the Chicago production of *Mary, Mary*, and had several small roles on Broadway and innumerable industrial shows. Though it would be some time before I had John for every show, he and Cleo, Ken Senn and Ann Blager were the backbone of the Old Log acting company.

In the spring of 1963, Andy Devine, the motion picture and television actor, was looking for a young boy to play *On Borrowed Time* with him in Milwaukee. On Edgar Meyer's recommendation, he asked Tommy to take the role. School was still in session; Tommy was attending St. John's School in Collegeville. When the headmaster, Father Cuthbert, heard of the invitation to Tommy to appear in *On Borrowed Time*, Father immediately gave his permission for Tommy to be away from school for the short run of the show. He felt it would contribute more to Tommy's education than would those same weeks in school.

During rehearsals and the run of the show, Tommy and Andy Devine became close friends—it was a friendship that lasted until Andy's death.

As I recall, it was shortly after Christmas of 1962, when I was attempting to complete our schedule for 1963, that I had the idea of repeating *Mister Roberts* with Dave Moore, not repeating his role as Ensign Pulver, which he had done so beautifully, but rather playing the title role. I knew that the play was one of Dave's favorites and knew that he had enjoyed enormously the companionship with the other members of the crew. Since I saw Dave almost every day at the station (Channel IV), it was easy to start immediately my campaign to get both Dave and the station management to agree to his being away from his usual schedule. In only a few weeks, a three-week run was set with the opening to be August 21.

Dave, in the role of Mister Roberts, was magnificent. He had a sense of love and compassion for the crew of the ship that I felt was even superior to that of Henry Fonda. When in 1979 we again repeated **Mister Roberts**, I was hoping Dave would again be able to arrange his schedule with WCCO-TV so he could play the Doctor. He would have been the only actor to ever play all three of the leading roles. It was unfortunate that it could not be arranged.

Before leaving 1963, it is worth mentioning that in October we presented one of Neil Simon's first plays, the rarely produced **Come Blow Your Horn**. It starred Angus Duncan, who had joined our company in the fall of 1962. A graduate of Pasadena Playhouse, Angus had been successful in receiving role after role in national television, as well as playing Bing Crosby's son in the motion picture **High Time**. In his first appearance at the Old Log, he had been required to use the name Angus MacIntosh, because no two actors are allowed to be members of Equity with the same name. Upon our urging, Angus called the other Angus Duncan who was an officer in the union, now well along in years and highly respected.

Our Angus: Mr. Duncan?

NY Angus: Yes.

Our Angus: Mr. Angus Duncan?

NY Angus: Yes.

Our Angus: My name is Angus Duncan, too. My real name. I'm an actor—I've just gotten a job with the Old Log Theater in Minneapolis and so have to join Equity.

NY Angus: Good.

Our Angus: The Equity office told me I couldn't use my real name because there was already a member with the name Angus Duncan. You.

NY Angus: Correct.

Our Angus: They told me that you no longer acted and if you gave your permission, I could use my own name.

NY Angus: Yes, I think that's true.

Our Angus: Well, may I have your permission to use my real name?

NY Angus: Let me ask you a question.

Our Angus: Yes?

NY Angus: Are you a good actor?

Our Angus: Sir?

NY Angus: Are you a good actor?

Our Angus: Not yet, sir, but I'm doing my best to become one.

NY Angus: I'll tell the Equity office that you have my permission. And good luck.

For once in his life, our Angus had come up with exactly the right answer. And he was right for the juvenile in *The Golden Fleecing* with Judy Perle and Rupert LaBelle.

The second play of 1964 was an even more rarely produced play by Tennessee Williams and Donald Windham, *You Touched Me*. It is a story about an old sea captain's attempt to save the love between his foster son and his daughter.

The first week in August in 1964, the Old Log production was *Look Homeward Angel*, the American classic from the Thomas Wolfe novel, a story of a boy coming of age. It is one of the productions of which I am most proud.

The last play of the 1964 was to be a repeat of *Marriage Go Round*. There was only one thing wrong, we had absolutely no one to play Katrin Sveg, the Swedish femme fatale. I had gone through our files of photographs and resumes, called local agents, and then started making plans for a quick casting trip to either New York or Chicago. When our attorney at that time, John McNulty, heard my plans, he said "There is a beautiful, statuesque young lady in our office. I know she has had a lot of acting experience. Why don't I have her give you a call tomorrow? Her name is Anita Anderson—she has an absolutely beautiful voice." Anita was a great Katrin Sveg. Anita later became my secretary/assistant, and is still here.

Some time during the run of *Marriage Go Round*, Anita asked:

Anita: Don, you don't remember the first time we met, do you?

Don: The first time we met? I guess I don't.

Anita: It was during the run of *Mister Roberts* with Dave Moore as Roberts. I was in the audience. The whole experience was embarrassing.

Don: Oh?

Anita: I was the guest of Tom Boright; we were sitting in the front row. Every time Dave Moore started to give a line, Tom Boright would say it first.

Don: I remember. Dave wasn't really very happy with the situation.

Anita: At intermission, you were much kinder than I would have been. You told Tom you knew that he loved the play or he wouldn't know all those lines. You just wished he'd give Dave a chance to say them before he did.

Don: Oh, it wasn't that bad. As I remember, Tom never said another word during the show.

Anita: That's right. But it was still embarrassing. Shortly before our presentation of *Mister Roberts*, Fred Sammut, our designer at that time (he was one of the sailors in *Mister Roberts*), came to me with a list of tools that were needed for our scene shop. There was no doubt they were needed, but I explained to Fred that there was no way that we could afford them.

Fred: That's what I thought your answer would be. How would you feel about it if the shop earned some extra money—would you let us use that for tools?

Don: Well, sure. But how are you going to earn this extra money?

Fred: I'm not going to tell you. It'll be a surprise.

It was only a few days until I learned. Through several seasons we had saved every plug that we had made. (Plugs were the small pieces of scenery to go over a door or over a window—they looked very much like stretched canvases on a frame that artists use.) It was probably this similarity that gave Fred and his crew the idea. They placed all of these plugs on the floor of the scene shop, and then each member of the crew took a can of different colored scene paint left over from previous sets, and they went around from plug to plug, brushing or dripping paint as they willed. It was painting "by committee" with no plan, no pattern, just keep it colorful and fun. After the paintings dried, they added "T. Crew" in the corner, then hung them in the lobby.

Audiences were delighted by their discovery of a new "modern artist whose work was more exciting than anything at the Walker."

John Sherman, the music, drama and art critic who had gained permission to review *Mister Roberts*, praised the work of this T. Crew and even asked if he could meet him—his work was excellent. Fearing that John might write a review, I told him what we had done. "Well," he replied, "this may have done by committee, but it was a committee with strong creative minds and talent."

I've wondered what his review might have been.

We sold over $1,600 of these "works of art" but only did so after we had told the buyer what they were.

Wayne Field, one of our regular attendees, was particularly drawn to the largest of those hanging. He told us that it was probably too large to hang in the empty space on his office wall, but said he'd measure and call us back. The next day he told us that in truth, it was too large. I asked him if he'd like to have us cut it in two and sell him both pieces for the same price. He was extremely pleased and sent a check immediately.

Whoever it was who said "beauty is in the eye of the beholder" was correct, but I want to add that I thought the beholders on this show were correct. I liked two of the T. Crews so much that I took them and still have them.

The design crew got their tools.

The same year, 1964, I had a call from the Skylight Club, an organization that was founded in 1890, and with membership that included University professors, newspapermen, artists, authors and businessmen with interest in the arts and the state of society in Minneapolis. But there were no members from any branch of theater. Theater men, it seems, were considered businessmen—

Mister Roberts; Ennis Johnson, Dave Moore, Jack Bacon, Jerry Donlin, Fred Sammut, Joel Stohr, Peter Stolz, and Richard Dix.

Catch Me If You Can; Ross Bickell, John Varnum, and Rhonda Hopkins.

PeterPat; Cleo Holladay and John Varnum.

more interested in attendance at their theaters than the contemplation, with their fellow citizens, the social, cultural and artistic being
of their city. That changed with Oliver Rea of the Guthrie Theatre
and Don Stolz of the Old Log were taken into membership. Legend
has it that these two were approached with the following invitation:
"If you feel you would be comfortable being members of Skylight, it
probably will be all right, if you care to join."

By 1965 it seemed we were in the habit of finding somewhat
obscure plays by well-known playwrights. One of our plays was **South
Sea Bubble** by Noel Coward. The year 1965 was also the year in which
we first presented two plays that over the years would have repeat runs.
The first was **Never Too Late**. Senn was magnificent. The second was
Catch Me If You Can, a mystery comedy. It's one of the very few plays
so described that really fulfills both "comedy" and "mystery."

In May of 1965, Mel Jass, who had become a good friend while
he was still at Channel Four, had asked me to be a guest on his new
show at Channel Eleven. As something of a "go-for" and sometimes
assistant on the air, Mel had engaged a very pretty, extremely well
poised teenager, Nancy Nelson. In one of the breaks, Mel introduced
Nancy and suggested that I should ask her to come out to the Old
Log and audition. I did. And one way or another, Nancy has been
connected with the Old Log ever since. During those same years she
developed, wrote and appeared on her own TV shows, eventually
becoming in, the '90s, the most recognized and most popular of the
national infomercial presenters. When Nancy first came to the Old
Log, she had just graduated from Roosevelt High School. Her first
play here was Samuel Taylor's **Beekman Place**, in which she played
Cleo Holladay's daughter.

In 1966, the play for children (again, as the Union states—"The
Theater for Young Audiences" was **The Dancing Donkey**. The four
leading characters were played by ubiquitous Richard Paul, Rex
Partington (borrowed from his job as Production Stage Manager at
the Guthrie), Valedia Hill and Jeanne Whittier (my sister). Soon
after the play is well under way, the four are to sing a quartet. During
rehearsal we soon found that there was danger; only one of the four

performers could actually sing. The organist played a few notes of introduction; the four singers began the quartet, each one singing in a different key. The organist attempted to find a key that they all could settle on; mercifully the singing soon came to an end. There was no applause from the audience, but there was a small voice in one of the front rows: "Boy, that stunk."

Some time during the run of **Donkey**, Valedia Hill asked if Richard Paul could take her lines for one performance—could "sub" for her. She had to go downtown Minneapolis to get her divorce.

A play, **PeterPat**, that I would not have mentioned were it not for this wonderful photograph of Cleo Holladay and John Varnum. In a picture has been captured the entire play.

The Odd Couple; Ken Senn (standing) and
John Varnum.

In 26 years of the Old Log Theater—from 1940 until 1966—
no actor had ever missed a performance, regardless of how tired, how
ill, they were. Never did we have an understudy. In May of 1966, the
play, **Goodnight Mrs. Puffin**, starring Ken Senn and Jean LeBouvier,
had just opened. Jean was a houseguest of the Snells. Early in the
morning, Jean had gotten out of bed, and in finding her way into the
bathroom, she had fallen and broken her leg. Waiting until morning,
Jean awakened Marge and told her that she, Marge, would have to
go on for her that night. Marge, always a quick study, did. The next
night, Jean was back on stage with a cast on her leg and walking with
the aid of crutches.

Since that time, there have been, though remarkably few, a
number of occasions when an unscheduled replacement was necessary, a replacement that quite often fell on me.

The highlight of the next season (1967) and the highlight of
seven other seasons was **The Odd Couple**, starring Ken Senn and
Edgar Meyer. As I mentioned elsewhere, Ken and Edgar were absolutely the best Odd Couple that ever played the roles. In 1967 it ran
for 13 weeks. It was such a box office success that it probably should
have run for 13 months.

"CALL HUBERT HUMPHREY"

I don't remember what year it was that I did my first work with National Car; it was so long ago that their home office was located in the lower level of a building that is now a mortuary. From the years I worked with them, there are several memories that are still fresh and firm. In a morning meeting in the president's office we were served coffee. Frequently being a klutz, I spilled some of my coffee on the office's newly laid carpet. When I knelt with the hope of sponging the spill, one of the other klutzes at the meeting unkindly asked me what I was going to do if the spot didn't disappear. I remember saying, "if the spot doesn't disappear, we pick up the president's desk and move it far enough to cover the stain."

Perhaps my favorite recollection about National Car has nothing to do with the Old Log's work. The convention was at the magnificent Coronado Hotel, just across from San Diego. Sunday, everything was absolutely ready for the Monday opening. Joan and Tim and Jon (the two boys were working the show) and I went to Old San Diego. There we ran into Joe Sullivan and his family. Joe was a senior executive with National Car. When the bells in the old town cathedral announced the Sunday mass, the Sullivans and the Stolzs all went to morning mass. It seemed a special blessing.

Years later when our family was going to Memphis and knowing that we would return with quite a bit of luggage, I called Joe Sullivan and asked if he could possibly arrange for us to pick up a station wagon at Memphis, which we would drive back to Minneapolis and drop off. One way station wagons were not a frequent rental. Joe made the arrangements. When we arrived at the Memphis airport and went to the National Car Rental desk, the young lady could find absolutely no reservation for the Stolzs at all.

Girl: What was that name again?

Don: Stolz.

Girl: I'm sorry—I still can't find any reservations.

Don: It was for a station wagon, which we would drop off in Minneapolis.

Girl: When did you make this reservation?

Don: I didn't make it. Joe Sullivan made it.

Girl: Who's he?

Don: The Vice President of National Car Rental.

Girl: Oh—that reservation. Of course we have it. It's special—we were expecting a much older man.

Of much more importance.

In a meeting to plan the upcoming convention that would include all the holders of the national franchises, the Canada people and the Hilton Car Rental from England, someone suggested that the convention should open with a welcome from the Governor of Minnesota. A call was made to Governor Wendell Anderson's office. When asked the date of the convention, the Governor replied that he was sorry, he couldn't be there because he was going on a fishing trip.

The committee wasn't pleased. I said, "Why don't you get Hubert Humphrey to make the welcome?"

Committee member: Humphrey's in Washington. He wouldn't come back for that.

Don: We don't know that. Why don't you call him?

Committee member: You call him.

Don: All right, I will.

When I talked with Humphrey's Washington office, they said they would give him the request immediately. Humphrey called back that afternoon saying that he had to come back to Minneapolis some time soon and he could very well arrange that time to be the opening day of National Car Rental's meeting.

The morning of the meeting before he went to the podium, Humphrey thanked me for calling his office. Then went to the podium. I so well remember his opening remarks that the following is almost verbatim:

"Good morning. I know in this audience there is only one man who would ever vote for me for anything. That man is Zollie Frank (Chevrolet's biggest dealer in America and one of National's most important members). But when I heard that you were coming to Minnesota from all over America, Canada and England, there was no way I was not going to be here to welcome you to my state."

By the time he finished his speech of welcome, I don't doubt at all that those "who had never and would never vote for him" would now have elected him president if they could. This state is, and should be, proud of the heritage of Hubert Humphrey.

National Car, through its advertising agency, had arrived at a contract with Don Rickles to be the lead spokesman on a number of television commercials. Rickles' agent, in an effort to complete the agreement, had included in the contract that Rickles would entertain at their annual franchise banquet in Minneapolis.

Rickles arrived happy and in good form. He glowed with anticipation of the success and admiration (and possibly even "adoration") that would be his.

Rickles performance started well. Very well, with substantial laughs except from the table immediately adjacent to stage center. It was a table that had been reserved for Zollie Frank, Mrs. Frank and their family. At that time, Zollie was America's largest Chevrolet dealer, and National Car's Chicago franchise, the most profitable in the National Car network.

Rickles, flushed with the success that came from the rest of the room, stopped stage center, pointed at Mrs. Frank and said, "Lady, if you don't start laughing at me, I'm going to lower my pants and fire a torpedo right at you."

Zollie, Mrs. Frank and their family, without a word, rose and left the room.

Don Rickles never made another commercial for National Car.

For their next franchise annual meeting, National Car was back in Florida, this time at the glorious Miami Beach Hotel, formerly the

Playboy Plaza, from which, originally, the Jackie Gleason show was televised. In the showroom was every piece of equipment you could ever ask for: a revolving stage which raised and lowered; two complete sets of lighting equipment—one, as explained to us, was for television, the other set for live production. The room had everything but a good piano. In the orchestra pit was an old upright which they could not have sold for more than $35.00. It certainly was not left over from the Jackie Gleason days.

Left, however, from the Jackie Gleason days was his trumpet player—and the only brass instrument Gleason ever used on his recordings. Not only did he play glorious solo on every musical number, but he was also used by the arranger as a strong voice between violin and cello. His name was Don Goldie. Already a legendary player in Florida, he had been retrained by the hotel as the leader of their house band and their musical contractor. When we told the hotel we intended to hire several local musicians in addition to the ones we were bringing with us, they informed us that we must talk to Don Goldie and make the necessary arrangement through him. When we called Don, he suggested that the committee come for dinner at the hotel, when his house band would be playing; when he was at break, he would sit with us and decide what was needed.

The committee and I agreed, went to dinner at the appointed time, had a great meal, listened to great dinner music and sat waiting for the orchestra's first break. This pleasant, friendly looking gnome-like man approached the table and greeted us:

Goldie: Hello—I'm Don Goldie, the world's greatest trumpet player.

Stolz: A few years ago, you couldn't have said that.

Goldie: *(Challenging)* Oh? Why couldn't I?

Stolz: Because a few years ago, the world's greatest trumpet player was with Paul Whiteman and his name was just Goldie.

Goldie: He was my father.

Stolz: I know. I have a copy of almost all the recordings he made with Whiteman.

Goldie: You're right. He was better than me.

Stolz: But he was older, too—you may catch up.

Goldie: I'm trying.

Stolz: Good.

We told Don the instruments we needed, and asked if he could be one of the players in our band, to which he eagerly agreed.

The next morning at the musical rehearsal, Don was delighted with the musicianship of the players from Minnesota and before the morning was over, declared that pianist Jeanne Peterson was as good as he had ever heard and better than anyone in Florida. As the rehearsal continued, it became evident that Don was not accustomed to reading; he was so gifted that it was something he ordinarily didn't have to do. At one point, Jack Gillespie, our trumpet player from home, turned to Don who had just erred slightly—and jokingly asked:

Jack: Say, Don—

Goldie: Yes?

Jack: When are you going to learn to read?

Goldie: *(Not jokingly)* I'm going to learn to read about the same time you learn to play jazz.

The two during the first moment of rehearsal had already become admirers and remained as such through the years.

Rehearsals went well; we were ready for the show the next morning. The show opened with a musical number—band and singers—an overture of sorts. It ended with one of the singers introducing the president of National. This morning there was first a company speaker, then a skit, which humorously but seriously introduced the subject the next speaker would then address. The third National Car speaker was Bob Twersky, Vice President Licensee Relations. Bob always worked extremely hard to be properly prepared for his appearance on the program. He always felt that he deserved the steaming acclaim that would be his.

The morning had gone well—extremely well. Not a cue had been missed; not a wrong note played. It was time for Bob, as the third speaker, to move to the podium. Just as he, almost trembling with anticipation, got to his place behind the lectern and opened his mouth to extend his personal welcome to the audience, someone, and to this day we don't know whom or how, turned off the spotlight, leaving him completely in the dark. Bob's shocked reaction was immediate; fortunately many of his protests were not understandable. It was at least a minute before the difficulty was corrected, the light went back on and Twersky began his presentation. Somewhat shaken, the presentation was not quite what he had hoped it would be. By the time he finished, we had hastily made arrangements for a short added scene, which started with son, Tom, crossing the stage carrying his suitcase. He was followed by the head of the hotel's stage crew:

Stagehand: Hey, Tom—

Tom: (*Stopping center stage*) Yeah?

Stagehand: Where are you going, anyway?

Tom: Home. Back to Minneapolis.

Stagehand: What?

Tom: Yes, I just got fired. I was the guy who turned the light out on Twersky.

(*End of scene*)

Two days later, it was with sadness that we saw the show come to an end. The musicians wanted to take Don Goldie home with them and he wanted them all to stay in Florida. He kept suggesting to Jeanne Peterson that if she stayed, the two of them should find a bass player and organize one of the great jazz trios of all time. This idea he held for years even including the years he spent at the Jockey Club. In the years that followed, we hired Don whenever we were in Florida and needed an added trumpet player. Whatever correspondence I had with him, I always addressed to "The World's Greatest Trumpet Player," and it was always correctly delivered. Of course having the right address helped.

When National Car was purchased by Household Finance, those planning the next convention wrote the president of Household Finance and stated that they would like very much for him to come to Minneapolis for the meeting and speak for 20 to 25 minutes. He wrote back saying he would be delighted to do that—what did they want, 20 or 25 minutes? I suggested we settle for 23. We did.

And believe it or not, that was exactly the time he used.

When the Minneapolis slate of owners and officers of National Car left to purchase Dairy Queen, I was taken along with them. The convention for Dairy Queen operators that soon followed came at a time of transition and varying opinions. What could have been disaster was changed when Ken Glazer, Dairy Queen's remaining president, started the meeting of the first day, as he always did, with a prayer asking for guidance, unity and blessing.

As International Dairy Queen grew, the pageantry of the opening session grew. After a few years, DQ had stores in locations all over the globe. They had photographs of the stores in Alaska with customers arriving at the drive-in window with dog sleds; camels and riders in Saudi Arabia lined up outside a DQ waiting for their turn to purchase "the cone with the curl on top."

Our stage productions for DQ became bigger and bigger.

After St. Louis, we went to Boston. Bob Pyle, of Campbell-Mithun, was making his advertising presentation as a magician, skillfully using pigeons that magically disappeared and reappeared. It was attention getting and relevant to the points he was making. There was only one thing wrong, throughout the tour, Ken Senn and I were the custodians of the two pigeons, who spent every night in our hotel rooms "cooing." Nor was the cooing reduced when we took them on the plane to the next stop.

Because I was responsible for the staging and lighting and sound in each city we visited, Ken and I always traveled at least a day ahead of the rest of the cast. Regardless of what city we visited, regardless of what airport we were in, always—always—people would ask me if that wasn't Zero Mostel I was with. After weeks of this, I became so tired of saying "I'm sorry, it isn't," that I changed my response to "Yes, it is, but please don't tell anybody."

These were not the first times Ken had been mistaken for Mostel. Several years before this when Ken and his wife, Muriel, were visiting London, they walked into a very swank café, where a strong orchestra was playing for the dinner guests. When the leader saw Ken, he stopped the orchestra and had them play "Fiddler on the

Roof." Ken understood why the orchestra had done this, so he most graciously stood and acknowledged the orchestra and bowed to the other guests.

Another year the convention was scheduled for New Orleans. Ray Komischke, as always our musical conductor, had designed an opening number that included not only the presentation of the flags from every country, but also special choruses celebrating the New Orleans location. He had engaged Pete Fountain, world famous jazz clarinetist, to play a chorus of his theme—then the arrangement had a chorus of transition into a chorus by the legendary Al Hirt. It was a long, complicated, pertinent and beautiful overture, played by an orchestra that included a complete section of string instruments. The afternoon orchestra rehearsal went well indeed, including the section for Al Hirt, who at that time was at the height of his reputation for being constantly drunk. At this rehearsal, Al Hirt reported on time and sober. I remember casually saying to one of the local string players:

Don: Things look all right with Al—he's here and he's all right.

Violinist: Well, that means only one thing.

Don: Oh?

Violinist: Tomorrow morning he'll be here terribly drunk or he won't be here at all.

With his knowledge of Al, Ray had anticipated just that, so he had arranged with me if, on the morning of the show, Al showed up too drunk to play or didn't show at all, to give him a cue on a light arrangement we had rigged in the pit, and he would skip section D (the Hirt solo) and go directly to section E. The morning of the show, Ray informed the orchestra of this possibility and urged them to be alert.

The next morning, the time for opening the show arrived. Searching back stage, I found no Al Hirt. As Ray led the orchestra through sections A and B, I signaled him "no Hirt." During the orchestras playing A and B, I went to the other side of the stage, and there sitting with his horn between his knees was Al. I ran back to my post, signaled Ray that Al was there. When his cue came, Al strode on stage looking perfectly sober, played beautifully, exited, came off stage sat down on the steps to recover.

My favorite Dairy Queen show and the one I think was the greatest, was the one we prepared for the 1976 convention to be held at the Waldorf Astoria in New York. It was, again, a large show: 24-piece orchestra, eight dancers, eight singers, and a cast of Dairy Queen executives, augmented by six or seven professional actors from Minneapolis. After the opening number, which included a presentation of the flags of all the Dairy Queen countries, we introduced a skit showing the attempt of the founding fathers of the United States to write a constitution. In 1976, Dairy Queen was going through some questions and disagreements about policy, and the opening skit showed that even in the important job of writing a constitution for the young country, there were disagreements, even though all the principals involved had the same desire, the same goal. The cast of DQ executives was beautifully costumed, and having given it long rehearsals, performed well.

When it was time for the bearded Harris Cooper to introduce himself as Benjamin Franklin, I had written his first line to read:

Franklin: Few of you, I am sure, recognize me, but I am Benjamin Franklin. As I said, "few of you will recognize me," for I know of no history book nor any historical photograph that reveals that at one time I wore a short beard.

As the show progressed through the history of the United States, each character spoke of the similarity between a problem of his time relating it to a problem then facing the Dairy Queen organization. Gordon Huber, as Daniel Boone, spoke of "pioneering and expanding into new territories."

Probably influenced by the involved reaction of the Dairy Queen people, a literary agent who was seeing the show as an invited guest, reported that it was the best show he had seen in New York in five years.

The DQ was a hit, indeed. The next year, though the meeting was in Hawaii, there were so many requests for a repeat of the New York show, that we added some Hawaiian music and acts in the overture and then, with very few other changes, repeated the 1976 show.

"Just Talk With These People"

I have absolutely no recollection of who was responsible for the call we received asking us to prepare a show for Arctic Cat that would be taken to five or six different markets. The cast, along with the speakers and company staff, would be flown from meeting to meeting in the company plane, which would be well stocked with food and liquor.

All remember our performing at and staying in the legendary Chateau Frontenac in Montreal, and sitting in the lower level bar with all six musicians and me in one large booth. Musicians have wonderful stories and tell great jokes. I can remember several.

The Inn on the Park in Toronto was another gracious engagement. A Toronto trio of violin, bass and accordion had been hired to play the reception. The violin leader played a five-string instrument and with it, produced remarkable jazz. When I mentioned to him that he reminded me of violinist Joe Venute, he replied that Joe was his God and two weeks later, mailed me a photo showing the two together.

By now, all the musicians were suffering from chapped lips. Reuben Ristrom announced that he had heard from a Toronto musician that there was a certain cure. In the center courtyard of the inn were several llamas, and if you approached one of them, lifted its tail and kissed it directly on the rectum, it would cure your chapped lips. When asked how that could possibly work he said, "Well, it will keep you from licking your lips."

The show in Toronto went very well. Save for one thing. At the intermission, the musicians had left their instruments on their chairs and gone to the lobby with everyone else. Bruce Neilson, backstage and eager to get out to the lobby, had walked between the scenery and the front curtain. His passage knocked over the tall Bose speaker, which fell onto Komischke's chair occupied now only by his saxophone. It was destroyed, bent double. Had Ray been sitting there, it might well have killed him. Ray, always insured, took it in good spirit and moved the saxophone to a special place in the lobby with a sign that read "For Sale—played previously only by a little old woman."

When Clyde Fessler, who had been in charge of the Arctic Cat shows moved to Harley Davidson in Milwaukee, he called me.

Clyde: Don—

Don: Yes—

Clyde: This is Clyde Fessler.

Don: How do you like your new job with Harley Davidson?

Clyde: It's great. That's why I'm calling you. We're getting ready for our first big convention and I would like very much for you to produce the show.

Don: For motorcycles? Clyde, I don't think so. I guess I'll just have to say "no."

Clyde: Don—just wait a minute. I have the names here of five dealers. I'll send you the list, and I want you to visit them and if you say no after that, I won't bother you.

Don: Clyde—I just don't—

Clyde: I'm sending you the list. At least telephone these people. Then give me your decision.

Reluctantly I called the first of them.

Elderly woman on phone: Yes, I'm still operating the dealership that my husband and I started 55 years ago when we were first married.

Don: The same shop?

Woman: Oh, yes—and I still live in the apartment over the shop.

Don: Do you like that?

Woman: Of course I do—I love it. I wouldn't think of moving. Selling motorcycles has been very good for me.

I've had a happy life. I've put three children through
college all because of Harley Davidson.

Don: Mrs. Watson, how old did you say you were?

Woman: I don't think I said—anyway, I'm seventy-eight.

Don: Seventy-eight. Tell me, did you used to ride a Harley
when you were younger?

Woman: What do you mean, did I used to ride? I still do—I
have a beautiful machine that's just mine.

**By the time she finished telling me of her life with Harley
Davidson motorcycles, I could hardly wait to make the
second call. It was to a young couple.**

Man: I've told you how proud I am to be selling Harleys. I
want you to know I'm just as proud to own one. My wife
owns one, too.

Don: Do you ride them quite often?

Man: Every day to work and then back home every day.

Don: Did you build a special garage at home for your two
Harleys?

Man: Are you kidding? I wouldn't think of keeping our
Harleys in a garage.

Don: Oh. Well, where do you keep them?

Man: In the living room, of course.

Clyde had selected the perfect list. I could hardly wait to call
Clyde and tell him "yes."

Our first show was in Chicago. When you've just written a
show, whether it's an industrial show or a play at your theater, your
anticipation and dread are truly heavy. After the first performance in
Chicago, the reaction of the audience and the reaction of the Harley
people told me that we had done well.

The first audience member who reached me was an elderly lady,
not the one I had interviewed, but another dealer with similar experience. I shall always remember what she said: "You have just told the
story of my life. Thank you."

We went to five different cities across the country with our show.
Dealers and other Harley enthusiasts had their choice of attending any

one of the five. Some, traveling together, attended all five. One dealer had organized a group of past middle-aged riders, half of whom were women. They rode specially painted Harleys—pink—and they dressed in pink. This group attended three of the meetings. Regardless of what you may have heard about motorcycle riders, I tell you Harley Davidson riders are great people. They are filled with joy that is difficult to find anywhere else.

AGAIN HONEYWELL

Though Honeywell was the company for whom I had my first industrial show experience, I was still doing productions for their various divisions. One is particularly memorable. We had done a first show in Minneapolis, the second in Carolina (both for different companies), followed by a third for Honeywell at Breezy Point. The evening before the day of the show, the troupe arrived at Breezy exhausted. In looking over the room, we discovered there was no piano; the only piano anywhere at the resort was a large grand in the dining room of the lodge, which was two blocks from the building in which our show was to be performed. We immediately received permission from the management to move the piano. In short time we had recruited about twenty men to help carry the piano to the show room. Ten would pick up the piano, carry it until tired; the other ten would take over and they would carry until tired. It was a successful move; the show was even more successful.

In 1965, Honeywell asked me to come in for a conference. Their project was a training film on quality, built around Deming's "Fourteen Points of Just in Time Manufacturing," to reveal the difficulty, the conflict and, often, the pain involved in "change." They wanted me to write the film script, "Right the First Time."

As soon as I agreed, which was soon, I was handed copies of the 12 quality lectures by Dr. Myron Tribus, a strong advocate of Doctor Deming, and a professor at M.I.T. A week later, they called Doctor Tribus and made an appointment for a visit by me and Honeywell representative, Bob Schwartz. Tribus was on the cutting edge of Just in Time Manufacturing and quality achieved through Deming's 14 points. He was direct and simple in explaining his views; his suggestions for the film were most helpful.

I wrote the script; it was approved; it was produced. Honeywell wanted it to be at least 45 minutes long. I kept telling them if they were going to use it for training, it should be no longer than 20. The client may not always be right, but he usually has great influence on the final decision. *Just in Time*, not only the working title but also the final title, when completed was 45 minutes long.

I don't know how successful it may have been for training Honeywell personnel, but I do know that a year later it was purchased by J. Arthur Rank of England.

All of this, and we were still operating the Old Log Theater 52 weeks a year.

Industrial Theater Revisited

Northwestern National Life decided they should change their usual format of meetings for their leading brokers and agents. Because of our close relationship with the company, it was natural that they would call us to see if we would be interested. The meeting was to be in London. They knew we'd be interested without waiting for our answer. Our cast included several actors, four singers and pianist Jeanne Peterson. Before we left the states, we had, by telephone, hired three London union musicians: bass, drums and guitar. They, as musicians do, marveled at Jeanne's great talent. Working with them could not have been easier nor more pleasant.

NWNL had arranged for all of us attending the London meeting to be their guests at a performance of *Midnight Express*. The next morning at our rehearsal, the London musicians asked Jeanne and me how we had liked the show. After we told them we enjoyed it greatly, they said, "all right, name or hum just one of the songs." Even Jeanne with her remarkable musical memory could come up with only one, "The Light at the End of the Tunnel." "That's always the only one any audience member can remember, and it's an adaptation of an old gospel number." At that time, the three London musicians were not great admirers of Andrew Lloyd Webber.

For Joan and me, neither of us had ever before been to England, the trip was a great adventure.

Another great adventure with NWNL was their request to write and produce a show, again for their brokers and agents, on a cruise ship to Alaska.

Whenever NWNL did anything, it was always elegant and

absolutely first class.

Across the river in St. Paul, Minnesota Mutual had heard of our shows for NWNL, so they called associates there and asked if they would have any objection to our doing a convention for them. There was none, so we were able to write and produce a show for Minnesota Mutual—a show that took us to Paris. I have heard other visitors to Paris complain of treatment by the French people, but Joan and I saw nothing but friendly courtesy. Whether we were walking or catching the Underground, there seemed always to be people who were happy to help. As a contrast, when we were taken on a splendid tour of the Chateau Country, I was embarrassed by the rudeness of some of the Americans on the bus. Even considering that, it was a trip I would like to repeat.

The next year, Minnesota Mutual took us, along with their leading salespeople, to Hawaii.

While the meeting in Paris had been exhilarating and something in which we could take pride, the meeting in Honolulu, even today, is a painful memory. There is no way you can fly young salespeople and their wives from a cold winter to the beautiful sunlit islands and expect them to be happy in a long sales meeting. But this was not the only problem. Three officers had presentations to make. From the very first day, I explained to each of the three that their presentations were too long. The feeling of each of them was, "well, have the other two shorten their part of the program." I knew we were in trouble, but no one was willing to do anything about it. The result was exactly what you can imagine, if you can imagine bad things. It was one of the two unhappiest business days in my whole life. I knew that if I was as good as I had always felt myself to be there was some way I could have handled the problem. I'm not certain that the three men didn't also feel I could have done something. Everyone of them took even longer to deliver their presentation at the actual performance than they had taken at dress rehearsal. The show was long, and compared to the wonderful sunshine outside, was boring. The loss of attendees was more than a few. It was devastating. I wasn't sure I would ever recover.

The second of "the unhappiest days of my business life" was a show we did for Pillsbury. The Pillsbury meeting was held in the Orpheum Theater on Hennepin Avenue. (The Orpheum-before-remodeling Theater.) When Dean Thomas, the Pillsbury officer in charge, indicated that he would like to have, as a part of the presentation, a very up to date, multi-image, multi-screen audiovisual presentation (which was, at that time, just receiving attention), I recommended Empire Photo Sound, a company doing splendid artistic and creative work.

The Orpheum was operating as a motion picture house, which meant that we couldn't move our show in until some time after 11:00 p.m. As we were moving in other units of the show, Empire Photo Sound was holding its last rehearsal. A rehearsal which, for the first time, resulted in the new system of correcting cueing slides for all the projectors. We connected our sound and lighting equipment, which would cover the live portions of the show. When at last all lights and speakers were hung, we were ready to test our lighting switchboard. The test went well but the electronic equipment was now malfunctioning. By 7:45 the next morning, we felt we had everything under control for the opening at 8 a.m.

The opening number—orchestra, singers, dancers—went exactly as it should. The first skit was well received. Then came the first major speech of the morning, the President of Pillsbury. He spoke with pride of Pillsbury's accomplishments; he spoke with pride about their assets. He spoke with great pride about the company's young officers who were "Pillsbury's greatest assets." When he spoke of the stable of young officers, the picture that came up on all three screens was of natives in Africa carrying, over their shoulders, sacks of Pillsbury Flour. It is fortunate that there was no convenient and immediate way of killing myself. Had there been, I would have done it. Though the rest of the morning went without any major misfortune, I knew that everyone even remotely connected to Pillsbury would scorn me forever. I was wrong. Most of those in attendance thought that it had been a clever insertion of humor. Those of the company who knew better, were kind enough to keep still. The shame of this show I overcame more quickly than I had for the show for Minnesota Mutual in Hawaii.

My life has not always been one happy, successful presentation after another. There have been times of shame, humility and anguish. Even now I am eager to attempt to replace the memory of those two shows with one more pleasant.

Ralph Blattner and his wife were regular attendees at the Old Log Theater, all during the years that he was one of the top officers of the Carlson Companies Communications Division, which produced shows (ordinarily audiovisual shows) for their clients. A new client was the Gravely Tractor Company of North Carolina. In talking with Blattner about their upcoming dealer meeting, they had indicated that they would like to consider not only audiovisual, but also a live section for their presentation. Blattner asked if I would accompany him to Gravely to determine if they would be interested in a production from us. They were extremely interested. The resulting show was outstanding.

The next year Gravely called me direct and asked me to do another dealer meeting. When I asked about Blattner, they replied that they had decided on a supplier other than Carlson. I told them under those circumstances, I felt that I should first check with Blattner to make certain he had no objection to my doing a production without Carlson. Blattner's reply to my question was memorable: "If we didn't do a job last year that made them want to use us again, we don't deserve the business. Take the job." We did. Joan and I and the rest of the company had greatly enjoyed our first visit to the Carolinas and we looked forward to returning. Another notable and relevant show.

For both Gravely shows, a part of our job was to present the entertainment for the evening banquet. The first year, one of the favorite numbers was a tap dance by Nancy Stewart. She was a large woman with a beautiful face, and when she danced, she was a picture of fun and joy. The night of the second year, Nancy was closing her tap dance with a series of twirls, which carried her across the stage. That night it also twirled her off the stage, which was at least four feet from the floor. An attendee in the first row saw her fall, jumped up and caught her before she could hit the floor. By the end of the evening we had rigged a medal and presented it to him for "Action Beyond the Call of Duty." He explained that he was a farm boy accustomed to catching bales of hay thrown down from the hayloft.

The Old Log was engaged to produce an industrial show for the King Koil Mattress Company. The company officers were efficient, pleasant and helpful. They heartily approved the script and the show that resulted. They had planned for a long luncheon break between the morning and afternoon sessions. The St. Paul Hotel, the location for the meeting, had been told to plan an elegant menu, for during the luncheon they had on display their new products. When they asked what I would recommend for music for this special occasion, I asked for a day to plan before I offered any solution.

By the time I got back to my office, I had decided that the perfect music for this "elegant" affair would be a trio of harp, cello and violin, even though there was in existence in the Twin Cities no such trio. I telephoned Don Anderson first. When I told him of my plan, he said the only way it would work is if we could get Cliff Brunzell. I next called Cliff; he said, "the only way it will work is if you can get Don Anderson on harp and Vince Bastien on cello." When I telephoned Vince, he said, "it's a great idea if you can get Cliff Brunzell and Don Anderson." The trio was a marvelous and a beautiful success.

How I had obtained the King Koil job, I have no idea. Of all the hundreds of other industrial shows we did, I knew very few who had initiated the client to call us. Unless we were asked to, we never made a presentation or sales call on a single company. And the only advertising we did was a direct-mail piece, more in humor than a serious request for business. The piece took the form of a legal subpoena and was mailed in a plain envelope with no return address. The direct-mail piece was a lot of fun and caused a lot of talk, but not a single request for presentation resulted.

I do, however, remember clearly the origin of several shows. One came through a telephone call to me so early in the morning that I was still home. The caller was an executive with the local office of Standard Oil.

S. Oil: I understand you help write scripts for company meetings.

Don: Yes, I do.

S. Oil: Well, we have a meeting coming up next month. I have part of a script, but I think it needs some help— some rewrite or something.

Don: I see.

S. Oil: Do you have a portable typewriter?

Don: Yes—I do.

S. Oil: Well, bring it with you. Come to my office and I'll pay you fifty dollars.

Don: I'll be glad to come over and talk with you, but I won't bring my typewriter and I won't do anything for $50.00

S. Oil: Well ... all right, I guess. But be sure you don't talk with anyone else or say why you're here. Is that okay?

Don: I guess so—sure.

S. Oil: All right. 8:30 tomorrow morning. We're on Highway 12.

Don: I know where your office is. I'll be there tomorrow morning.

The next morning at his office, I learned what I had already suspected was true. He had agreed to write a script and then found he just couldn't do it. I suggested that he tell the others involved that he had decided to get some help. We arrived at a fair price and all went well.

Another industrial show that I remember how it originated was for the Semiconductor Division of Motorola in Arizona. Their regional sales manager for the Upper Midwest lived only two miles from the theater. When he suggested to the home office in Phoenix that we be engaged for their next sales meeting, the National Vice President of Sales requested that he bring me to the upcoming meeting of the company's nine regional sales managers, so I would have a good background for preparing the script, should I be hired.

I shall long remember the meeting: the Vice President of Sales, the nine regional sales managers and I gathered in a small meeting room at the Wigwam Resort. Early in the afternoon, the Vice President announced that to sell the new products just developed, the company had developed two different sales campaigns: Plan A and Plan B. He outlined both plans in detail, then announced:

Vice President: Now the home office and I have decided that whether we follow "A" or "B" will depend on your vote. The plan that receives the most votes will be the sales campaign for the year. It shall be determined in a democratic way by vote.

One of the Regional Sales Managers: You mean that here, this afternoon, our vote will decide whether we follow "A" or "B"?

Vice President: Exactly. You men are the "field" and no one knows better than you the best way in which to approach our prospects.

Another RSM: And we're going to vote now?

Vice President: Exactly. You have the information, we will now vote. All right. Those in favor of Plan "A."

(After vote)

Vice President: None in favor of Plan "A." All right, those in favor of Plan "B." *(Pause while counting)* Nine in favor of "B." All right, the vote has been taken. This coming year we will follow Plan "A."

Brave RSM: Just a minute, sir, I thought you said that the campaign would be determined by a democratic vote.

Vice President: Yes, I did.

Brave RSM: Well, there were nine of us and we all voted for Plan "B." Nine votes.

Vice President: I know that. The nine of you voted for Plan "B." What you're forgetting is that I, as Vice President, have ten votes. It will be Plan "A."

During the next several weeks, we prepared a script, rehearsed it with actors, singers, dancers and a small band. The show, presented at the Wigwam was so enthusiastically received that the company decided, with a few additions, it would be presented once again at a meeting that included the wives, aboard ship on a Caribbean Cruise. Included were all of our wives—wives of actors, singers, musicians and dancers. It was a glorious trip for all of us.

During the voyage, I was to write and rehearse another script, which would be presented at the hotel in our last scheduled port. It was only a short time since the island's control had been turned from the British to local citizens. Even at the hotel the change of command had not been fully realized. While we were rehearsing on the ball-room stage of the hotel, the captain of the dining room was trying, desperately, to find a wait staff. He had gone to the street to enlist everyone he saw.

Early in the afternoon, the haphazardly recruited prospects were herded into the dining room. If they found a uniform that fit, they, regardless of experience, were hired to serve the Motorola banquet that night. Watching them serve was like watching an old Laurel and Hardy comedy. The banquet resulted in evening gowns permanently ruined and men's formal wear that would not be cleaned until our return to the States.

The return to the States was in itself another adventure. A few miles out of Miami, the home port, two of the crew had jumped ship and swam ashore. This raised such wonder that when the ship finally docked, no crew or passenger could leave the ship until the port authorities could determine why the two men had jumped and what they may have taken with them and what they may have left behind. We were delayed for hours; it was Saturday early afternoon. Most of the singers, actors and musicians had jobs scheduled that night in Minneapolis; they had no choice but to catch their booked plane back to Minnesota. Their luggage was still aboard ship, so we urged them to catch the waiting bus for the airport and Ray Komischke, Russ Moore, Joan and I would bring their luggage home.

When the cast and the other passengers had left the dock, there were waiting for us 62 pieces of luggage. Of course, all chances of a new flight back to the Twin Cities was impossible. When the 62 pieces of luggage were loaded aboard the second bus, the bus waiting to take the four of us to a Miami hotel, we looked down the long pier to make certain we had loaded everything. Sixty yards from where our luggage had been stacked was a lone briefcase. Though it was not near where our luggage had been stacked, I had to see to whom it belonged.

I walked the sixty yards, checked the tag; it belonged to Bruce Neilson, our lead singer, and it contained all the music used aboard ship and at the final banquet.

When the four of us boarded the bus, the driver reported that he had been prepared for forty people and since there were only four of us and since we would be staying at a local hotel, and since we had helped load the bus, he was going to take us on a tour of Miami on the way to delivering us to the hotel.

The next morning when the four of us and our 62 pieces of luggage arrived at the Miami airport and the luggage loaded on two four-wheel carts, I told Russ to hold the carts back until I had a chance to talk to the Northwest desk about the extra luggage. At the desk, I happily discovered a young man who, for several years, had worked at the Twin Cities International Airport.

Desk: Good morning, Mr. Stolz. Have a nice trip?

Don: Yes, thank you. But I have ended up with a bit of a problem.

Desk: Well, perhaps I can help you.

Don: I certainly hope so. We were hired to do a show on a cruise. Coming back to Miami, the ship was delayed several hours. The musician and singers had to be back in Minneapolis for night jobs, and I was left behind with all their luggage.

Desk: That's no problem. They all had tickets. You're talking about their luggage so there won't even be an extra charge.

Don: Well, I certainly thank you.

(With that I signaled for Russ and Ray to bring up the two four-wheel carts—all 62 pieces.)

Desk: Oh, my God. All that? Oh, God. *(Pause while he collects himself)* Don't worry. I told you I'd take care of it and I will.

(End of Scene)

I did not check Bruce's briefcase and the music with the rest. I made it my carry-on.

This was not the only time during our travels that Bruce and his briefcase of music were separated. One cold and sleeting night as we were leaving Billings, halfway to the airport Bruce suddenly announced that he had left his briefcase back at the hotel. The taxi dropped the rest of us at the airport and took Bruce back to the hotel. He had not returned by the time the flight we were catching had landed and was disembarking passengers. The time of departure had arrived; no Bruce. The musicians and singers did everything they could to delay boarding the plane: emergency trips to the restroom, an unfinished phone call, a delay in receiving the cup of coffee they had ordered.

Finally the airport staff announced that if we weren't getting on the plane, they were leaving without us. We embarked as slowly as we could. Still no Bruce. The doors of the airplane were closed, the engines were started and the plane began its slow cross to the runway. Looking out the port window, one of the singers saw Bruce, now with briefcase, running, still with the hope of catching the plane. When he caught up and knocked on the tail let-down door, the crew very thoughtfully and accommodatingly stopped the plane, lowered the door and somewhat less than heartily welcomed him aboard.

Bruce and his luggage were not a good combination. When another meeting for Dairy Queen brought us back to Miami, Bruce, as had the rest of us, picked up his suitcase from the luggage carousel. At the hotel he opened it, and though it was an exact duplicate of his suitcase, it turned out to be the sample case for a spectacle salesman. During this time the spectacle salesman, at his hotel, had opened his case and found there Bruce's tuxedo, pajamas and music. Thank heavens, some way a quick exchange was made and we had music.

Medtronic. I have no idea how long ago it was when we did our first industrial show for Medtronic. Nor do I remember who first called us. Though most of the shows we did for them were at their headquarters, or an adjacent school auditorium, several were scheduled at attractive out-of-state locations such as the one at Frank Lloyd Wright's Taliesin West. It was a lovely museum, with one wing, however, in which file boxes were stored without order or care. Several of the executives of Medtronic thought it would be a great idea for Medtronic to donate $10,000 to the museum with the understanding the donation would be used to put the wing in order. One wise head said it was a good idea, but the idea might be insulting to the museum staff.

One year the communication staff of Medtronic had the idea that the show should contain a videotape of a space ship (*Star Wars*) with their three top officers, Bill George, Glen Nelson and Art Collins, guiding the ship through space. I wrote the skit, showing these three men discussing, then arguing, about which one of them was to be at the "con" (in charge of the flight). It was fun; it was funny. On the day we were to tape the scene, Bill George said to the other two, "We can't do this. This shows that the three of us don't agree about who's running the company." To which Glen Nelson replied, "That's just about true." "All right, but we don't want our people knowing that." Again Nelson replies, "Bill, if Don Stolz knows it, everybody knows it." The videotaped skit showing the three costumed and wearing the proper ears was a big hit with all of Medtronic.

"It's Not a Very Good Car" —Bob Aden

Early in July of 1967, Bob Aden, after several years as the director of the National Theater of South Africa, returned to the Old Log. A good friend—a dear friend—a good actor was back. The first show of the new year, 1968, *Luv*, starred Bob with two other great performers, John Varnum and Cleo Holladay. The author, Murray Schisgal, describes the locale as "New York City. A bridge." *Luv* may well be an interesting play, but I could never get over the fact that the second act, with very few changes, is just like the first act.

In the middle of the action, if one can describe what happens in *Luv* as action, while the characters are sitting on a bench on the bridge, a stray mongrel dog enters, moves to Harry Berlin (played by Bob Aden), raises his leg and urinates on the character's leg, then chases him across the stage where the actor climbs a bridge lamppost to escape further treatment.

Several weeks before rehearsals were to start, Bob Aden, being a lover of dogs, wisely suggested that since he was the one to receive this special attention, he should be the one to find the dog and train it. Bob went to the local veterinarian, Doctor Hotvet, a friend of his who had for years taken care of all of Bob's dogs. The veterinarian had already in his possession what he described as a very bright little animal that occasionally was used as the donor in canine blood transfusions. Aden took the little black mixed breed home with him, and in only a few days had trained him to approach him at the right angle, then follow him as he ran away. The training was successful beyond expectation. Bob climbed the pole; the dog remained at the base. The dog never urinated either on Bob or the lamppost, but hundreds of people would swear that they had actually seen it happen. Every night after the play I was asked two questions: How did you ever train the dog to lift his leg? Do you have to have Bob's trousers cleaned after every performance?

I can't leave *Luv* without telling what is to me a glorious example of an actor's dedication to the show. John

Luv; Cleo Holladay, Bob Aden, and John Varnum.

Varnum was to dive over the bridge's railing into what the audience imagined to be the river below. There was no way that I was even going to ask John Varnum to endanger his bones and flesh to perform such an act. I felt already guilty about exposing Aden's legs should little Twinkle make a mistake and actually urinate. So I went to a downtown gym and found there a young man who greatly resembled Varnum and was the same size. I dressed them both alike. It was a remarkable duplication. Every night, John would exit stage left. At the cue, the acrobat would run on, dive over the rail, and land out of sight on the mattress below. Needless to say I was quite proud of what I had worked out. Then one night it happened. What I had secretly worried about ever since *Luv* opened: the young acrobat was trapped in an automobile accident on the way to the theater. There were no cell phones in those days. All we knew was the acrobat was not there. We kept hoping he would appear at any moment. Finally we could hope no longer. I found John Varnum backstage and said, "John, he just isn't going to make it." I shall always remember John's reply: "Don't worry, I'll make the jump myself." I watched this actor whose exercise in the last ten years had been limited to walking, make a beautiful dive over the railing. It was the end of the act before I could determine that he landed safely—and with pride. The actor's belief that the show must go on was not yet dead.

For the second play in 1968, we found a comedy, *The Girl in the Freudian Slip*, that would rival *Under the Yum Yum Tree* in box office popularity. On dress rehearsal night there occurred one of those marvelous accidents that are so real and so funny that they become a part of the show for the entire run and all revivals thereafter. Bob, playing the part of a psychiatrist, is mixing a drink for a female nympho patient, who is calling on him not as a patient but rather as a woman who knows the doctor is attracted to her. When she asks him a question, Bob turns toward her, gestures with the hand holding the glass with the three ice cubes. The ice cubes, of course, go shooting across the room, with Bob, still attempting to maintain his professional sophistication, crawling after them.

Indeed, Bob Aden was back. The audience loved him as did every member of the cast and staff. Bob was home!

As the years have passed, I have concluded, that though there are close and lasting friendships in every business and profession, there are, to my thinking, three professions in which the friendships seem closer, stronger, and probably more lasting. The three professions are professional sport teams, musicians and actors. Friendships are so strong that every act of another is understood and if necessary, forgiven and accepted. With athletes and musicians, these strong friendships are a little easier because the different levels in skill are recognizable and measurable. That is not true with actors. Their skills are not measurable with the result that every actor thinks every part ever written is perfect for him; there is no actor in the world better than he.

But despite this, we are occasionally lucky enough to have passionate, long and enduring friendships. For the Stolz family, that friend is Bob Aden. It's not just that Bob was the man who hired me out of graduate school to come to the Old Log—it's the years we have spent working, laughing and crying together. There were times when I could have killed him too, but managed not to.

Early in the 1960s, Bob purchased a little house adjacent to the rear of the Old Log property. He made of it a delightful home, and was always building, always changing, always improving it. I had just returned home after a long weekend presenting an industrial show for Dairy Queen. The second I saw Bob, he said:

(Into scene)

Bob: Oh, Don, I'm glad you're home. How did the show go?

Don: Fine, just fine. We had some good …

Bob: *(Interrupting)* I want to show you something—
   something I've just done.

Don: *(Out of scene)* He walked me to the back of the theater
   lot to his lot.

Bob: There it is. What do you think?

Don: Well—

Bob: My new garage.

Don: Yes—

Bob: What do you think of it?

Don: Well, I'm surprised.

Bob: I thought you would be,

Don: You've built your garage on theater property.

Bob: I know that, but I didn't think you'd mind.

(End of scene)

And you know, I really didn't mind. Not until the late '70s when Bob sold his property to someone else and moved to Texas. He hated Minnesota winters.

Early one year, I wanted to present a new play, which had a great role for Bob. I telephoned him in San Antonio, and he responded that he would love to be in it, but could only stay for three months. He had another engagement that he couldn't change. "All right," I told him, "It's such a perfect role for you that I would really like for you to open in it, get the word of mouth going, and we would replace you after three months." He liked the idea, and I sent him a copy of the script. Bob arrived on schedule; we rehearsed and opened the show. It was a fine production. The first week of the run was not completed when Bob came to me and said:

Bob: Don, I think maybe I forgot to tell you that next week I'm going to New Orleans for Mardi Gras.

Don: You're what?

Bob: Going to Mardi Gras.

(Don is stunned)

Bob: I've got it all figured out. It will be simple. You have to have a replacement for me in three months—whoever you're going to get for that, have him replace me for the week I'll be gone.

The only thing I could think of was "murder." We had just opened a play, now we had to go back in replacement rehearsal. Since I didn't have with me any proper weapon for murder, I just walked away. I didn't speak to Bob for three days. Not feeling very happy with my attitude, I decided I should wish Bob an adventurous Mardi Gras. I found Aden in his dressing room.

Don: Bob, you're leaving tonight or tomorrow morning?

Bob: Tomorrow morning.

Don: Well, if you need a ride to the airport, I'd be very happy to drive you there.

Bob: Oh—I'm not flying.

Don: Oh. How are you getting there?

Bob: I'm driving your car.

And he did. I'd like for you to know what he said a week later, when he got back from New Orleans.

Bob: Don, that car of yours?

Don: Yes?

Bob: It's not a very good car. The gas tank is too small and it doesn't get good mileage.

Bob was a dear friend, generous, loyal, fun, and a splendid actor. You can't say more than that about anybody.

When our five-year-old son, Peter, was in Eitel hospital after a tracheotomy, Bob went to Dayton's and bought an electric train. He delivered the train to the patient in the hospital, tied a string to the

Treasure Island; (on bridge) Mark Bradley, and Jan Puffer; (on deck) Tim Sharp, Russ Konstans, and Chris Richards.

Treasure Island; Bob Aden and Chris Richards.

locomotive and led Peter up and down the hallway pulling the train. He pleased Peter tremendously and displeased the nurses the same amount. The incident also resulted in Peter's being released from the hospital a week early.

Another time, for three-year-old Timmy, Bob again walked into the toy department of Dayton's, purchased a giant red rocking horse and carried it out to where Joan was waiting in the station wagon.

When Bob was 80 years old, he came to Excelsior, hoping we'd have a role for him. Anticipating this, Will Kenzie, an Old Log associate in charge of matinee sales, had found a wonderful one-character English play, entitled **Old Herbaceous**, the story of a gardener at one of England's finest manor houses. Bob was wonderful. Jon and Tim built a temporary stage in the dining room that was just exactly right. With Anita O'Sullivan's help, I directed, ran the sound board and the light board. Opening night was special. The audience sat at the dining room tables, on which we had placed small pots of flowers. They were enchanted before we ever opened. Aden was in great form. As I was following the script, I suddenly became aware that Bob, some way or other, had lost his way and was now in the middle of the second act, having skipped entirely the intermission. Bob's performance had been so charming—so winning—that only two people asked how they had missed intermission.

I should add, despite Bob's 80 years, he not only performed **Old Herbaceous** on Monday and Tuesday nights, but also appeared twice a day for six week days in our play for children, *Treasure Island*, in which he played two different characters.

These were not the performances of a tottering old man—they were the performances of an able, compelling actor, the soul of the Old Log.

Bob died June 1, 2005. He had requested that his ashes be scattered on the grounds surrounding the original Old Log building. This we did on the first anniversary of his death.

In his book *The Way It Was*, his story of the first three years of the Old Log Theater, Bob wrote: "Though I may avoid Minnesota winters, my heart is bound to this little spot of the world."

When I look back at the cast lists of those plays in the '60s and see listed Bob Aden, Ken Senn, John Varnum, Richard Dix, Warner Lahtinen, Cleo Holladay, Ann Blager, Valedia Hill, Marge Snell (as well as other available performers), I can't but believe—I can't but "know"—that we had assembled one of the most talented, capable companies that was ever put together. And every one of them loved by the audience. They were so versatile that casting and producing every show was a joy. And it was easy. As I have said again and again, "Nothing helps a director more than having a good cast."

During the winter of 1968–69, there were two Viking football players who became regular patrons of the Old Log: Tommy Mason and Bill Brown. Immediately our young sons, particularly Timmy, became great fans. And for good reason. Brown and Mason would pick up their tickets, leave their dates in the lobby and go with the

Star Spangled Girl; Richard Paul, Nancy Nelson, and Tommy Mason.

boys back to what is now the dining room and discuss the upcoming Viking season. Never have two players done more to deserve their following.

Some time in March, Timmy suggested that Tommy Mason had told him he had always wanted to be in a play, and Tim suggested "it would be nice" if that could happen at the Old Log. I liked the idea. Tommy Mason had been an All-American running back at Tulane, was the number one draftee in the first NFL draft, had been named all-pro, and was engaged to a Lake Minnetonka girl. He was an exciting player to watch.

For his play, we selected *Star Spangled Girl*, not the best of Neil Simon's writings, but with a good role for Mason. He attacked his role diligently, determined to give a good performance. He appreciated the help of the other two members of the cast, Nancy Nelson and Richard Paul. *Star Spangled Girl* was a box office success that ran for seven weeks.

For some years, Breezy Point Resort, and a number of citizens of the neighboring Nisswa, had repeatedly requested that we do a short summer season at the resort. With the cast of *Star Spangled Girl* requiring only three actors and leaving our "strong regulars" not playing, we decided that the summer of 1969 was the time for a season at Breezy Point. In finalizing the arrangements, we found that there was only one cabin for rent and that the only way to secure living quarters for the men in the cast was to buy a cabin—which we did, and sold at the end of the summer for a small profit.

We scheduled three plays for the Breezy Point season: *The Girl in the Freudian Slip*, *Marriage Go Round* and *Star Spangled Girl* (without Tommy Mason, of course). The actors who spent the better part of the summer there included John Varnum, Bob Aden, Julie Hines, Valedia Hill and Anita Anderson. No one enjoyed it more than did Bob Aden, who loved living in our new lakeside cabin.

Back in Excelsior, the play scheduled to follow *Star Spangled Girl* was a third production of *Life With Father*. The four oldest Stolz sons played the Day sons. To my knowledge no production of this play anywhere has ever had the Day sons all played by brothers.

Along with Ken Senn (Father Day of course), they all again had to have their hair dyed red. Since the play ran until the middle of August, they all returned to school with hair that was an ugly mixture of faded red, bleached blond and traces of the original brown. Little Jon, who had no desire whatsoever to have his hair bleached and then dyed, did, however, feel left out—the only Stolz son not in the play. We found an easy solution when we were reminded that the Roosevelt family had lived only a few doors from the Day family. We had Jon come in while the Day family was having breakfast and asked Mother Day:

Jon: Mrs. Day—

Mrs. Day: Yes, Franklin?

Jon: After breakfast, can Harland come out and play?

Mrs. Day: Certainly.

(Jon leaves)

Father: Who was that, anyway?

Mrs. Day: You know who it was—little Franklin Roosevelt.

Father: Oh, yes.

In preparing to cast **Cactus Flower**, the next play on our schedule, I looked over our "talented, capable, versatile" and discovered that the one thing lacking was a juvenile—a young leading man. I went through the resumes we had received over the last months preparing for New York auditions, and made reservations on Northwest for the trip to Manhattan.

PHONE RINGS

I happened to be in the box office and answered.

Don: Good afternoon, the Old Log Theater.

Nick: I'm calling from Arizona and I'd like to talk with Don Stolz.

Don: This is Don.

Nick: Well, I'm an actor out here at the Arizona Rep. They keep telling me about Bob Aden and you and the Old Log, and I'd like to work there.

Don: How old are you?

Nick: Twenty-six.

Don: Are you a member of Actor's Equity?

Nick: No, but I'm eager to join. I can come there for an audition.

Don: Well, let me say, I was leaving the day after tomorrow for New York to audition for a young leading man. If you can be here before then ...

Nick: I'll be there tomorrow.

Don: You sure?

Nick: Very. See you tomorrow.

Don: Just a minute—

Nick: Yes?

Don: You never gave me your name.

Nick: Sorry, guess that's important, isn't it? My name is Nolte—Nick Nolte.

As you may already know, in 1960, Nick came to the Old Log and played Igor Sullivan, the young leading man in *Cactus Flower*.

Nick was here for the better part of three years, and appeared in seventeen different plays. The two most outstanding of those roles was David in *Catch Me If You Can* and in that great Ayckbourne play, *How the Other Half Loves*. A third memorable performance was his appearance as a prince in the play for children.

Nick became immediately a member of the community. He played on the Excelsior baseball team and on one of the touch-football teams. Nick could kick the football farther than anyone I have ever seen. He was a hard-working actor: diligent and studious. He was never late for performance; never late for rehearsal. He liked to rehearse. I liked having him in the cast; if there is anything a director likes it's an actor who likes to rehearse. Nick Nolte worked hard, Nick Nolte played hard. There isn't a young lady in Excelsior who doesn't say, "I used to date Nick Nolte." And there isn't a one of them who's lying. Again—it was an exciting time.

Cactus Flower, which ran for six weeks in 1969, was followed by a new release, *Lovers and Other Strangers*, an evening of four one-acts. The first starred our new young leading man, Nick Nolte and Nancy Nelson. Bob Aden and Felicia Soper played a married couple

How the Other Half Loves; Adrian Kent, Cleo Holladay, John Varnum, Nick Nolte, Ken Senn, and Ann Blager.

The Christmas Show for children. Nick Nolte is Prince Charming standing behind the King, Jim Horsewill flanked by Malcolm Dick. The Princess is Shelly Chall.

who were arguing about whose turn it was to start making advances. Bob Aden had desired, with my approval, to wear a hairpiece. It worked well until on opening night, Bob leaped out of bed and the hairpiece went flying. During the loud and long lasting laughter that followed, Bob and Felicia just stood looking at one another. After the show, Felicia told her fellow actors, "it was like looking deep into the soul of the other actor." It worked well, as I reported, opening night; it worked just as well every night during the five-week run. Later in the run, after leaping out of bed and losing his hairpiece, Bob finds that the zipper on the pair of trousers that he is attempting to hurriedly put on won't zip, so he, in his anger, ties the two sides together. It's a shame that he didn't discover this hilarious bit of business earlier in the run.

During 1969, the most popular theater presentation across America was a little musical based on a comic strip by former Minnesotan, Charles M. Schulz, *You're a Good Man Charlie Brown*. Wanting always to increase our reach, I started inquiries concerning the rights to produce it at the Old Log. I wrote Arthur Whitelaw, the New York producer. Mr. Whitelaw, after telling me that no such rights were available, suggested what he considered a great idea— bring the number one road company into our theater for a run of six weeks. He, himself, would come out to review the show, to make certain that it was absolutely fresh, and would bring with him the original set designer to make certain that the sets, though limited to "set pieces," would also be fresh and attractive. Negotiations led to agreement.

Mr. Whitelaw was even better than his word; he also brought with him one of New York's finest publicists, who came close to suicide when he could not get one word of publicity through the *Star Tribune*. The paper refused to even announce that the production was coming to town. Not one word. Why? I do not know. At the suggestion of the publicist, we took out a large (large for us) ad for the Sunday edition. Again for reasons I do not know, they printed the ad upside down. It was obvious that the *Star Tribune* did not like what we were doing and were going to show us so. *You're a Good*

Man Charlie Brown was not reviewed until next to the last week; it was not favorable, even describing the freshly painted set pieces as "worn and tacky."

It was an experience to be remembered. In addition to the lack of publicity, January of 1970 was the coldest in Minnesota history since the winter we were in the Woman's Club. We lost $50,000. Thank God the plays that followed were box office successes.

One of the largest of these "box office successes" was our fourth production of *The Odd Couple* starring Ken Senn and John Varnum. It was certainly an appropriate choice; we knew it would be good box office—and it marked the 25th anniversary of Ken Senn at the Old Log. Ken Senn was the first actor in the history of American theater ever to be at the same theater for 25 years. Since then every Stolz at the Old Log has equaled that mark, but in 1970, Ken's 25th anniversary stood alone. For the printed program I wrote: "For a quarter of a century, Ken has amused, delighted, charmed, moved, enlightened and inspired Old Log audiences and his fellow actors. I think he is one of the country's most gifted performers, and to his work he has brought the talent of a genius, the sensitivity of an artist and the dedicated commitment of a man who lives his vocation." I wrote what I knew to be true.

Ken's father had for years been a leader in the Minnesota Republican Party. Ken followed in his footsteps, so it was absolutely to be expected that someone (not a member of the Old Log and not Ken himself) sent a copy of the program praising Ken to President Richard Nixon and asked that he send an autographed picture to Senn. Nixon was happy to do this and on the photograph wrote: "To Ken Senn. Congratulations on your 25 years' performance at the Old Log Theater, and best wishes. Richard Nixon."

Ken, of course, had the photograph framed and hung in the lobby close to the box office. He would stand near the picture every night before going backstage to prepare for the evening's performance.

I decided it was time for payback, so I wrote Hubert Humphrey telling him that I felt in my own theater I was entitled to equal time, and asked him to send an autographed picture with the following inscription "To Don Stolz. Congratulations on your being able to put up with Ken Senn for 25 years." Humphrey immediately complied with the message written on a charming picture of him and his wife, Muriel. In an accompanying letter he said, "Thank you for giving me the opportunity of keeping the Old Log Theater bipartisan."

Today, both pictures and both letters are famed and hanging in our lobby.

The Odd Couple was followed by a light (very light) comedy, *Love and Kisses*. It marked the first appearance at the Old Log of a very pretty young lady, Julie Hines, in the role of Rosemary. She had auditioned the summer before and we had cast her in our Breezy Point production of *The Girl in the Freudian Slip*. In *Love and Kisses*, there were two actors who would within a few years find success in Hollywood: Julie Hines who would be featured on the Bob Newhart show and Nick Nolte about whom no more need be said.

It should be mentioned that by 1970, we were serving "light suppers," which featured steakburgers or ham on a bun, served with either potato salad or baked beans. And they were delicious.

Also it was in the late '60s that the log cabin across the drive from the front entrance to the theater was converted into the "Too Much Too Soon" bar. The chief difficulty with the "Too Much Too Soon" bar was that it attracted drinkers who had been asked to leave the bars in downtown Excelsior.

The year 1970 ended with a repeat production of *Don't Drink the Water*. In the fall of that year, we knew we were going to need more good male actors, so we asked our friend, Richard Dix, if he could return for the winter season. He replied he could; all he needed was a nice apartment for him and his wife, Nancy. We told him to prepare for his return even though we knew that "nice apartments" were not easy to find in Excelsior. We learned that there was an apartment available in the building that had been the Catholic Church. When I telephoned the manager of what was now an apartment building, he said that yes, there was an apartment for rent, so I asked him if

I could come over and look at it. When he agreed, Joan and I drove her car and took Henry, our Basset Hound with us. (When we got in her convertible, the dog jumped into the car, too.) We looked at the apartment. It was clean and "nice." We told the manager we would like to rent it for a couple that would be coming into Excelsior the next week. He agreed; it was settled. Then he said:

Manager: What's your name again? I'm sorry, I've forgotten it.
Don: Don Stolz.
Manager: Don Stolz. And what do you do?
Don: I operate the Old Log Theater.
Manager: The Old Log Theater—what's that?
Don: We present plays—live actors—plays.
Manager: Well, where is it?
Don: Well, if you're driving to Lyman Lodge, you go right by it.
Manager: Oh. I drive past there twice a day.
Don: Stop by some time.
Manager: I'll do that. I'll walk out to your car with you. Your name again was … ?
Don: Stolz—Don Stolz.
Manager: Oh, yes.

(By then we were outside. Henry was standing in the front seat of the car with his front feet resting on the padded dash. The apartment manager took one look at the dog and enthusiastically said:)

Manager: Why, there's Henry. Hi, Henry.

I couldn't get over it: the Old Log had been in existence since 1940; the manager had never heard of it; I thought I was one of Excelsior's best known citizens; the manager had never heard of me, but he knew my dog by name. I suppose it's good to have one's self-esteem punched every so often. Driving home, Joan couldn't stop laughing at the man who had never heard of me but knew Henry.

In truth, I should not have been surprised. Everyone in town knew Henry and loved him. There were no leashing laws then, so Henry was free to roam. Almost every day he walked into Excelsior where he visited the butcher shop, where he was given a bone and then on to the pet store where he would pick up whatever treat he wanted. At the end of each month, the pet store would send me a bill covering everything Henry had selected.

Henry liked to spend his time in downtown Excelsior, usually on one of the wooden benches. But occasionally he would lie down in the middle of the street. The police would then call Joan and say, "Mrs. Stolz, we think your dog has hormone troubles. He's in the middle of the intersection and we can't get him to move. You'd better come get him."

Henry was a true hound; true to his breed. He knew where every female dog in the area lived and exactly when he would be welcome to call on her. If he was not home at nightfall, I would get in the car and go looking for him. After a time, I, too, knew where every female dog lived.

One morning—two o'clock in the morning—the doorbell rang. I looked out the window and there in the drive was a police car. I knew all of our sons were home, so I couldn't imagine why they were there. When I answered the door, Big Charlie said, "Don, I have a friend of yours in the backseat of the car. I picked him up for being drunk and disorderly. It's Henry."

One night when I was out looking for Henry, I was again stopped by Big Charlie, the policeman. "Well, Don, out looking for your dog is better than being out late at night looking for one of your sons."

We had by now another dog, a Siberian Husky—a beautiful dog. She had been given to me between acts at the Old Log. She never left our yard, except the few times she accompanied Henry into town, I think with the hope that she could get him home at a proper time. The weekly paper took a picture of the two on Water Street and published it in their paper with the caption "The two ambassadors of Excelsior."

In 1971, we repeated some of my favorite shows, *The Biggest Thief in Town, Look Homeward Angel, The Girl in the Freudian Slip*. Looking back, I am most proud of having selected Arthur Miller's *The Price* and then presented what, even being modest, was a tremendous production. Though *The Price* had been done at a number of theaters in New York as well as the Guthrie, none of them could compare to our cast:

Love and Kisses; Julie Duffy (a.k.a. Julie Hines)
and Tom Stolz.

The two Stolz dogs, Tania and Henry, on
their daily inspection of Excelsior.

Play It Again, Sam; Cindy Subby, Loni Anderson, Don Ruble, Holly Melser, Linda Wohlrabe, Margo Weckesser, Nancy Nelson, and Susan Hammond.

The Patrick Pearse Motel; Loni Anderson and Ross Bickel.

Richard Dix as Victor Franze, Felicia Soper (an absolutely stunning actress, one that Charlie Boone called the best he had ever seen) as the wife, Esther, John Varnum as the brother, Walter, and the perfectly cast Bob Aden as Gregory Solomon.

In 1972, as the third play of the year, we presented *Relatively Speaking*, the first Ayckbourne play to be seen in the United States. Not only was it a memorable play by a magnificent playwright, but it was also responsible for another of Bob Aden's accidents that were so natural and so funny that they became a part of future productions. Bob, as master of the manor, was sitting on the terrace having breakfast. His belt had caught in one of the ironwork curls of the back of the chair; when he stood, the chair came right up with him.

In late May of 1973, it was time to cast *Play it Again Sam*, not the first time we had produced it. I list this play because in some way, we had been able to collect one of the most beautiful groups of young women ever seen on the Old Log stage: Cindy Subby, Nancy Nelson, Linda Wohrabe, Holly Malzer, Susan Hammond, Margo Wickesser and the then dark-haired Loni Anderson. As a brunette, Loni was more exotic than ever she has been since being a blonde. Loni had the most beautiful and natural smile. One could point at her and say "smile" and she could and look absolutely natural doing it. She was a beauty. I remember John Varnum, who was more than a few years older than Loni, said, "Loni is about as beautiful an OLDER woman as I have ever met." We featured Loni in our next play too, *The Patrick Pearse Motel*.

FARM:
GOOD DEED BECOMES A TRAGEDY

The mortgage on the new Old Log building originated in 1960 and was to be paid in full by 1970. Up to the mid-sixties, payment had gone reasonably well despite an occasional past due monthly payment. Northwestern National Life was always considerate and understanding; the last thing they wanted was a foreclosure.

It was some time in 1966 that Harry Kuechle told us that when the mortgage was satisfied, it might well be that he and Grace would like to sell the property to us, so Joan and I, for the first time, started attempting to save money. We weren't as unsuccessful as our future life might reflect.

During the next three years the Kuechles said nothing more about selling the property, until one day Harry told me that he probably would sell the property to us some day, but would prefer to postpone that action. What we had carefully saved we decided to carefully keep for when the day to buy might come.

For the first time in our lives Joan and I had a little money in the bank, and for the first time since we were married, we had no dog. The beautiful bloodhound we had purchased several years earlier from a small kennel west of Chicago had been hit by a speeding car. The woman who had bred and sold to us this wonderful dog, had moved to somewhere near Baraboo, Wisconsin.

That fall, Joan, Tim, Jon and I were driving to South Bend to visit Joan's parents and to see a Notre Dame football game. And we had hoped to look for a dog when we approached the middle of

Wisconsin. So when we reached a small Wisconsin town just a few miles west of Baraboo, Joan suggested we stop and see if anyone knew Hilda, the Bloodhound lady. By then it was ten p.m. so the only place open was a typical tacky, small town bar.

We ordered some beer and asked the three Wisconsinites present if they knew where we would find Hilda and her bloodhounds. One of the men replied that he didn't know Hilda, but he drove a delivery route up County Road E, where he often heard baying, something he had long ago determined to be bloodhounds.

When he continued to assure us it was County Road E—just off of Highway 12, we quickly swallowed our beer and went on our way. Near the Baraboo Munitions Works, we found County Road E and followed a pickup truck as it turned off of 12. A mile or two up County E, the pickup truck turned into a farmyard. I decided to follow him up his drive to ask him if he would know where the bloodhounds lived. He certainly did, but there was no way he could give us directions that would enable us to find it. If we followed him, he would guide us there.

Though it was almost midnight, we found the house lights on and saw activity inside. Hilda invited us in and introduced us to a friend, the wife of the other couple living in the same house and working the farm with them. The two men, having to go to work early the next morning at the Munitions Works, were still working in the field.

Hilda showed us her kennel of hounds, none of which was for sale, but she was expecting a fine litter from the bitch that was pregnant. After some time with the dogs, every one of which Joan liked, Hilda told us the men would soon be coming back to the house and urged us to please wait to say hello to Felix, her husband, and meet the other man. By the time Felix and the other man got in, it was so late they urged us to spend the night. It was the coldest, most miserable night we have ever spent. The next morning at breakfast, we met five foster children that the two families were caring for.

The next day, as we continued our drive to South Bend, I said to Joan and our two boys, "Last night was an important illustration.

These two men, working a full and sometimes overtime schedule at the Munitions Factory, out until midnight working in the field, taking care of five foster children, all living in the same house—it sure proves that ambition and the desire to find a living still exists in this country."

During the next two years, Hilda and Felix would occasionally visit us at our home in Greenwood. They became even better friends. As I remember, it was the year after that when Joan and I visited Hilda and Felix at the farm they shared. During our visit they told us of a great dairy farm next door that had just been offered for sale. We drove to the farm. I suppose it needed some work, but to Felix and me it looked good. When I asked Hilda and Felix why they didn't buy it, they replied that they would certainly like to. After all, two families living in the same house wasn't an ideal situation, but there was no way they could afford it. They had no money for the down payment. They could meet the monthly payment, but had nothing to put down.

That night when Joan and I were alone, she suggested that we should take what we had saved and make the down payment; we could then sell the farm to them on a contract-for-deed.

The next morning we met with Felix and Hilda. They assured us that if we were so helpful as to do that, they would have no trouble paying both the mortgage and the contract-for-deed payments.

We then went to the Baraboo National Bank. I introduced myself to Robert Kent, the President, told him what we wanted to do and asked him to arrange the purchase the mortgage and the appropriate contract. Mr. Kent agreed to take care of everything. One of our financial references was Jack Haertel a broker in Minneapolis. When the president of the bank called Jack, he was told, "If you won't lend them the money, I will." That's all it took. I never realized banks were that easy.

The closing date was arranged. We met in the conference room of the bank: the elderly man and wife selling the farm, the man and wife buying the farm, the man and wife making the down payment, and the banker, Robert Kent.

The elderly farmer seller told us of the 125 years his family had spent as dairy farmers on the property, and as he was finishing his story he started to weep. I don't mean "cry." I mean "weep." It was heartbreaking. Finally, I could speak:

> **Don:** Now, please, please, know if you don't want to sell, don't. It won't bother us. Felix and Hilda can wait until another nearby farm is for sale. So don't sell.

> **Farmer's Wife:** He'd better sell. I'm not living on that damn, god-forsaken farm another day. If you don't buy it, someone else well. So he's selling.

The papers were signed with sobs still racking the farmer's body. He sold. It was a dreadful picture I couldn't forget. The next week, I called the banker and told him how I regretted the whole transaction, and I asked if he had seen the farmer since. He replied that he wished I hadn't called. Just that morning, the farmer had taken his shotgun, put the end of the barrel in his mouth and shot his head off.

Joan and I couldn't but feel we were responsible.

Months passed. Felix and Hilda had not only not paid us anything on the contract, but they also had not made even one mortgage payment. After six months the bank called me and urged that I foreclose; that the farm was worth thousands of dollars more than the price we had paid. If we wouldn't foreclose, they would have to. We told them to arrange for a meeting with Felix and Hilda and us for the next Wednesday at the bank.

Our attorney at that time was John McNulty, who kept telling me that he didn't know how I could be so stupid as to get into this buying a farm for another family. He stopped such talk when I reminded him that it wasn't many years before when he had co-signed a loan for me. Appeased he might have been, but not enough to keep from insisting that he was going to Baraboo with us, and to make the trip as quickly as possible. He and Bill Kuechle would fly us there in the plane of which they were two of the owners. Joan and I were almost looking forward to the flight until we learned that John was going to practice "instrument flying" from takeoff to landing. It was not a pleasant trip, topped off with the roughest landing ever made at any Wisconsin airport. Even Bill Kuechle was a little shaken by the number of bounces off and back on the ground. After we were definitely and finally on the earth, Bill, now able to breathe, said "John, you have to remember the comfort of your passengers."

The meeting at the bank was even rougher, only this time it was not McNulty who was responsible for the turbulence. This time the turbulent maker was a newcomer to the group, someone we had never before met—Felix's father. Even before we had time to taste our bank-provided coffee, Felix's father announced that he was buying the farm for his son and was ready to make whatever payment was necessary to clear the title and have him recorded as the owner. Not Felix, but him. There was nothing to do, but do it.

While flying home from Baraboo to the Flying Cloud Airport, I couldn't clear my feeling that what had transpired at the meeting was not leading to a happy ending. Two weeks later we learned that Felix's father had thrown Felix and Hilda off the farm and rented it, with the option to buy, to another dairy farmer. Four weeks after that, Felix and Hilda divorced. But even this was not the end.

During the months from our first contact with the Baraboo Bank until the sale to Felix's father, the Stolzs and the Kent family found a warm and easy relationship. I think it started when, shortly after meeting Mr. Kent and his wife, Amanda, I had suggested they be our guests for dinner and theater at the Old Log. They had heard about the Old Log and were pleased to accept. The first visit was followed by several more. One thing about operating a theater—it furnishes an easy way to extend an invitation to people you like and an easy acceptance by the invitee. We enjoyed the company of Bob and Amanda.

They in turn invited us to the Baraboo Community Theater's production of **South Pacific**, which was to be presented in the Ringling Theater. The Ringling Theater had been built during the most prosperous times of the Barnum, Bailey and Ringling Brothers Circus. In those years the theatrical road companies liked to stop in Baraboo for a number of performances because Baraboo was halfway between

Chicago and the Twin Cities. The theater building had been beautifully maintained, with the red upholstered chairs still in place in the boxes, and the red with gold trim front curtain.

The Baraboo Community Theater production of **South Pacific** was amateur, of course, but it was good. And most enjoyable. The chorus of nurses in the production, played mostly by Wisconsin farm girls, looked exactly like the nurses I had met in the Pacific during World War Two.

The middle of the next summer after the sale to Felix's father, I walked from our house on Meadville to the theater, happily accompanied by our Siberian Huskie, Tanya. It was a bright, sunny, delightful morning. As soon as I walked into my office, my secretary handed me a note with the name and telephone number of a Minneapolis banker. "He said you didn't know him but he would like very much for you to return his call just as soon as you got here."

Don: Mr. Peterson—Ray Peterson, please.

Ray: This is Ray.

Don: This is Don Stolz, returning your call.

Ray: Thank you. I have bad news, but I thought I should call you, rather than letting you read it in the paper. I understand you and your wife were friends with the Kents of Baraboo.

Don: Yes, that's right.

Ray: For years the Kents and their bank have been business associates with our bank. Well, late yesterday afternoon, Bob and Amanda got in their new RV to start on their two-week vacation. Just as they turned onto Highway 12, a speeding truck hit them. Both Mr. and Mrs. Kent were killed instantly.

What Joan and I had thought would be a good deed turned into a tragedy from the beginning until the end.

If we learned anything, it was that one shouldn't save money, because you'll probably only do something stupid with it.

Box Office One: Did You Ever Dedicate a Flagpole?

Back in the early seventies, the Old Log Box Office was still controlled—and I mean "controlled"—by Rupert LaBelle, who was also our number one character man. If Rupert was not in the current play, he would arrive by taxi from his quite attractive apartment over the Super Value Store. Rupert had established a definite routine with the cab company; they were to pick him up on Water Street in front of the steps leading to his second floor dwelling every day at exactly 1:50, so he could arrive at the theater before two o'clock. Once there, he would stay until the show was over.

Rupert was, unapologetically, a lover of cats. And, as quite often happens in such cases, cats loved him. Demonstratively loved him. Since the landlord at Rupert's apartment did not allow pets, Rupert's cat lived at the Old Log Theater. Rupert unwaveringly insisted that the cat was toilet trained, using the same toilets as did our customers in the evening. Though there were some of us who doubted this, we never found any evidence to prove otherwise.

As stated, the cat loved Rupert. Each day the cat waited impatiently for Rupert to arrive. When the taxi brought his master to the theater, the cat knew when that cab crossed St. Alban's Bay Bridge. The cat knew. His impatience became a frenzy, which was not relieved until Rupert walked through the theater door. Whatever Rupert's first task, it was always performed while he sat on a high stool behind the box office counter. As soon as he was seated, the beloved and loving cat climbed to his usual position—curled up around Rupert's neck across his shoulders. He stayed there for hours. One night the cat found its way through the door to the outside. No one noticed. The next morning, its body was found on Minnetonka Blvd., where it had been run over.

In some manner, Rupert concealed his grief. I do remember so well his saying to me, "I miss him. I greatly miss him, but I'm never going to have another cat. It hurts too much when you lose them."

Two days had not passed before a cat, never seen before, appeared, walked into the theater and climbed up on Rupert's lap. None of us ever questioned how, when or why. You don't question anything that may be heaven sent.

From his first rehearsal on that original three-week contract, Rupert LaBelle was a favorite of his fellow actors. In the box office he was a favorite of every customer who ever came to the Old Log. It is no wonder then, that one summer when we were still in the original building, Rupert, in a capricious mood, shaved off half of his mustache to see who would be the first actor to notice. Two days passed and no one had noticed.

In the box office, Rupert had a remarkable talent for combining the face with the right name. The second time you came to the Old Log, the chances were that Rupert would remember your name and have your tickets in his hand as you approached the counter. If you were an attractive woman, it happened after your first visit. On stage, it was not the same. When doing a new show every week, actors will tell you that the last thing they memorize is the names of the various characters in the play. They seem to hold to the dogma that if you learn the rest of your lines, God will guide you through the maze of proper nouns. Not necessarily so.

One memorable night, Mr. LaBelle—on stage—as a most important part of the play, was to place a telephone call to a Senator Harrison. As Rupert was dialing, he suddenly realized that he couldn't recall the Senator's name. Even worse, he had no idea what his own name was supposed to be. Full of hope and a belief in the supernatural, Rupert kept right on dialing. After the appropriate interval he was ready and came out with the show-saving line, "Hello

Senator … oh, good, you recognized my voice."

This was not the only time that Rupert failed to remember the name of the character he was playing; it was not the only time that quick wit came to the rescue of slow memory. Several years later, we were doing the classic comedy, **Harvey**, with Rupert cast in the role of the doctor at the institution to which the aunt of Elwood Dowd was trying to get Elwood committed. I hope you remember the scene when Elwood first reported for an admittance exam. Doctor Chumley is questioning Elwood to properly fill out the necessary forms. After a series of somewhat indifferent questions, Elwood suddenly starts questioning the doctor. "Who are you?" asks Elwood. Every night Rupert would turn and look at the door of his office downstage right, and read his name right off the door: "I am Doctor Albert Chumley." All was well, until the night when the crew in changing the set forgot to put the doctor's sign on the door. This night, when the question came, Rupert, as usual, turned to the door down right, expecting to see there his name. No sign. Hesitating no more than a second, he replied, "Who am I? I—I am—I am the head of this institution."

We first presented **Never Too Late** in 1965. (We repeated it in '67 and '79.) In his exit speech in Act One, Rupert omitted one of the lines. At intermission, the young actors, delighted to have something with which to bedevil Rupert, all quoted the line exactly and reminded Rupert that he had omitted it. After hearing enough of it, Rupert said to them, "All right—just forget it. Tomorrow night I'll get the line in twice." And he did.

I usually arrived at the theater a little before six, in time to help Rupert handle the dinner crowd. I suppose right here I should explain that in the theater, "crowd" is really an oxymoron. To us, "crowd" means anyone who happens to come in. And all too often the true meaning of "crowd" never applies.

I have arrived at no possible way to demonstrate what, on a busy night, the box office is like. Unless you have worked in the box office, there is no way you really know either your theater or its audience. In the '70s, Rupert was the box office.

In the following scene, the dinner "crowd" has all been checked in and ushered into the dining room; it is almost 30 minutes before the show-only guests begin to arrive. There is time to answer the phone and check the ticket envelopes, with a few minutes left over in which to exchange ideas.

Rupert: *(Just finishing a phone conversation. He is not too happy.)* You're welcome. *(Hands up)* The moron.

Don: One of those, hmm?

Rupert: I sold her two seats in the second row. "The second row? The second row from the front?" No wonder this country is in the mess it is—we've been dumbed down.

Don: I don't know, you may be right. Yesterday a woman called. She didn't know where she wanted to sit; she just wanted the best seats in the house.

Rupert: Middle of the seventh row.

Don: That's what I gave her. You know what she said? "Oh, I was thinking more like row eight."

Rupert: Women. You know when this country made its big mistake was in 1918. We should never have given them the right to vote.

Don: Rupert, expressing that view might very well get you killed.

Rupert: I know. I offered this same opinion last night to Pam Danser in the women's dressing room.

Don: Oh, boy.

Rupert: She said, "You mean you think we women have no rights." Of course I do. I think every woman should have the opportunity to select the one or two men to whom she is going to submit. Beyond that, nothing. I was lucky to get out of there alive.

Don: Rupert, you like women.

Rupert: One thing has absolutely nothing to do with the other.

Don: Pam's still speaking to me. I think she is.

Rupert: When you answer the phone, be very careful.

Don: Oh?

Rupert: I just had a call. When she asked what the play was this week, I said, *You Know I Can't Hear You When the Water's Running*. "Oh, I'm sorry, just hold on and I'll turn it off." Ten minutes before that call—almost the same thing. "What's the name of the play now playing?" The same answer: *You Know I Can't Hear You When the Water's Running*. Only this time she said, "Okay, I can hold on—you go turn it off." So when you answer the phone and they ask that question—I've learned my lesson. Just say, "The name of the play is _____."

Don: It's almost as bad as when they're standing right here. Last night this very pretty young lady came up and asked, "Can you tell me what the next play is?" I was busy pouring coffee, so I very quickly said, *Not Now Darling*. For a moment I thought her boyfriend was coming after me—right over the counter. He was big, too.

Phone rings

Don: Good evening, the Old Log Theater.

Woman: Yes.

Don: May I help you?

Woman: I hope so. We've been having an argument. I know you're busy, it's almost time for the show to begin, but I have a question and I just couldn't wait until tomorrow to ask you.

Don: I understand. What's the question?

Woman: Well—back in the early sixties you had just moved into the new building, as I remember, and you did a show that had the name of a big animal.

Don: The name of a big animal?

Woman: Yes. The big animal didn't have a thing in the world to do with the play, but the play was named after this big animal. I think the big animal was an elephant. My husband says it was a water buffalo. So my question is—and I do hate to bother you at this busy time of night—

but which was it, an elephant or a water buffalo? The animal had nothing at all to do with the plot. It was either a water buffalo or an elephant. I remember it as an elephant.

Don: How about rhinoceros? *The Rhinoceros?*

Woman: That's it. I knew it wasn't a water buffalo. And thank you. I think I should also tell you—I really didn't care for it.

Don: I'm sorry.

Woman: Thank you anyway. *(Hangs up)*

Don: Sometimes you wonder—why?

Rupert: And sometimes you just wonder. You think "The Elephant"—we could sell to Republicans?

Don: Did you bring that thing with you?

Rupert: The thing I wrote?

Don: Yes.

Rupert: I did, but I don't know. It's old fashioned. Out of date. People don't feel like that anymore.

Don: Well, they should. That's the reason I asked you for a copy.

Rupert: You're not going to read it to the actors, are you?

Don: I don't think so. I might.

Rupert: Uhnnn. *(Objecting)* That is not what I think is a good idea.

Don: Did you bring a copy?

(Pause)

Rupert: All right. But if I were you, I would just put it in my pocket and forget it.

Don: *(Reading it)* "The first time I stepped before an audience and accepted its time and money for any training, talent or personality I possessed, I forfeited all right to privacy. They bought the whole package, not just 20 or 30 minutes of my time."

Rupert: Well—

Don: You actually believe this—

(Phone rings)

Don: Good evening, Old Log Theater.

Woman: *(On phone)* I'm wondering—

Don: Yes?

Woman: This show of yours, *You Know I Can't Hear You When The Water's Running*—is this show all right for youngsters?

Don: Well, how old are they?

Woman: Nineteen and twenty-one.

Don: Nineteen and twenty-one. Yes, it is. They'd enjoy it a great deal. A very funny show, very funny.

Woman: Is it a comedy?

Don: Yes, it is. It's a very funny play. Would you like to make a reservation?

Woman: No, not yet. I'll have to check with the children and see if they're available.

Don: Thank you for calling. If you like to laugh, don't miss it.

Woman: You sure it's a comedy?

Don: Very funny comedy.

Woman: Thank you. *(Hangs up)*

Don: *(To Rupert)* You actually believe this?

(Phone rings)

Rupert: I'll get it. *(Into phone)* Good evening, the Old Log Theater. May I help you?

Woman: *(A different voice on phone)* Yes—

Rupert: The Old Log Theater.

Woman: Yes. Is this a recording?

Rupert: No, ma'am. This is Rupert Labelle. Live and ready to help. Would you like to make a reservation?

Woman: No, that's why I'm calling. I have a reservation for tonight and I'm calling because I have to cancel—I had forgotten—this is the day my husband had to have all his teeth pulled out. So please cancel.

Rupert: I'm sorry. May I have your name?

Woman: Oh, of course—Terwilliger, Mr. & Mrs. J. C.

Terwilliger.

Rupert: Is that T as in Thomas?

Woman: No—T like in Tom.

Rupert: I see. Thank you for calling—and give our best wishes to your husband. *(Hangs up)*

Don: *(Pulling tickets)* Terwilliger—with a T as in Tom. *(Pulling envelope)* Here it is. Two fewer for tonight. If this becomes a trend, the actors will outnumber the audience. Now—*(holding up the piece of paper he got from Rupert)* You still haven't answered—you believe this—I mean really.

Rupert: You didn't read the last sentence.

Don: "If I didn't believe this were true, I would feel as important as a loaf of bread … bought, eaten, digested and forgotten." You saying that actors—and others—entertainers—have no right to their privacy?

Rupert: No.

(Phone rings)

Rupert: *(Answers phone)* Good evening, the Old Log Theater, Rupert LaBelle—may I—

Woman: *(On phone)* Yes.

Rupert: May I help you?

Woman: I hope so. This is Mrs. O'Connell. I'd like to reserve four seats for a week from Saturday.

Rupert: *(Writing on ticket envelope)* O'Connell … initials, please.

Woman: Initials—"C" for Colleen.

Rupert: And your phone number, please.

Woman: WA 6-1408.

Rupert: Would you care to join us for dinner?

Woman: No, thank you, not this time. I do love that roast beef.

Rupert: Thank you. Remember, we don't take credit cards—check or cash, please.

Woman: *(Hurriedly, fearing that Rupert is going to hang up)* Where are my seats? I'd like to have seats just as close to the front as possible.

Rupert: *(Checking as he talks)* All right—I have four for you, right in the middle of the first row.

Woman: Oh, no. Not that close. How about four in the middle of the tenth row?

Rupert: All right, Mrs. O'Connell. Four in the middle of the tenth row. I can do that.

Woman: Good.

Rupert: The show starts at 8:30, so please pick them up by 8:15.

Woman: 8:15—in the morning.

Rupert: No, that same night.

Woman: Oh. Thank you. *(Hangs up)*

(As he hangs up, the other phone rings)

Don: Good evening—the Old Log Theater.

Voice: Wrong number. Sorry.

Don: Call again when it is the right number.

Voice: *(With a chuckle)* Thank you.

(Both hang up)

(Phone rings)

Rupert: Good evening, the Old Log Theater

Woman: Would you please tell me what kind of stage you have there at the Old Log—is it theater in the round?

Rupert: It's a proscenium stage, the way God intended theater should be.

Woman: Oh, it isn't theater in the round?

Rupert: No, it isn't, thank Heavens.

Woman: Don't you like theater in the round?

Rupert: I hate it. It's bad enough to have all those people in front of you without being surrounded by them.

Woman: Oh, you don't like theater in the round.

Rupert: I'm sorry, but I don't.

Woman: You should try it some time.

Rupert: I already have. Thank you.

Woman: Well, thank you. I was just wondering.

(Both hang up)

Don: I don't know why that would remind me—I didn't tell you, at 6:30 this morning I had a telephone call.

Rupert: Oh?

Don: Some woman who said, "Do you realize there's no one in your box office?"

Rupert: What did you tell her?

Don: I told her I was sorry and took her order for two tickets. I've already put the tickets in the envelope. *(To Rupert)* Back to this. *(The thing Rupert has written)* I asked you if you believed that actors had no right to privacy.

Rupert: What I am saying is—we have no right to expect our—following—not to be interested in our private lives.

Don: And they have the right to know—

Rupert: Within proper limits, yes.

Don: All right. What are "the proper limits"?

Rupert: I haven't written them yet.

Don: I see.

(Don dials phone)

Rupert: Who're you calling?

Don: Clellan. He wanted to know if he could pick me up a little earlier tomorrow afternoon. *(He is finished dialing)* Line's busy. Don't let me forget to call him later.

Rupert: How is Clell?

Don: Great. Great on the show. Driving home he became a little melancholy. Came out with the same melancholy question that he asks about every six months. You know, "Don, don't you wish you had done something worthwhile with your life?"

Rupert: You realize he's really asking that question of himself, don't you?

Don: Oh, sure. And so does he.

Rupert: You should have told him my story about the two actors.

Don: Oh?

Rupert: You remember—there's this elderly man and wife—
actors. They haven't worked all year. Finally agent
Clarence Brown calls them to say that they have a job—
both of them—in the Staten Island weekly stock
company. All week they keep hoping that it will be a hit
and held over for at least another week, but it wasn't. So
after the last performance, out of work, they gather up all
their clothes—in those days actors had to furnish their
own wardrobe—and board the ferry for Manhattan. It is
a cold, miserable rain and sleet-filled night. When the
ferry draws up to its Manhattan dock, the old couple is
already wet and cold. As they walk carrying their clothes,
down the passenger gangplank next to the exit ramp for
cars, they pass beside a huge puddle of muddy water.
Coming down the ramp at that moment is a large black
chauffeur-driven limousine. Sitting in the backseat,
comfortable and warm is an elderly couple probably of the
same age as the heartsick thespians. As the limousine
comes down the ramp, it goes through the puddle,
throwing dirty spray, completely covering the two old
actors and the clothes they're carrying. It is too much.
The wife can restrain herself no longer; she starts crying.
Her husband, though burdened with his now dirty
clothes, embraces her as best he can and comforts her
with these words: "Just remember, dear—they can't act."

Don: I'll tell Clellan. I'm not sure it will help.

(Phone rings)

Rupert: It's mine. Good evening, the Old Log Theater,
Rupert LaBelle speaking.

(Other phone rings)

Don: Good evening, the Old Log Theater.

(Ken Senn enters, as third phone rings)

Ken: I'll get it. Hi—the Old Log.

Woman: We're coming to the theater tonight and I'm
wondering if you could tell me how to get there.

Ken: Sure. You come out Highway Seven—

Woman: *(Interrupting)* You mean Highway Twelve.

Ken: No, it's Highway Seven.

Woman: Just a minute—*(She obviously talks to husband)* My
husband says it's Highway Twelve.

Ken: If you knew how to get here, why the hell did you call?

(Hangs up)

(Don and Rupert are shocked)

Thank God you have already met Ken. Ken Senn was one of
the most talented and personable actors I have ever known or
watched. In addition to that, he would do absolutely anything to help
the theater.

And he had promotional ideas, which he himself would put into
motion. In the summer after we moved into our new building (that
would be 1961), we had put in a flagpole between the edge of the
parking lot and the theater building. Ken, a staunch Republican and
a very patriotic man, decided that the flagpole should be dedicated.
Without telling me, he telephoned Hamm Brewing to donate several
cases of beer, Oscar Meyer for several dozen wieners and the local
bakery to donate the same number of hot dog buns. Having secured
these commitments, Ken decided to take it to the next level. He
telephoned the Washington, D.C., office of Minnesota Representative Clark MacGregor to ask if Mr. MacGregor would preside at the
ceremony. The invitation was warmly accepted. It was only then that
Ken told me what he had accomplished. Thinking that Representative MacGregor had accepted with the idea that there would be an
audience of several hundred supporters and important Minnetonka
Personages, I telephoned his office the minute Ken left my office. I
explained that there had been no promotion, that no one outside the
theater family knew of the dedication and that if he wanted to cancel,
we all would certainly understand. In the warmest words I have ever
heard, MacGregor said it made no difference how small the audience
or who they were, if there was a flagpole to be dedicated in his
district, he wanted to do it.

The ceremony was scheduled for 1:30 on a Tuesday afternoon.

It developed into the hottest day in the history of Minnesota summers. We took folding chairs, placed them in two short rows in the parking lot, called all the neighborhood children, and several sympathetic adults. At the appointed time, there were six members of the Old Log company, twelve young children and Mr. Kuechle, who owned the property. MacGregor's driver dropped him off at the theater entrance, where I took him aside to apologize for our unintentionally misleading him. He dismissed it with six words: "Don, I'm glad to be here."

Still filled with embarrassment, I led him to the site of the execution. He warmly welcomed those in attendance—and it was a hot day, remember. Then he went on to say much of what he had said on the telephone: how proud he was that in his district there was a theater organization—a theater organization—that was so patriotic and so loving of their country that they wanted to express it in the placement of a flagpole on its lawn and dedicate the flagpole properly. He spoke simply. Nobly. I don't remember hearing any speech since that so relieved me, warmed me, and made me proud. When he finished, he asked if there were any questions he could answer. Immediately Mr. Kuechle's hand went up. "Yes, Mr. Kuechle, what is it you would like to know?" The answer: "Why are my taxes so high?" After our dear Representative answered that, we all went into the theater for hot dogs and beer. Most of the audience was too young for the beer; they had to be happy with a hot dog and a Coke. Again, one of Ken's crazy ideas had been a huge—well, not huge in number—success.

The dedication of the flagpole was not the only promotional idea Ken had. Though the actors of the newly formed Guthrie Theater and even Mr. Guthrie himself, were attending the Old Log every Sunday night, Ken felt a softball game between the two theaters would bring us even closer together. Ken knew very well the Twins executive organization, so it was easy for them to agree to furnish the umpire and actually attend. The game was scheduled to be played on a nice field now covered by an apartment for seniors. The wives of the Twins' executives not only attended, but were

The Honorable Clark McGregor.

Rapunzel; Teri Deaver and John Shuman.

enthusiastic rooters for the Old Log. A former Twin was announced as the umpire, a duty he performed as if this were one of the games in the World Series. There is no record of the final score, nor even the winner, but we all remember it was a long game with many runs scored.

When fall came, Ken decided it was time for a touch football game between the two rivals. John Kundla would referee. The Old Log team showed with an offensive and defensive line (we played both ways) as heavy and impressive as me and Richie Davis. The Guthrie team had not one actor, but instead their stage crew, all large, fast and determined. Richie Davis and I played on the right side of the Old Log line. Though this was supposed to be a "touch" game, there was no "touch" to our opponents on the line. Again and again and again Richie and I were smashed by men weighing at least 150 pounds more than did we.

During the second half, Richie said, "I don't care what happens, let's you and me both go after the one son of a bitch that has been particularly brutal." I agreed. We got the son of a bitch though it damn near killed both of us. Our opponent left the game, Richie and I remained. We had no second line. The high point of the game was when our leading man, Walter Boughton, dropped back to punt the ball. It was a terrific punt. Unfortunately, the ball hit Ken Senn, who was playing center, squarely on the butt, and the ball took a terrific bounce backward and over the goal line that we were protecting. The game did nothing to promote friendship between the two theaters; Richie and I couldn't move without pain for two weeks. At that time the Guthrie stage crew wasn't even union.

Ken was a star. On Broadway he would have been the toast of New York. He was a big, rotund, jovial man who, as I have previously written, looked exactly like Zero Mostel, only more so. When he appeared in our plays for children—which he did, every one of them—he loved the kids and the kids loved him. Every word he spoke, every move he made was a special jewel created just for them. One morning performance they were especially delighted with one of his little pieces of business—so delighted that one of the young boys couldn't restrain himself and expressed his pleasure by saying, "Oh, shit." This was so many years ago that it was the first time that word had been heard inside the Old Log. It would be several more years before it would be heard from our stage.

In those years of Senn, there was hardly—no, let me change that—there was never a children's play in which Ken Senn's special and memorable moment did not occur.

During a Wednesday morning performance of ***Rapunzel***, there was a ten-year-old boy in the right side of the front row who kept making noises and saying words that were entirely irrelevant to anything that was happening on stage. Senn finally could stand it no longer. He stopped in the middle of a speech, stepped downstage toward the boy and said, "If you don't be quiet, I'm going to come down there and turn you into a toadstool." Everyone—even the troublemaker was stunned into silence. Just as Ken turned to cross back to his position, the miscreant, to save his pride, could not resist giving a taunting "Yeah, yeah, yeah." It was quiet, but it was there. Without a word, Ken came offstage, down the steps, took the boy by the hand and led him backstage, where he picked up a giant mushroom prop, which Ken then put in the seat just vacated. It was a winner. The stage manager took the young boy outside, around to the lobby and put him in a good seat in the rear of the theater. I hate to admit it, but it worked so well and added so much fun that we incorporated it in every performance, each day selecting a young boy and giving him the instructions so he could properly play the role.

In ***Two Pails of Water***, a delightful play from Holland, Ken played, with considerable authority, the lazy but likeable village constable. When that day's scalawag became unruly and loud, Ken, since there was no giant toadstool backstage, just stopped, walked downstage and said to the young man, "If you don't behave, I'm going to come down there and spank you." Silence. As Ken turned back upstage, the boy finally had a reply: "You do and I'll tell my mother." But he did, from then on, behave.

Ken Senn and Edgar Meyer were the best Odd Couple that ever appeared in the Neil Simon comedy. I mean the best anywhere—

here, New York or in the motion picture. Ken and Edgar were the best. Oscar, stamping his feet and telling Felix to "Go to your room"—was a moment I shall always cherish. Ken and Edgar. God bless them both.

Two Pails of Water; Steve Pringle, Don Fallbeck, Tom Stolz, and Barnie Erhardt.

ACCIDENTS BECOME A PART OF THE ACT

In January of 1973, Terry O'Sullivan and Anita Anderson married and immediately established their home in Excelsior. It was great comfort to have my old friend and my secretary assistant both available. Before the year was out, Terry joined Bob Edwards and Ross Bickell as the regular male members of almost every cast.

This began with our first show in 1974, *Uproar in the House*, a show we would repeat twice before the seventies were over. Then *Don't Drink the Water*, followed by a starring role for Terry in *The Happiest Millionaire*.

Early one September morning in 1973, Ralph Blattner telephoned me and said he would like for me to meet him at the new Plymouth Radisson at the intersection of Highway 55 and 494. He wanted me to see and critique the meeting room/theater that was being built in the hotel. I was not much surprised at the telephone call because we had become good friends working together in several industrial shows for the Gravely Tractor Company of Winston-Salem, North Carolina. In 1973, Ralph had not yet retired from the Carlson Company Communication group.

The theater was a delight. It seated just under three hundred and had a small stage, ideal for intimate productions. Before the week was over, we had signed an agreement with the Carlson Company, selected our first play for the new theater, *Play it Again Sam*, to open on January 20, 1974. On January 17, the worst ice storm to hit the Twin Cities had descended and stopped everything. Everything! Our crew, comprised of Peter, Dony, Timmy and Jon Stolz already at the Playhouse, were trapped. The Highway Department closed all roads and highways. There was to be no traffic. For three days the boys were the guests of the new Radisson. By the 20th, some traffic was allowed and some way the cast and crew finally met on stage and managed to keep the opening night schedule. There were even a few in the audience, who had braved the storm to attend.

The second show was **Barefoot in the Park**. Ann Blager, who had played the role of the mother in our original production some years earlier, felt that she could repeat the role despite her having since had a stroke; she was still walking with a cane. On the opening night of the production, Ann slipped and fell on stage, but managed to get up and finish the show. Curt Carlson, who was present with Mrs. Carlson and several of his family, went backstage after the performance, congratulated Ann and told her that her overcoming her difficulty of falling and then getting up, had inspired him. He would remember always her courage and her commitment.

We finished our stay at the New Plymouth Playhouse with two more productions, **Butterflies are Free** and **Promenade All**.

Without much doubt, we would have continued appearing there, but the temporary head of the Chicago Equity office demanded that we pay the same salaries and observe the same minimums there as we did at the Old Log. It was an impossible situation. I should have taken my requests to the New York office. This was the only time in our long history with the union that we had any difficulty that couldn't be negotiated.

In July at our Excelsior theater, we opened **No Sex Please, We're British**, which would have four more productions in the next ten years.

When I first read **No Sex Please**, I found it very funny. How would we play the two ladies-of-the-evening? In London, as I understand, the roles had been played by two beautiful girls uncovered from the waist up. Even if we could find their duplicates, this, I knew, would never work at the Old Log. I finally decided that the two ladies should be played by Margaret Christopher, a pretty but very heavy comedienne paired with Jeanne Whittier, who, though beautiful, sounded like one of those young ladies with little mind. It

No Sex Please, We're British; Jerry Newhouse, Margaret Christopher, and Jeanne Stolz.

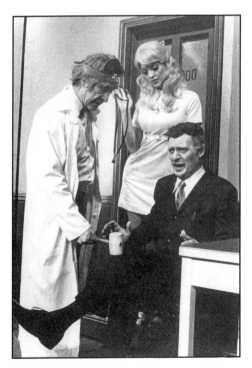

The Sunshine Boys; Bob Aden, Sharon Anderson, and John Varnum.

worked. They were a wonderful pair. As funny as is the whole script, there were several moments never to be forgot. After the girls have established themselves in the apartment to which they think they have been called, Margaret enters from the bedroom down left with Tommy on her shoulders headed for the bathroom up right. As Margaret runs through the door, Tommy is caught, hanging on the millwork on the upper part of the door. He remains hanging there for several minutes—long enough for the audience to collapse with laughter. Another never to be forgotten piece of business took place every night of the run, when Jerry Newhouse, playing a bank inspector, hoping to be led astray, is in his pajamas, leaning unconsciously on an upstage walk. He remains there while the action of the play continues. His pajama trousers creep lower and lower until the laughter of the audience makes impossible any other action on stage.

In 1974, shortly after President Nixon resigned, new President Gerald Ford was scheduled to make an appearance in the Twin Cities. Apparently it was difficult for the committee to decide just who should introduce him. As each name of a prospect came up, again and again that person was eliminated because it would give that part of the Republican Party prestige that others would resent. The only solution was compromise. They could think of no one more compromising. I introduced President Ford, having never met him before nor after the meeting. However, several days later, I did receive from him a gracious letter and an autographed photograph.

The theater season of 1975 at the Old Log started with a January production of *Finishing Touches*, written by Jean Kerr—a simple, delightful family comedy. After 14 weeks, we opened *Uproar in the House*, which we followed with another production of *Life With Father*. Ken was gone; I played Father Day with the boys all playing the Day sons. I'm not sure that I didn't enjoy it more than the audience. After four weeks of *Life with Father*, we presented a Ray Cooney farce, *Move Over Mrs. Markham*. One of the biggest laughs, and there were many, had absolutely nothing to do with Mr. Cooney's delightful script. Ross Bickel, at a point in the second act is supposed to say, "I was peeking at the key hole." One night during

The Happiest Millionaire; Terry O'Sullivan.

The Pursuit of Happiness; Merle McDill, Terry
O'Sullivan, Frank Scott, Don Fallbeck, Ray Belander,
and Rebecca Lundahl.

the seven-week run, Ross said, "I was peeing through the keep hole." On stage with Ross were Terry O'Sullivan and Jerry Newhouse—not one of the three expert in controlling unscripted laughter. All three, collapsed on stage. The laughter in the audience lasted for minutes.

We closed 1975 with Neil Simon's *The Sunshine Boys* for a good solid run.

For May of 1976, I had decided a simple and certainly not flamboyant way to celebrate the hundredth birthday of our country was to present *Pursuit of Happiness*. In a relatively small part, Don Young was marvelous.

I suppose the most unusual selection of 1976 was *Enter a Free Man* written by Tom Stoppard, even today has not been widely produced, probably because it is difficult to see either the humor or value in telling of the failings of its central character.

The box office success of 1977 was *Absurd Person Singular*, written by Alan Ayckbourn. It ran for 14 weeks. In the cast was Toni Gilman, an actress with truly extensive Broadway credits, and year after year in the first class road companies. I had seen her in San Francisco during the war years as a young ingenue in *Ten Little Indians*. Her appearance in our play was as brilliant as her war-time appearance in San Francisco.

During the '60s and '70s, Shirley Moore, the wife of Dave Moore of Channel 4, came to the Old Log quite regularly. Since Dave was on the air most of the nights, Shirley usually attended with several of her girlfriends. In those days, Shirley had long auburn hair—below her waist. When she would take her seat in the theater, rather than sitting on her own hair, she would, naturally, throw her hair over the back of the seat. One memorable night her assigned seat was directly in front of a large, very heavy man. During the first act, this man, to make himself more comfortable, slackened his belt and unzipped his trousers. All was well until intermission, when a couple to the man's left wanted to go to the lobby, which necessitated the fat gentleman to stand to let them through. When he stood, he zipped up his trousers, catching quite a portion of Shirley's hair. Try as they would, there was no way they could separate zipper and hair while in the auditorium, so they came to the lobby—the man holding his trousers up—Shirley bent almost double holding onto her long hair. Even with a pair of scissors the situation took time to solve. From the first, Shirley, with her usual sense of the ridiculous, was laughing. I'm not certain the zipper man has even yet laughed.

Back to the plays of the '70s.

For two years I had been receiving letters from friends who had seen, in London, what they described as "the funniest play they had ever seen," *A Bedfull of Foreigners*. I sent for a copy of the script and, after reading it, started a search for the broker or agent who might control the rights for production. New York brokers advised that it would be years before it was available in the States, but my determination led me to the author's London agent.

I telephoned him, told him that Joan and I would be in London the next week and asked for an appointment. The agent suggested lunch two days after we were to arrive. It was a most pleasant lunch at a "quaint"—and I use "quaint" after considerable contemplation— café two doors from his office. Conversation started even before we had sat down.

He told me that the American rights had not been sold and "it would be great fun to arrange a contract with the Old Log, a theater well known in London for its productions of English farce" and more admired in London than in the States. Arrangements were made, the contract signed, payments arranged, and for a time we held the exclusive American rights to this masterpiece written by Dave Freeman, a former writer for Benny Hill. We found Dave Freeman to be a delight and a charming man of television and theater.

As soon as we returned to Excelsior, I wrote every professional theater in the United States telling them of this wonderful new comedy, which was now available.

Whenever, in future years, we were in London, we had dinner with Dave Freeman and his wife. They remained our friends for the rest of their lives.

Bedfull of Foreigners tells of a young British couple who have decided that driving through France might be a more exciting vacation than going as usual to a nearby beach. It ran for 19 weeks.

By 1976, our annual presentation of the David Preeves String Quartet had become a tradition. Vince Bastian, who was actually the spine of the Preeves Quartet, came to my office, as he usually did, to discuss the upcoming program for the Sunday afternoon concert. Vince was a son of the legendary Bastian family; his mother was a highly respected pianist and teacher; one brother was on the west coast where he was sought after as a most versatile musician; another brother was a gifted trombonist in the Twin Cities. And there was another musician brother, Biddie, whom Ray Komischke almost always used in our industrial shows.

Our son, Peter, who happened to be home from San Francisco at that time, wandered into my office while Vince and I were finishing the plans for the concert. I introduced Peter to Vince with the remark that Vince was Biddy's brother whom Peter knew and admired greatly. The introduction was hardly completed when Peter started telling Vince how great his brother was. "He's probably the best player in the country; I've never heard any other bass player who is even close," and many other such remarks. When after several minutes Peter paused, Vince felt he had to reply. He came up with a line that among musicians in the Twin Cities has become classic: "Yes, Biddy is about as good as a bass player has to be."

Though I was no longer producing commercials, my relationship to a number of the top advertising agencies in the Twin Cities had remained strong. Early in 1979, an account executive of Campbell Mithun telephoned to ask if I would have time during the next week to meet with their new client. It was not only a new client, but was actually a new business, and yet not exactly a new business.

For some years, Jim Riggs, the editor of the magazine *Better Homes and Gardens*, had believed that with the magazine's popularity among homeowners, the company should be in the residential real estate business. Jim was so strong in his belief that he resigned his position as editor to become the president of the Better Homes and Gardens Real Estate Division. In the months that followed, he convinced hundreds of brokers and agents that they would be a part of his dynamic idea. They now were ready for a convention to which all of these new "partners" would be invited.

When I eagerly agreed to meet with the representatives of BH&G, it was suggested that the meeting be at the Stolz home at 5120 Meadville. The account executive from Campbell Mithun felt that Jim Riggs, as former editor of the magazine, would be interested—even "impressed"—by the Bloomberg architecture.

After a brief—brief—tour of the house, which Riggs did appreciate, we met around the dining room table. Present were Jim Riggs; Randy Schwager, an enthusiastic former radio announcer; Rick Prenger, also young and enthusiastic; and the representative from Campbell Mithun. Riggs believed, and rightfully so, that the convention show should begin with an audiovisual listing of all the member realtors. He realized it would take time and suggested that during the long audiovisual listing that we have on stage right a trampoline with one or two young women exercising. Riggs knew magazines, and while he certainly did not yet understand show business, he was quick to learn.

When Riggs learned that I would be writing the script, he said, "Good. For your own comfort, I think you should know that although I have left my position as editor of the magazine, I have not yet lost my inclination and desire to edit anything that I read." (He changed only four words when he went over the first draft.)

The first show for this exciting new company was in Las Vegas. We, of course, took Ray Komischke and his orchestra, the Bruce Neilson singers and Old Log actors who were not in the show in Excelsior. Jim, Randy and Rick were all strong in their approval when I suggested we bring from Miami eight of the June Taylor dancers. All three remembered that these were the dancers who had appeared weekly on the Jackie Gleason show.

I don't remember much more about that first BH&G show except that it was an extremely successful production, and the joy it was to work with Riggs, Schwager and Prenger for they were familiar with every popular song of the previous 20 years.

The officers of BH&G Real Estate Division had determined that the convention had been so successful, they should have another one in 18 months. The 1981 convention was scheduled for Montreal. Shortly before the opening day of the meeting (too short a time to cancel or postpone), the air traffickers of Canada declared a strike. Company executives, cast, crew, musicians and attendees all were determined to get to Montreal in some way. They came by train, by bus, by private automobiles. They were so looking forward to the meeting that I wouldn't be surprised if some hitchhiked. It was on this trip that I re-confirmed how difficult it was for musicians to cross the border, regardless of how they might travel. Their instruments were almost taken apart by the border inspectors looking for drugs. In addition, the serial number of each instrument was taken to make certain that everything entering Canada also leaves.

In looking back over the industrial shows, I'm always a little surprised by how vividly insignificant items return to mind. I remember going down to the meeting room very early the morning of the show, and there was Randy Schwager playing his trumpet. He is a good player, but he would never agree to being a part of the show orchestra.

In 1983, back to Las Vegas. Again, the insignificant memory. Randy and I turned down the cocktail hour to have an ice cream cone just off the hotel lobby. This meeting of 1983 was so heartily approved by those in attendance that Riggs determined we should have another convention the following year not wait for 18 months. The meeting was in Boston. After the show, a few of us had enough time to become typical tourists and visit Old Ironsides.

In 1986, just the day before we were to leave for San Francisco, Joan had a heart attack. I postponed my departure, but when the doctor told us things were well under control, Joan insisted that I leave for California the next day. Terry Smith, who always did the audiovisual work, had everything well organized by the time I checked in at the Fairmont. The show went well, even though the attendees were still mourning the death of their truly beloved leader, Jim Riggs. BH&G had brought in a bright, young, ambitious man, Allan Sabbag, to replace Riggs as president of the real estate section. Allan, when he learned that my son, Peter, lived in San Francisco, invited him and his young son, Andrew, to be guests at the cocktail party. Allan, for the party, was dressed in his usual too tasteful to be called "sartorial splendor." Eleven-year-old Andrew, already tremendously interested in men's clothing, was approvingly fascinated. Everything Allan Sabbag was wearing—his suit, shirt, tie and shoes—was combined perfectly. After viewing this perfection for some time, Andrew could not resist. While Allan was talking to a group of men, all holding cocktails and chatting warmly, Andrew very quietly knelt beside him, lifted his trouser leg just high enough to make certain that Mr. Sabbag had done as well in his selection of stockings.

Though Joan remained in Abbott Northwestern Hospital for about two weeks, her carefully guarded recovery was extremely successful and she attended every convention that followed.

Eighteen months later, we were in New Orleans. When we met in Des Moines to review the first draft of the script, Allan Sabbag, wanting to display his newly acquired knowledge, stated that he had been reading about scripts and had learned that every script should have a beginning, an ending and a middle. When he asked if this script did so, before I could answer, Terry Smith replied, "Of course it does. Don wrote it. The first page is the beginning, the last page is the ending, and everything in between is the middle." Though Allan did not particularly approve of Terry's answer, he let it go.

The show we did in New Orleans was one of the best that we have ever done for anyone. The plot was clearly understood by every one in the audience. It was the story of a young, not very successful, real estate agent who is working for a company other than BH&G. When his employer calls him into his office to discuss the young agent's lack of success, the young agent replies that his widowed mother is about to sell her home and he knows he'll be able to get that listing. When he calls on his mother, she informs him that she's sorry but she has already given the listing to a Better Homes and Gardens real estate agent. When he asks in despair what he can do, his mother replies that she will answer him the way his Marine officer father would have—"If you can't beat them, join them."

Five-foot-five Tommy Stolz played the son; six foot one Claudia Wilkins (a fine, fine actress), played the mother. She has her son stand; she stands and sings "The Ballad of the Green Berets" with special BH&G lyrics. On the last four bars she embraces her son, lifting him off the stage floor. Seldom have I heard such applause. We truthfully could not continue the show until Claudia and Tom had repeated the scene. I saw Claudia only a few months ago. She stopped me and sang "The Ballad of the Green Berets" with the BH&G lyrics she still remembered.

I think it was the huge success of the New Orleans show that convinced Sabbag they should return to a convention every year. The year 1989 was in Scottsdale, 1990 we were at the Las Vegas Hilton, 1991 Honolulu.

Wanting to pursue a different format, Randy and Rick sold Allan on the idea that the show should be built around our own version of *The Honeymooners* with Steve and Tommy playing the two roles.

I have never cared for industrial shows built around an established TV or radio show. I've always felt that it introduces a step that has to be taken by the audience before the material truly applies. But a sponsor is a sponsor. And Randy and Rick are bright, clever and creative.

For *The Honeymooners*. I decided that we needed a fragmentary but realistic setting of their home and another setting for a real estate office. I wrote the company in Honolulu that we always used to supply staging, lighting and sound. They wrote that if I sent them a drawing of the sets, they would build them in their shop. When I arrived early in Honolulu, I discovered that they had built the sets, but weren't sure how to paint them. I told them that if they would supply the paints and brushes, I would be out the next morning to do the painting. It worked well. The show worked well.

During the day of the performance, the young man who represented the stage supplier said that his wife was a teacher at the
University of Hawaii, she was the head of the graduate school of
theater. She had asked him to ask me if I would agree to come to her
class when the show was over and talk to them about the Old Log.

The students in the class were all graduate students of theater,
eager to learn about theater management. The first question asked
was, "Every theater we have ever heard of, including those not-for-
profit organizations as well as those supposedly interested in making
a profit—every theater is operating in the red. How does the Old
Log support a cast of Equity actors and still stay in business?"

I couldn't think of a proper answer. I told them that I would
think about it and answer later, and led into other questions. On the
plane coming home, I couldn't forget the question. By the time we
landed, I had reached something of a conclusion. "The Old Log had
succeeded because in every part of operation we always put the audience first. This did not mean that we asked them what plays they
wanted to see; it did mean that we selected our plays based on
whether comedy or drama, it had anything to say to the audience.
Parking lot boys, box office help, ushers, set design and execution—
all were determined on making attendance at the Old Log a memorable occasion."

I telephoned the teacher to give her and her class my delayed
answer.

In 1992, Better Homes and Gardens and the Old Log went to
San Antonio. Since Bob Aden was living there, we asked him, and
he agreed, to be a member of the cast.

In 1994, back to New Orleans. In 1995, Orlando. Without the
leadership of Jim Riggs, the real estate division of Better Homes and
Gardens had not succeeded as he had dreamed. When the company
was sold, we did no more work for them. But when Randy Schwager,
Rick Prenger and Tom Smith all joined the Consumers Club organization in Valpariso, the Old Log did shows for them.

In the years since, these three, with Joan and me have managed
to get together and recall with tremendous pleasure and joy the work

we did together.

In 1978 and 1979, all but three plays were repeats of past successes—and again they were good box office. The two new plays in 1978 were *90 Day Mistress* and *There Goes the Bride*, and the new play in 1979 was *California Suite* by Neil Simon.

The author of our 1980 new play, ***Chapter Two***, was also Neil Simon. It was beautifully performed and well received. Over the years it has remained as one of the plays of which I was particularly proud. In the cast was Ross Bickell, a fine, fine young actor who had appeared in over 20 of our plays by the time we produced ***Chapter Two***. Playing the other male role was also a fine actor, Don Amendolia, who was making his first appearance at the Old Log. The two young women were Cynthia Subby, who had begun her professional career at the Old Log when she was sixteen, and Judith Robinson, a beautiful young actress who had received her training at Carnegie Mellon and Boston College.

In November that same year, we presented Alan Ayckbourn's London success, ***Bedroom Farce***. It was a great but entirely misleading title. Our patrons knew well what "farce" was supposed to be. There was a bedroom, certainly, but the only farce in the entire script, I fear, did not come from the writings of Mr. Ayckbourn. People arrived thinking they were going to see a Ray Cooney type show; it failed to deliver what they wanted. Despite the results, I truly would like to do it again.

In 1980, our designer and oldest son, Peter, told us that for the benefit of his family, he felt he should move to San Francisco. Tommy would take over; he had almost the same background in design and technical theater as did Peter. The concern for Joan and me was Peter's going to the West Coast without prospect of a job.

We were pleased, certainly, when Peter told us that he had already prepared for work in San Francisco. Several months earlier, he had designed and built an outstanding trade show display for the Pond Company. Peter had been suggested for the job by the Brede display company, who would transport the setting (the exterior of a large colonial house) and engage the crew in Memphis, where the trade show was booked. At the end of the trade show, the Pond Company sold the display Peter had built to a Memphis firm for more than the original cost to Pond.

When Brede heard that Peter was considering moving to San Francisco, they offered to write a letter to a company they knew well. They went further than that; they sent a copy of the detailed blueprints that Peter had drawn before building the Pond display. As a result, Peter started work as soon as he arrived in San Francisco.

Several weeks after Peter started his new job, a visitor came to the shop where he noticed Peter working on a project involving somewhat complicated blueprints. The visitor approached Peter and asked, "Can you read plans?" Before Peter could answer, his boss said, "He not only can read and work from them; he can draw them, too." The visitor then told Peter, "I'm from Industrial Light and Magic, the special effects group for Lucas and Spielberg, and we'd like for you to come to work for us.

Peter: When?

Visitor: Immediately.

Peter: Well, I'd certainly like to work for you, who wouldn't? But I couldn't possibly leave here until I've finished this job.

Peter couldn't have given a better reply. When he finished the job, Industrial Light and Magic was there for him.

At ILM, Peter was guided into "pyrotechnics," and after considerable study and experience, received his first-class license. He worked on almost every one of the Indiana Jones motion pictures, but the assignment of which he was most proud is probably the one when he and two friends did all the special effects for *Top Gun* and were nominated for an Academy Award.

Bedroom Farce played until the second week of February 1981, when we opened *Romantic Comedy* by Bernard Slade. Slade was also the author of our next presentation, *Tribute*, in which Ross Bickell gave a stunning and emotional performance. Cleo Holladay was also in the cast, her first role in years at the Old Log.

Chapter Two; Cindy Subby and Ross Bickel.

The Kingfisher; Mary Seibel, Ken Graham, and Bob Aden.

We followed *Tribute* with another new play, *The Kingfisher*, a beautiful play with a cast of only three, that included Old Log veterans Bob Aden and Mary Seibel, with a Minneapolis veteran of the theater, Ken Graham. In the program notes is included this statement: "Ken Graham's career has spanned a line of tremendous growth in the performing arts and he has done much to further that growth both locally and nationally."

After *The Kingfisher* came *Da*, written by Hugh Leonard. *Da* was one of the most distinguished plays of the decade. It has received the Tony Award for Best Play, the New York Drama Critic's Award, the Drama Desk Award and the Outer Critic's Award. The *New York Times* called it "a humane and honest memory play with great affection and humor." A little bit more about *The Kingfisher* later. The Old Log's production of *Da* was excellent, featuring Tom Stolz, Don Fallbeck and Bob Aden. It ran for eight weeks. It was followed by a first-class presentation of *Not Now Darling*.

I Ought to be in Pictures was the first play in 1982. Of all of Neil Simon's plays it is the one for which I have cared the least, for it was difficult to admire any of the three characters. *I Ought to be in Pictures* was followed by *Lunch Hour*, written by Jean Kerr, the author of several hit plays and a best-selling book, *Please Don't Eat the Daisies*. She was married to *New York Times* drama critic, Walter Kerr.

We closed 1982 with *Not in the Book*, described by London critics as "the best comedy mystery in many decades." One of the actors was Will Kenzie, making his first appearance at the Old Log. He has been with us ever since—a confidante—and the best group salesman in the business. No one can sell matinees as effectively.

The year 1983 was a successful year. The year 1984 is memorable because during that year we presented two of Old Log's four musicals, *Cotton Patch Gospel* and *They're Playing Our Song*. Also in that year was Ayckbourn's play *Taking Steps*, which was worth seeing just for a tremendously funny scene between Bob Aden and Tom Stolz.

Key for Two had been running in London for over two years. It was not yet available in the States, but because of our friendship with

Da; Mary Seibel, Don Fallbeck, Paul Eidie, Tom Stolz, Louisa Kerry, Bob Aden, Spencer Beckwith, and Katy O'Toole.

Da; Louisa Kerry, Don Fallbeck, and Bob Aden.

Dave Freeman and our success with *Bedfull of Foreigners*, Dave was able to convince the co-author, John Chapman, that the Old Log be given the rights to be the producer of its first appearance in this country. We were concerned about *Key for Two* because it presented a woman rather than a man as the center of sexual misbehavior. By careful playing, it worked. One of the most humorous scenes ever witnessed was Tom Stolz, playing the role of a young veterinarian, who has gotten terribly drunk—so drunk that he tries to give breath-to-breath resuscitation to a fox fur neckpiece. To the 19 week run in 1984, we added 21 weeks in 1988, for a total run of 40 weeks.

In 1984, Bob Williams, the Old Log's publicist and head of group sales, and his wife, Patty, had visited London and seen *84 Charing Cross Road*, written by Helene Hanff, adapted for the stage by the renowned English playwright and director, James Roose Evans. The action of the play is set in the New York apartment of Miss Hanff and in Marks and Co., Booksellers, 84 Charing Cross Road, London. The lovely and romantic story spans the years of 1949 to 1971. For the better part of a year, Bob had been after me to check the rights for production. I was finally able to get Alene Hussong of the Samuel French organization to secure for us "special permission" to produce the play. Laurel Ollstein played the role of Helen Hanff; Ross Bickell played Frank Doel of the bookstore. Included in the cast were several characters with no spoken lines but whose presence on stage was important. One of the roles, a worker in the London bookstore, was played very well by Jimmie Wright, who created a most memorable moment in theater. We have had any number of actors who, for one reason or another, have missed an entrance, but Jimmie is the only actor in our more than sixty years who missed an exit. As the character in the play, he was working at his desk. He became so involved or was so sleepy (we don't know which), that when his cue came to leave the stage, he ignored it. The desk and Jimmie were so close to the stage left wall that the stage manager could whisper for him to come off stage. Jimmie's being on stage a little longer than usual did nothing to harm what was a beautiful production.

Key for Two; Tom Stolz and friend.

84 Charging Cross Road; Laurel Ollstein and Ross Bickell.

There have been few plays over all of our years that were as loved by the audience as was *84 Charing Cross Road*. Would I like to give it again? I'm not at all sure I would. I'm not sure we could do it as well.

Again it was Samuel French, playbrokers, who granted "special permission" to produce our next play, *Squabbles*, a new American comedy that was one hilarious squabble after another. One critic wrote, "It is a heart-warming comedy which has the appeal of *On Golden Pond* and the sizzle of Neil Simon." Bob Aden and Pam Danser were the center of a good many of the squabbles. Tom Stolz played Hector Lopez, the couple's handyman whose work is everlastingly interrupted by the need to visit the restroom. Tommy's young son, Patrick, looked as Puerto Rican as Tommy, so someone (I think it was Tommy) had the idea of having young Patrick come on stage, late in the second act, and whisper in his father's ear. The father would then direct him to the restroom. When Playwright Marshal Karp came from New York to see the production, he was surprised to learn that his play now had an extra cast member. Marshall was delighted and asked if he had our permission to suggest it to whatever producers might be offering *Squabbles* in the future.

In 1984, shortly after Lawrence Roman's comedy, *Alone Together* opened in New York, I telephoned Samuel French and asked for a reading copy of the play. I liked the play, liked it very much. For me, there was one large objection. In the middle of a quiet, romantic scene between husband and wife, the husband, when questioned by his wife, admits to and describes a past affair. I couldn't believe that the husband would ever admit such a transgression of several years earlier and I strongly felt that it did nothing to further the comedy or the plot. Without even communicating with Larry Roman, I cut the 2-1/2 pages that I disliked and scheduled a run of 11 weeks.

To follow *Alone*, I had set George Kelly's comedy, *The Torchbearers*, which had opened its original New York production in 1922 at the old Vanderbilt Theater. Though I had hoped for a long and successful run, as the rehearsals progressed, I began to realize that it was never going to work for us. I was inclined to blame my belief that women don't play farce too well, and all the good roles were written around women. The true fault was that I found no way to make an audience of today realize that the play was a satire of amateur theater and not a report. The night we opened I posted a notice and told the crew to save the set of the play which had just closed. All furniture and props from *Alone Together* were put aside, where they would be easily available. The notice-to-close had to be given two weeks warning, but after only two weeks, we reopened *Alone Together* and held it for 15 weeks.

Years later when we had just witnessed the opening of a new Ray Cooney play in Windsor, England, Ray asked a dear colleague of his, Nimo, who had driven to Windsor to give us a ride back to London so we wouldn't have to take the late train. Nimo was a well-known English actor who had expanded his activity to include the production of shows at theaters across Europe and Asia. He revealed that he was having difficulty in finding a comedy for his upcoming season, so I suggested *Alone Together* and told him I would mail him a copy as soon as we returned to the States.

When I sent him the copy, I also included the suggestion that he cut the same two pages as had I. *Alone Together* became his play for his next season. He was so delighted with it that he telephoned Larry Roman in the States and told the author he was making arrangements for Larry and his wife to come see his production in Shanghai. Time and again I have reminded Larry that he owed me; I was responsible for his wonderful trip to Shanghai. We have done *Alone Together* many times here at the Old Log, and Mr. and Mrs. Roman have come to see our production. Whenever he finishes a new script, he sends me a copy and asks if I care to be the first to produce it.

During the Lenten season in 1986, the Old Log presented something new—"The Off-Night Series" productions. In 1986 it was a one-man show starring Tom Stolz, in *The Gospel According to St. Mark*. It was a dramatization and memorization (word for word) by Tommy of the entire King James version of this, the most stirring gospel. During this holy season it was presented every Monday and Tuesday night. Tommy has performed it every Lenten season since then, and all through the years he has taken *The Gospel* to churches all over the country, to England, France and, just last year, to Israel. It's a remarkable and spiritual performance.

September the next year, 1986, there was Neil Simon's *Brighton Beach Memoirs*. Simon's autobiographical telling of his growing up as a 15-year-old boy in the Depression year of 1937. *Brighton Beach* had been named "Best Play of 1982" and described "Simon's finest and most artfully wrought play." We had a good cast which included two of our grandchildren, Allison and Theresa. Some 20 years later, both are doctors.

For the first 27 weeks of 1987, it was a revival of *No Sex Please, We're British*. During those weeks, we had received the rights to Simon's latest play, *Biloxi Blues*, which as we started production, soon became my favorite Simon memoir rather than *Brighton Beach*. I was determined to have a fine cast and, though the play did not open until September, started auditions in July. For the servicemen, I auditioned over a hundred young men. I knew Tom was to play Eugene, the autobiographical Neil Simon. Though Hal Atkinson had appeared only in musicals (*Cotton Patch Gospel* and *They're Playing Our Song*), I knew he would be a great Sgt. Toorney. And he was. After auditioning, I cast Steve Zahn, a freshman at Gustavus Adolphus College, as Don Carney. (After finishing college, he became a well-known New York and Hollywood actor.) Rehearsals with this diverse cast with a complicated script were strenuous and exhilarating. The result was one of the finest productions the Old Log has ever had; one of the finest productions of *Biloxi Blues* ever had. "The finest production I have ever seen"; "The best play I've seen in the last ten years," etc.

Of course the 26-week run carried over into 1988 and was scheduled to continue 26 weeks into the new year. What the next play would be, we were not sure. Early in February, I had a request from an actor then living in Iowa to hear him in audition. I agreed, as always. The day he came for the audition there was a matinee, so

Alone Together; Bob Reid and Mellissa Kenworthy.

The Gospel According to Mark; Tom Stolz.
(The sweater he is wearing was knit by his mother, Joan.)

it was impossible to hear him on stage, which I certainly preferred. But not wanting to detain him, since he was returning to Iowa that afternoon, I took him to the veranda. As soon as he finished his audition, I asked him when he might be available. He answered, "any time." I said, "I don't know what the next play will be, but I do know you're in it." His name is Steve Shaffer and now, almost 20 years later, I'm so thankful to say he's still with us. One of the finest actors in the country.

"We don't know what the next play will be, but you're in it" turned out to be *Doubles*, a good script about several men who meet to play tennis. The setting is the men's locker room. Though it was funny and well done, it didn't draw the audience that we had hoped for. There was, in 1988, just as there is today, a great deal of local interest in tennis, so we were surprised that it didn't do better. I think the play would draw better today, but I have no desire to produce it again. Attendance increased immediately when we reopened *Key For Two*.

The next year was special, very special. During 1989 we were to celebrate the Old Log Theater's 50th anniversary. It was special in other ways as well.

Every person we knew who went to London during the past eight years had come back telling us about "the funniest show I have ever seen. It would be perfect for the Old Log." It was a repeat of our experience with *A Bedfull of Foreigners*. Only this time there seemed no possible way of even getting a copy of the script. The play was Ray Cooney's *Run For Your Wife*, which had played in London for eight years, and was not even considering closing. In past years we had presented at least six of the eleven plays that Cooney had written, so I had what I thought to be several leads—his agent, his play broker, his former collaborators. Nothing worked. Finally I had a call from Bill Kron, who was the manager of the downtown Minneapolis theaters. He assured me that he knew how to reach Cooney through a mutual friend. He was successful.

Run for Your Wife is the story of a well-meaning young cab driver, who through circumstances seemingly out of his control,

Biloxi Blues; David Lipp, Steve Zahn, Douglas Steindoff, Michael Tierney, Hal Atkinson, Scott Johnson, and Tom Stolz.

Doubles; Steve Shaffer, Jim Harris, John Patrick Martin, and Tom Stolz.

finds himself married to two young, attractive wives. Tom played the cab driver; Steve Shaffer played his friend and confidante. Though they had appeared in leading roles in **Doubles** and **Key for Two**, it was the long run in **Run for Your Wife** that really established Tom and Steve as a great comedy team.

When we opened **Run For Your Wife** the first of February 1989, I had hoped to find a play that I thought better represented the 50 years work of the Old Log. A show that would open the second Wednesday in June to celebrate the Old Log's anniversary. While I was searching for such a play, it had become obvious that regardless of anniversary or no anniversary, it would be foolish to close what was becoming every week a bigger and bigger hit. **Wife** ran for 52 weeks, the first play that ran for a whole year at the Old Log.

The precise celebration of the 50th was the second Wednesday in June, the true anniversary. And a celebration it was. The day started early in the morning with an hour WCCO broadcast from our stage, emceed by Charlie Boone and Roger Erickson. We were surprised by the number of audience members who showed up for the very first of the broadcast at 6:00 a.m. The radio audience was invited to phone in with any questions they might have for Boone and Erickson. WCCO had arranged for actors from previous years such as Nick Nolte, Loni Anderson, Mary Ellen Fedora and many more to telephone their congratulations. In actual attendance there were at least a score of actors who had, over the years, appeared at the Old Log.

In the afternoon there was an extended cocktail party, followed by dinner, then a short program before the presentation of **Run For Your Wife**. The "short" program included presentations by Equity (the Actor's union), the state's representative in Washington, the local mayor and several of the actors from past years.

Some time during the day—probably all during the day—we announced the first edition of *The Way We Were* by Bob Aden, and the occasion's Souvenir Program. The Souvenir Program was put together by Bob Williams, our Publicity and Marketing Director, with photographs and remarks from each of the five decades. Also included were unsolicited comments from actors who had been here sometime during those fifty years, knew of the anniversary and wanted to be a part, if only through the mail. I include several from the program—not as self-serving, but rather as a reflection of what the Old Log is.

> **Hal Atkinson:** "I was an established musician, singer and composer-lyricist when a phone call from Don Stolz asking me to play one of the leads of *Cotton Patch Gospel* changed my professional life. There is nothing more stimulating and rewarding than rehearsing and performing at the Old Log Theater."

> **Cleo Holladay:** "For me personally, my time at the Old Log Theater was some of the happiest years of my life. There was a feeling of family, and I loved the people of Minnesota and that lovely small town of Excelsior. Artistically, I truly learned my craft from Don Stolz. I learned more about comedy from him than any school I could ever attend. I love the Old Log audiences and those marvelous fellow actors—Ken Senn, John Varnum, Bob Aden, Ann Blager, Edgar Meyer and Terry O'Sullivan."

> **Ann Blager:** "I loved the Old Log so much and admired Don's direction so much that I purchased a house and moved to that beautiful Lake Minnetonka. I still dream about my favorite role as Vinnie in *Life With Father* with Ken Senn and the Stolz boys. The Old Log was always a happy family."

> **Lois Nettleton:** "The Old Log was a fun, wonderful experience, and I recall the great pride that I had in the quality of the work we were doing there. There was always great joy—and I remember it with great affection."

> **Edgar Meyer:** "I think of those early years with the Old Log Theater as my training ground with the wonderful direction by Don Stolz, the marvelous Old Log audiences, and the caring for each other by the actors. I miss them all, and I especially remember my favorite plays

there—*Sunrise at Campobello*, *Of Mice and Men*, *The Odd Couple*, and *Harvey*."

Dave Moore: "At age 16, I fell in love with theater at the Old Log. It was my first involvement with professional theater. Not many actors can say they're that lucky. I still have fond memories and cherish those wonderful times on the stage of the Old Log Theater. It has truly become a Minnesota institution."

Nick Nolte: "The Old Log brings joy and integrity to the theater. Without the challenges and the experience extended to me by Don Stolz while I was at the Old Log, I could not have achieved what I have now. I thank them always."

Richard Dix: "The Old Log Theater is one of the most wonderful and unique theaters in the world. When I work at other places, I tell them about the Old Log and they are spellbound. My years there were the happiest time of my professional life."

As I re-read these, they seem self-serving, but I think they honestly show the family that is the Old Log.

Before the week of the anniversary was over, we had a memorial service for every individual who had been at the Old Log, but had died. It was conducted at the Excelsior Episcopal Church; the service was patterned after the one held annually in New York for departed Equity actors.

Our 50th anniversary was a celebration.

MY TIME IN SANDSTONE PRISON

In all the years that the Old Log has been producing shows, we have done only four musicals: *They're Playing Our Song*, *Cotton Patch Gospel*, *Mahalia* and *Radio Gals*. When I remember that most of the thousands of industrial theater shows we have written and produced, almost all included music—musicians, singers and quite often dancers—it seems, even to me, a little strange that we haven't done more musical theater. The answer is simply that it is difficult to find musicals with small enough requirements—requirements of musicians, number of cast members, settings and royalty—to make producing them a reasonable gamble.

I remember directing two other musicals—productions that had nothing to do with the Old Log. One was the opera *Thirteen Clocks* presented at Northrop Auditorium, the University of Minnesota; the other was *Gin*, with music, lyrics, book all written by Jerome Carlson who also produced the show in downtown Minneapolis. No outside backers or partners. Had Mr. Carlson been a recent graduate of the Yale School of Drama rather than a middle-aged, Republican, successful businessman, the show would have had reviews praising this new writer-composer. I should have mentioned that Jerome played the leading role—he played it quite well and sang beautifully.

They're Playing Our Song, written by Neil Simon, with music by Marvin Hamlisch. It was years later when I discovered that the original London production was produced by our friend, Ray Cooney. At our production, Hal Atkinson played the lead, singing and playing the piano. We had a five-piece orchestra placed behind a scrim on an upstage platform. This enabled us to bring them into

From left, clockwise: Jay Hornbacher (Bob Branigan), Dominic Castino (Fred Blair), Bill Ewald (Harry Drayton) and Jerome Carlson (Jack Connery, kneeling) in the title song from "Gin," a new musical by Jerome Carlson playing at the newly restored Music Box Theatre, 14th and Nicollet. Runs March 26 through May 15, 1994.

Gin; Jay Hornbacher, Dominic Castino, Bill Ewald, and Jerome Carlson.

view when we wanted. Though *They're Playing Our Song* did not pay off the mortgage on the theater, it did contribute, at least, a small payment. I'd like to do the show again.

Cotton Patch Gospel—the gospel story told in today's backcountry Georgia language. It was based on the book by the Reverend Clarence Jordan, play by Tom Key and Russell T. Keys, and music by Harry Chapin. It tells the Gospel story of Jesus Christ with reverence and relevancy. Hal Atkinson played Christ and he was nothing short of magnificent. During rehearsals, the cast grew to believe he was Jesus and there were times when I suspected Hal did, too. *Cotton Patch* opened to great audiences, but I noticed that every night early in the first act, a considerable number of audience would stand—almost simultaneously—and leave the theater. Their ubiquitous exit was always right after Hal, as Jesus, sang, "It wasn't easy growing up to be Jesus, with no steady job and no steady girl." They had difficulty fitting this into their fundamentalist views. It was a disturbing situation. After giving it considerable thought, I concluded that I should tackle this problem in an announcement always made before the show. What I told the audience was to the effect that "we were all going to hear thoughts that may not have been a part of our experience. Early in the first act you are going to see and hear the character of Jesus singing, 'It wasn't easy growing up to be Jesus.'" "Frankly," I went on, "I had never thought of that before, but when we started rehearsals I became aware and strongly convinced that it wasn't easy growing up to be Jesus. It wasn't easy being Jesus. If it had been, we would not be worshipping him and honoring him as we are today."

What I said was not eloquent, I know; it was effective. After the announcements started, we never lost another attendee.

Cotton Patch Gospel was responsible for one of the most memorable days of my life. One of the members of the audience, a delightful lady who saw the show at least four times early in the run, came to us asking if we would consider doing **Cotton Patch** at Sandstone Prison. She had talked with her husband, a former banker, now a prisoner in Sandstone convicted of embezzlement—a charge that both he and his wife denied. I had little trouble believing them. She and her husband both believed that **Cotton Patch** would be a gospel of Good News that all of the Sandstone inmates should witness.

The entrance into the prison itself was not simple. All musical instruments, all lighting equipment and every part of the sound system was minutely examined. Then it was our turn. The actors/musicians and crew: all briefcases were carefully searched; all pockets emptied. As Hal was standing in line awaiting his turn, he suddenly turned and said, "I have to go back to the car, I forgot my harmonica." To this day I do not entirely believe what the other musicians claimed—that the reason for his departure was to remove the packet of marijuana from his shirt pocket.

After what was a slow and deliberate entrance from the door

into the inner space, we quickly set up lights and sound in a very attractive hall, which served as chapel and auditorium. The several hundred inmates were ushered into this room; most either despondent or morose at best. The grimmest audience I had ever seen. When all had entered, the heavily plated doors were locked with guards remaining at each entrance. In no way could it be considered a happy overture to what might take place.

What was to be our audience sat there, dejected, depressed and disinterested; some already asleep before the last door had been locked. Obviously this was going to be a show to remember.

"Something's Going on in Gainesville"—the overture. Only a few in that audience had any idea where Gainesville was, and no one had the slightest knowledge of "what was going on" there. But with Reuben Ristrom playing banjo, Cliff Brunzell, the great violinist playing fiddle, Bob Guck playing bass, the entire cast singing, the audience began to open their eyes, sit up and start to think this might not be a completely lost evening after all. By the time of the reprise, the audience was awake and eager.

The next two hours was a glorious mixture of tears, laughter, renewal and even conversion. When Jesus declared his innocence at the trial, they enthusiastically yelled their support of this man who was soon to be unjustly crucified. They understood Jesus, they righteously and indignantly objected to his punishment—and many for the first time understood what Jesus and his crucifixion had done for all of us. Including them. Sitting there. Being a part of what was that evening created.

At the end of the show, no one wanted to leave the room; the applause, the shouting for more continued and continued. They demanded and their custodians agreed, that the entire show should be immediately repeated. And it was. That event became one of the most glorious and inspiring evenings that anyone of us had ever known.

Finally it was over. It was time to dissemble, pack up and leave. A few inmates had been left in the room to help us in whatever way they could. One of them was the former banker, who, when working in the bank, had been known for his racial intolerance. At Sandstone he ironically had been assigned as his cellmate a very large and dark colored African American. His name was George. The banker was helping me take down the light trees. He called to his cell-mate, "Hey, George, come over here and help me." George almost ran to get there—"All right, what do you want me to do?" "Just hold up the pole." "Hold up the pole? That's the way I got in here."

My sentence in Sandstone was one of the most significant and happiest of my life.

Then there's *Mahalia*, based on the life and music of Mahalia Jackson. Again and again, wherever I go, people ask me, "Of all the plays you have done, which is your very favorite?" In my answer I tell the truth. When you produce plays, you have several favorites for several different reasons—(1) Because the play made a lot of money when you needed it most; (2) When you liked the message or content of the play—and (3) When you felt close to and loved the cast. When we presented *Mahalia* in 1994, we did excellent, excellent box office. Reason number one was satisfied. I loved the message of *Mahalia*—its deep and honest religious conviction. I was stirred by the gospel music. What really underscored reason number two for me was the fact that *Mahalia* had been written by our son, Tom. *Mahalia* was overwhelmingly strong in reason number two. Reason number three for making a show a favorite—the cast. All the roles were played by three actors—people I immediately loved, still love and will always love.

Mahalia was Jearlyn Steele Battle—I should properly say Jearlyn Steele Battle WAS Mahalia. I had for years used her in our industrial shows. Her rapport with any audience was unbelievable. The minute she appeared on stage you felt her warmth and her love. When she sang her first note she touched your soul.

Her brother, Fred, played all the male parts including Martin Luther King, Jr. Each character was clearly defined and well rounded. He played the Hammond organ with Leslie speaker—(and when you do those gospel numbers it has to be a Hammond with Leslie speaker.) No one ever duplicated the meaning of a scene better than he did. No one ever played those gospel numbers as he did. Fred was a handsome, successful young man, a respected member of the community who still remembers what it was like growing up "in the neighborhood." Many times he had been a part of our industrial troupe.

Then there was Gloria James, who played all the feminine roles other than Mahalia—and played the greatest stride piano I have ever heard.

My favorite play? *Mahalia* qualified in all three points.

Since our original production, *Mahalia* has been presented on several different national tours always successfully, and the Old Log has had four different productions—all with the same great cast. *Cotton Patch Gospel*—two productions, both extended runs. *They're Playing Our Song*—only one production for eleven weeks. And we so far have had only one production of *Radio Gals*; a production that had a successful 18 weeks.

This small musical, *Radio Gals*, is set in the twenties, a time when small radio stations were popping up all over the country. One of those stations is WGAL, established in the front parlor of music teacher, Hazel C. Hunt, who, in her operation of her station, doesn't ever hesitate to wave jump (infringing on others assigned frequency) hoping to find a clear channel.

With good luck we were able to assemble a wonderful cast— Barbara Davidson as Hazel, Nancy Lillis as an old friend and classic vocalist, Amy McDonald and Colleen Everett as two of her students. Traditionally the play is produced with two of the musician singers as men dressed as women. They are not female impersonators, but rather two minor criminals attempting to escape by posing as women. They are also the piano and bass player. We were able to hire Jay Albright and Russ Peterson for the two roles. Jay was excellent on the piano; Russ, one of Minnesota's most versatile musicians, played bass, saxophone and everything else. He was invaluable as a coach whenever anyone was to play any instrument other than the one in which they were already skilled. Furthermore, both boys were very funny—never once "camping" or overplaying their roles.

Everyone in the cast was an excellent singer and musician and was capable of learning to play other instruments. We had the best drummer in the Twin Cities complete Amy's relatively small knowledge of drums—she already played violin and guitar, as did Colleen. All, it seemed, could play piano, including Peter Thomson, whom we cast as the government inspector who had come to WGAL to close it down, but his decision is changed when Hazel discovers that he is a closet tenor and accordion player. We had the legendary Larry Malmberg, probably the best accordion player in the country, give Peter whatever accordion lessons he needed. It was fun.

Radio Gals, too, is a musical I would like to repeat.

In July 2003, my friend and co-worker, Will Kenzie, handed me a book saying, "This isn't for your birthday, which is tomorrow, but it's a book I thought you would appreciate." The book was *The Mousetrap Map*, an autobiography written by Peter Saunders. Saunders started his career as a publicist for small bands playing in the cities surrounding London. After World War II, he longed to be a London West End producer and began working toward that end. Saunders eventually achieved great success, including becoming the man who produced *The Mousetrap*, the forever long run champion of world theater. I found the book so remindful of our early days at the Old Log that I took it home and read a section of it to Joan every night.

In his book, Saunders tells of his early days of trying to become a producer in London's West End. Though his struggles took place in a more costly venue, in a city more the center of his nation's theater, I could identify with many of the things he tried. On one of his first attempts to bring a play into London, opening night was just three days away and when he examined the box office, he learned that fewer than twenty tickets had been sold. No way could he allow the critics to come to his play with no one in the audience. He gathered all the actors, the stage crew and the staff to a meeting, issued them all a large number of tickets and told them that their future and his depended on their giving these tickets for the night the critics were to be there. All of his fellow workers complied; they filled the house. Only one thing was wrong, the critics were not coming until the next night.

Mahalia; Gloria James, Jearlyn Steele, and Fred Steele.

Radio Gals; Jay Albright, Colleen Everett, Barbara Reese
Davidson, Russ Peterson, and Amy McDonald.

On occasion—let me change that—in the early days, Saunders almost always found it difficult to get any press from London's newspapers. I admired what he tried, even though there were times when nothing worked. It reminded me very much of the times—frequent times—when the Old Log could get no mention at all. No publicity. The cost of display (theater page) advertising was prohibitive; small "personal" ads were affordable. So I wrote such personal ads as "Tom, my husband is out of town this weekend, so meet me Saturday at the Old Log Theater. You know who." I'm not sure these brought in any customers, but they were fun and I felt I was at least trying to get some attention.

Sometime in the early seventies when, again, we were not being covered, not even a review, I thought of a plan to get a little attention. I hired two young men, not actors who would be recognized, to go to downtown Minneapolis and visit every tall building with elevators. They were to enter the elevators separately, as if not knowing that the other one was even in the area, and then have the following conversation:

Jim: Bob, how are you?

Bob: Fine. Haven't seen you in a long time. What have you been up to?

Jim: Last night I took Jane out to the Old Log Theater. It's the funniest show I've ever seen.

Bob: Really?

Jim: Yes, it's called *Whose Wife is it Anyway*—God, it's funny.

Bob: Who wrote it?

Jim: I haven't a clue. Who cares—it's really funny. You should go out and see it. I'm going back next week to see it again. *(The elevator stops at a floor nearing the top.)* Call me. Nice to see you, Bob.

Bob: At the Old Log, right?

Jim: Right.

Commercial theater in London, commercial theater in Excelsior, have a lot in common.

THE BARBER SHOP,
THE MORTUARY, DULUTH

Like most men—I think probably all men—there are two things I just hate doing. One is going to the filling station to get gas. Nothing has ever happened on that subject to change my mind—even using a credit card right at the pump. The other thing I hate doing is getting a haircut. Once I'm in the barbershop, everything is wonderful. It's one of the places in Excelsior where I feel I'm really a part of the town. I like Ed—I like the way he thinks and I guess I like the way he cuts hair.

How does Ed think? Well! Since time began, actually since 1949, Ed's father, Tony, operated Tony's Barbershop, from the Number One chair—the chair closest to Water Street and the window. Three months after graduating from high school, Ed began cutting hair at the Number Two chair—the second from the window. Fifteen years ago Tony died. In all the years since then, Ed has never moved to his father's Number One chair. He is still cutting hair at the chair second from the window.

When you walk through the door, it's like stepping back into the 1920s. There are the works of several good taxidermists: a mounted red fox, an albino squirrel, and several different breeds of ducks. Above the mirrored wall is a collection of what are now rare antiques—15-foot cane fishing poles. On a shelf below the poles, carefully placed in line by size, is a gathering of used shotgun shells of every gauge from 410 to 8, and empty cartridges of every caliber, from 22 caliber to 20 millimeter. In the back hall leading to the lavatory, hanging from a shelf on which has been placed dozens of liquor bottles of various sizes and brands, is a string of much used duck and geese decoys. On two tables, piled high, are newspapers and magazines—some of which are as outdated as those found in the family waiting rooms at Abbott Northwestern Hospital. The only publication missing that would have been there in the 1920s is *The Police Gazette*.

One of the features of Tony's Barber Shop—that's still its name—was the daily or twice daily visit of Jimmy Hutmacher. Many of you might know the truths, the half-truths and the legends surrounding this 65-year-old gnome. For those who don't know him, he is Excelsior's slow-minded, one of a kind, who every day, regardless of the weather, happily wanders the street, talking to himself or to anyone polite enough to listen. He is beloved by everyone who lives here. If you don't know Jimmy, you're from out of town. An outlander.

I got to the barbershop a few minutes before eight—just in time to catch Ed coming across the street from the bakery with a Styrofoam cup of coffee and a chocolate Bismarck. After Ed unlocked the door and took yesterday's page off the daily calendar from the Chanhassen Bank, I climbed into the Number Two chair, knowing it would be a considerable wait while Ed finished his breakfast and talked.

At 8:45, Ed was still cutting and we were still discussing the Excelsior Chamber of Commerce and how the newcomers—primarily ladies with blue hair and wearing tennis shoes—were planning on how they were going to change the town—beginning with main street.

Don: *(In chair)* Well, what do you think is going to happen?
Ed: Probably nothing. They'll have a couple of meetings and then nothing.
(Enter Jimmy H. Unshaven, four layers of clothes and an unlit cigar in his mouth)
Ed: What do you know—what a surprise, it's Jimmy.
Jimmy: *(Laughs)*

Ed: A little late this morning, aren't you?

Jimmy: Since the drug store closed, I just can't get started.

Ed: Try the bakery.

Jimmy: They don't let me charge.

Ed: Have you asked them?

Jimmy: Not yet.

Ed: Good luck.

Jimmy: *(to Don)* You were Tallulah, the cat on TV, weren't you?

Don: And Towser, the dog, too.

Jimmy: Clellan Card was a good man, wasn't he?

Don: Best man I ever knew.

Jimmy: Funny, too.

Ed: Yes, he was.

(Jimmy sits down, moving his cap forward over his eyes, puts cigar back in mouth.)

Ed: Hey, what are you doing now?

Jimmy: *(As if this were the dumbest question in the world)* Taking a nap. *(And he does so)*

Ed: *(Referring to cigar)* Well, don't burn yourself.

Jimmy: It's not lit.

Don: Jimmy was right about the drug store, wasn't he?

Ed: I went there every morning before opening. Its closing was the worst thing that ever happened to Excelsior.

Don: The restaurant that moved in—

Ed: The Chinese place?

Don: Right. How are they doing?

Ed: All right, I guess. You been in yet?

Don: Once. Joan and I went in for lunch a day after they opened. Our waiter had a whole bunch of body rings— one of them in his tongue. I've had trouble getting Joan to go back.

Ed: I don't think he's there any more. Didn't seem like a part of our local culture.

Don: What about the building across the street?

Ed: The Ace Hardware Store.

Don: Anything new there?

Ed: No, it's still the same. The owners are waiting for the city to build a parking ramp and the city is waiting for the owners to pay for it.

(Pause)

Don: How's your daughter?

Ed: Which one?

Don: Your oldest. The one who graduated from college last year.

Ed: I guess I forgot to tell you the last time you were in here. After graduation she took a job in Des Moines. Sort of an advocate in a home for abused women. And a few abusers as well.

Don: You didn't tell me.

Ed: Two weeks ago we drove down to Iowa to see her.

Don: Everything all right?

Ed: She was awfully quiet. You know—withdrawn. And that's not like her. It worried me. I had trouble sleeping. Early the next morning, I mean really early, I got up—quietly— and went down to the kitchen to make myself a cup of coffee. *(All of the above is broken up by intermittent cutting of hair, readjusting position, etc.)* Ellie came in and I poured her a cup too. For a while we just sat there. Saying nothing. Finally I asked, "Ellie, what's bothering you? I know something's wrong, what is it?" "Oh, I'm all right," she said. "Is it your job?" "What?" I said, "Is it your job?"

Then she told me it was. She was frightened; her life had been threatened twice and she had been struck, I don't know how many times. She said "What's worse, I don't feel I'm helping anyone. I've failed." So I said, "Ellie, you have a lot to be proud of—you completed college— you got yourself a job in what you thought was the right field. You have a lot to be proud of. I want to tell you, though, you're too young to spend the rest of your life in a place that frightens you—a place you don't like."

Don: What did Ellie say?

Ed: Nothing for a while. Finally she said, "But what would I do?" So I said, "Come home. Just remember, our house is your house just as it always has been. It is your home just as much as it is your mother's and mine." Last night she telephoned—she's coming home next Wednesday.

(Enter a man. The way he is dressed and the way he carries himself, he is obviously a successful businessman, from out of town.)

Ed: *(Dryly)* Good morning.

Man: How many are ahead of me?

Ed: Just Don—and I'm almost through with him.

Man: *(Pointing to Jim)* What about him?

Ed: Him? Oh—that's Jimmy. He's not waiting for a haircut. He's—he's our Quality Control Officer.

(The man glares, but goes and sits down. Nothing is said for a few minutes)

Ed: *(Finishing job)* There you are. All set.

Don: Thank you.

Ed: Your getting a haircut usually means you're going out of town on business. Have a good trip.

Don: Thank you, but I'm not going out of town. I'm going to a funeral.

Ed: Sorry. Well, have fun—that's not right, is it. *(Rapidly correcting what he said)* Have a good time—that's not right, either. Oh, hell, you know what I mean.

Don: Sure. And thank you.

Ed: Anyone I know?

Don: Probably. Shirley Johnson.

Ed: One of Hugo's daughters—married Chester's son. Funeral's not at Huber's, is it?

Don: No, that place in town on fiftieth.

Ed: Well—have a good funeral. *(The next is not a question)* That's all right, isn't it.

Don: It is.

THE MORTUARY

So with my fresh haircut, I went home, changed clothes and Joan and I drove to Warness Brothers Mortuary, for "the good funeral." And I guess for Shirley it was a good funeral—strange, mixed up and different. Soon after we entered the chapel, the unseen organist began her pre-service concert.

MUSIC: Organist playing "Up, Up and Away"
(As music fades under) **You may not believe it, but that was actually the first number.** *(Quite a long pause here as this number ends)* **The second bit of music was—and you won't believe this, either:**

MUSIC: Organ plays "Raindrops Are Falling On My Head"

MUSIC: *(Under as Stolz continues)*

For the next fifteen minutes the recital continued with music just as aptly and tastefully chosen. Not one even semi-religious number. As the concert came to an end, the pastor started his role as master of ceremonies, and, though the deceased's family had never been close to becoming Evangelical, jumped immediately into the most flamboyant revivalist sermon I have ever heard. He closed his thirty-minute homily threats with these remarks:

Minister: So again I say—Be warned. Be warned. There are many of you here this afternoon that are traveling—who of your own choosing—are traveling the road to hell. Turn back, I say. Turn back now and repent or you shall go through eternity in the fires of hell. Do not—I say, do not follow the path of our poor sister who died not in a state of grace, but still following that path to eternal damnation. Be warned—turn back—repent.

(He pauses, recovers his composure, then goes on)
And now—now I am going to do something that I rarely do at funeral services. In fact, I don't think I've ever done it before. I'm going to play my saxophone.

(He crosses, picks up saxophone as we hear a saxophone playing "Rock

of Ages." Lights fade on him)

For seven minutes—at least seven minutes—without accompaniment, he played "Rock of Ages" with variations. Did he play well? Well, this fundamentalist minister played his saxophone better than as a saxophonist he preached a homily.

DULUTH

As we were driving home after the service, I found myself thinking of one of Rupert Labelle's greatest stories. I think it was perhaps because of the saxophonist I'd just heard.

As Rupert's story went, a young member of the Minnesota Orchestra was hired to go to Duluth where he was to rehearse the amateur orchestra for four weeks, and to lead them in their concert appearance. It was a job the young musician gladly accepted; in those days the jobs with the Minnesota Orchestra did not include summers.

Musician: I was the young musician. And I was delighted to be offered the job. The chairman of the search committee—and they hadn't searched very diligently—in wanting to be completely straightforward, had reminded me that it would be quite a change from the Minnesota Orchestra. The Duluth musicians were businessmen, professional men, school teachers, housewives. They all had other jobs—other work. Rehearsals would be somewhat less than professional. Their other work would delay them, they would get there when they could.

Well, it was much worse than I had been told. *(Elderly man enters carrying a violin which he is tuning)* Every night—and I mean every single night—there was only one—there was only one musician who was there at the scheduled time. The last night, the night before the concert, he was the first player there. I thought this is probably my last chance to thank him.

Musician: *(Now to elderly violin player)* Good evening.

Violin Player: *(Nodding)* Good evening.

Musician: When I took this job and came up here to Duluth, I was told that most of the musicians would be late. And they have been. But you—you have been here every night, at the scheduled time, prepared and ready to play.

Violin Player: Well—

Musician: I'm not complaining, not at all. They told me it might be like this.

Violin Player: Well—

Musician: Well, I want to thank you. As I said, you have been here on time—on time—every single rehearsal. And for that, I thank you.

Violin Player: Well, thank you. But I thought it was the least I can do since I can't be here for the concert.

"Avoid Even White Lies"

In 1974, we were presenting *There's a Girl In My Soup*, starring John Varnum and Sharon Anderson, who later became a prominent voice of KSTP Television. Late in the day—better stated—early in the evening, we learned that John Varnum was ill. In no way could he even get out of bed. Though I had directed the play, which would ordinarily mean that I had a reasonable grasp of the roles, there was absolutely no way I could play the part without holding a script in my hand. There, in my mind, was but one way to go ahead with the performance. Holding the script in my hand, I went in front of the curtain and told the audience that John Varnum was ill and that I wanted to introduce them to this book since they would be seeing it for most of the evening, because I was going to read the part. "They could either leave now, go to the box office and get their money back, or they could see the entire show and pretend that they had had a great evening."

There's a Girl in My Soup opens with the character I was playing and the character Sharon Anderson was playing, sitting on a sofa engaged in a passionate and prolonged kiss. For this I did not need a script, but I thought the audience should immediately know what the rest of the evening would be like, so while embracing Sharon with my right arm, I had extended my left arm, holding the book behind her head. Never had the show opened with a bigger laugh. I was ridiculous and they loved it. Later another occasion allowed for great laughter when I took off my trousers while reading from the script. No one left; no one asked for his money back. Over the years enough people have told me that they were there that night that the total number would fill the Old Log three times.

The first time we presented *Over the River and Through the Woods*, the ingenue misread her schedule, thought there was no matinee that week, and had gone fishing in the Boundary Waters. There was nothing to do but for me to again explain to the audience and read the role. Randy Berger, who played the young romantic interest opposite the missing ingenue, was as sincere and as straightforward as always. And I was the same. I will admit, however, there were a few lines when the dialogue got unintended laughs.

Most of the time when a sudden replacement had been necessary, the roles have been small male parts in which anyone close to the script could be ready to perform with only a few hours to prepare. This is especially true if you have, within the past week or two, directed the show.

In 1981, we opened what developed into a beautiful production of *The Kingfisher*, a three-character play with Bob Aden in the leading role as the squire and master of the house; Mary Seibel, having by now developed into a handsome older leading lady, as the woman he loved; and Ken Graham as the butler who unrequitedly loved the master of the house. Dr. Graham was a handsome and talented actor who had returned to professional theater after retiring as a professor in the School of Theater at the University of Minnesota.

During his tenure at the University, the Guthrie Theatre was established in Minneapolis, and Doctor Graham revered and cherished it as only an academic could. At the time of his retirement, the primary target of his adoration was the current Artistic Director of the Guthrie, Livieu Cheuli.

Anyway, back to the Old Log and *The Kingfisher*, a delightful play with a strong cast.

We had just opened the play when Ken Graham came to me and said that—unexpectedly to him—his son was getting married; the wedding was to be on the East Coast in two weeks. Was there any way we could arrange for him to be able to attend the ceremony?

Since it had been little more than a week since I had directed the show, the blocking was still solid in my mind, and the lines were more than slightly familiar. Since I knew how much it would mean to the son for his father to be there, I assured Graham that I would play the role during his absence. I went on to suggest that since I had to prepare for the Saturday performance, why didn't I do it for the whole week? Then it would be possible for him to attend the groom's dinner, and whatever pre-ceremony functions there might be. He was delighted.

The first of the next week, our production company left for Canada where we were presenting an industrial show for Harley Davidson motorcycle dealers. On the flight back to Minnesota, Joan, who always knew the schedule, asked me if I knew what the next day was. Wednesday, I said. "Correct. It is the Wednesday when you replace Ken Graham as the butler in *The Kingfisher*. Fortunately I had the script with me. For me, the week's run was a pure delight—appearing once again with Bob Aden and Mary Seibel—two of the Old Log's all time favorites.

Doctor Graham returned to the theater to tell us that his trip to his son's wedding was a wonderful experience. He was so happy—as was his son—that he could be there. When I gave him his payroll check for the weeks he had been gone, he was close to tears, and said: "Don, this is the nicest experience I've ever had in all my years of theater. Thank you." How do you reply to a statement like that in a situation like that? Thinking humor would be the best path, I replied, "Well, it was a very nice experience for me, too. One night Livieu Cheuli was out and so captured by my performance, he asked if there was any way that I could get away from the Old Log and do a role at the Guthrie."

What I thought was so obvious a lie that no one would believe it turned out in Ken's mind to be the truth. He believed it so strongly that I could think of absolutely no way to tell him the truth. And in the years that followed, I never could. So many times since Doctor Graham's death, I have thought of that delightful theater man and dear friend going to his grave still thinking he had missed his great opportunity to star at the Guthrie.

To my memory, there comes no lie that I have ever told that I have regretted more than what I thought would be readily seen as a joke. I suppose that what has augmented and sustained this feeling was something that took place a few weeks later. The Guthrie Theatre, after the death of Tennessee Williams, scheduled in his memory a service in which every theater in the Twin Cities was to send a representative to present a reading or short performance from one of Williams writings. I did two short cuttings of Tom's role in **The Glass Menagerie**. I had years earlier played the role and delivered what the audience accepted as a subdued but brilliant performance. After the memorial service, Livieu Cheuli sought me out and asked the question that I had long since told Dr. Graham that he had—"Don, is it possible you could get away long enough to do a role here at the Guthrie?"

Since then I have attempted to carefully watch what mis-truths I might utter. Let me quickly add that in all the mis-truths of which I have been guilty, not once have I ever praised an actor's performance if it was not good, but many times I have hidden behind the expression I had learned from Lee Mitchel: "You know, it was an interesting performance."

NEITHER OLD LOG NOR
INDUSTRIALS—WHAT ARE THEY?

On the afternoon of January 14, 1976, Wheelock and Irene Whitney arrived on the appointed hour at our home at 5120 Meadville. Joan and I had met both Wheelock and Irene some years earlier at the home of Wheelock's sister, Sally Pillsbury.

Joan had hardly finished serving coffee before the Whitneys announced that they had a great idea they hoped would include me. They began by telling of Irene's struggle with alcoholism, the help she had received from an Episcopal priest, Rev. Vern Johnson, who had experienced the same struggle. He suggested to her that she go through treatment as he had. Irene's recovery was equally successful. In the years that followed, the Whitneys became so eager to help others with the same problem, that they helped start the Johnson Institute and began working with a trained counselor, Betty Trilegi, out of a rented second-story space on south Nicollet Avenue. Helping others subject to chemical dependency had become their avid vocation. I knew something of what they have been doing but was not really aware of the intensity of their commitment.

Their "big idea": they intended to rent the Metropolitan Stadium some night in June—whenever it would be available—and in the stadium present a celebration to be called FREEDOM FEST. They were well aware that 1976 was the two hundredth anniversary of the founding of the country, but in no way was this to be a celebration of anything other than a celebration of those who had broken free from either alcoholism or other chemical dependency. A celebration with orchestra and singers, but no patriotic music. It was to be a celebration of a different freedom.

Every treatment center in the state was to be invited; individuals would be welcome; there would be thousands of people celebrating being free from the use of drugs.

Irene and Wheelock said they would engage the speakers and help with the script, but would like for me to hire the musicians and singers, co-write the script, establish the proper sequence for the speakers, direct and stage-manage the production. Considering their enthusiasm and the importance of the event, there was no way I could not agree to do whatever they wanted. In the months that followed, I met with the Whitneys and their staff several times a week.

With the exception of what few government officials were to be asked, all speakers were to be those who had endured the struggle with addiction and won, though it was to be remembered not always did victory endure forever. The date of FREEDOM FEST was set for June 23. June 23, 1976.

As soon as the date was set, I hired Ray Komischke and his orchestra, Bruce Neilson and his singers, and Jan Gillespie and her dancers. In the meantime, the Whitneys had reached a number of nationally known entertainers and speakers, most of whom were recovering alcoholics, who in speaking, would "witness" their freedom.

They had asked, and he had accepted, Dick van Dyke to be the Master of Ceremony. Wheelock made arrangements for me to meet with Dick at Dick's home in Coronado Beach, California, to find how he wanted to handle his assignment. It was a warm, delightful, informative meeting of a few hours after which I returned to the airport for the trip home. Dick's house, I remember it well, was so much like Dr. Mark Sloan's house in "Diagnosis Murder" that I have always suspected it to be one and the same.

On the night of June 22, the day before FREEDOM FEST was to be staged, a violent summer storm hit the Twin Cities. It rained for hours; the late news weather forecast was for an increasing storm all through the following day. It was still raining when all involved reported early next morning for the last rehearsal. There was not one indication that the forecast of increasing winds and more rain was incorrect.

I remember Wheelock saying something to the effect that it was too bad that after all the work in preparing FREEDOM FEST, no one would face the storm to be there. Nobody would be there. I remember Trilegi replying that many of her friends weren't going to let a storm keep them away ... to them, FREEDOM FEST was the truest and greatest celebration of the century. In mid-afternoon, a miracle: the rain stopped and the sun came out. The infield of the Met was mud and the outdoor stage stood in a pond that covered second base.

As Wheelock said about all of us who were rehearsing, instead of drowning we were going to have a show. Though we were not going to drown, we were covered with mud and there was no time to either change or wash. Though a huge stage had been set up, there was no backstage from which to work. I stage managed, standing ground level, still covered with mud. During a musical number on stage, Don Newcomb, the major league baseball pitcher, though he was to be one of the speakers, was stood beside me in the mud and said, "You know what I'd do with those white shoes you're wearing? When I got home, I'd throw them away."

The speakers and entertainers all sat in the baseball dugouts until it was their turn to appear. Then they walked through the mud to the stage.

Governor Wendell Anderson welcomed the celebrants of Freedom, followed by Hubert Humphrey, who spoke with even greater grace and warmth than usual. Fran Tarkenton, though not himself a victim, had great knowledge of the program. He said that being an alcoholic was like being a football player: you would get knocked down, then you would have to pull yourself up only to be knocked down again. But if you kept on getting up, sooner or later you would win.

Dick van Dyke did a masterful job of introducing each speaker. Art Linkletter spoke with great feeling about "thoughtless acts."

Gary Moore appeared, spoke briefly, and then with Dick van Dyke sang and danced to a song we had written for them—the first two lines of which were:

"How can you believe me when I say I'm sober,

When you know I've been a drunkard all my life."

With those two, it was a show stopper.

Dick introduced the Senator from Iowa, Harold Hughes, who was known as one of the nation's strongest speakers on the subject of alcoholism and chemical dependency. He was even more effective and inspiring than I had anticipated.

It was a celebration of over 40,000 happy, sober—and happy to be sober—people celebrating being free from the use of drugs. The event became the glorious celebration the Whitneys had hoped for.

In 1982, when he was urged to run for Governor of Minnesota, Wheelock asked if I would give him some suggestions on the content and delivery of his campaign speeches. I was pleased. Wheelock is a man I truly admire and for whom I have great affection.

METHODIST GENERAL CONFERENCE

In the early winter of 1952, I had a telephone call from Ed Viehman, WCCO Radio producer and chief announcer. The fact that he called me was not extraordinary, for he was accustomed to calling me whenever he was preparing a dramatization for broadcast. What was unusual about this telephone call was that he asked if I could meet with him that afternoon at the station.

When I arrived at the station, I was surprised to see that Joyce Lamont, a co-worker with Ed at the station was also in Ed's office. Joyce was both a writer and on-the-air personality; she had the best female voice I have ever heard on radio or television.

Both Ed and Joyce seemed concerned and eager to talk.

Ed: Don—

Don: Yes—

Ed: Joyce and I—well, we need your help.

Don: Well, if there's anything—

Ed: *(Interrupting him)* There is something. Something I know
   you can do if you will.

Joyce: Don, you must.

Don: Well, what—

Ed: Let us start at the beginning. Next spring—

Joyce: This coming spring.

Ed: The Methodist Church is holding its world wide General
   Conference here in Minneapolis.

Joyce: At the Auditorium.

Ed: Well, the committee formed by all the Methodist
   churches in Minnesota has decided that the history of the
   Methodist Church in Minnesota is such an important
   part of the state's history—

Joyce: So they decided this history should be the opening of
   the worldwide conference.

Joyce: And presented in the form of a colorful and inspiring
   pageant.

Ed: Then this committee came to WCCO about five weeks
   ago and made an agreement with the station that the
   station would write and produce this pageant.

Don: Sounds like a good idea.

Joyce: It does, doesn't it?

Ed: They arranged for Wally Olson and his big concert
   orchestra, all 26 pieces. And engaged Vince Bastien to
   write an original score.

Joyce: Whatever the writers and director would want.

Don: It is a big project, isn't it?

Ed: Yes. And the station has assigned Joyce and me to write it.

Joyce: The trouble is—

Ed: We can't do it. *(Pause)* We don't have the time.

Joyce: And if we did have the time, we still couldn't do it. We
   wouldn't even know where to start.

Ed: So, Joyce and I have decided that you should write it,
   produce and direct it.

Joyce: We'll help you in every way we can.

Don: Where would I start?

Ed: The Chairman of the committee is the Rev. George Chant out at the Richfield Methodist Church. Go see him.

Joyce: You'll like him. He's a fine man.

Ed: And smart.

I did like the Reverend Chant. And he was smart. Gave me all the material on the history of the Methodist Church in Minnesota and "turned me loose."

Not only did the Reverend Chant give me the material he had collected, he also gave me a list of other ministers with whom I should talk. All were excited and cooperative.

As I started outlining the script, I very soon decided that there would be short dramatic scenes, tied together by narration. Each scene would be played by members of the congregation of the various Methodist churches in the Twin Cities. In that way they could hold rehearsal for their individual scenes in their own church buildings. I decided on two narrators: a "reader" who would work at a lectern stage right, he would read the selected scripture; a "narrator" stage left would cover the secular material.

It wasn't long before I could meet with Vince Bastien. We discussed several powerful traditional sacred music numbers that he would orchestrate. We discussed the use of instrumental pastoral music and arrived at the conclusion that it would be effective to have two voices of the same theme—a string version and a woodwind. These were to be used to bring together the various scenes. When I mentioned that there would be sections of "movement" as the state and church progressed, Vince suggested he write what he termed "travelogue" music.

One very small detail I remember well: Vince and I wanted the sound of a concertina during the French voyager's scene. Jeanne Peterson, who, as well as her husband, Willie, was in the orchestra, told me "You bring me a concertina and I'll learn to play it." Vince did a remarkable job of writing and arranging. The music was glorious. I'm afraid it did more to inspire than the words I wrote.

When Doctor Pennington, pastor of the large Methodist Church on Hennepin Avenue, heard how the pageant was progressing, and knowing that my father as a Methodist minister would especially be pleased by my work, he wrote my father in Kansas, inviting him and my mother to come to the General Conference to see the pageant and said his church would gladly pay their expenses.

Meanwhile, at the national headquarters of the Methodist Church, the Board of Foreign Missions had requested a time at the General Conference when they might present "The History of Methodism in India." Arrangements had long since been made for a chorus of singers and dancers from India to be the spine and primary attraction of their pageant.

The script had been written by a man well established as a leader in the field of religious drama.

The local committee, knowing that I had a full list of all the churches taking part in the Minnesota Pageant and was aware of any church groups that would be available for the dialogue section of the script for India, suggested that I direct it. I accepted the job knowing that there was no way it could equal the Minnesota production. But it did succeed.

It, too, was produced at the Minneapolis Auditorium, with its wide, wide stage. At the time of the pageants there was no intercom from one side of the stage to the other, so I appointed an assistant stage manager to be on the opposite side to follow closely the script to see that the actors entered on cue.

The cue for the first entrance of the dancers and singers from India came, and my stage-opposite assistant stage manager misread the cue and sent out Doctor Rolland Beck, who was playing one of the speaking roles. He had been costumed with an exact copy of the robes being worn by the chorus. Beck was just entering, even though he knew it was not his cue, when the chorus of dancers and singers entered with him. It didn't take Beck long to determine that there was no way he could continue moving and chanting with them, so he stepped off a few paces to the side and acted as a native spectator enjoying the work of his friends. Thank God, it worked. However it was weeks before Beck stopped getting calls from his fellow actors, asking if he was available for native dancing.

Several of the pastors from Oklahoma who were attending the conference were so moved by the Minnesota Pageant that two years later, they asked me to come to Oklahoma and write and produce the history of the Methodist Church in Oklahoma. They didn't realize that I had spent my boyhood there.

The Reverend Fisher Blanton, Chairman of the event, wanted me to follow the same format (they would line up the various churches), and whatever I did, use the same music. Oklahoma didn't have Wally Olson, but they did engage musicians from the Oklahoma Symphony Orchestra. Two of the musicians had played in the same Guthrie High School band, as had I.

I made a number of trips to Oklahoma to rehearse the various scenes at the designated churches. One scene, a Native American Indian scene, was to be performed by the Native American Methodist Church in Oklahoma City. I went to the church at the appointed time. No one was there. I began to wonder if I had the wrong day or the wrong time. After waiting for a while, with the appearance of not a single actor, I decided that the house next to the church was probably the parsonage. The door was answered by the Native American pastor of the church. When I asked him if I had the wrong date or the wrong time, he explained, "Oh, no. Two o'clock was the time. And it was for today. What no one told you is that it was two o'clock Indian time. Which means that they'll get there when they can." They finally arrived and the rehearsal went well.

The dress rehearsal with orchestra and cast at the Oklahoma City Auditorium was a long and strenuous afternoon. My most vivid memory of the day occurred during the congregation's singing of the first hymn. I went to the edge of the masking drapes and looked out. Directly in my eyesight was a group of almost a hundred deaf people all "signing" the words that others were singing. I couldn't recall ever seeing anything so graceful and so inspiring.

They Knew Lincoln

In the spring of 1966, Art Hustad, one of the city's leading insurance executives, had engaged his friend, Carl Sandberg, to speak at the Minneapolis Rotary Club Nine on the Friday closest to Lincoln's birthday in 1967. As the 1967 date approached, the program was announced, included in the weekly bulletin, and members were urged to bring wives and friends.

On the Wednesday before the great Friday, Art received a call from Sandberg's personal representative telling him that Carl was seriously ill, would not be in Minneapolis for his speaking engagement, and accurately forecasted that it would be Carl's terminal illness.

That was Wednesday morning. Wednesday afternoon, Art called me and said, "Don, we have to have a Lincoln program the day after tomorrow. I know you are well informed on Lincoln, so I'm relying on you." Wednesday afternoon until Friday noon. The Old Log didn't have, nor did I know of any actor who looked enough like Lincoln to go in that direction. I had known the Gettysburg Address since high school, but that wouldn't suffice either. It was too late to write a play with dialogue and expect the actors to memorize and rehearse it before Friday noon.

After dinner Wednesday, I knew I had to do something. How could I use several different actors without involving them in lengthy memorization and blocking rehearsals? The answer—have each actor represent a friend or person who had known Lincoln. Each actor would tell briefly (and this would be memorized) how he knew Lincoln, and then read from one of Lincoln's speeches he had personally heard. I could start work; I had many books on Lincoln's life, and I wrote a short presentation for the President of Rotary to read as an introduction in which the problems of today paralleled the problems of Lincoln's presidency.

After that introduction, five male actors and one female entered and sat in chairs lined across the stage. All were dressed in appropriate costume. All listened and responded to their fellow friends of Lincoln.

I was the first. I played Lincoln's law partner, William Herndon. After the lengthiest story in the script (and I admit I read some of it), I introduced the next character, Illinois merchant Joshua Speed, who told of his long relationship to Lincoln, and ends with reading a portion of Lincoln's remarks as he stood on the back of the railroad car preparing to leave Springfield for Washington.

Next was a reporter for Horace Greeley's newspaper. He ends with reading the closing remarks of Lincoln's inaugural address. Then I, as Herndon, introduced Mrs. Bixby, who spoke only to read the letter Lincoln had written to her as the mother who had lost five sons in the War. Next was a reporter from the *New York Herald* of the 1860s, Mr. Thomas Coate, who closed his remarks by reading several paragraphs of Lincoln's second inaugural speech.

The last of the performers was introduced "not as a personal friend of Mr. Lincoln's," but he had seen him, he had heard him speak. This speaker told of living in Gettysburg as a boy and being in the first row of spectators as Abraham Lincoln said ... and then this actor READ the Gettysburg Address.

What had begun as an emergency had turned into a blessing. For the first time we heard the Gettysburg Address, and other thoughts of Lincoln without wondering, "Did Lincoln sound like that? Did he really look like that?" All of a sudden we were listening to what he said—the words he used—the thoughts that were his.

Since that original staging, we have presented the Lincoln program over 300 more times.

THE HINCKLEY FIRE

A friend for a good many years, Don Engebretson, called to ask if I could join him for lunch at the Lafayette. As I recall, it was January of 1994. When I arrived at the club, Don and a young woman were already seated. He introduced her, the curator of the Hinckley Minnesota Museum. The curator explained that the focus of the Hinckley Museum, though it contained other material, was primarily concerned with the history of the Hinckley fire, the most devastating fire in the history of this country. Don interrupted her story to say that when he had first visited the museum, he found it so well organized, so well labeled, so well executed in every way, that he asked to meet the curator.

In their conversation, she had told him that they were preparing to celebrate in September, the 100th anniversary of this fire, if they could find someone to write the script. Engebretson replied that he knew exactly the right person and he would introduce us as soon as she could come to lunch at Lafayette.

The first thing I asked the curator was, "did she want a pageant?" Her reply was no, she wanted a 50-minute play. When I remarked that a play depicting the fire would not be easy, Engebretson suggested that I should start by visiting the museum and several of the sites where lives were lost and saved. I made an appointment to visit Hinckley the first of the next month.

My visit to Hinckley proved one thing: it was going to be difficult to write and difficult for them to produce a play depicting the fire. The curator showed me the small "auditorium" at the museum in which the play would be presented and suggested the cast be limited to no more than ten people. Despite the limitations, I agreed to attempt to produce a script.

After much thought and many changes in outline, I finally arrived at a form around which I could write a play.

First scene: A home in Hinckley before the fire—
approximately 16 minutes in length.

Second scene: A symbolic scene representing the fire—two
minutes.

Third scene: The receiving depot in Duluth to which the
people of Hinckley were taken to escape the fire—
15 minutes.

Fourth scene: A home in Hinckley after the fire—16 minutes.

Feeling that the significant story and emotion of the play would come through dialogue, I decided narration would be used in only three places.

In scene one, the narrator was the mother.

In scene two, no narration, no dialogue. I suggested that five or six people would be used to change the furniture, rearrange set piece. They would be seen in silhouette only against a background of fluctuating red light. They would move in dance-like movement, symbolically representing fear, despair, pain, burning and death. During these two minutes, a sound tape would be played. We spent a great deal of one day in Cookhouse Studios in Minneapolis, producing a really remarkable tape that contained the frightening wounds of the all-consuming fire and the sounds of attempts to escape.

In scene three, the narrator is a reporter from the *Duluth Times* newspaper as he interviews the survivors from Hinckley who have arrived at the Duluth depot, and helps families search for children separated in the wild race to escape.

The narrator of scene four was Mary, the daughter we met in the first scene. She tells of the courage of the many families moving back to Hinckley, making the most of small homes hastily built, not yet complete.

Realizing that in a small place the sense of smell can add much, I suggested that in the first scene, a gentle odor of burning wood be introduced; and in the scene from the first makeshift meal in the home to which the family is returning, I suggested a strong odor of brewing coffee be used.

In scene four, when the family inquires of their pastor, whom they have asked to join their humble meal, what his text will be for the first church service in Hinckley after the fire, he replies:

Pastor: Well, I thought I'd start the service with this bit of scripture:

"And there are some of whom there is no memorial. But these, too, were men and women of mercy, whose godly deeds will not fail. Good things continue with their seed; their posterity are a holy inheritance, and their seed hath stood in the covenants. And their children for their sakes remain forever; their seed and their glory shall not be forsaken. Their name liveth unto generation and generation. Let the people show forth their wisdom, and the church declare their praise."

Father of the family: (Speaking of its appropriateness, hardly more than a nod of his head in agreement) Yes.

Pastor: And then ask them—as I ask you now—to join in singing—
(Family joins almost immediately. They know this favorite church hymn)
Bless'd be the tie that binds
Our hearts in Christian love
The fellowship of kindred minds
Is like to that above

Pastor: (At end of song, the Pastor, without any announcement, starts praying): Our heavenly Father, bless this family here tonight—(A pause, then continues) And bless forever, Hinckley, this town that is our home. Amen.

After each presentation, the people of Hinckley in attendance felt that they were among those so blessed.

"Actors—They're a Favorite Race"—Cervante Quixote

Again and again I have said that one of the reasons the Old Log has been able to keep going is because we have always been fortunate in the actors we've been able to hire. Not only through our regular auditions in New York and Chicago, but also from recommendations. As an example, Dr. David Itken, head of the Goodman School of Theater, would call us each spring at graduation time to tell us he had a number of graduates we should see.

At the Old Log, we have always heard, in audition, everyone, regardless of experience or lack of, who wrote or telephoned asking to read for us. On occasion this has added some excellent talent to our cast.

"One of the reasons the Old Log has been able to keep going is because we have always been fortunate in the actors we've been able to hire." The same can be said of all our help that we've hired. Just as Dr. David Itkin recommended actors with unusual talent, just so did the head of the Design Department of the Yale School of Drama, recommend young designers. He sent us Gene Tunezi, who, after several years at the Old Log, was hired by CBS. Next was Peter Wingate, a good designer and a uniquely talented painter, who painted elaborate wallpaper designs with both hands simultaneously. Wingate became an established designer of Broadway shows. Some of our staff came without any recommendation.

As we moved into the new building, and as we moved into our new home at 5120, there was often carpentry work that needed to be done, so we often hired contractor Augie Ofstead to do whatever was necessary. After two years of this, he came to us and said that it was too difficult to find carpenters, too difficult to do the new required governmental forms; he was retiring. When I remarked that we would miss him, he said that if the job wasn't too heavy, he could handle it alone. The discussion ended with our putting him on our payroll. I thought Augie was 70; we soon discovered that he was almost 80. We put Augie in charge of all construction that the scenic designer needed, which meant that he was in charge of the young men who were apprentices. Never could there be a better arrangement.

Augie Ofstead was an ethical, moral and religious person. In his quiet way he guided these boys under him into the right path by simply saying, "I don't think you're right. I wish you'd think about it." How many of these boys he turned away from disaster? Well, it was all of them.

Following Augie came Herb Leffler, who was hired by either Rupert or Dony.

Herb, in age, was over sixty. Whatever his age, he looked older. He was slow both in movement and mind, but he was steady and, as I have said, willing. Wherever he was, whatever he was doing, Herb was smoking his pipe. His official assignment was "janitor and maintenance" but being "willing," he would do whatever he thought needed doing. If the box office phone rang and no one else was there to answer, Herb became "box office" and answered the phone, not always with desired results. During the run of *Ten Little Indians*, Herb answered the phone, and when asked about the play, he told the caller: "It's about this judge who has killed all these people, but nobody knows about it."

Timmy in later years was also very good at talking with prospective help. I heard him tell a young man who wanted to work with the scenery crew, "And of course there are also fringe benefits." "Like what?" was the question. "Every strike night Bob Wang goes into Excelsior and brings back pizza." I wish I could say that I was the one who could see beneath a coarse exterior a loyal and willing person. When Timmy attended Blake School, he was assigned a writing project. He wrote a three-act play about the Old Log and its people. He included this scene of Herb answering the phone. Timmy was severely criticized for including in his play a scene in which there was a person doing something that no person was ever so stupid as to do.

On another occasion, early in the morning, Rupert LaBelle was in his usual position behind the box office desk. Herb was sweeping the floor immediately in front of the box office counter and Rupert was just ending his telephone conversation:

Rupert: I told you that? . . . Well, I was wrong. I'm sorry. Thank you. (He hangs up) Hell.

Herb: Something wrong?

Rupert: I've been here ten years and that was the first mistake I've ever made.

Herb: (Continuing sweeping the floor) Well, you know, if you don't do much, you don't make many mistakes.

Rupert had a great gift for answering any question that a caller might ask. We all remember a caller asking him, "Does Nancy Nelson use dope?" Rupert didn't lose a beat. "That," he said, "is the most impertinent question I've ever heard." And hung up.

Herb's assistant, Mike, was just as slow as Herb physically and perhaps even slower mentally. Mike was a good and loyal worker. I doubt, however, if any assistant janitor has ever gotten along well with his boss. Herb and Mike didn't fight; they just never spoke to one another.

One late morning I could find neither Mike nor Herb. When I went into the dining room seeking to find either one of them, I found them both. Herb was sitting in a dining room chair, smoking his pipe. Mike was kneeling at Herb's feet shining Herb's shoes. Mike looked up at me: "This afternoon Herb has to go to a funeral."

The winters in the sixties and seventies brought much more snow than recent winters. Several times each winter there would be a great accumulation of snow on the roof of the theater. Fearing a buildup of too much weight, we would shovel and sweep the roof clear. We, for some crazy reason I can no longer recall, would always do this at night after the show. Joining us, always, were Herb and

Mike. They enjoyed it. On several occasions, Herb, standing on the peak of the roof, would lose his footing and start a slide on his back down to the lower veranda roof. Always, he would joyfully shout, "LOOK OUT, here I come." We began to suspect that his falls and long slides were intentional. I do know Herb never missed a "shovel snow off the roof night."

A special moment: when, Carol, Rupert's assistant in the box office, complained to Herb that the toilet tissue in the ladies room was rough and harsh. She told him when he next ordered to get something softer. Herb said not a word to Carol, but as she walked away, Herb turned to Anita and whispered, "Carol's delicate."

And then there was Quentin Morello. Quentin worked for his father in the family-owned bar in Chicago, but would come to the Old Log every summer as a part-time actor and full-time assistant to everyone. After spending two days helping to carry heavy platforms from the shop to backstage at the theater, Quentin said, "We may not be the best company, but I can tell you we have the longest arms of any crew in theater."

I'm certain you have heard story after story about chefs, cooks and their helpers. Having operated a theater that serves meals, I assure you that all the stories you have heard are true. The Old Log has served food from the very beginning. Beginning in 1940, hamburgers were prepared and served out of the attractive gazebo just outside the box office door. After the war, we continued still using the "logburger" peanut dressing that Mrs. Kuechle had developed. During the 15-minute intermission between acts, there were quite often three of us working the stand. It was a busy place; the orders had to be taken and filled as quickly as possible. In the late '40s, the fastest and best hamburger expert we had was Al Burns. One intermission, I was, as usual, busy selling and opening Coca-Cola, 7-Up and Dr. Pepper. Just as the outside lights blinked to signal that the audience should return to their seats, one of them ordered five hamburgers. Al went into flank speed to deliver the order before the curtain for the next act went up. In only a few minutes he served the man his five hamburgers. When the man opened one to add ketchup, he discovered there was no meat. On examining the other four, none had any meat. When he brought this to Al's attention, Al's reply was "I'm sorry—why didn't you tell me you wanted them 'with.'" The five hamburger patties were on the grill ready to go.

After we moved into the new building, the gazebo was, for the most part, left empty and unused. We asked Bob Aden, who had operated a restaurant in Manhattan and owned three restaurants in Arizona, what he would suggest. His idea was to serve "Light Suppers" with the choice of hamburger or ham bun, served with either potato salad or baked beans. Bob volunteered to cook and get the operation under way. "Light Suppers" were an immediate success.

When there were groups who wanted a more hearty meal, we arranged with the catering service of Aggie Klotter, who also served as the pastry chef for the Lafayette Club.

By 1970, our original mortgage loan from Northwestern National Life had been paid off, so with Bob to advise us, we decided to ask for another mortgage loan with which we would build a full kitchen and laundry. Bob and Joan created the first menu—a menu that we still follow today. Our goal was to keep the menu simple, concentrating on quality and service. We soon gained a reputation for having the best walleye pike and prime rib dinners in the area. Bob tried several suppliers of fish before settling on one; our roast beef was always government graded "prime."

Aden was responsible for hiring our first kitchen staff and I very quickly learned that all chefs, including Bob, are "different"—on occasion, "weird." All are proud of their skill and their ability to produce good meals. You can question them, but be prepared for strange answers.

The parade of Kitchen Kings over the years include Denny Henderson, who was as proud and weird as any of them, but by far the most loving. Denny, now retired, was as big around—well almost—as Robert Robinson, the gospel singer. Denny loved to eat, particularly liked to eat food that he had prepared. He was and is a favorite, wanting to love and be loved by everybody, including all friends of the Old Log.

While Denny was still early in his career at the theater, Terry O'Sullivan, dressed in his usual good taste, came to the theater looking for his wife, Anita. After Terry and Anita had discussed whatever it was that Terry came to discuss, Denny went to Anita and asked her who that handsome man was. Anita answered, "Why that's the man that married me." Denny misunderstood exactly what Anita meant, so for months after that referred to Terry as "The Reverend."

Denny was a gift giver and unbelievably generous. Whenever a grandchild was born, Denny sent the child a complete wardrobe. When Christmas came, every person at the theater received a gift, carefully selected, carefully wrapped. When Bob Aden died, Denny ordered and had planted a tree in Bob's memory. Another year, another tree in memory of another Old Log family member. Denny is, and always has been, a giving person.

Chico, though not a chef, was a kitchen worker who was proud and weird, but like Denny, loving and lovable. Chico is an elf-like person who every morning salutes me, saying "Good morning, Sir Don." I always reply, "Good morning, Sir James" (his given name). I once lengthened the conversation by saying, "Chico, you're a good man" (and he is hard working, loyal and never complaining). Chico replied, "You're a good man, too, Don." After a pause, Chico added, "If either one of us was really a good man, we wouldn't be here."

At present our chef is Chris. He and his assistant have organized everyone in the kitchen so well that there is truly nothing but happiness. Whenever possible, Anita and I both become a part of the "line" when there are large crowds for lunch. When working there we know that we have accomplished something.

We have discovered only one "weird" thing about Chris—he left the kitchen of the Minneapolis Club to come to us at the Old Log.

Whether it was Rupert or Dony who hired our priceless staff isn't at all clear. Most of them, excluding Chris, were people who anyone else would probably not have hired, but both Rupert in the '70s and Dony now had a unique ability to see into the soul of those who were applying.

ENGLAND WITHOUT LONDON

In the telling of our success with the Cooney farces—I still maintain Ray saved the American commercial regional theaters—I omitted the telling of other attractions that took us to London.

One beautiful summer morning, Dick Wilson, an advertising executive and writer of wonderful jingles, telephoned me to say that there was a marvelous show coming to the Hennepin Center for the Arts. It was a show built around the life and the mission of St. Francis, and was performed by a world famous pantomimist, Nichel Ortherin. It had been put together by a London theater man, Hugh Williams, for an idealistic group that had taken the name Moral Rearmament. He felt strongly that I would be pleased with the show.

He was correct; I did like the show. I found its unusual format, of one actor (basically a pantomimist) and a small orchestra, interesting and relevant to the life of St. Francis. I returned for a second viewing, taking with me our former parish priest, Father William Bullock, who by now was an Auxiliary Bishop. He, too, was moved.

After the show, as Bullock and I stood on Hennepin Avenue to say our goodnights, we were approached by a somewhat intoxicated derelict.

Drunk: Father—

Bullock: Yes—

Drunk: I just want to tell you I love the Virgin Mary.

Bullock: Well, I want you to know and remember that she loves you, too.

Drunk: Thank you, Father.

I can't remember ever hearing a shorter, more effective homily.

Back to St. Francis.

I again found it easy to invite the St. Francis company to the Old Log for dinner and the show. While having dinner at the Old Log, they reminded me that their show of St. Francis had been produced for and by the group Moral Rearmament.

The group had been started during World War One by an American chaplain serving at Oxford. When he explained to students that he believed that if the members of every religion would lead their lives on the principles and guidelines of the religion in which they claimed to believe, the problems of the world would soon find solutions. In the beginning of the organization, since all members were students of Oxford, it was called "The Oxford Group."

Understanding that I was genuinely interested and seeing that my life was theater, they told me that for years they had owned and operated a professional theater in London, called the Westminster, where they presented plays that if not religious, had at least a moral standard.

Moral Rearmament's chief spokesman for this discussion was Hugh Williams, the author of St. Francis and an already established playwright.

Before the evening was over, I promised to let Hugh know when next we were in London and he gave me two phone numbers, making certain I'd be able to reach him. And I did.

Over the years that followed, High and Dell were responsible for English adventures that without them, we would never have experienced: a tour of Windsor Castle followed by high tea, a visit to one of the earliest fishing villages in Wales, very much the same as it had been for centuries; a weekend at a friend's cottage in Wales; a visit to Winston Churchill's home at Chartwell, where he did most of his painting; a fabulous weekend in County Kent; and then the most surprising.

After a weekend at their home, Hugh and Dell were driving us to the nearest rail station, when he said, "We're just coming to something I think would interest you." He turned into what appeared a long drive across a field. No building, nothing in sight, except the field. Finally we reached a small church to the side of which was a cemetery with headstones dating back to the 1600s. Inside this church, miles from any settlement or even any neighboring houses, was a man tuning an immense white Bougandorf piano. There was to be a concert there the following Thursday. A priceless instrument. A truck could have driven up the narrow road, loaded up the piano and stolen away. Nobody would ever have seen them.

Hugh brought our attention to the stained-glass window in back of the altar—a Chagall. The window had been commissioned by a prominent, affluent family as a memorial to their young daughter who had been killed in a boating accident. The family, the parish, all who ever saw the window, were so pleased that the family had replaced every window in the small church with a Chagall work of stained glass. It was unbelievable in this little country church miles from anywhere. Knowing I would never forget the experience, I recorded the name of the church: "Tudely Church, County Kent, outside the Tombridge Village."

In 1993, Hugh and Dell came to Excelsior for their third visit. In our library, Hugh noticed the shelf of books about Abraham Lincoln. There were very few that Hugh hadn't read; he told me of the adoration that the people of Great Britain had for our sixteenth president. It was something I had not realized. The English felt that Lincoln represented to the world a democracy and freedom that they did not yet fully enjoy. "Lincoln's beliefs, if known, could change the world."

To that end, Hugh had written a play, *Old Abe*. He had hoped to present it the next year at the Moral Rearmament international meeting at Coux, Switzerland, where the organization owned and maintained a former great estate. But though the play, *Old Abe* had only two characters, to produce it with professional actors in London would be more costly than the organization would invest. When I told him I'd like to read it, he said, "I'll send you a copy as soon as we're home."

Old Abe was a brilliant play expressing all the beliefs, the philosophy, and the political morality that was Lincoln. After the reading the play, I wrote Hugh and told him that I would produce the play here at the Old Log without cost to him, if he could provide transportation for the two actors to Switzerland. Agreement was immediate. I cast Jim Wallace, whose frame and facial expression, even without makeup, had a remarkable resemblance to Lincoln; and Jim Harris I cast as the second actor who played several roles. Hugh and Dell returned to Excelsior for the last few rehearsals and the two performances at which we hoped to raise enough money to pay the actors.

Between London's West End and Moral Rearmament's Westminster Theater, Joan and I had experienced heady times.

Box Office II: There's Only One Way to Know Your Theater

In 1970, Rupert, at age 75, decided it was time for him to go into semi-retirement. We gave quite a large party at the theater and presented him with a three-week, expense-paid trip to London, his favorite city. If you ask why we didn't give him a gold watch, we had presented that to him the Christmas before. He was in London less than a week, when we received a cable: "I have overestimated the time I should be away from home. Please see that my apartment is ready for my immediate return."

On his return he was busy as ever in the box office and on stage. Two years later, Rupert went into full retirement. He felt, however, that since we assured him of a weekly salary—needless to say a small weekly salary—he would want to do something for the Old Log. He decided that "something" was to be his numbering of the tickets with row and seat. Every few days he would call to report that he had another set or two of tickets, and we should send someone over to pick them up.

We heard from Rupert daily. Then one day, no call. When we attempted to telephone him, there was no answer. There had always been a key to Rupert's apartment in the safe at the theater, so Dony took it, asked little Jon to go with him to see if Rupert was all right. They climbed the stairway, knocked on the door, and then, with growing apprehension, unlocked it and walked in. Indeed, something was wrong: there sat Rupert leaning over, his head resting on the kitchen table, felt-tip pen still in hand, a third of the way through numbering a day's set of tickets. He appeared to be reaching out with his left hand to his old blue enamelware cup, still half-filled with yesterday morning's coffee. How many, many times must Dony and Jon have relived that morning of discovery.

That night, Jon came into our room. "Is it all right if tonight I sleep with you and Mom?"

If only I, instead of Jon and Dony, had gone to see if Rupert was all right.

After Rupert retired, the box office, just as Rupert had planned, was taken over by Dony. After more than 25 years, has "being in the box office" changed? Not much.

The following section is "being in the box office" with Rupert. This time we're in the box office just 15 minutes before curtain time.

Now I can't tell you that all of these incidents happened the same night, but I can tell you that every one of them is real. They actually happened. And some of them happened every week.

Please remember that they occurred while we were selling 350 or 500 other seats. Well, sometimes maybe a hundred other seats. With almost everyone saying how they are so glad that we're still here, or they had their first date here 20 years ago, or their grandparents brought them to the Children's show every Christmas—always something that made you happy that you were still here. It was an opportunity to greet old friends, many of whom had attended every play for years. All of this made working in the box office, in spite of everything—including these "incidents"—a time of joy and fulfillment.

Woman: *(Approaches counter)*

Dony: Good evening, Mrs. Harrison. *(With tickets in hand)*
Here are your tickets, two in the center of row seven. The best in the house.

Woman: I know. Thank you.

Dony: Have a good evening.

Woman: Thank you. Oh—I have a question for your father.
You're too young to remember.

Dony: Maybe not.

Woman: I think so. *(Now to Don)* Back in—I think it was 1961 or 1962, we saw a play here that was funny. I mean really funny. I can't remember the name.

Don: Do you remember what it was about?

Woman: Well, all I really remember is that there was this room where a young couple—well, whatever—and living across the hall from them was a real—well, I think he may even have been their landlord. Anyway, the first we see of him is early in the play he wants to get the bottle of milk left in the hall, so he reaches out with his leg to get it within reach, and all the leg has on is a red sock.

Don: A red sock—

Woman: That isn't much to go on, is it?

Don: It's all you need. The play was **Under the Yum Yum Tree**.

Woman: That's right! Successful, wasn't it?

Don: The first time we did it was in 1961, and it was the first play we ever ran for three weeks. After that, we did it every year for eight years. Yes, it was very successful.

Woman: Thank you. That's what it was all right. **Under the Yum Yum Tree**. *(Starts for auditorium)*

Don: Have a good evening.

Woman: I'm sure I will. Thank you.

Dony: It was a funny show, wasn't it?

Don: It was. When I first read it, I hated it.

Dony: Why did you do it?

Don: Because Arthur Godfrey had spent weeks talking about it. Someone in his cast was appearing in it.

Dony: So?

Don: Joan insisted with that publicity, it couldn't lose. Just another time when she was right.

(Phone rings)

Don: *(Answering)* Good evening, the Old Log.

Voice: *(Woman's voice over cell phone)* I'm on my way, but I'm lost. Can you tell me how to get there?

Don: I'm sure I can, if you can just tell me where you are.

Voice: *(Not happy)* If I knew where I was, I wouldn't have to ask you how to get there.

Don: Yes—Well, are you somewhere on Highway Seven?

Voice: I think so. *(To driver of car)* Are we on Highway Seven? My husband says he thinks we're on Highway Seven. Yes.

Don: Are you going east or west?

Voice: How am I supposed to know that?

Don: Well—let's see—when you pass a landmark, you know, or a special building—tell me what it is and maybe I can figure out where you are.

Voice: Just a minute, there's one now—

Don: What is it?

Voice: A brown house.

Don: I see. Was it on the left or the right?

Voice: *(Of husband)* Is it on the right or on the left? *(Pause)* It's on my right if I'm facing the front of the car—on my left when I'm turned around and looking out the back window. Just a minute—we're passing a street sign.

Don: Good!

Voice: It says, "Lake Street."

Don: *(Pause)*

Voice: Did you hear me? It says "Lake Street."

Don: *(Not really wanting to ask)* Is that Lake Street in Minneapolis or Lake Street in Excelsior?

Voice: How the hell do I know? Why do you think I called you? Is there anyone else there that I can talk to?

Don: *(Hands the phone to Dony)* Here. I'll sell the tickets. Good luck.

Dony: Good evening. May I help you?

Voice: I certainly hope so. That other idiot couldn't. I just told him we passed a Lake Street sign and he stupidly asked me—

Dony: I know, I heard him. Well, let me ask how did you get on Lake Street.

Voice: We turned off 494, onto Highway 7, and the first thing we know, it's Lake Street.

Dony: Which way were you going?

Voice: I don't know. We passed the Mall of America, then the Radisson and then—

Dony: So when you came to Lake Street—to Highway Seven—you were going north.

Voice: I don't know. If you say so, yes.

Dony: And you turned to your right on Seven.

Voice: Yes.

Dony: Well, you should have turned to your left.

Voice: Oh, sh… *(and she hangs up before the whole word is heard)*

Dony: Hello—hello—

(Other phone rings)

Don: Good evening, the Old Log Theater.

Dony: I think she hung up.

Don: May I help you?

Voice: *(This is a new voice)* What time is your curtain tonight?

Don: 8:30.

Voice: 8:30—it's almost 8:30 now.

Don: That's right.

Voice: Could you please hold the curtain for about 15 minutes. My daughter and her new boyfriend just left for there.

Don: Well, it's raining so we'll be a little late in getting started anyway.

Voice: Thank you. They're already on their way. Hold that curtain.

(Hangs up, shaking his head in wonder)

Dony: *(Having overheard enough to know the conversation)* What happened to your policy of "always tell the customer the truth, regardless of what happens"—?

(Phone rings)

Don: OK. Good evening, the Old Log Theater.

Voice: *(An elderly woman)* Oh, hello. I was hoping you might answer the phone because I want to ask you, and I know it's almost 8:30 and time for you to go into the theater

and make your announcements. The question I want to
ask, is this play that you're presenting now—is it one of
your risqué plays?

Don: *(Looks at Dony and knows he has to tell the truth)* I'm glad
you asked. Yes, I'm afraid I must tell you that it is.

Voice: Good. I'll take eight tickets.

Dony: *(Taking phone)* I'll take the reservation.

Don: Always be honest with the customer.

Dony: *(On phone)* This is Dony—eight tickets for what night?
(Phone rings)

Don: Good evening, the Old Log Theater.

Man: *(On cell phone)* I need help.

Don: Maybe I can help you.

Man: I'm lost.

Don: Where are you? Maybe I can help.

Man: Well, I was at Maynard's—

Don: Yes?

Man: Either they gave me the wrong directions or I didn't
understand them. So I went to McDonald's. I couldn't
find anyone there who could speak English.

Don: Are you still at McDonald's?

Man: Sort of. I'm at that stop sign between McDonald's and
Maynard's, facing Maynard's.

Don: All right, that street right in front of you is Minnetonka
Boulevard—Old Log Way. Turn right there, you go two
blocks, and there we are on the left-hand side. See you
soon.

Man: Just a minute—would you stay on the phone and help
me until I'm there? I don't want to be lost again.

Don: I can do that.

Man: I've just turned right on Old Log Way.

Don: You're doing great.

Man: I'm now crossing a bridge.

Don: You're fine.

Man: There's something called St. Albin's Bay Boat House.

Don: You haven't much farther to go.

Man: Don't leave me.

Don: Still here.

Man: There's something on my left—with a lot of lights.

Don: That's us.

Man: Do I turn in here or go on straight?

Don: You'd better turn in or you'll be lost again.

Man: I'm turning.

Don: Good.

Man: I'm in the parking lot.

Don: Can you find your own parking space?

Man: I think so. And thank you. God bless the cell phone.

Don: Yes. "God Bless the Cell Phone." *(Not meaning it) (Now off phone)* The worst thing in years to hit the box office is the cell phone. A couple of weeks ago someone asked me if "being in the box office" had changed in the last 50 or 60 years.

Dony: And you probably said no. And you were right except for the Internet, the charge card, ticketmaster, online sale of tickets—except for those things, you were right.

Don: You should have added the cell phone. Just six years ago that man who wanted you to guide him to the parking lot wouldn't have thought of it.

Dony: No, he would have gotten his directions when he ordered his tickets and wouldn't have been lost.

Don: The cell phone has eliminated the necessity of knowing where you're going. You can always call and find out how to get there when you're already on your way.

Dony: Who was that old baseball player who said, "if you don't know where you're going, any road will get you there?"

Don: I don't remember.

Man: *(Approaching counter, throwing his tickets on counter)* When I called the box office last week, I asked for the best seats in the theater. And when I get here tonight, I find that this is what they gave me—11 and 12 in the 7th row.

Don: What seats did you want?

Man: The best seats in the theater.

Don: Well, these are the best seats in the theater.

Man: Oh. Well, I'd prefer seats 13 and 14. In the 7th row.

Don: We can do that.

Man: You sure these are the best?

Don: Yes, they are.

Man: All right, then.

Don: Thank you.

Man: Thank you, too.

(Woman is talking on her cell phone a few steps away from box office. She is having a quiet argument with someone on the other end. She approaches Dony in the box office.)

Woman: Pardon me—

Dony: Yes?

Woman: *(Handing him her cell phone)* My husband won't believe me. Will you tell him how to get out here?

Dony: *(Taking phone)* Sure.

Woman: And tell him to hurry!

Man: *(Approaching box office)* Not many cars in the parking lot. George Harrison *(This is his name, he is asking for tickets)*

Dony: It's a little early yet.

Man: What's the matter, the show's not any good?

Don: I think you'll like the show.

Man: I hope so.

Don: *(Handing him tickets)* Two tickets. That will be $48.00, Mr. Harrison.

Man: $48.00, huh. I'd better like the show. *(Handing him money)*

Don: You will. Thank you.

Man: I loved the last one. That's what we need—laughter.

Man: *(Approaching box office)* Before we left home, my wife told me you didn't take credit cards—and I forgot my checkbook. Do you have an ATM machine anywhere?

Dony: I have an idea that's easier than that. Just send us a check tomorrow. Here's our address *(Handing him a ticket envelope)*.

Man: I'll do it first thing in the morning. And thank you. I appreciate it.

Dony: You're welcome. Have a good time.

Woman: *(Approaching counter)* I picked these tickets up earlier, and I'd like to exchange them.

Don: Certainly. Where would you like to sit?

Woman: *(Not hearing this)* I beg your pardon?

Don: I was just asking, where would you like to sit?

Woman: I'm sure these are great seats, but I really have to have something close to the front. You see, my husband is hard of hearing.

Don: Here you are. *(Exchanges tickets)*

Dony: Her husband is hard of hearing?

Don: In all the years I've been here, the person ordering the tickets is never the one that's hard of hearing.

Woman: *(Approaches box office, directly in front of Don. She looks around to make certain that no one can hear her, then she whispers her question.)*

Don: May I help you?

Woman: I hope so. *(Looks around again then whispers)* Can you tell me, is Don Stolz still alive?

Don: *(Looks at her for a moment and then says)* Just barely.

Woman: *(Understands but still says)* Thank you. I thought you'd know. *(She leaves)*

Dony: I heard that. Very funny.

Don: I thought it was funny, too. You know what I'm going to do? When I make my announcements before the show,

I'm going to tell the audience exactly what happened, and then ask this dear lady to stand.

Dony: You don't think she'll do it.

Don: She'll love it—probably wave at the audience.

Dony: As you have said so many times, there's nothing like working at the box office. Speaking of your announcements, *(He looks at clock)* it's about time for you to do it.

Don: Yes, it is.

Dony: My favorite is still the one you made on the opening night of the new building.

Don: Which one?

Dony: You remember. You told the audience that when we moved into the new building we took the seats out of the old building. Then you went on to say that you knew the legend was that they were made of split logs, but that wasn't true. The benches were made of two-inch planks and the benches had backs on them.

Don: Which most people don't remember.

Dony: At that time, 1960, neither the parking lot nor the driveway had been black topped. They were mud.

Don: They were mud! Real mud! In trying to make the walk into the new building less unpleasant, we had placed the planks from the former seats over the worst potholes.

Dony: You remember, don't you? You apologized to the audience for the mud, said you hoped the plank placement had helped some, and then you added—"Just remember the planks that you walked on tonight were the planks you sat on last summer."

Don: Mud and all, those were good times.

Dony: *(Hands note to Don)* In your curtain speech, don't forget this for Paul Najarian.

Don: Thank you. I hope it works.

Dony: It's a funny idea—if it does work.

Don: I understand why. His mother told Paul that when he's

going to propose, it would be nice if he selected a
romantic spot at which to do it.

Dony: And to Paul that meant the Old Log.

Don: Well you can understand that. His mother and father
have been bringing him out here since he was a boy.

Dony: And he's been in how many plays here?

Don: I think it's four.

Dony: Anyway—why wouldn't it be where Paul would want
to propose?

Don: Well, let's hope it works.

Dony: What happens if she refuses?

Don: Thank you for your reassuring question.

(As Don leaves box office to talk again directly to audience)

Dony: Good luck.

Don: *(Directly to audience)* Don't get the idea that just because
it's time for the curtain to go up that the phone calls stop.
They don't.

(Into scene—still in the box office with Dony)

(Phone rings)

Dony: Good evening, the Old Log Theater. May I help you?

Young girl: *(Crying)* Would you please call my mother to the
phone, her name is Mrs. John Harrison.

Dony: Well you know she's in the theater. The play's already
started.

Girl: But I have to talk with her. This is an emergency.

Dony: Maybe I could help.

Girl: Just get my mother to the phone.

Dony: There's no way I can page her at this time.

Girl: I have to talk with her, this is an emergency.

Dony: Like life threatening?

Girl: Yes, it is.

Dony: Do you know where she's sitting?

Girl: In the theater.

Dony: All right. I'll try to find your mother. What shall I tell
her is wrong?

Girl: Just tell her I have to talk with her. In my homework there's a question and I don't know the answer.

Dony: I understand. I'll tell you what we'll do. We'll find her at intermission and have her call home. That all right?

Girl: Well, just don't forget. Thank you.

Don: *(Direct to audience)* Sometimes the emergency call is for the father, not the mother.

(Into scene—back in the box office with Dony)

(Phone rings)

Dony: Good evening. The Old Log Theater.

Another young girl: *(Also crying)* Hello, is this the Old Log Theater?

Dony: Yes, it is.

Girl: Oh, good. I've got to talk to my father right away.

Dony: And his name?

Girl: Harry Williams. He's seeing the show.

Dony: You're crying. Is this an emergency?

Girl: A terrible emergency.

Dony: Well the play has already started and I have no idea where your father is sitting.

Girl: I have to talk to him. It's terrible.

Dony: If I can find him, what shall I tell him is wrong?

Girl: Well, before my mom and dad and their houseguests left for the theater, I asked my dad if I could have one of his old shirts and cut off the sleeves like all the other girls are doing. So I did.

Dony: Well, he told you that you could, didn't he?

Girl: Yes, he did, but you don't understand. I made a terrible mistake and cut off the sleeve of one of the houseguest's shirts. I have to talk to Daddy before they come home.

Dony: Now don't worry. You said your father's name is Harry Williams. We'll page him at intermission and have him call you.

Girl: Don't forget. It's a matter of life or death.

Dony: Don't worry, he'll call.

Girl: Thank you.

Don: *(Again direct to audience)* Long before either of these calls, I was backstage and had checked with Tim about the Paul Najarian thing, then went out before the curtain.

(Don is now in front of curtain, beginning his curtain speech) Good evening, and once again welcome to the Old Log Theater. I want especially to welcome two people who have been dear personal friends and friends of the Old Log for many years. And I know they're friends of yours, too—Doctor and Mrs. John Najarian. Sitting with them in the front row is one of their sons, Paul, and Paul's lovely girlfriend. Paul, would you please stand? I want to ask you a question.

Paul: *(Who is now standing)* All right.

Don: Paul, why haven't you married that lovely young lady who's with you tonight?

Paul: Maybe it's because I haven't proposed yet.

Don: Don't you think it's about time you did?

Paul: I suppose so. *(Starts to return to his seat)*

Don: Just a minute. Don't you think you've put it off long enough? I suggest you do it now.

Paul: You mean now—and here—

Don: I mean now and here.

Paul: It's a good idea, but I can't do it tonight.

Don: Why not?

Paul: I'm not prepared. I haven't any candy, and if a guy's going to propose he should have candy for the girl.

Don: Candy? Well, we can handle that. *(Reaches back between the curtains. Tim hands him a candy bar.)* Here's a Snicker's bar. That takes care of the candy.

Paul: I still can't propose. I haven't any flowers.

Don: *(Again reaches behind curtain. Tim hands him a terrible crushed imitation flower)* Here's the flowers.

Paul: Well—

Don: Now don't tell me you don't have a ring, because we've furnished the candy and the flowers, but we're not going to furnish the ring.

Paul: I have a ring.

Don: So—

Paul: *(Somewhat reluctantly)* All right. Honey, will you stand here with me?

Girl: *(She does)*

Paul: I love you very much and have for a long time. Will you please accept this ring?

Girl: I will. *(They kiss)* And I'm glad you asked me in front of your parents and this audience.

Don: And I'm sure that John and Mig and the audience are glad too. Congratulations and best wishes.

(Now Don moves on to other announcements)

Earlier this evening a lady, a former old-time resident of Excelsior, asked me nicely, quietly and secretively, "Could you tell me if Don Stolz is still alive?" When I answered, "Just barely," she had the answer. Will that lady please stand so we can properly thank her for her concern.

Sometimes my announcements are not that much fun, fun either for me or for the audience. Usually the announcements are concerned with greeting groups, announcing birthdays and congratulating couples on their anniversary, but always I try to make the audience welcome, hoping to leave them happy, in good spirits and looking forward to the play.

Talking to the audience before the play was something that I thought was important—and, all right—it was something I enjoyed. Most of the time. And sometimes there were announcements that were necessary. An example? *(After a second of thought)* Well, in 1969, we had a beautiful production of **You Know I Can't Hear You When the Water's Running**. You may remember that was one of the titles that Rupert mentioned earlier, one of the titles that caused some misunderstanding on the telephone. It was a collection of four beautifully written one acts. Together they were in the words of the critic of the *New York Daily News*: "Captivating, touching and explosively funny."

The third of the plays, *I'll Be Home for Christmas*, shows a father and mother discussing the sex education of their almost grown children, a son and a daughter. It was a discussion that could have taken place in almost every home in America, with language just as open and just as frank. But on opening night, I knew we were in trouble. And I wasn't pleased. The second night when making my pre-show announcements, I told the audience: "Tonight you are going to hear words in our theater that you have never heard from our stage before. They are all words that if you heard them from your doctor or even from your minister from his pulpit, you would not be offended. So I'm hoping that all of us will hear these words with the same acceptance that we would give our doctor or minister."

What would have been a failure, I think primarily because of my announcement, *You Know I Can't Hear You When the Water's Running* became a big ten-week hit—the second longest Old Log run at that time.

Then in 1981, September 1981, we were presenting Hugh Leonard's beautiful and wise play, *Da*. One of the characters was shown as a young man, and then as an old man. They were played by two different actors. In the program they were listed separately as "young Charlie" and "old Charlie." Quite a few in the audience never read the cast of characters carefully. And to them the play became confusing. No one was offended, just confused.

Confusion is also something that doesn't help attendance. It was such a beautiful play. So my evening announcements very briefly brought to the audience's attention that there were two Charlies— young Charlie and old Charlie. We all felt happy with the play from then on.

The first time we presented Ray Cooney's *Run For Your Wife*, I wanted to really emphasize that the next show about which I was talking was really great—one of the best—probably the funniest. It had run for eight years in London. So I guaranteed it. I said, if you come to see *Run For Your Wife* and you don't think it's funny, you come to the box office after the show, and I'll be there, and I'll—I'll

Beau Jest; Barbara June Patterson, Steve Hendrickson, Teri Deaver, Mark Bradley, and Neil Kobin.

Funny Money; Steve Shaffer, Susanne Egli, Tom Stolz, and Jan Puffer.

try to figure out what's wrong with you.

In 2003, we were doing **Out of Order**—another great Ray Cooney show that had won the Laurence Olivier award for Best Comedy of the Year. We were doing well with it and then the snow and below zero temperatures came. The audience size still wasn't too bad. To be there at all they had to be crazy, wonderful people. So I said to them, "You can see that because of the weather, attendance isn't what it really ought to be, so I'm going to ask you to help the Old Log. If you like the play, and I'm certain you will, I'm going to ask that in the next few days you call all your friends—people you like and tell them that they have to get out to the Old Log and see **Out of Order**. Now, if for some reason I can't imagine, you don't like the show, you can still help me. Call all the people you don't like.

Then there was my effort. *(Holding up brochure)* Everytime the printer would deliver our new brochure listing the plays for the coming year, I would say to the audience: "I'm going to ask you to do your share to help the Old Log by taking a handful of these brochures with you. If you would leave them at the checkout counter at Cub, the lingerie department at Target, oh, yes—church pews on Sunday. My feeling is that there is no place in the world where you could leave one of these where it wouldn't be doing me more good than where it is tonight."

In 1995, these schedules I was urging the audience to help distribute, featured **Beau Jest**, a delightful play that covered the warmth of the Jewish family tradition. In 1996, I emphasized that Ray Cooney would be back with a new comedy, **Funny Money**. In 1997, was a return of Neil Simon's **Odd Couple** starring Steve Shaffer and Tom Stolz. Then in 1998 a play we had seen in London and then Door County, **A Perfect Wedding**.

So, please remember that sometimes I think I have a reason for those stupid announcements that I make.

A Perfect Wedding; Emily Dooley, Sean Dooley, Tim Sharp, Amy Colon, Breean Julian, and Russ Konstans.

The Odd Couple; Tom Stolz and Steve Shaffer.

Whose Wife is it Anyway; James Harris, Steve Shaffer, Tom Stolz, John Seibert, and Lisa Todd.

381

THE TRUE INTERNATIONAL THEATER

About six months into our year-long showing of ***Run For Your Wife***, late in the summer of 1989, Ray Cooney (the playwright) and his wife, Linda, received our invitation and decided they should accept and come to Minneapolis to see what kind of a theater this was that was now into its 26th week of his play and still going strong.

Though the correspondence between both families was cordial, and occasionally even humorous, and though we had been warm in our invitation to stay with us in our home, the Cooneys, not quite sure, I'm certain, of what kind of theatrical animals we might be, replied that they would prefer to stay at some nearby hotel or B & B, explaining that they then would have more control of their personal schedule. We made reservations for them at the refurbished Christopher Inn, with which they were delighted. They thought that Mrs. Johnson, wife of Howard Johnson, owner and manager, was, with her high cheekbones, one of the most beautiful women they had ever seen. Anyone who met her couldn't but agree.

Alleen Hussung, the Cooney's specific agent with the Samuel French Play Brokers, had informed the Cooneys that she had seen the Old Log's production and much preferred it to the New York production, which had Ray Cooney as one of its stars. Surprisingly, both Ray and Linda, after they saw our production, agreed, though both did have some suggestions that they thought would make the production even better. These suggested changes we made immediately.

The third day the Cooneys were here, Joan suggested that we have a picnic on the theater grounds where we had some good picnic tables. Linda said she thought the picnic idea was great, she loved the grounds of the Old Log, but we would have a picnic the way the English did—we would sit on a blanket. It was a bucolic, arcadian afternoon, which brought the two families even closer.

Before the Cooneys left for London, Ray told me he had a new comedy; he would send me a copy and if we liked it, we should come to London, then go to a beautiful theater in Leatherhead for one of the preview performances and then be the sole producers of the play in the United States.

Joan and I had no question about whether or not we were going—we were going. We checked our passports to make certain they were still valid and made reservations on Northwest's night non-stop to England. We did not anticipate that the date we had selected was the same week as the Chelsea Flower Show; there just were no hotel rooms available. When we telephoned, Ray said not to worry, that his assistant, Hymie Udwin would find something for us. The something he found was the Athenum, one of the most elegant of the mid-size London hotels. The bed sheets were actually linen and changed daily.

Ray was correct. The theater in Leatherhead was lovely; his play, *Whose Wife Is It Anyway*, was a delight. We scheduled to open the last week of June 1990. It would be September before it opened in London.

Some time between the preview performances in Leatherhead and the opening night in London, Ray and his staff decided that the title *Whose Wife Is It Anyway* would be confusing for both those who had seen and those who had not seen *Run For Your Wife*. So they changed the title for London to *Out of Order* in reference to the large clock in the tower of the House of Commons.

Our *Whose Wife Is It Anyway* had a most successful run of 42 weeks, which meant it was also the first play of 1991.

As we did every year since first presenting it, we offered Tom's performance of *The Gospel According to St. Mark* on dark nights during the Lenten season.

In June of 1991 we presented Neil Simon's play, *Rumors*. Our

Not Now, Darling; Bob Aden, Paul Eidie, and Tom Stolz.

Rumors; Tom Stolz, Steve Shaffer, and Jackie Ross.

play for children that year was **Rapunzel and the Witch**. We were surprised that several groups cancelled their reservations because they thought it was immoral to even consider the possibility of ghosts or witches. As I have said before, when operating a theater, one finds unexpected and sometimes hard-to-understand viewpoints.

In December of 1991, during the run of **Rumors**, Club 9, Minneapolis Rotary called and asked if there was any way that we could once again perform **They Knew Lincoln** on Lincoln's birthday. Of course the answer was "yes." Some Rotarian had invited Kelvin Miller of Primarius Productions to attend. The next week, Kelvin telephoned to make an appointment so we could talk about a project that he was preparing for Cargill. Kelvin wanted me to portray W. W. Cargill, the founder of the company, to appear in a video production covering the 100-year history and to appear live at several locations, including the introduction and book signing of *Cargill, Trading the World's Grain*, written by Wayne G. Broehl, Jr., of the Amos Tuck School of Business, Dartmouth College, and published by the University Press of New England. As is probably apparent, I eagerly accepted.

Primarius ordered for me a tailor-made, authentic period suit and overcoat. It took little more than a mustache to turn me into a remarkable likeness of W. W. When they gave me a packet of business cards, I was W. W. Cargill. I copied his signature so thoroughly that by the end of the book signing, no one could have told that it was a forgery.

Of course Dr. Broehl, Jr., the author, was present when the employees were told if they wanted to purchase a copy of the book, they should do so now and it would be autographed by the author. I appeared so much like photographs they had seen of W. W. Cargill, that not taking into account that W. W. would now be 130 years old, some standing in line holding their copy of the book and waiting to get the author's autograph, decided it would be great to have W. W. Cargill's signature as well. Dr. Broehl heard several such requests and calling me aside asked if I would mind autographing the book along with him.

It Runs In The Family; Steve Shaffer and Tom Stolz.

Every year since then, when the Cargill retirees come to the theater in a group, I am asked to wear the W. W. Cargill suit and mustache when I welcome them to the Old Log.

Also, sometime during the run of **Rumors**, Ray Cooney wrote to say that he had a new comedy, had "workshopped" it several times, re-written it several times (Ray always went through this meticulous procedure before opening a new farce), and was going to have preview performances at the Royal Windsor in Windsor. We assured Ray that we would be there sometime during the preview performances.

It Runs in the Family is set in the doctor's lounge of a large hospital. It contains not one of the distasteful and objectionable bits of so-called humor that the doctor's lounge suggests; in fact it had some especially tender and pleasant moments in scenes between a young boy and his mother. The audience of the Royal Windsor was enthusiastic, and the local critics declared without doubt, it would be a big hit in London.

Ray had asked that we meet him in the bar lounge after the performance, along with some other people interested in arranging for performances at their theaters. It was at this meeting that I began to realize that few people in the States, including New York, have a good idea of what "international theater" is. At this after-the-show reception, there was an agent from Germany, a producer from Holland, and the head of the National Theater of Israel. And of course, the two people from Excelsior, Minnesota. No one was surprised that we were there.

The Old Log, with Ray's blessing, opened *It Runs in the Family* before it opened in London, as we had with *Whose Wife is it Anyway*. Opening night was September 9, a successful run of 24 weeks carried the farce over into 1993.

On these two visits to England just and in subsequent visits, Joan and I almost always arranged a full week away from home. We scheduled as many London productions as we could, often as many as ten in seven days. We, perhaps foolishly, always scheduled our first play of the visit on the afternoon we arrived in London after an all-night flight from Minneapolis. One of those "first" plays was *Don't Dress for Dinner*. As soon as we were seated, we began to doze off. I have from time to time said that the third best place to sleep is in the theater. First is your own bed, second is church, theater is third. During the performance of *Don't Dress for Dinner*, Joan and I were brought suddenly awake by the loud sounds of laughter. Quite frequently, Joan would ask me what they were laughing at and I couldn't reply. We decided we should come back the next night. I'm glad we did, for *Don't Dress for Dinner* has provided the Old Log with two fun and successful runs.

Several other plays that we saw during our London visits have very special places in my memory. *Blood Brothers*, the musical by Willie Russell, is one of those. Joan and I had tickets for a matinee performance. Sitting next to us was a young girl of perhaps seventeen years. Before the opening curtain she asked us if we had seen *Blood Brothers* before. When we said no, we hadn't, she replied, "Well, you'll love it."

"You've seen it before?"

"Oh, yes, this is the fifth time I've seen it. I save my money each week and when I have enough saved to buy a ticket, I come back to see **Blood Brothers** again."

When I looked at my program and saw that the opening musical number was titled "Marilyn Monroe," I sarcastically said to myself, "Oh, yes—this is going to be just great." But as soon as the curtain opened, I knew that I was wrong and the young girl right. It was a passionate show about twin brothers separated at birth. Some have accused it of being melodramatic. My reply is, "So what? Which of Shakespeare's tragedies was not melodramatic." One of the lead characters is the narrator. I would love to direct **Blood Brothers** with Hal Atkinson playing that role.

On another occasion, Joan and I were having dinner with Ray and Linda Cooney. When they asked what play we were seeing that night, I told them we had tickets for **Dead Funny**. Ray said, "Don't go, you will hate it." When I asked if he had seen it, he said no, "But believe me, you will hate it." Later that night at the theater, I understood why he had so advised us. In the first five minutes we heard the frankest language I have ever heard in a theater, and the leading man was absolutely nude. But with all the problems being endured by every character in the show, when the cast hears that Benny Hill has died, all of their personal problems are forgot. They decided to have a party in memory of Benny Hill and to that party, as their guest of honor, they invited an actor quite often on the Benny Hill show, an actor whom we had met through Ray Cooney because he is quite often in the cast of a Cooney show.

During the party on stage, Henry McGee telephones to say that he'll be a little late because the curtain of the Cooney play in which he has been appearing was a little late. Then after being assured that that is perfectly all right, he asks if it would be all right to bring Ray Cooney with him. Of course neither one of them ever appears. I haven't often found Cooney wrong in his recommendations, but I found **Dead Funny** to be interesting, memorable and even worthwhile.

During the following years, the Cooneys continued to visit us; staying with us at our home at 5120 Meadville and later at 4765 Regents Walk, and it became our custom to stay at their home at least one of the nights when we were in London.

As we were planning one of our summer trips to England, our son, Tim, informed us that he was open and could go with us. Our plans became greatly enlarged. We would rent a car (Tim had had experience driving in the British Isles when he attended school in Wales) and drive through the Lake Country and up around the Northern edge of Scotland.

Our first stop was to be at the White Moss Inn, about which we had read ads in *Gourmet Magazine*. It was a small inn: five rooms and an unattached cottage. Joan and I had a large, comfortable room; Tim, a smaller room just down the hall. The three of us eagerly awaited the announced cocktail hour in the living room of the central house, expecting to have the interesting experience of getting acquainted with people from the surrounding area. It developed that every single person booked at the Inn was from the United States. It was still fun and the dinner that followed was everything that *Gourmet Magazine* had said it would be.

The next morning, Tim got up early, walked down to the lake-shore to take pictures. Without knowing it, one of the pictures he took was from the exact point at which a photograph had been taken for an elegant book, which he gave us the following Christmas.

After a glorious breakfast at the White Moss Inn, we were off for Scotland, driving along the very narrow road with a high hill to the left and a steep decline on the right. Early in the afternoon as we went along this road, a boulder—well, actually a large stone—came rolling down the hill and hit the left rear tire, which it destroyed. We stopped. There was no shoulder on which we could move over; we had no idea where the spare tire was (we finally found it underneath the car); we were blocking traffic for what I'm sure was miles. As we were looking for the spare tire, a Scottish highway patrol officer managed to reach us, as the cause of the traffic jam. He expressed his sympathy for our situation and immediately started the process of changing the tire. I can't imagine anywhere in the United States where you could hold up traffic as long as we did on that road in Scotland without an ensuing riot. In Scotland there was little honking, and I heard absolutely no swearing.

With the tire changed, we drove past Loch Ness and arrived at our hotel in Inverness in time for dinner. During dinner I asked the middle-aged waitress if she had ever seen the "monster" in the lake. She replied, "No, I haven't, but I've never had a quart of whisky before breakfast either."

Beginning with the kind officer who helped us change tires, we had begun to notice how difficult it was to understand the people in Scotland. On occasion, it was impossible. At breakfast at our Inverness Hotel, when I went to the buffet to replenish my plate for the third time, Joan remained with Tim at our table. When I returned, Joan whispered to me: "You see those men at the next table? While you were gone I listened and I didn't understand a word they spoke." I listened for a few minutes and then reported, "Joan, no wonder you couldn't understand them. They're speaking German."

In Glasgow we stayed at the large and comfortable Railroad Hotel and ate dinner at a recommended restaurant. Getting up early the next morning I went to the lobby, which also served as the waiting room for train traffic, and asked the on-duty officer the best way to get out of town onto the road at Edinburgh. He said, "I'll show you," and took me into the security office to trace on a large hanging map the route I should take. When I spoke of the long wait we had experienced the day before at the stop lights his reply was, "They are 'teejous' aren't they?"

We reached Edinburgh the day after the Fringe Festival had closed. The concierge at the hotel informed us that there was a glorious play at the city's finest theater, and there were, he knew, tickets available.

It was an historical Scottish play with a cast of tremendous size. After the first act, I turned to two elderly women sitting behind us and asked if the play was being performed by the Scottish National Theater. She replied:

Woman: Oh, no, it's the best play of the Fringe Festival held over in this theater.

Don: Thank you.

THE TRUE INTERNATIONAL THEATER

Woman: Are you folk from London?

Don: No, we're from the United States.

Other Woman: The United States, the United States—well, may I ask you a question?

Don: Certainly.

Woman: Could you understand the dialogue—I mean with the Scottish brogue and all?

Don: We had no difficulty most of the time. When they had the large mob scenes with the townspeople, we had some difficulty.

Woman: The mob scenes? Don't worry about it. We're from here and we didn't understand a word they were saying.

All over the world, theater is the same.

The next morning we took the traditional walk from the castle to the palace. Standing in the palace entry, two young women came up and asked what was playing at the Old Log. Turned out they were the friends of Hugh and Dell Williams the couple from Westminster Theater.

That night we dropped our rental car off at the railway station. Someone should write a play or at least a song about the night train from Edinburgh to London. Before retiring, we were asked by the conductor what we would like in the morning, coffee or tea, and what time would we like it. When I asked when the train arrived in London, he replied that that really wasn't involved, we could have our tea or coffee whenever we wanted it, and could stay aboard the train as long as we wanted. That train ride was one I would like to repeat.

CRETEX

Early in 1996, I received a telephone call from the Cretex Company in Elk River, telling me that the Bailey family had decided that they should have a record of their company and asked if I would come to Elk River to meet with them and discuss whether or not I was interested in writing that history.

After meeting with John Bailey Sr., Alfred Bailey and Arnold Fuchs, I was eager to write the story of these truly remarkable people. Never in any way was compensation discussed, nor did I care; I was eager to start. I learned that the company that started with the two partners was now a national family of companies that supplied a world market with products as diverse as heart pacemaker components to prestressed bridge beams; a company that had seventeen wholly owned subsidiaries, with 34 manufacturing facilities.

It was thrilling—and I mean "thrilling"—to learn that though the company had grown and become diverse, other things had not changed. Cretex was still committed to the founding qualities:

Manufacture and deliver a quality product at an equitable price.

Extend to every customer concerned care for his needs and deliver service that reflects that care.

Use imagination and innovation to better serve.

Establish leadership that gives the best to the employees and demands the best from them, giving them the opportunity to use their innovative skills and organizational ability.

Be generous.

Have a joyful journey.

One of the junior officers in his summary offered a quote from

Proverbs: "Of a good beginning cometh a good end."

While gathering information from various employees, I learned what John Bailey would never admit—his total generosity. There were stories about his financing hospital stays and the care of the families during the illness—story after story, none of which John wanted in the book. Still, we sneaked in a few.

Each of the various Cretex plants had its own president. I believe the quickest way to tell you how they felt about John Bailey, Sr., is to quote from page 112 of the book. At one of the annual meetings, after the closing dinner, one of the presidents stood and said:

"I'd like to have everyone's attention for just a minute or two. I suppose, John, I should start by saying how glad we all are to be here. But that's only the beginning. Just before we came down to dinner, my wife and I were talking about what a great group of people this is, beginning with you and Rosemary. Then we got to talking about why we thought this company of ours, this family, if you wish, was so successful and so happy. Well, it starts with the fact—and John, you just have to accept this—it starts with the fact that we have a great commander. If you prefer, I'll call it good leadership. You have been, always, generous with us. Very generous. And in turn we have tried to be generous with our efforts and our work and our time. Next, you have always hired the best. Now that may not sound very modest, but we are the best. You have hired people with the same goals and the same ideals, but at the same time, you have let us run our business as if it were our very own. And the truth is, we think of it as our own. We have done a pretty good job with this business of yours because we feel just as you do, that there is nothing more important than our customer, and we're going to do everything we can to give him the service that a good customer deserves. I would like to say more, John, but I can tell by looking at you that there is just no way you're going to let this go on any further."

Perhaps the best way to summarize the effect of my working on the book is by including here what I wrote in the Foreword and Acknowledgments.

"As I first started learning about Cretex, I found myself wishing

I had been a member of this remarkable company. As I continued learning about them, I found myself believing I was a member of the family.

"Cretex, a family of companies, is what business should be: they love what they are doing, and they love the people with whom they are doing it.

"What more could anyone want?"

"I must first acknowledge the tremendous help and sure guidance that Albert Bailey and Arlon Fuchs brought to the project. Without them, I would have been lost. To say that these two Cretex stalwarts have a sense of humor is almost belittling, for what they have is joy that is fostered by patience, understanding and love.

"I want to thank Ann and Barbara Longfellow not only for graciously telling me of the Longfellow family, but also for giving me the privilege of reading the book written by Dwight Webster Longfellow, *Letter From the Philippines*.

"Then I want to thank and bless every member of the Cretex family, not only those with whom I talked, but also those who I haven't even met.

"Then there is my secretary, Anita Anderson O'Sullivan. If ever you are looking for energy and loyalty to a project, just find Anita. But please leave her where she is. Thank you."

Cretex Times was published and distribution had begun and still there had been no discussion concerning compensation to the writer. The secretary to John Bailey, Sr., called and asked if I could have lunch with John, Alfred, Arland and John, Jr. As soon as we'd ordered our meal, the conversation began:

John Bailey, Sr.: Don—

Don: Yes—

John: I understand you haven't presented an invoice.

Don: No, I haven't—

John: Alfred and Arland have told me of the fun the three of
    you had in writing it.

Don: That's right.

John: Well, I think you're a great deal like me, and I know when you've enjoyed something that much, you just don't know want to charge. So I've solved the whole problem. Here in this envelope is a check which, along with our thanks, is your fee.

Later, when I opened the envelope, I discovered that statements concerning John Bailey's generosity had certainly not been overstated.

The memory of the entire experience is something I shall always treasure.

IF YOU'VE SEEN A GOOD PLAY,
LET OTHERS KNOW

When the 1993 hit, ***Don't Dress for Dinner***, ended its run in 1994, we opened Tom's play, ***Mahalia***, about which I have already written. We followed with a 23-week return to ***Run For Your Wife***, which carried us to September, when we presented *Déjà Vu*.

A New York literary agent, Earl Graham, whom we had known for years, wrote and then telephoned me to tell of this wonderful comedy written by one of the authors he represented. *Déjà Vu* was to be presented at the Barter Theater of Virginia, and since he felt it would be perfect for the Old Log, we should make arrangements to be there some time during its scheduled run. He and the author would meet us there. Aside from staying and dining at the Martha Washington Hotel, I recall very little of pleasure from the whole experience. The play, however, received such approval from the audience that it was not difficult for Earl to persuade me to schedule it for the Old Log. Though we managed to get by for 25 weeks, under no circumstances would I direct it again. For the most part, Old Log audiences don't find the subject of sex change terribly funny.

In 1995 *Déjà Vu* was still running. It ran until March when we opened ***Beau Jest***, a delightful play about a Jewish family, whose daughter they fear might marry a Gentile. There were 32 wonderful weeks followed by another Ray Cooney play, ***Fools Rush In***, set for 23 weeks.

In March of the following year, 1996, we returned ***Mahalia*** for five weeks followed by 22 weeks of *I Hate Hamlet*. We had gone to

Chicago to see a production of this play and found it truly interesting. A young actor is faced with the tremendous challenge of having to play Hamlet. In his despair at the prospect, the ghost of John Barrymore appears to guide him through this difficult time. Obviously, we needed a "John Barrymore." The only person in the Twin Cities I could imagine in the role was David Brinkley who was appearing in a musical at the Chanhassen Dinner Theater. How, I brought myself to do it, I don't know, but finally did call Michael Brindisi, the Artistic Director at Chanhassen, who most graciously agreed to replace David. This is but one of the more than a few actions for which I am going to have to find some way to repay Michael. I just hope he never asks for Tommy and Steve.

After *I Hate Hamlet*, we presented what we found to be one of Cooney's funniest and most successful farces since *Run For Your Wife* and a perfect show for Tom and Steve. *Funny Money* is the story of a mild-mannered accountant, who, on the train home, picks up the wrong briefcase. The briefcase is filled with money—money that he decides is illicit. Reaching home, he tells his wife that they must drop everything and leave immediately for Barcelona. If she doesn't like Barcelona, they can go to Bali and buy it. Before they get out the door, the doorbell rings.

After 49 weeks, we opened in September of 1997, *Radio Gals*, one of the musicals about which I have already written.

Early in 1998, we decided to star Tom and Steve, the "two best comedic actors in the country" in Neil Simon's *The Odd Couple*. It ran a solid 36 weeks.

Early in the summer of 1998, we received a letter from Jim McKenzie, the producer/director of the Peninsula Players in Fish Creek, Door County, Wisconsin, recommending a play that they were going to present early in their summer season. We had quite often exchanged ideas during the years we both had been open. Furthermore, we had a letter from the author, Robin Hawdon (another English writer), saying that he, too, thought it would be a good fit for the Old Log.

We seemed unable to arrange our schedule to make the trip to

Door County until the last week of the run. If we were going to see *A Perfect Wedding*, it had to be now. From all we had heard, it was going to be worth it, even though we knew going to Door County without lodging reservations was more than a bit risky. But a new play is a new play.

On our way, we stopped in Milwaukee to visit our granddaughter and her family and spent the night there so that we could leave early the next morning. When we arrived in Fish Creek we were able to secure a room in a small hotel for one night, and a good B & B the second night. We were set.

The management at the Peninsula Players had made arrangements for complimentary tickets, so with lodging arranged, we explored the city of Fish Creek. Every other house the owners had turned into an "antique and collectible" shop, most of them containing primarily the same merchandise. But it was fun. The unique experience was lunch at a restaurant where, while you ate, a small herd of goats was grazing on the roof.

French's catalogue, once they had received the leasing rights, described *A Perfect Wedding* as "a rare combination of riotous farce and touching love story." Not only was it a pleasing and funny play, but it also needed neither Tom nor Steve in the cast. Scheduling it would give an opportunity for both of these actors who just finished a strenuous schedule to have several weeks of vacation.

At Peninsula Players, a recent major operation had kept Jim McKenzie from directing, so his daughter had done the job instead. Jim was rightfully proud of her work, though I did think the curtain call she designed was one of the most ridiculous I had ever seen. But that certainly was not important. We met briefly with playwright, Robin Hawdon, whose demeanor I admired. I told him with his approval we would be performing his play in the early fall. We bade farewell to Jim McKenzie, wished him an early and easy recovery, and returned to Fish Creek for a pleasant night.

When fall arrived and we began what resulted in 25 weeks of *A Perfect Wedding*, Robin Hawdon was pleased and impressed. Our relationship has continued; he has sent us every play he has written, and one of them we will be presenting sometime in the future. Robin Hawdon is an excellent playwright.

After *Axel and his Dog* had played at the History Theatre in St. Paul, we had been receiving requests to present it on home territory at the Old Log. Though we had some misgivings, we scheduled it with Ron Peluso coming from St. Paul to direct. The result was a good 23 weeks. I have already described the play so will not do so again at this point. The Old Log is again receiving requests to bring it back to our stage.

At the close of *Axel and his Dog*, we opened **Cash on Delivery**, a new farce, not by Ray Cooney, but by his son, Michael. It concerns a successful con man who has duped the welfare authorities for years by claiming every type of benefit from the innumerable people he claims live at his address. When investigators finally arrive, they are so impressed by his ability to get around every rule that, instead of having him imprisoned, offer him a job as the agency's fraud investigation unit. Thirty-six good box office weeks carried us until April of 2000.

In April we opened a play that I had found both funny and relevant. **Over the River and Through the Woods** is a warm and comfortable story of a grandson who divides his time between his maternal grandparents and his paternal grandparents who live next door to one another. The second act contains one of the longest and best build-ups to a great joke that I can remember. The four grandparents and their grandson are playing a game of Trivial Pursuit. How the one grandfather arrives at the proper answer to a particular question is one of the biggest laughs I have ever heard.

Late in September we repeated one of our past hits, *A Bedfull of Foreigners*. In truth I must say, for reasons of which I am not at all sure, I just wasn't able to get the gloss that could have brought it up to past performances. Disappointing.

The year 2001—ordinarily sequels to plays are no bigger success than sequels to motion picture. But Ray Cooney was able to write a sequel to **Run For Your Wife** that resulted in what the *Daily Telegraph*, London, called: "A sheer joy from beginning to end. The

Cash on Delivery; Steve Shaffer, "The Body," and Tom Stolz.

A Bed Full of Foreigners; Randy Berger and Eden Bodner.

funniest play of the year." Other reviews were just as full of praise. The sequel title: *Caught in the Net*. In sequel time, it is eighteen years later, but the bigamist taxi driver is still keeping two households going. The difference is that during those eighteen years, there have been some changes. One wife has a teenage son; the other wife a teenage daughter. The two teenagers have met on the Internet and, having the same last name, and both having fathers that are taxi drivers, the two are eager to meet in person. This puts John Smith in a truly threatening position. The play is as funny as the review said it was. We opened the play March 7 and ran it with big box office results for 50 weeks.

The year 2002 opened with two reruns of my favorite productions: *Mahalia*, for a very short run (all the time that Jearlyn Steele had), then *Cotton Patch Gospel* for nine weeks. During the run of *Cotton Patch*, I received one of the most peculiar letters of my long years at the Old Log. Remember, *Cotton Patch* is deliberately set in contemporary Georgia. That is its premise. The letter objected strenuously and bitterly that the characters all spoke with Southern accents and that none of them was dressed in any Biblical costume.

I then made a mistake for which I even now have not forgiven myself. I scheduled *My Husband's Wild Desires Almost Drove Me Mad* for a run of 25 weeks. The playwright and his wife were delighted with the production; I was not. I did admire the performances of the members of the cast. I found Steve Shaffer in a turquoise blue dress with high-heeled pumps to match, very funny, not campy. He was excellent. When I scheduled the play, I knew there were difficulties, but I was filled with confidence (perhaps even vanity) that I would be able to give the production a focus that would make even the offensive material relevant. I don't think I succeeded, even though each night before the curtain I would explain that the play was not offering itself as a guide to the way we should live, but was instead intended to show the results if we attempted to solve our problems the wrong way. To any of you who saw *My Husband's Wild Desires*, I most sincerely apologize.

How happy I was, how happy everyone at the theater was, when

Moon Over Buffalo; Steve Shaffer, Tim Sharp, and Katherine Ferrand.

we next scheduled that classic of American theater, **Arsenic and Old Lace**. We, perhaps, did not have as good a cast as we had for **My Husband's Wild Desires**, but we certainly had a better play. It was great box office.

During the run, I found it interesting how many of our audience would say, "I was in **Arsenic and Old Lace** when I was in high school." "Very interesting. What role did you play?" "The cab driver." (There is no cab driver, but some high school director found a way to make the cast even larger.)

With the presentation of **Arsenic**, I felt better. I no longer was planning the best way to burn the theater.

On March 16, 2003, we opened **Moon Over Buffalo**. We, as do most regional theaters, solved the problem of the first scene, which the playwright intended to be played in a full set, by playing it in front of the curtain. It worked well. Steve played the megalomaniac actor; Katherine Ferrand played his leading lady.

I don't have to tell how delightful they were. In the play, the entire future of this little acting company depends on what impression they may make on Frank Capra, who, supposedly, is coming to the performance that night. By curtain time, the leading man (Steve) tries to bury his sorrow in drink. He is under the impression that the play that night is *Cyrano*, so makes his entrance onto the balcony where other members of the cast are well into the balcony scene of *Private Lives*. The result is one of the funniest scenes in contemporary plays.

Moon Over Buffalo ran for 26 weeks, after which we opened *Out of Order*, which we had produced in 1990 under the title *Whose Wife is it Anyway*. As mentioned earlier, when Ray took the show into London he changed the title. *Out of Order* it was named the 1991 Olivier Award Winner, Best Comedy.

After 22 weeks of *Out of Order*, in 2004 we brought back our big hit of 2000, *Over the River and Through the Woods*.

During early spring, Cooney sent me a fax, then a letter, saying that he and his son, Michael, had written a new farce, *Tom, Dick and Harry*, and a manuscript was on its way to the Old Log. I immediately, but tentatively, scheduled it to open here in the middle of September. I found *Tom, Dick and Harry* to be the hilarious story of three brothers. Tom and his wife are hoping to adopt a baby, and the two brothers are eager to also make a good impression on the woman from the adoption agency. But each has problems that Tom knows nothing about. When the play opened in Windsor, one of the reviews read, "No wonder Cooney's farces attract packed audiences; they know they are going to have a good time." And so did our audiences, for *Tom, Dick and Harry* ran for 26 weeks.

After *Weekend Comedy* and *Murder at the Howard Johnson's* in 2005, we brought back, in 2006, our hit from 1993, *Don't Dress for Dinner*. It was great reassurance to have both Steve and Tom in the cast, and I'm glad to say that both were happy to be back in a true farce. R. Beard, critic for the *Star Tribune* gave it a great review and we were off for a good 46 weeks. This offered us time to prepare two really great shows for young audiences: in the summer, *Wind in the Willows* and for the holidays, *Snow White and the Seven Dwarfs*.

Some time during 2005, I received a fax from Ray Cooney telling me that he had taken one of his old scripts that he had never felt was right for production, had rewritten it and turned it into a musical. He also informed me that he was forwarding me a script and hoped that we, Ray and the Old Log, would be able to produce and present the first performance.

The script arrived. Story and book by Ray Cooney, music by Christ Walker with lyrics by Mary Stewart-David.

The action begins in Guildford in 2005, where Steven, a young solicitor, works for the firm of Pilsworth and Pilsworth. He is engaged to his boss's daughter, whom we find domineering and bossy. His father-in-law-to-be demands that Steven stop smoking and sends him to a hypnotherapist for treatment—a treatment which results in his regression to a previous life in Chicago where he worked as a getaway driver for the Bugs Moran gang. Between treatments, he switches back and forth from 1929 to 2005.

Producing it with Ray was a challenge that I was eager to accept. As I started work on the script, I soon found that there were 12 principal characters, 24 roles played by the "ensemble," plus at least six musicians. It was not difficult for me to figure out that there was no way I could possibly finance such a venture. So I did something I had never before done: approached investors. Ray Cooney immediately was in for $50,000 and the first person I called on in Minneapolis told me he'd match Ray's investment.

Before going further, I knew it was time to take another and closer look. In addition to 36 actors and six musicians, there were 13 sets. Even though many could be done with nothing but suggested props, there were still 13. I began to realize, despite my weeks of planning, that to produce this musical on our stage was impossible. We didn't have room for 36 actors and six musicians backstage, to say nothing of dressing room space. We had no orchestra pit; our wing space was limited. After weeks of exchanging plans and ideas, I finally wrote Ray and told him it was impossible. "It's time I stopped daydreaming."

I shall keep forever his reply. He had, I'm sure, anticipated my decision, but the sentence I treasure was: "Don't ever give up your daydreaming. That's the reason we're in this crazy business, isn't it?"

UNIVERSITY OF MINNESOTA FOUNDATION

Though I was in no way an alumnus of the University of Minnesota, through the years I had come to know many of the faculty and, with the rest of the citizens of the state, admired greatly what the University was and shared its dreams of what it could become.

In 1986, I followed with interest, though making not even a small donation, the University Foundation's Campaign, under the leadership of Curt Carlson and Russell Bennett, to raise an astonishing 365 million dollars, creating 127 endowed faculty positions.

In 1996, it was announced that the Foundation would initiate another drive with Carlson's daughter, Marilyn Carlson Nelson, and Russell Bennett as co-chair. The goal—and it still seems like an impossible dream—was 1.3 billion dollars. Yes, they were dreaming!

After the campaign had been announced, the Executive of the Foundation decided that the drive should begin with a kickoff in Northrop Auditorium, a dinner function to which every influential and affluent alumnus would be personally invited.

As happens so often in Minnesota, whenever anyone has a big dream, they call Paul Ridgeway, who has built the reputation for bringing to fruition other's big dreams. I suspect that when Paul was in grade school, he made a celebration of the exercise of dusting the blackboard erasers. Whatever, Paul adds his own big dreams to those that he has been handed.

Paul, having met our son, Tommy, at meetings of the Christian Fellowship for the study of the Bible, was a true admirer. Paul, knowing Tom's ability in the theater invited him to the first meeting of the committee-in-charge of planning this foundation's function. Tommy invited me. Tommy's schedule did not allow him to attend more than the first meeting; I was in it for the entire game.

It was at the second meeting that the work began. Paul and the young man who was to be his writer presented the outline of what they were recommending as the format and script for the show. Present were all of the members of the planning committee including a young woman, who, after Paul's reading, took charge of the discussion that followed. Linda Berg was there to directly represent the foundation. A few weeks later, I learned that this knowing, clever woman was Garrison Keillor's sister.

The first thing Linda did, as she took over, was to ask each member of the committee what had been their reaction to what they had just heard. The replies were varied. None criticizing, none praising without reservation. I answered that though it was humorous, it was in questionable taste, and to some would be offensive. I felt there were other ways, just as humorous, of announcing their goal and setting in motion the action they needed to achieve it. Linda Berg strongly and almost emotionally agreed with the points I had made. The young man was not happy, but Paul was far from being offended. He and Linda asked if I would bring to the next meeting an alternate outline.

Paul then announced his plan for the setting of the kickoff dinner. He had arranged for the opera seats of Northrop to be removed, platforms would be built to establish various levels of flat floors, tables and chairs would be tastefully decorated. Though Paul had not arranged for the catered meal, he assured us that it would be delicious and elegantly served.

When we all gathered for the next committee meeting, I suggested that the program for the evening would begin with a stunning opening number that would involve an orchestra comprised of students from the University's School of Music, eight singers also from the School of Music, and eight dancers from the University's recently established School of Dance. I also suggested other songs and skits with which to introduce the various speakers and various subjects. Linda announced that the Hollywood actor, Peter Graves, an alumnus of the University, had agreed to be the Master. Garrison Keillor, also an alumnus, would speak.

We were under way.

The next day I called Dean Sorenson, head of Instrumental Music, a man who occasionally had played in Ray Komischke's orchestra. Dean asked if Ray had orchestra charts for the music I'd suggested. When I told him "yes," he said that he knew Ray would be happy to give him the use of them.

Next I arranged for the Vocal Music Department to select and train eight singers. The School of Dance, after studying the style and the timetable, reported they could not be a part of the program. I immediately telephoned Michael Farrell who conducts a sophisticated school of dance, and asked if he could furnish and costume eight girls from his upper classes of teenage dancers. He was delighted to do so.

One of the songs we had indicated was a re-write of "It Had to Be You" to "It Had to Be 'U.'" I had intended for University Professor, Vern Sutton, to sing it with the eight singers. When I asked him if he could and would do it, he was enthusiastic but said he was going to be out of the country until the day of the dress rehearsal. If, however, I would mail him the music and lyrics, he would come to dress rehearsal fully prepared. At the final rehearsal, Sutton was on time, he was fully prepared, and made of the song a charming and relevant message.

At the performance, Farrell's young dancers looked like University underclassmen—beautiful and talented.

Peter Graves was an excellent emcee.

Garrison Keillor spoke with both humor and passion about what he had achieved because of his attending the University. Then he spoke of the dreams he had for its future.

In total it was a gloriously emotional evening that left the audience ready to contribute to the financial goal and ready to convince others to do the same.

The week after the performance, the last week in October, our family's internist, Dr. Eugene Ollila, had scheduled my annual physical. Everything was fine until he asked if there were any changes since my last exam. I reported that on my way to one of the committee meetings at the University, I couldn't find a place to park and during the long and overly hastened walk that resulted, I had felt a pressure of fullness between my shoulders. Ollila immediately made an appointment with the cardiologist, Dr. VanTassel. I failed the stress test. VanTassel refused to let me go home, sent me by wheelchair to the connected Abbott Northwestern Hospital, and scheduled an angiogram for early the next morning. It was another test that I did not pass; apparently the angiogram showed that I was a candidate for bypass surgery. I suggested if it had to happen, let's get it over with. Two days later the surgery was performed. Every medical and staff person at Abbott was remarkable in their care. I can truthfully report that I remember absolutely no pain.

If you ever need bypass surgery, approach it without dread. Today it is hardly more than routine.

Celebrating the Victory of the U's Goal

Celebrating the achievement of the goal was set for the Coffman Auditorium and once again Ridgeway called Tom and me to assist in the Victory Celebration. The audience will ever remember Russ Bennett's announcement that the campaign had gone beyond their goal and had raised 1.6 billion dollars.

The high points of the celebration were Bennett's announcement, a relevant but humorous skit showing three janitors objecting to all the new spaces they would now have to cover. The three janitors were Tom Stolz, Reuben Ristrom and Vern Sutton. The third high point was Marilyn Carlson Nelson's closing speech. She ended the evening with a speech that praised and thanked all who had been a part of or had contributed to the campaign:

"And in our celebrating with you and thanking you, we hope you will continue your great generosity; that you continue to give some measure of your accomplishments, and that you continue to invest in the future of the University of Minnesota. Our future.

"There are those donors present here tonight whose names we know and hold dear. But in words from the Old Testament, we say 'there are many others of whom there is no listing. And they, too, were men and women of mercy, whose generous deeds will not fail. Good things shall continue with their seed, and their posterity shall have a blessed inheritance of knowledge. Through their actions, their children and our children shall prosper.'

"Let us include those not here with us tonight and those not listed—in our thanks and in our praise this evening.

"In closing this evening, I'd like to ask President Bruininks and Susan Hagstrom, Jerry Fischer, Russ and Beth Bennett and the rest of the Campaign Steering Committee to join me here on stage as we sing 'Hail Minnesota.' We'll be joined by the University Choir, directed by Kathy Romey."

BOONE AND ERICKSON

I made the note that in 1967, we first presented *The Odd Couple* with Edgar Meyer and Ken Senn, and that over the years we have presented *The Odd Couple* seven more times. One of those times was in 1980. Bob Williams, our group sales and promotion manager, suggested that it would be fun and good box office to have Charlie Boone and Roger Erickson play Felix and Oscar.

Charlie and Roger were the most popular radio duo that the Twin Cities has ever heard. On the air they were already established as the odd couple—one from the East and the other a farm boy from Minnesota. Both had been trained in theater. Charlie, the son of a minister, was raised and educated in the East. Roger grew up on a farm 40 miles west of Minneapolis and attended the theater and radio department of the University of Minnesota.

When I first met them, Charlie was a sophisticated disk jockey at KFGO in Fargo. Roger was working at the radio station in Stillwater, Minnesota. WCCO Radio was celebrating Minnesota's anniversary—part of that celebration was an extended series of radio dramas. The producer always had Rupert LaBelle, Ken Senn and Don Stolz from the Old Log, Irv Fink and Sheldon Goldstein, formerly with the University Radio Station, and Roger Erickson from Stillwater. Roger was assigned roles from young boys to elderly women. As I remember, we had a whole year's work (only once a week, however).

When the producers at WCCO TV started looking for someone to play Bozo the Clown on an upcoming children's show, I suggested they audition Roger. They did, and he was wonderful. Whatever

Roger did, he meticulously prepared. He still claims I got him started in television.

I met Charlie through his wife, who at that time was working at WCCO TV while he was still out west at KFGO.

There have been people who have asked, "Who played Oscar and who played Felix?" In my mind, there was never any doubt about this. Roger was Oscar, Charlie was Felix. When they were in the third week of their four-week run of *The Odd Couple*, they would frequently be asked, as I'm sure most TOC couples were, "Wouldn't it be fun for you two to switch roles for a week?" Before they could even consider it, I said, "No—and besides, you'd have to memorize a whole new set of lines." That ended the discussion. If an actor fulfills the image of a character that is the character he should portray, nothing, not even talent, can replace type casting.

Boone and Erickson had been acting off of radio scripts for so long and ad libbing when necessary or desired, that whatever skill they once had in memorizing lines was no longer but a remnant. For them, learning lines was what Louis Lytton called, "mental ditch digging." Boone and Erickson were serious and in earnest about doing the play. It was to be done to the very best of their ability; there was no ad libbing, there was no falling back on the ridiculously funny material of radio. They did a good and legitimate job.

The box office was great.

This was the last performance of Boone and Erickson on our stage (other than radio remotes) until 2000. Though Roger had retired somewhat from WCCO radio, they were still the biggest attractions in Minnesota. When Lou Holtz, the legendary University of Minnesota football coach had to cancel a date in 2000 for a personal appearance at Willmar, the organizers telephoned Boone and Erickson and said, "We'll pay you two the entire Holtz fee if you would put together a show and bring it to Willmar on the scheduled night. They hired their friend, Reuben Ristrom, musician beyond belief, to put together a five-piece orchestra to take with them. It was a tremendous hit. Someone among our crowd or theirs suggested that they do the same show at the Old Log.

The Odd Couple; Rolland Beck, Jim Wallace, Roger Erickson,
Charlie Boone, and Peter Stolz.

We scheduled it for two nights; and even though those two nights were a Monday and Tuesday, we were immediately sold out. So we scheduled it for another Monday and Tuesday a week later. Again sold out. And being greedy (and needing money), I suggested a Monday and Tuesday in August.

Every summer since then Boone and Erickson have come back, at my urging, with a new show put together and written around a different theme. The year 2001, 60th anniversary of Pearl Harbor, 2002, Boyhood days with radio

As with the other shows, the 2002 show included a unique old radio memory. This time the memory of a show sponsored by Hartz's Mountain Bird Seed. The program was one of music with domestic songbirds singing along. Boone and Erickson had the audience do the bird whistling while Russ Peterson played a lovely bit of music on the flute. I couldn't believe the wonderful volume of audience bird sounds.

Radio in the '60s

WCCO Radio's Anniversary

Old Log Theater's 65th Anniversary

Radio Revue

Don Stolz's 90th Birthday

Regardless of the theme, Boone and Erickson always had to include "Minnesota Hospital," a ridiculous skit full of puns and other comedic writing. As they put each separate show together, they featured the jokes of that period and the music (more or less) of the same period. Reuben always had the finest musicians with him: Joe Polic, Bob Guck, Russ Peterson, the very best brass player available, and vocals by Dianne, his wife.

No way in this world is it possible for an outline of the show to demonstrate the effect of the show. Because it had been some years since their daily appearance on WCCO, the primary audience for these shows was always a little past middle-aged. Earlier, I said Boone and Erickson were "the most popular"—that doesn't even begin to tell the story. They were loved. They were adored. And Boone and Erickson deserved every bit of that adoration. During all those years they never turned away from an invitation to appear at every event in the Twin Cities that supported any worthwhile endeavor. They were at the heart of the community. They were WCCO's "Good Neighbors."

Every night the audience left the Old Log filled with love and joy in their hearts. This is what entertainment should be. As everyone in the cast:—Boone and Erickson, Dianne, Reuben, the other members of the orchestra and even the sound man—said, "Aren't we fortunate to be able to bring so much happiness to so many people?"

In 2003 we presented our first annual concert reading of *The Christmas Carol*.

Early in the winter, Bob Williams reminded us that he had once seen on public television a concert reading by two actors, of *The Christmas Carol*. The actors were in full dress—white tie and tails—and the entire story was tied together by a narrator. It was not a new idea nor was it unique. It was always *The Christmas Carol*, that people most often wanted to hear when reading his works. Dickens was good at these readings, he enjoyed it.

At first, Roger did not see the desirability of the full dress, but then he realized that it removed the performance of the ordinary and made of it a "concert."

I, like most Americans, have seen four or five different dramatizations of *The Christmas Carol*, and have liked them all. But to me, the best of all is the concert reading; you get more of Dickens' actual words—and who better could use words. And I, as narrator, attempted to show the terrible conditions in England that made Dickens write the piece, and what he was truly saying with every scene.

After their years of radio, both Boone and Erickson were excellent readers. Always the audience left the Old Log feeling that now, truly, the wonderful Christmas season had begun.

Boone and Erickson are good men. As I said, and have said many times, they deserve all the adoration they receive.

Boy Scouts

Last month, in answering a letter of complaint from a woman who didn't like the play, I began my letter with this sentence: "Nothing is as hurtful as knowing that we have disappointed a customer." And it's true. I have given so many examples of the joy that has been mine, but I should tell you that there have also been moments of disappointment, embarrassment and even pain. I know full well that regardless of what you do, it is impossible to please everybody; but still, when we have disappointed or offended a member of our audience, I can't help feeling that I have failed.

This feeling of failure is not restricted to the reaction to our theater productions; it is ever present when I am asked to give a speech, as I often am, at some club or business meeting. I always hope—hope desperately—that I have not disappointed the audience or failed to deliver what they expected.

I would think by now, after all the thousands of speeches I have given, that I would be more self-assured. In 1954, George Grim, who was that year the Chairman of the Speaker's Bureau for the Community Chest (now the United Way), booked me for 150 presentations (that one year), just for the Community Chest. And in 1960, a writer for the *Minneapolis Star* included me in his list of the city's ten best speakers. But still—always—after every speech I find myself questioning if I have done as well as I should have. I think instead of a lack of self-confidence, I harbor an unhealthy desire to please.

One of the organizations for whom I have yearly given several speeches is the Viking Council of the Boy Scouts of America. I name them, for if ever there was one speech with which I had more or less succeeded, it was the one I delivered at the meeting honoring those boys who had achieved the rank of Eagle.

The Council had selected a nationally known speaker, the Reverend Rounder, pastor of the Colonial Church and a missionary to Africa, to give the keynote address. A week before the function, he had to tell them that it was going to be impossible for him to be there, even though his appearance had been highly publicized. The committee asked if I would take his place. I accepted.

Since I delivered a speech that I thought was suitable and one for which I had few misgivings, I have taken the liberty of including it.

Boy Scouts—April 2001

When I was nine years old—three years before I could join the Boy Scouts—the summer was one I shall always remember. My father was a Methodist minister and we lived in Miami, Oklahoma ... just across the border from Joplin, Missouri. Miami, Oklahoma ... and we called it "Miami," too. Anyway, early in the spring, it was announced that in the second week of September, Barnum, Bailey and Ringling Brothers combined circus would pay our little town a three-day visit before its ten-day engagement in Joplin.

Unless you have lived in Oklahoma, there is no way in the world that you could imagine how exciting that news was. Especially if you were nine years old.

Overnight large posters, three and four sheets, appeared in every store window on Main Street. They pictured all of the wonderful acts that would appear—trapeze artists, trained elephants, leaping magnificent tigers, a hundred clowns all pouring out of miniature automobiles. It was breathtaking. And to me the most breathtaking of all was a picture of a very large brown bear roller skating around the center ring. I could hardly wait until the performance date.

Finally the circus arrived. Even more magnificent—more glamorous—more wonderful than I had imagined. I was so excited I could hardly breathe. One glorious act followed glorious act until it was time for the trained brown bear on roller skates. I was shivering in anticipation when the ringmaster got the attention of everyone in the audience and announced that the troupe of Roller-Skating Bears had become indisposed—whatever that meant—and they would be replaced by a group of trained monkeys. I had seen trained monkeys two years earlier when the 101 Ranch Circus had come to town. Instead of the wonderful Roller-Skating Bears, what I now was to see was a little trained monkey.

That is very much the position in which you people are tonight. You had been promised the wonderful, internationally famous Reverend Rounder—and what you're getting is just a trained monkey.

A year later—no connection at all—my brother, Fred, who was two years older, joined the Boy Scouts, and I could forget the Roller-Skating Bears. I was now absorbed in my brother's Boy Scout Manual. I borrowed it whenever he wasn't looking. Before I was eleven, I knew the Scout Oath, the Scout Law and could tie every knot—even the double carrick bend, though I still have found no use for it.

It was one week before my twelfth birthday, the day I could join the Boy Scouts. I could hardly wait. I had talked with the Scoutmaster and the Assistant Scoutmaster—which was easy because the Assistant Scoutmaster was also my father. I had volunteered that I didn't care which patrol I was going to be in, as long as it wasn't the one my brother belonged to.

By now we lived in Cleveland, Oklahoma, a day's drive from Tulsa—the nearest city where Boy Scout uniforms were sold. Two days before my birthday, the family got in the Ford sedan and we headed to the big city of Tulsa—and to all of us it was the "big city." At last we arrived at the store with the uniforms. There I was fitted with shorts, stockings, shirt and neckerchief. In my mind no Scout ever looked more handsome. At this point the clerk, actually a very nice man, asked for my Boy Scout card. When he was told that I lacked two days of being twelve and a Scout, he, with some regret (but not enough, I thought), reported that he could not then sell them until the two days had passed.

It was one of the saddest moments of my young life. An adult standerby—obviously not a Scout himself—suggested that since there was an older brother who was a Scout just say that we were buying the uniform for him. It was a moment of enormous suspense and hope. Then my father spoke. He said, "But that wouldn't be true—and a Boy Scout is always truthful."

It was a lesson I shall never forget. A Boy Scout is always truthful.

We went home to Cleveland. And even though I became a Scout in three days, it would be two years before I had official shorts, shirt and neckerchief.

A Boy Scout is always truthful.

I never forgot. Even today I remember "A Boy Scout is always truthful." Just remember, however, whenever you are determined to tell the truth, sometimes the results are not what you really expected. Just last week I was walking through the lobby at the theater, the third phone rang—everyone in the box office was busy on the other two phones, so I picked it up. "Good Morning, the Old Log Theater." The elderly lady said, "Oh, I'm so glad you answered the phone—I wanted to ask you personally ... is this one of your risqué plays?" Well, I thought only a moment—then I remembered, "A Boy Scout is always truthful"—though the play wasn't naughty at all, I have to tell the truth and I said, "I'm afraid I must tell you that it is." "Good," she said—"I'll take six tickets."

We never know where the truth will get us.

Back to my boyhood in Oklahoma. The troop meeting place was in a relatively small room in the church basement. That meant, of course, that it was right next door to our home, the church parsonage. I remember the room so well—a permanent platform at the end of the room where the entrance door was—which meant that no one ever arrived late if he could possibly help it. I remember hearing my father say on a couple of occasions that he was tempted to make the same arrangement in the sanctuary—then everyone would arrive on time for church.

The Scoutmaster was an accomplished artist, so he got the

idea of taking the Boy Scout Trail as pictured in the handbooks of that time and painting it as a border around the top of the four walls. Remember the Boy Scout Trail? It took us from Tenderfoot clear up to Eagle. I wish today's handbook still pictured the trail in the same way.

Memorable occasions included the many times I attempted to pass the "fire building test." My father was so demanding that I thought I'd have to build the fire with no matches nor equipment of any kind. Having a father who was both the minister and assistant Scoutmaster was not always the easiest relationship.

Two years later we moved to Guthrie—the West Side Methodist Episcopal Church. Methodist ministers in Oklahoma moved a lot in those days. And again there was a Boy Scout troop sponsored by the Church. Troop 66 met in a wonderful gym that was a part of the church. It was a great place for holding Courts of Honor not only for Troop 66, but for other troops sponsored by other churches in Guthrie. I remember well winning the annual knot-tying contest every year, but remember more clearly losing the bugling contest.

In a town of ten thousand, some of the merit badges were easy to master. You were close enough to the country that you knew farm life as well as city life—and all those animal husbandry, poultry raising, egg-laying things were not far removed. I was always somewhat proud of my knowledge, but I must tell you I have not found that any of the merit badge requirements helped me find my career.

I cannot say, as did Paul Douglas last year, that some of these merit badges led me directly into my profession. Oh, there was the merit badge for theater—but at that point in my life, theater people seemed sort of wimpy, so I never fooled with this badge. That would be a good goal for me now—try to pass the theater merit badge.

And I had no idea that I would enroll in college as a pre-med. student—so no merit badge in this field either.

Shortly after I became an Eagle Scout, I became the Cimarron Valley's youngest assistant Scoutmaster. During all that time—all those years—I never attended a week-long camp or jamboree. I couldn't afford it. From the time I was thirteen I always had full-time summer jobs.

When in college, I got a job working on the stage in the school's theater. Every knot I knew, I used—though the double carrick bend was primarily for show-off time.

Later, during World War II when the Navy sent me to Notre Dame's midshipmen school, knots were something I already knew and didn't have to learn. Once aboard a ship, I never tied a knot in anything other than my shoelaces. But I knew my knots.

I remember at the end of the War—World War II—when our country was facing years of challenging change, President Truman declaring, "What a great nation this would be if the principles of Scouting could be woven into our daily lives."

I was filled with deep admiration—and yes, pride—in the organization of which I had been and was still a member—the Boy Scouts of America.

If I were asked—"Aside from the fun, the companionship, the character development, did Scouting do anything for you?"—I would be furious if asked such a question. How can you put aside fun, companionship and character building ... but I would answer it anyway: "Yes."

Yes, Scouting has done a lot for me. I learned a lot ... a lot of what I learned, I have used a lot.

My way from Tenderfoot to Eagle was a time of glorious adventure and diversified learning. I should be grateful for the opportunity and so I am. And so, I am sure, are you.

Being a Boy Scout—becoming an Eagle Scout has brought to each of us significant and special opportunity.

Significant and special opportunity

One thing I learned in Scouting and have had confirmed my entire life since is that when we have had special opportunity and special advantages, we also have placed upon us added responsibility and obligation. I agree with John D. Rockefeller, Jr.'s statement: "Every right implies a responsibility; every opportunity an obligation—a duty."

A duty to see that President Truman's hope became reality; a duty to see that the principles of Scouting are more often and more thoroughly woven into the everyday life of this country.

As Eagle Scouts, you and I have that responsibility and that obligation. You are young. As the poet Emerson wrote, "When duty whispers low 'thou must', then youth replies, 'I can.'" You are young—you can.

Let's begin talking of responsibility and obligation with remembering the Scout oath—

"On my honor I will do my *best*"—your best. Not anything that will get you by, but your best.

We all know—that we are committed to doing our BEST. Our oath is "I WILL DO MY BEST." I will do my best to do my duty to God. Not just to a rising cloud of smoke from a camp fire ... not just the glorious sound of flowing water ... not just to the soaring bird ... the rushing deer ... not just to some vague "spirit" but, rather, to God. He who created the smoke, the flowing water, the bird and the animal, and you and me. To God. The Creator of the Universe.

"I will do my best to do my duty to God and to my COUNTRY." Our country—our United States of America. The country that has given us our freedoms and our rights—and our opportunities. Including the opportunity to become Eagle Scouts.

Let me again remind us that perfecting ourselves and our own behavior is not enough. We are indebted to our country and to others to bring them this opportunity—this great adventure that is Scouting. Bringing Scouting to every boy is our responsibility. Our duty to see that President Truman's hope becomes a reality—a duty to see that the principles of Scouting are more often and more thoroughly woven into the everyday life of the country.

It is our duty.

William Tyler Page in 1918 wrote the American Creed, which was adopted by the House of Representatives. It closes with these words: "I believe it is my duty to my country to love it"—to love it—"to support its constitution, to obey its laws to respect the flag, and to defend it against all enemies …"

Remember we have taken the Oath, the oath that says, "On my honor I will do my best to do my duty to God and my country, and to obey the Scout laws, to help other people at all times, to keep myself physically strong, mentally awake and morally straight."

RETIREMENT, ANNIVERSARY AND BIRTHDAY PARTIES

I can't remember when the first one was, or who it was for, but doing small shows celebrating retirement, anniversary or birthday was, from 1960 until now, a steady moneymaker for the Old Log. I do know that the first few retirement shows were so well received that they established a pattern that I continued to follow. The pattern required a quartet of singers, a trio of good musicians, a sound, lighting and projection man. I served as narrator. Seldom were there skits with actors. Only two come to mind at this writing. One was the retirement of Bill Craig from AAA; the other was the retirement of Phil Larson from Northwestern National Life.

Several weeks before the party, I would have met with the retiree's wife, other family members, employers and fellow workers and friends. I would visit the home of the employee, where his wife would go through all of the photograph albums including those that covered his childhood. From his baby and childhood pictures you could always find some expression, some pose, that would remind you of similar characteristics now at the time of his retirement. The wife and I would select photographs that we thought presented, with fun and relevance, the decades of the man's life. Though the company usually furnished a complete biography of the man, the wife usually had treasured choice memories to add.

I would borrow the photographs, have slides made, then start writing the presentation.

Our show almost always followed a well-planned, well-executed dinner at some special location. During dinner, our instrumental trio would provide soft background music. The show began with an opening musical number featuring the four singers, accompanied, of course, by the trio. The two women and two men would be dressed in today's attractive formal wear.

My narration following this opening number would lead through the reason for the party, the welcoming of family and friends, and the history of the period of time in which the subject had been born, which led directly into a musical number reflecting that period. During the narration, the four singers had changed into costumes of that period. This was especially effective if the honoree had been born before the turn of the century.

Then followed the second section. Again with narration that often included national and local historical facts of interest, more slides from the life of the man during those years and led into the next musical number by the four singers. Each decade would be covered in this fashion; each time with music from the period sung by the singers with a change of costume for each decade. With each decade, the narration revealed little humorous facts from the man's life.

The show closed with words of thanks and sincere praise for the many contributions the honoree had made to the community, his family, his company and to us, his friends. Usually this was followed by the president of the company with a very short introduction of the honored person, who was then given a chance to reply. In the several hundred of these parties that we performed, no man was ever offended, no family or employer was ever disappointed in the results. There were several that had to be handled more carefully than others, but with these we were also successful.

One, which involved special care, was the retirement of Phil Harris, Chairman of the Board of Northwestern National Bank. Mr. Harris was a gentle, beloved man, whose wife had died only a few months before. The bank considered postponing the party, but decided that would simply prolong the situation. The committee booked Woodhill Country Club for the occasion. They knew how elegant and proper would be the cocktail party and dinner. The Board of Directors of the bank and their wives, the senior officers of the bank and their spouses, and the remaining members of Phil's family were sent invitations, which noted that it was a "black tie dinner." The board of the bank and the officers of the bank represented well the leaders of the Twin Cities. Few have been the times that I've seen a more sophisticated gathering.

The show went gloriously and well, with wonderful reaction. The evening was to close with a speech by a former chairman of the board, John Moorhead. (I had written his retirement party years earlier.) John was a clever man who since retirement had a lot of time to do whatever he wanted. For Harris's party, he wanted to deliver a special speech. As I said, John was clever. He decided his speech should be delivered in poetic rhyme. I envied the skill with which he wrote. More than halfway through his speech, he delivered to this elegant and sophisticated audience this couplet: "Phil Harris is a gentleman, always proper and very meek; the only man I've ever known to step from the shower to take a leak." There was a pause, then the boisterous laughter never before nor since equaled at Woodhill. John paused with a look of boyish innocence as if to say, "I'm wondering who put those two lines into my speech." By noon the next day, there wasn't a businessman in Minneapolis who hadn't heard the two lines.

The year that Northwestern National Life had their meeting aboard an Alaskan cruise ship, was the year that John Pillsbury was to retire. Part of my assignment was to write and produce a retirement party for John and Kitty during the cruise. The material available was voluminous. That coupled with my true admiration and affection for the Pillsburys brought special pleasure to the writing.

After the return from the cruise, NWNL asked me to do another Pillsbury retirement party that would include the company's employees at a special meeting. Knowing that it would also include many from the cruise, I had the challenge of changing the pattern as much as I could and still follow the true path of John's life. I think it went well. Almost immediately, less than a month later, there was to be another retirement party for John and Kitty at the Lafayette again including many of those who had attended at least one of the previous parties, some having attended both. How successful I was in making it "different." I'm not sure. I do know that again it was well received.

When young Jack Stafford became president of Pillsbury, the company decided that they would observe that occasion with a "this is your life" celebration. I met with the chairman of the committee in charge of the function gathered the material he had, and started planning how we would divide the show to accommodate not only me as a narrator, but also two young officers of the company as fellow narrators.

My advisor then suggested it might be well if I talked with Mrs. Stafford, who would make available the photographs that we would need. He telephoned her immediately, explained why he was calling and then handed the phone to me. Mrs. Stafford suggested rather than her carrying the heavy albums to an office downtown or the theater, it would be better if I visited her at their home. When I agreed, she said, "I'll give you the address, but you'll still have trouble finding it. You see, we live in the old Country Club section of Edina.

Don: I know where that is.

Wife: Well, the street we live on, is just two blocks long—almost hidden away.

Don: What street is it?

Wife: Moorland.

Don: I know Moorland quite well.

Wife: You do?

Don: Yes.

Wife: Well, we live at 4615. Do you think you'll be able to find it?

Don: I should, I used to live there.

Wife: That's impossible. Only two families other than us have ever lived in this house.

Don: That's not quite right—it's been lived in by three

families.

Wife: Are you sure?

Don: Reasonably so, yes.

The most recent of requests for a celebration of this kind came from John Morrison, for whose retirement I had made one of our presentations. John telephoned to ask if I was still doing such work, and when I said yes, he replied that he would like for me to prepare a little show for his wife's 80th birthday. It would be at Woodhill, of course. He came to my office at the theater bringing several albums of photographs from her baby pictures to the present day. Two of the pictures I will always remember. One was of a seven-year-old girl, standing, leaning back against a large tree. In someway it showed what a delightful woman she would become. The other photograph was of her at twenty years. She was sitting at a courtside table, resting from a game of tennis just finished. It was a perfect example of the grace and beauty of those years.

Here's an interesting example of how change comes with time. After I had selected the photographs that I wanted to use, I had great trouble finding a company that would make slides of them. Slides were a thing of the past. Finally, a company on 44th and France agreed they could make them. Next was the projector. I had long since given my projectors away. I telephoned AVS, the Fuller and Pearson audiovisual experts whom we had frequently used for industrial shows, to inquire about renting a projector. They said they wouldn't rent me one; they had forty that they never used; they would give me one. For me, PowerPoint projection is certainly more convenient, but much of the crispness seems gone and colors have faded. Change is not easy.

The "show" closed with a gracious short speech by John in which he expressed very well his love and his wish that they share many more happy birthdays. Mrs. Morrison was just as gracious and charming in her response. All of Morrisons guests were quick to extend to Jane their personal congratulations and birthday greetings.

As I was helping clear our sound and lighting boards to ready for the dancing, Mrs. Morrison interrupted me to say that the program had been a great tribute and a wonderful birthday gift. While she was talking, her brother-in-law, Clint Morrison, joined up and said, "Well, Don, have you been out on the Lake lately?" (then to Mrs. Morrison) "You know, Jane, if it hadn't been for me, this party would never have happened. If it hadn't been for me, Don would still be outside in the middle of Lake Minnetonka." Then he told her about rescuing us years ago.

After the show section of the Morrison birthday party was over and the dancing had begun, Tom Markle, a friend from Fox and Hounds, told my crew that John Morrison had asked him to take us to the lounge on the lower level and make certain we had whatever food and drink we wanted.

It's understandable that after working with friends and family of the honoree, gathering information and photographs, I always felt as if I were an old and close friend of the family. And I think that they, in most cases, felt the same.

CHANGES IN THEATER

In the years that I have been in theater, have I seen changes? In the last 70–75 years, what hasn't changed! In the commercial theater, even the form of the plays has changed. During the first years—no, let me change that—just let me say that until a decade or two ago, all of the commercial plays were written (and produced) in three acts with two intermissions. All of them. So much so that there was, I remember, a wonderful book on playwriting with the title "How's Your Second Act?," meaning: without a good second act there was no way the third act could perform a rescue. Today, one rarely sees a play other than those written in two acts. And in past years, the plays were longer: two-and-a-half hours to three-and-a-half hours. Today the audience is happy to be on its way home after just two hours.

Why? Today's busy schedules, attention span, interest span, the desire to get home to see on television the last three innings of the baseball game. Which of these? Probably all.

Change? There are fewer plays being written for the stage. Good playwrights are finding the television and motion picture markets more certain, more rewarding and less open to destructive reviews of the critics.

To further reduce the number of desirable plays, too many young authors have been guided into thinking that being "different" is synonymous with delivering "quality." Playwriting for the commercial theater has almost become a club of members writing so-called "serious plays" for the approval and delight of their own narrow-view members. "Being different" is often equated with the use of language not often heard, bringing on stage words we haven't heard at home or even at work. Again, I remember well the time "shit" was first said on our stage. It was not that many years ago.

The chief problem, however, is that the New York or London production of plays has become expensive beyond reason. Why write a play if it has no chance of finding a producer?

Has there been a change in the actors? Yes. There are more actors to choose from—actors with good training, but fewer with adequate professional experience. There are still actors willing and happy to make the commitment to long hours, insufficient financial reward and the sacrifice of personal interest, but the ability for them to find a company with which to make that commitment is increasingly difficult.

As much change as there has been in theater, there is something that has not changed nor will it ever—the purpose of the whole thing. "Theater is and will always be a celebration of the spirit of man—a celebration which can, and often does become, an act of worship."

STRAY THOUGHTS

In theater, as in every aspect of life, there are sayings, ideas, thoughts that are so common and ever present that they become trite. I have to remind myself that quite often they are repeated again and again and become trite because they are true. May I list a number of them that, though I may not have heard them again and again, I have experienced them again and again.

- Remember: in theater, "Why" is a legitimate question, whether asked by the director or the actor.
- The art of acting is the art of listening.
- Cherish the actor who likes to rehearse.
- It has been said that nothing helps the actor as much as repetition.
- There must be in every performance moment of repose.
- It is true that an audience likes to see an actor eat, but even more, they like to see an actor think.
- (This one comes primarily from outside the theater) Beware the speaker or performer who tells you he works better without a script.

Following are a number of reflections on stage movement. These reflections become rules. I know "rules" are to be broken, but you'd better have a good reason for doing so. Movement reflections:

- Tell the actor to move on the verb—the word of action.
- When beginning the cross (the movement), start with the upstage foot.

- A stage prop should usually be handled with the upstage hand, but don't let this common knowledge so influence the actor that he handles a weapon or a drink in his left hand.
- In giving a toast, or replying to one, the glass should be in the right hand.
- Never touch the leading lady for any reason other than to hit her or kiss her.
- Be careful with crying—it may be stealing the role of the audience.
- If the actor's reading of a line seems strange or uncomfortable to him, the chances are that he may be underscoring the wrong words. Emphasis, almost always, should fall on either the verb or the subject noun.
- If the actor's delivery has become dull and uninteresting, remind him of the way we all, in our personal conversation, secure variety and maintain interest: by the change of volume, the change of speed, the change of key, underscoring the important word, pausing before and after important ideas.
- The gesture should come on the climax of the spoken word.
- Watch carefully the way young women sit. Most of them have had no training in proper or graceful movement.
- In the handling of weapons on stage, make certain that guns are never pointed directly at audience.
- Never underestimate the difficulty of blocking a group around a dining table. Give it much thought before going into rehearsal.
- Make certain that your designer has all the doors on the set open off stage and hinged on the upstage side. This, of course, does not apply to the "front" entrance, nor does it always apply to a number of other situations such as in many of the Ray Cooney farces.
- Under normal conditions, the actor, when entering through one of the doors, should close it with his downstage hand.
- Make certain that the correct actor is in the middle. Some-

times there is still a "middle" if references or attention is being given to an actor who has gone off-stage through one of the doors.

- Each actor should be reminded that the first few lines he has in a scene must be clearly and understandingly delivered. Give the audience a few minutes to "tune him in."
- Make certain that all actors know the climax of the scene; all actors know when is "the moment of repose."
- Remember, please, that when the actor is first "off book" and working with hand props, it is a difficult time for him. For many it seems that everything he has accomplished has left him. Be gentle.
- A part of the director's job includes telling the actor if he is going in the wrong direction with his characterization or with his acting. Never criticize or correct him if he is not present. In return, you can expect the actors (and tell them you expect it) not to criticize one another behind their backs. Theater is a difficult profession made possible only by people working together.
- Keep reminding the actors and yourself that everything we do is for the benefit of the audience.
- Keep control. Inform the actors and stage manager that no change in interpretation, movement, costume or makeup is to be made without your approval.
- Nothing is as satisfying as seeing order come out of disorder. Never lose sight of the fact that theater is a celebration.
- As with everything in life, in theater there isn't anything as destructive as indecision. And may I add, "you arrive at false philosophies when you're out there fishing."
- Without the possibility of failure, there can be no success.

I have other pieces of great wisdom—rich nuggets of insight and truth. They have, at first glance, nothing to do with theater, but anything that has anything to do with anything has something to do with theater.

- Nugget one: Very few handsome men are funny—they don't have to be.
- Nugget two: There are two groups of people who believe they should be in control of every activity: former school-teachers and choir directors.
- Few things are as ugly as a used banana.
- If a good deed is the result of someone having acted in nothing but habit, it's still a good deed. And if you think the good deed was done just to impress, it's still a good deed.

I have also discovered:

- You can't water your entire lawn without getting some on the sidewalk.
- You don't put your pants on standing up.
- In the winter, don't walk outside with your hands in your pockets.
- If there is a hand railing, use it.
- If someone says to you, "I'm an honest man, look me in the eye and you'll see I'm an honest man." He's either a high school sophomore or a liar.
- If you're an actor, don't ask the set designer, "Is that the color it's going to be?"
- Nothing is as hard to break as a bad habit.
- For every concave there is a convex.
- Your chance of having a big funeral is greatly increased if you die young.
- It would diminish us if everyone else were perfect.
- There isn't anything that builds character like being unwanted.
- In listening recently to a speaker at a gathering of church people, I discovered that "Pride in your humility diminishes your humility."
- I believe—I know—"That heaven is not going to be a place where we learn the details of our friends and our family's transgressions and misdemeanors. Nor will we want to hear of them."

One final set of "great truths":

- The reputation for being clever is not easy to maintain.
- The reputation for being charming is even more difficult to maintain.
- The reputation for being funny is even more difficult to maintain. Don't try it.
- Remember what I wrote earlier, "Theater is a celebration." Celebration is not a word that today we hear often—only at services for the dead.

Epilogue

I can't remember that I ever questioned Heaven. Or even often wondered what it was like. It was there. "In my Father's house are many mansions." That's all I needed to know.

At the time of a friend's death, those seeking to console were always heard to say, "Well, now, he's in a much better place." For reasons I couldn't understand, that, for a moment or two, bothered me. I didn't know why. I didn't know why until Joan's death.

"In Heaven there is no death, no illness, no suffering, no pain, no tears, no sorrow. Heaven is a paradise where everything is perfect."

In my present sorrow that's not good enough. I want Heaven to be what my life has been—with Joan just the way she's always been. And with me working to make her and our audiences happy. I need difficulties to overcome, disappointments to wipe away and happiness to be achieved only by striving through and overcoming barriers.

During the years Joan and I were married, there were times of great sorrow; but there were also times of great joy. I'm not ready for a perfect world, one without challenges that hold the possibility of defeat.

I want Heaven to be what I have already had.